ad
man
mad
man

ad man mad man

Unapologetically PRAHLAD

PRAHLAD KAKAR
WITH RUPANGI SHARMA

HarperCollins *Publishers* India

First published in India by HarperCollins *Publishers* 2023
4th Floor, Tower A, Building No. 10, DLF Cyber City,
DLF Phase II, Gurugram, Haryana – 122002
www.harpercollins.co.in

2 4 6 8 10 9 7 5 3 1

P-ISBN: 978-93-5699-832-2
E-ISBN: 978-93-5699-833-9

Typeset in 11/14.5 Scala (OTF) at
Manipal Technologies Limited, Manipal

Printed and bound at
Replika Press Pvt. Ltd.

This book is dedicated to my beautiful wife, Mitali, who if she knew any better, would not have got on my back and unfailingly whipped my ass to write my memoir. Now that the genie is out of the bottle, we all shall have to learn to live with it!

The detailed notes pertaining to this book are available on the HarperCollins *Publishers* India website. Scan this QR code to access the same.

Contents

Act III

Act IV

Act V

The Last Act

Always take the initiative. There is nothing wrong with spending a night in a jail cell if it means getting the shot you need. Send out all your dogs and one might return with prey. Never wallow in your troubles; despair must be kept private and brief. Learn to live with your mistakes. Expand your knowledge and understanding of music and literature, old and modern. That roll of unexposed celluloid you have in your hand might be the last in existence, so do something impressive with it. There is never an excuse not to finish a film. Carry bolt cutters everywhere. Thwart institutional cowardice. Ask for forgiveness, not permission. Take your fate into your own hands. Learn to read the inner essence of a landscape. Ignite the fire within and explore unknown territory. Walk straight ahead, never detour. Manoeuvre and mislead, but always deliver. Don't be fearful of rejection. Develop your own voice. Day one is the point of no return. A badge of honour is to fail a film theory class. Chance is the lifeblood of cinema. Guerrilla tactics are best. Take revenge if need be. Get used to the bear behind you.

—Werner Herzog[1]

Foreword

Prahlad writes the way he talks—good-humoured, laughing loudly at his own jokes and skillfully disguising his sharp no-nonsense and pragmatic intellect behind his bluff exterior.

I was told that while he was still in his teens, and probably up to no good, his mother—worried about his future—asked Jog Chatterjee to take him under his wing. At the time, Jog Chatterjee was a highly reputed advertising professional heading a prestigious agency called ASP (Advertising and Sales Promotions Company) in New Delhi.

Jog could never say no to anyone even if there was nothing he could offer in his agency. He took Prahlad and assigned him a position which, in advertising circles, is known as Gofer—it stands for someone who is made to go for this or go for that.

Jog Chatterjee did not have enough work in ASP to occupy Prahlad's time. So he shunted him off to the head office in Mumbai, where he was initially assigned as my Gofer in the film department.

Prahlad never said no to anything assigned to him. His enthusiasm was proverbial, despite his inability to spell words correctly.

Prahlad soon took wing and became a huge success as an advertising professional. Over the years, he has succeeded in a whole range of fields as diverse as scuba diving in Lakshadweep and the Andamans.

Prahlad is an outstanding entrepreneur. Even though I grudgingly say so, he is full of enthusiasm, going from one successful project to another, which includes teaching advertising and mass communications at institutions that he himself has created.

Prahlad Kakar is quite a colourful character. I wish him well.

Shyam Benegal
12 October 2023

Jean-Paul Sartre—Who am I? Why am I here? Where am I going?
(The Song of the Existentialists)

1

'I Want a Nalki'

As far as I can remember, I have always—without exception—been thrown out of respectable institutions for being at the right place at the wrong time, and for not being able to keep my mouth shut. The glee I got from it came much later when I decided to have fun while being thrown out. The first incident, if you want to call it that, happened at a haloed kindergarten school on Lodhi Road, New Delhi. It was named Kumkum School after the principal's spoilt, precocious five-year-old named Kumkum—or should I say, Princess Kumkum.

The principal was a senior bureaucrat's wife and had decided to appropriate the sprawling government bungalow to enhance her social status and make some extra money. I was an active general's grandson, so I was allowed into the hallowed premises. My peers were kids of Indian Administrative Service and Indian Foreign Service officers, or socialites' children. I found another child who didn't quite fit in, and Naveen and I became good friends. He was a fair, good-looking boy, and I was a scrawny, geeky-looking kid with a fertile imagination. Kumkum, the princess of the school, had her beady eyes on poor Naveen, who was a bit embarrassed at being singled out for unwanted attention.

Naveen and I found a small hidey-hole in the tall hedges bordering the school, and we used to disappear into it during breaks, much to Ms Kumkum's chagrin. One day, the sneaky young lady followed Naveen and discovered our secret retreat. She demanded to be made privy to our private club. Naveen was no match for her guiles and, despite my vehement objections, he caved when she said, 'It's *my* school, therefore *my* hedge.' She threatened to tell her mother about it if we refused. In our defence, I had told her it was a boys-only club and no girls were allowed.

Her retort was, 'What's the difference?' I kept quiet because I wasn't too sure. And so it came to be that Ms Precocious Kumkum became a member of our boys-only club. On a sunny afternoon, we were lolling around in the cave, when Ms Kumkum flounced in and accused us of being boring. We never let her into our conversations, hoping that she would lose interest and go away. Casually, I asked her what kind of exciting things she had in store for us, considering we were such bores. She perked up and said brightly, 'If you show me yours, I'll show you mine.'

We weren't particularly interested as we didn't know the difference anyway, but she launched into a bolshy temper tantrum. I watched in dismay as Naveen lowered his shorts and underwear to calm her down. She glared at his pinkish nunu for some time. Then, turning to me, she ordered me to follow suit. She was about to throw a fit, so I gave in, at which point the little vixen ran off at high speed, completely reneging on the whole deal. We nervously covered our delicate nether regions and emerged sheepishly out of our cave, only to be summoned to her mother's office. Ms Kumkum stood there, shedding crocodile tears, stamping her foot and saying, '*I want. I want. I want.*'

Her mother looked at her placatingly and asked, 'What do you want, my baby?' Kumkum truculently said, 'I want a nalki.'

Her mother somehow managed to keep her voice under control and asked, 'What nalki, baby?'

'A nalki like Naveen's and Prahlad's,' she said plaintively.

To which her mother, who looked like thunder at this point, asked, 'How do you know they have a nalki?'

'*They showed me!* Now I also *want!*'

Shit hit the fan, and nobody was interested in our version of events at all. Our parents were summoned, and we were both rusticated with dishonour from Kumkum School. Naveen and I slunk off the premises with our parents as Ms Kumkum looked on, smirking triumphantly.

Nobody told her that when she grew up she could have her own collection of nalkis.

After this disastrous episode, I was busy skulking around the house, sure that the adults in the family looked at me as some kind of pervert, when my grandfather, Major General K.N. Saigal, retired from active service as the deputy director-general of the Medical Corps, and we moved lock, stock and barrel to Dehradun's verdant, lush greenery. We ensconced ourselves in a lovely stone bungalow on 6, Old Survey Road, built by Ruskin Bond's grandfather, who was a railway engineer. It was a fabulous house with about two acres of lychee and mango trees, and a slightly overgrown front garden full of flowers, heady jackfruit, guava and sour plum trees. It seems Ruskin Bond's book *The Trees of Dehra* spoke of these very trees from my childhood home.

The Doon valley is known as the retirement hub for those in the services. The Dehradun I knew was a peaceful paradise of green Himalayan foothills, crisscrossed by rivers and canals, flanked by Mussoorie on one side and Rishikesh on the other—full of wildlife, fish and pristine forests. As you crossed the Mohan Pass from the dusty plains, you got transported to a scenic valley known for its academic institutions, basmati rice, flora, fauna, fruits like lychees and so much more.

My grandmother, Dr Sonutai Saigal née Patwardhan, immediately took charge of the house with a phalanx of gardeners, and set about civilizing and taming the garden. She was also a doctor, and a brilliant one at that. She was a pure Konkanastha Chitpavan Brahmin from Nagpur, Maharashtra, who had met my grandfather at Grant Medical

College and had fallen completely in love with this tall, handsome North Indian from Allahabad. Though things took a turn for the worse and became acrimonious when the Allahabadis were unable to accept that a woman could be a doctor and accused her of being a lowly midwife or dai, who had phasaoed this well-to-do, innocent boy with her charms.

My grandmother was a mild, grey-eyed woman, all of four feet, eight inches, a steel hand in a velvet glove, and when you lit a fire under her, by god, she became a seven-foot-tall spitfire. Even my grandfather, who was five feet, eleven inches, would cower before her fury. Well, that's exactly what happened—she was furious with his typical UP Kshatriya side of the family and, like a good, obedient boy, my grandfather eloped with her, and both families cut off all ties with them. Inter-caste marriages were unheard of in those days. I am talking about 1915 here. She was a topper, and he was not. He joined the Royal Army Medical Corps and she ran the house, with its two kitchens, the non-vegetarian one for my grandfather and a pure vegetarian one for herself.

Though she was a strict vegetarian herself, she learnt to cook all the non-vegetarian food in his kitchen. She treated all the neighbourhood poor in a free clinic at the gate of every place that they were posted. Once, she even delivered the neighbourhood mali's wife's baby on our dining table during a severe storm, using sterilized kitchenware as it was a caesarean. The lives of both the mother and the baby were hanging by a thread. My sister, Mandakini, and I witnessed this first-hand. We were frightened out of our wits by the thunder, lightning and the pouring rain outside, and the blood and gore on our very own table inside. She skillfully saved both the mother and child. Her reputation was so legendary that she became a part of local folklore wherever she went.

I was also in genuine awe of my grandfather—he was a towering figure, at least for a nine-year-old. I had been fed on stories of his long walk from Rangoon to Kohima, which was then in Assam, with General Slim's shattered army, living in and off the jungle, constantly under attack by the advancing Japanese. My grandfather kept the Indian troops from his medical corps together, and ensured that their morale and fighting spirit never flagged. He was once taking a bath in an abandoned tub when a Zero fighter started strafing the unit with machine guns and cannon fire. The troops disappeared into the jungle in panic, and my grandfather continued bathing as if nothing had happened. The group then returned sheepishly and never again ran for their lives leaving their officer behind.

He was a man of habit and discipline. I remember his batman, Drighman, who had also retired at the same time, waiting outside his door at 9.15 a.m. sharp, holding a steaming mug of hot shaving water. He would, alternately, blow on it to cool it and then test it with his index finger for the exact temperature at the precise time, and only then would he knock on the door. 'Suh! Shave!' This ritual I witnessed every morning in Dehradun—so you can imagine the habit of a man who spent his entire adult life in the spit and polish of the services suddenly retiring, and not trying to regiment the household.

I find this in many a retired senior officer; they continue behaving as if they are still in service and order everyone around like recruits, especially kids. We used to stand in front of him at attention, in savdhan, while he lectured us on the finer points of discipline and detailing. Luckily, my grandmother was understanding of my dreams and was formidably territorial—nobody, but nobody trifled with her.

The next five years in Dehradun held several defining moments of my life. The valley had a significant impact on my growing-up years and inspired my love for forests. I was introduced to shikaar, or hunting, at a very early age. I spent my weekends near a forest block called Timli at a farm, where a formidable lady called Doris Carberry taught me to shoot. She was a crack shot. Doris and her husband, Aubrey, owned the farm and lived on it. We spent some of our weekends there as our school's bursar, Ivan Mann, had married their daughter, Jenny.

Mrs Carberry was a sparsely built, tall lady, who had spent her entire life outdoors, and it showed—she was tough as hell, with a head of grey hair. For some obscure reason, she decided to make a man out of me. Mrs Carberry taught me to respect all weapons, take care of them, strip them, clean them and never point a gun at any living creature unless it was for the pot. She warned me, time and again, never to be casual with a gun—it was not a toy, but a lethal weapon.

With great clarity, I remember how, after putting me through her usual drill, she let me take a shot with her shotgun. It was an old hammer-type twelve bore, which she had beautifully and lovingly maintained. I must have been twelve or thirteen, and the gun was as tall as me. I leaned forward as instructed, cocked the right barrel of the gun, aimed it at a distant wood pigeon and squeezed the trigger. There was a loud detonation and the kick of the weapon knocked me down on my bum, though I was still clutching the gun tightly. I dared not let it fall on the ground—that would have been sacrilege.

Till today, I have never forgotten the acrid smell of burnt cordite. It must be like mainlining. Many years later, I watched *Apocalypse Now*, directed by Francis Ford Coppola—a film about the Vietnam war. I could immediately relate to Robert Duvall's character, who is an air cavalry chopper pilot. After an attack on a Vietnamese hamlet, he gets down from the chopper, sniffs the air and says, 'I love the smell of napalm in the mornings.' It took me back to Dehradun, my bum on the ground, with a smoking twelve bore clasped to my chest, imbibing the smell of burnt cordite and getting high on it. I still do!

Mrs Carberry taught me how to love the jungle and stalk the most challenging game, namely foraging junglefowl, because you can't see them in the forest's dense undergrowth. I learnt to stalk them, crawling on my stomach, cradling the gun in the crook of my arm, and listening to the old guard hen protecting her flock as she kept a close eye and sharp ears out for danger, while the rest were pecking at the ground, noisily looking for grubs and insects. The old guard hen clucks like a metronome as long as everything is clear on the coast, but the moment she feels they're in any danger, she lets out a high-pitched squawk.

The jungle falls into a pregnant silence, the flock freezes mid-scratch and listens carefully, poised on the brink of instant flight. You have to freeze with them immediately and stop breathing—if you move even a whisker, the whole flock of murgis erupts into explosive flight and you have lost them. If you maintain stillness long enough, after an extended pause, the old hen starts clucking again, and you can resume the stalk until you are close enough to see them, through the roots and bushes, and only when you can line up two of them together, then, and only then, can you squeeze your shot and hopefully get two birds for the pot. I loved the whole business of being in the jungle, recognizing all the calls of the birds and animals in their habitat, and their breathtaking ability to become invisible at will.

Just like the ocean, the jungle has its own sacrosanct rules of dos and don'ts. The underlying feature of natural phenomena, be it mountains, seas or the forest, is respect and humility for all of its inhabitants. Only then will it reluctantly reveal its secrets to the acolyte.

While I was in Dehradun, I discovered that though I looked like a geek, I was not interested in my studies. I was this stringy kid with glasses, so everyone used to look at me and say, 'Oh, he must be good at studies!', and then would find out, much to their disappointment, that I was hopeless at academics. I selectively studied subjects that interested me and the truth is that I was an undiagnosed dyslexic—something I found out much later because no one even knew about learning disabilities at that time. Everyone assumed I was a lazy duffer.

I went to a very respectable school called St Thomas, which has an excellent faculty and is located bang in the centre of town. In our time, the school didn't have a sports ground to call its own. We went to the Forest Reserve Institute's field across the road for most of our events. It was a well-maintained, lush, green ground with a 200-metre running track lining its edges. We had a huge, muscular PT master called Mr Butlerwhite, who took us through the paces of gymnastics, sports and general discipline.

God forbid he caught you with your hair curling over your collar! His favourite method to punish this minor offence was to grab your hair by the end of your locks and pull it upwards, while you stood on your toes and squirmed in abject discomfort. The punishment was accompanied by a ditty that he forced us to recite with him, between our ows and ouches: 'When Mr Butlerwhite catches you hard by the hair, he snatches you. Wiggy! Wigg! Wigg!' For some reason, Mr Butlerwhite took me in hand and pushed me into things I usually would have avoided like the plague, such as athletics.

One day, he saw me running for my life from an unsavoury goon who hung around outside the school gates down the lane, out of sight of the teachers, to shake down nerdy kids for their tuck money. I was a prime target as I was a bespectacled, stick-insect type. I had been bullied by him once and was so terrified that it had taken me a few days to recover. The next time he tried to bar my way, I dodged him, and jinking left and right like a broken-field runner in a battle zone dodging bullets, I turned on the juice and sprinted down the alley, leaving behind a cursing, lumbering goon, who couldn't match my turn of speed.

I ran into the school gate, smack into none other than Mr Butlerwhite's stomach, and just about knocked him off his feet. He was surprised by my fleetness of foot. Anybody would have run like the devil if a goon were chasing him for his tuck money! He did not ask and I never told him why I was running full tilt, looking over my shoulder as if all the bats out of hell were chasing me. The next day, I was called at assembly to report at the games period to the athletics ground. I was a bit miffed as I had a challenge on for a game of kanchas, or marbles, with some of my scruffy, unathletic friends.

When I reported to the grounds, I realized that some sort of athletic trials were on and I was expected to compete with the best athletes of my school. We were divided according to age, and I was with a motley bunch of under-fourteens. I pretended I knew what was on and tried to warm up with the rest of the confident boys. Running in short bursts and limbering up, I noticed two critical things that day. The first was that most of the boys in my age group wore running shoes with spikes, whereas the lallus like me had Keds on that tended to slip on the turf. I would have preferred to run nange pair (barefoot), but was too embarrassed to ask.

The second was that the primary audience for the runners were schoolgirls looking adoringly at the likely champions—though I felt sure I wasn't going to be one of the winners. We took our positions on the racing line, with our hearts in our mouths, buoyed by a kick of adrenaline and nerves. Mr Butlerwhite was the starter and announced with considerable gravitas, 'On your mark ...' When he paused, my heart was beating so loudly it drowned out all ambient sound, including the cheering girls'. 'Get set!' He took another dramatic pause, followed by the explosive bang of the starting gun.

'*Go!*'

I don't remember taking off. I only remember that halfway down the 100-metre track, I felt the wind in my hair, my feet flew seemingly in slow motion without touching the ground, followed by the snap of the finishing tape as I rushed in and then it was over. Schoolgirls and some teachers were mobbing a tall, good-looking Anglo-Indian boy called Ian Howard. He had come first. Then, suddenly, a teacher accosted me and asked me my name. I was a bit perplexed because I was so sure I had come last, as there were no girls or fans around me, unlike the others. I was hustled off to a desk where they asked me to tell them my 'Name! Number! Class!'

Then I realized I had come second—an unknown dark horse, a last-minute runner, who had been entered by none other than a smiling, bald, hefty Mr Butlerwhite. Thereafter, Ian Howard and I became best buddies, and were always surrounded by the lovely ladies after winning races. I just loved it. Sports opened up a whole new world for me; my level of confidence shot up and I was ready for anything—long jump, triple jump, high jump and relay. Though I never managed to perfect the Western roll, a high-jumping technique where the jumper has to lift his body over the bar and make a three-point landing on the other side. When I had cannoned into Mr Butlerwhite that fateful morning, he had rightly predicted that I was a sprinter, as fast as I was skinny. As for the street goon, suffice it to say for now that he never managed to catch me.

Shortly after winning the race, on a whim, Mr Butlerwhite took me aside during the games period and asked me to take off my glasses. I wondered whether he had a touch of the sun; you know that old saying, 'Mad dogs and Englishmen come out in the noonday sun.' Anyway, he peered down at me, put up his hand and asked me to count the number of fingers he displayed. I counted them accurately each time. Satisfied, he asked me to report to the assembly hall in the afternoon. I reached the building and found a lot of tough-looking boys trying to put a boxing ring up. I shat bricks. Boxing? No way! I just wasn't comfortable with the idea of being pulverized by a bruiser. I wanted to get the hell out of there and to the safety of the athletic field.

Butlerwhite gave me a steely look, crooked his finger towards me and drew me to him like a wriggling fish reeled in on a hook. I jumped out of my skin as he barked at me, 'Scared?' 'No, sir,' I shook my head in denial, and then immediately changed my mind to avoid being put to the test and stuttered, 'Yes, sir.' He smiled lazily like a Cheshire cat and said, 'That's a good start. Fear is a good thing in a fighter. It gives you humility and respect for the sport and your opponent.' My mind kicked into a blue funk and I struggled to escape. 'Sir, I have an important tutorial to complete. I will come back tomorrow.' Not a chance! He just laughed. I put on the gloves and, thank god, was sent off to practice on the punching bag. Whew! Saved, I thought, at least the bag doesn't punch back.

During the next week, we were put through vigorous training—skipping, running, footwork, ducking, weaving and punching. 'Don't punch your opponent's face! Punch through it,' snarled Butlerwhite. 'Straight left from the shoulder; don't telegraph it, you blithering idiot.' That part of the dialogue made a lasting impact, and I imbibed it subconsciously. I still use his phrases—'blithering idiot', 'dying duck in a thunderstorm'. Since my athletic training had put me in great form, I had the stamina to take being trained in boxing; yet, I was scared shitless about the day I would have to face a real opponent and not a punching bag. Boxing, I realize in hindsight, is a true test of character. One has to face a real fear of combat, however civilized it might seem, to overcome it.

I remember my first bout with great clarity as Butlerwhite paired me off with a supercilious young boy, who thought he knew it all. He was good-looking and a bit of a snob. In my opinion, he thought he was god's gift to mankind. He always looked at me with great disdain. With a spasming, nervous stomach and a mind that had gone from colour and definition to dark and blank in panic, my movement was reduced to that of shuffling reluctance. The epicentre of the fear radiated in my nabhi, the navel. My body was heavy with the stench of fear, and I was sure my opponent could smell my panic. Everything was cumbersome, ponderous and slow. I breathed ragged breaths as if I was afraid somebody was going to shut off my air supply. My limbs were leaden with fear.

Suddenly, his left hand snaked out and collided with my nose. Stars exploded in my brain. Everything went into automatic mode as anger overtook my mind. I launched myself at my opponent: punching, kicking, biting, the smell of blood in my nostrils. All my pent-up animosity suddenly released with a whoosh, and I wanted to kill him—so I went at him with everything I had. 'Stop!' shouted Butlerwhite and physically separated us. He took me to a neutral corner and stared down my anger. 'You are in a boxing ring, not a street brawl,' he said. 'If you lose your temper in a fight, the fight is as good as lost. Never lose your temper. Never! Think clearly. This sport is as precise and scientific as anything you will ever do. Follow the rules. Don't brawl. Box on!'

What a downer! But now, I was no longer in a fear-generated paralysis and the many hours of training kicked in—straight left, straight left, feint, front right hook. Pedal, pedal, clinch, get off the ropes, circle, punch, punch, weave, duck, get up close, hook to the body, hook again. Two lefts and a right. The bell went 'Tong!' I didn't hear it. Butlerwhite separated us in our corners and soon announced, 'Time! Box on!'

Weave, feint, left and a left again, duck, right hook; now I was in a rhythm and I realized I was fast. Fast in, fast out, the fear of being hurt goaded my feet. 'Dance like a butterfly, sting like a bee' sang Cassius Clay in my mind. Those words started to make sense. The bout ended. We both flopped on to the stools, water poured over our heads and our sweat sponged off. I was still flying on my fear-induced adrenaline high. Phew! Never again, I thought. But I was wrong. I went back again and again like an adrenaline junkie. The fear, the first punch, the high, everything in slow motion, not feeling the punches, just floating effortlessly. I was fast when I was scared and earned the nickname 'The Ghost' because it was difficult to hit me.

Boxing taught me many life lessons. The fear of getting hurt and humiliated in front of peers, just making a fool of yourself, is a constant for almost anything new that you might try in life. But it is the fear of being beaten up in front of people that causes the most dread. If you want to achieve anything in life, the first lesson is to learn to face the fear and not let it paralyse you. The moment you are in it of your own free will, your instinct for survival kicks in, and you automatically rely on recalled training and instruction.

You start functioning at hyper speed after the first knock on the nose because of a rush of adrenaline, which is the body's response to the fear that equips you with a high, to help you think your way out of the danger area safely. Your first instinct is to think, fuck it! Run. Then kicks in conditioning, backbone, a lot of pride and maybe a touch of confidence to see it through. When a person decides to stand up and fight, it shows character. Then your belief and training kick in, and you are in for the ride of a lifetime.

One of the problems that I have had subsequently is that I became hooked to the adrenaline high and became a junkie for risk—this thrill-seeking attitude seeped into everything I did in life, much to the dismay and concern of friends, family and other animals. It was a dream when it worked. When I overstepped the mark, it was an ignominious landing into reality with a thud. What sets entrepreneurs aside from the ordinary Joes and the sweaty cookie-cutter millions is that the real entrepreneur never gives up. Success and failure are both different sides of the same coin, and both are impermanent and fleeting. It's the journey that is the greatest of all teachers and it takes you on a roller-coaster ride even as you hang on for dear life.

I realized much later in life the role that Mr Butlerwhite played in shaping my attitude to fear. He knew that fateful morning when I collided with his midriff that I was bloody fast on my lean legs and shit scared of messing up with a physically imposing opponent. Butlerwhite made me an athlete and built in me a reserve of confidence, self-belief and competitiveness, within my safer world of dreams and fantasies, and took the paralysis out of the fear.

The next time the goon tried to stop my cycle by standing in front of it, I didn't run. The only way to stop him from bullying me was to take a beating. That also gave me the confidence to get a few licks in. I must say it surprised the goon that I was willing to stand up to him and punch him back. With my training in footwork and a healthy dose of fear, I took the fight right to him and did not come out second best.

He never bothered me again. Fear is a crucial part of life and it makes you careful, but never let it grow in your imagination to make it all-pervasive and crippling—face it squarely because you can never outrun it. It's like a shadow attached to your mind, growing all the time. When I look back at those days in Dehradun, I realize how they shaped my character: my fantasies, my deep love for the forest, the heady feel of the hunt, my gut-wrenching fear of the boxing ring and being able to excel at it because of the adrenaline rush that kicked in.

~

The other person who cast a massive impression on my fourteen-year-old feverishly fertile mind was our principal, Mrs A, who had recently come from Bangalore to take over the running of the school. She was a brilliant and attractive lady, and I was utterly infatuated with her. Other than her administrative duties, she also taught English literature. So, of course, I worked extra hard and became excellent in English literature and poetry. As English was the language spoken at home, my vocabulary and enunciation were pretty good, and I soon managed to catch Mrs A's attention. She then put me in her elocution class, where we were coached to appear for the Trinity College of London exam for elocution. Of course, I was in seventh heaven, and I promptly rattoed all the poems assigned to us. I still remember them.

'Casabianca'

The boy stood on the burning deck,
Whence all but he had fled;
The flame that lit the battle's wreck
Shone round him o'er the dead.

—Felicia Dorothea

'The Tyger'

Tyger Tyger, burning bright,
In the forests of the night;
What immortal hand or eye,
Could frame thy fearful symmetry?

—William Blake

And:

'Ode to the West Wind'

Oh, lift me as a wave, a leaf, a cloud!
I fall upon the thorns of life! I bleed!

—Percy Bysshe Shelley

Outside of the classroom, where Mrs A exposed us to poetry and the classics, I read a lot of comics, adventure novels, action-based pulp fiction with characters like Bulldog Drummond and Leslie Charteris's The Saint Series, and books by P.G. Wodehouse. I dreamt up entire scenarios from nothing, a creative power born from my love for English literature. One of my favourite characters from the stories I read was William from the Just William series. He was a snotty little English boy, aged eleven. His curiosity and his approach to discovering life and people were very much like my own. A lot of what you see is not what you get—what you see begins in your imagination. In the books, as I recall, William lived in a village in the countryside and had an old farmer as his neighbour. For William, this old farmer, who was a reserved kind of person, had a house full of spooks and instruments of torture—at least that's what he imagined.

I was no different. We had an old widower as our neighbour and I would imagine that he was like one of the main characters from the novel To Kill a Mockingbird. Arthur, aka Boo Radley, lived in a seemingly haunted house—Radley Place—and he came off as sinister to the child protagonists in the book. Similarly, although my neighbour was a harmless old codger, sitting on his rocking chair, I imagined he had a darker side. Of course, he didn't.

Considering my love for the language, it was natural that at school, some of my best times away from the games field were in Mrs A's elocution class. Nothing else mattered: I was in the zone. I followed Mrs A with my eyes in her class, and I would like to think that she realized it. My fantasies knew no bounds. When I was alone, I talked to myself, and lived out all my dreams and desires—the fevered brain of a fourteen-year-old pubescent struggling in the throes of becoming a man-child.

During my middle school years at St Thomas, I discovered that other than Mrs A, I was beginning to feel a burning attraction to girls my age. I was drawn to the girls' athletics team captain, Nalini. She was a lissome, long-legged, high-breasted, young sprinter. Not only was she senior to me, but half the school was in love with her. I have always been a sucker for the impossible. The other girl who I had a crush on was a sardarni in my class, Dipika. She was also a damn good athlete, though not at the same level as Nalini, because she did not have the length of leg to be fast enough to beat her. What she lacked in speed, she made up for in sheer grit and determination. It was never a cakewalk for Nalini as Dipika's dogged pursuit always gave her a run for her money.

Dipika lived on East Canal Road, which was close to my home. Her father was a colonel in the army. My friends and I had formed a club inspired by R.L. Stevenson's book, *The Black Arrow*. We spent our evenings plotting and planning many adventures. Most of them were about raiding neighbouring gardens for lychees during the season and how to divert the hapless watchman's attention. But my courtship with Dipika was also one of the Black Arrow Club's support activities. In true Black Arrow tradition, we fashioned bows and arrows and painted them black. The arrows were iron-tipped, lethal and accurate. I was the ordnance officer of the club and crafted all the weaponry.

Dipika had a sprawling bungalow with a massive jackfruit tree in front of the porch. I wrote chits to her on flimsy rice paper, rolled it up and attached it to the arrow just behind the business end with a rubber band. We imagined her as a fair damsel in distress being held captive by her fierce warrior father, who was forcefully giving her hand away in marriage to the local toughie hanging around outside the school gate on his Bullet motorcycle.

Not to be left wanting, after all, we were the Black Arrow Club, we had concocted this elaborate drill of sending her little notes from me. We snuck up to her gate and shot the message-laden arrows at the base of the jackfruit tree after dark. She would join in the conspiracy by fetching the chits and reply by passing me a note in class the next day. There was no need for this tremendously action-packed exchange, as we met every day in school and on the athletic field. As far as possible, the path of true love shouldn't be straight or smooth. If it is, it invariably becomes boring.

On the other hand, Nalini was senior to me and I only got to see her in the running field during practice. She was always a little aloof and surrounded by admirers. I wondered if she noticed me at all. The scrawny geek with glasses, who just looked at her adoringly as she sprinted down the track like a gazelle. I thought of a plan because all young men with fevered minds generally have a Plan B. I still remember the ditty that started it all: 'With the sister to win, with the brother you must begin.'

Nalini had a brother, the apple of his father, Sethji's, eye. Sethji was an ex-zamindar type with all the vices of his lineage. Two wives of some royal blood, one from Nepal, who had eight daughters and one son. They lived right at the end of Rajpur Road, opposite the Blind School, in a crumbling haveli. Sethji was a dyed-in-the-wool shoukeen of nachnewalis and mehfils, which were organized regularly at his house. He even had a spool-style tape recorder, a Grundig—a rare find in the valley. All the programmes were recorded on the Grundig for posterity. He possessed a fabulous collection of guns. Nalini's brother, for some reason, had been nicknamed Cocko by his friends.

I only realized why much later, when I got to know him. He was slightly North by Northwest. In familiar parlance, he was cock-eyed. Despite that, he was a crack shot. His weapons of choice were a .22 Brno rimfire rifle and an unusual 20 bore ladies' shotgun, whose ammo was challenging to come by for wing shooting. Cocko entertained me, even though I was a junior, and that in school is a caste system by itself. I think he did because I was known for my wins at boxing and athletics. When he discovered my love for hunting, we spent many weekends together.

We often went to the Rajpur Road diversion, which was very sparsely populated—and one of its few residents was Pandit Jawaharlal Nehru's sister Vijaya Lakshmi Pandit. This road that led to Mussoorie was heavily forested, with scattered fields full of black partridge, wood pigeons and jungli murgas. We stalked and shot game for the pot there. Cocko would smuggle the .22 out of his father's cupboard as ammo was plentiful. I would pack some sandwiches and cycle up the hill to the diversion, and we would spend the day waiting for the distinctive call of the black partridge to begin our stalk.

One day, we came up short at the edge of a khai, where there was a dry riverbed, and further off on the other side, we saw a distinctive black dot. The partridge sat on a low bush at least 180 yards away. We didn't have a telescopic sight. We had to rely on good old-fashioned open sights, but we could barely see the bird. Right off the bat, Cocko rested against a tree and squeezed off the shot. The dot disappeared in a flurry of feathers and dropped. It took us an hour and a half to traverse the riverbed's steep slopes, curves and bends to retrieve the bird before it turned dark.

Though Cocko and I became good buddies, I never got to meet Nalini at home, as girls were not allowed to hang around their brother's male friends. During one of our summer breaks, destiny intervened and I saw Nalini shopping in Ashley Hall, the upmarket shopping place in Dehradun. I excitedly waved and yelled hello, and she replied, albeit not as enthusiastic as me. I crossed the street and chatted with her, and asked her for a kind of date the next afternoon at my place at Old Survey Road.

She looked at me quizzically and agreed. I was gobsmacked and wanted to yell, 'Eureka!' or 'Geronimo!' Thankfully, other than grinning like a lunatic, I said, 'Bye, see you tomorrow at 3 p.m.' I zipped off before she could change her mind and went straight home to find my grandma. I stood hopping from foot to foot in front of her as I tried to paraphrase my thoughts. She put down her knitting and stared at me, with her light-brown, almost grey–green, Konkani Brahmin eyes. 'You are trying to tell me something,' she stated.

'Yes, Naniji, you see, I have been pursuing this girl in school for a year.'

'So?' she said, looking me up and down.

'Well,' I paused and then blurted out, 'I met her today and asked her to come over for tea.'

'Very civilized. Do we get to meet her?'

'That's just the point,' I rambled on without a pause. 'You see, we haven't met each other in private all this time.'

'Oh?' she said with an arched eyebrow. 'So you want us to disappear discreetly?'

'No! No!' I vehemently declared. 'It's just that the guest room part of the house is locked. Could you please open it, and let me entertain her there?'

Gulp! I had let the cat out of the bag.

She looked at me very pointedly with her wise eyes and said, 'Okay.' I was about to hug her when she said, 'But! I want no hanky-panky.' I swear those were her exact words—hanky-panky. Now, what on earth had she meant by that? We hadn't even held hands yet. To date, holding hands is not a small thing for me.

The next day, the guest room was opened up and aired, all in preparation for Nalini's date with me. I was sure she would not show up, and nervously paced up and down, trying to find a plausible reason why she might not turn up. I was a nervous wreck, hoping against hope. At 3 p.m., the main gate opened, and there she was in a salwar kameez, looking stunning. I led her into our house's guest room, firmly shut the door and dared to look at her properly for the first time. She sized me up too, but I noticed that she was shy, which was out of character.

Usually, she was an outgoing and impulsive girl. I sat beside her and held her hands sweatily as if it were the most natural thing to do. We talked and laughed, still holding hands, and then, at an opportune moment, I leaned over and kissed her. I thought to myself, here comes the music—having grown up so far on films where the orchestra builds up to a romantic crescendo while the hero and heroine kiss each other: A lingering, shuddering, melting kiss.

Here we were lip to lip, feeling our teeth behind our mouths, our noses were in the way, and there was no bloody music. Just heavy breathing and my heart beating a wild tattoo in my chest. I waited, she waited; and nothing happened. Our lips were squashed against each other, teeth firmly closed as we took laboured breaths. There was no 'The Blue Danube', no foxtrot, no 'Sail along silvery moon', no 'La Paloma'. After a long pause, we parted and tried to pretend it hadn't happened.

I am sure she was disappointed and embarrassed because I sure was, and confused to boot. For some reason, she seemed as inept as me, which was strange considering the number of boys pining after her. Why was she as clumsy as me? Maybe she was testing me and I had failed the test. I still remember that first kiss as clammy and awkward because it was devoid of any background music. It was many years later, in college, that a young lady taught me the art of kissing—the whole nine yards of how it should be done.

Now came the not-so-exciting part of dropping Nalini home. She had a sunset deadline and it was an uphill ride for five kilometres; she sat with me, double-seated on a cycle with no carrier. She was sitting on the front bar of the bicycle, with her hair blowing in my face. It was supposed to be the romantic seat. Though, right then, there was no thought of romance and the deadline loomed large as I frantically raced against the setting sun. I huffed and puffed uphill. It took us twenty minutes to cover the distance. We arrived hoping against hope that she would get away with missing her deadline. She looked around, suddenly stiffened and whispered urgently, 'My father is waiting on the porch, you had better run.'

'What! Where?'

I couldn't see a thing. While Nalini hurried away, I caught a glimpse of the glow of a beedi in the gloom of the porch. For some obscure reason, the shoukeen Sethji's preferred smoke was a beedi. I caught my breath and hung around the gate, waiting to see her off safely despite her urgent warning. As she reached the porch, Sethji threw the glowing beedi and stepped out of the gloom. I saw the gleam of a shotgun in his hand. I remember him angrily shouting in a booming voice and that's when survival overtook chivalry. I jumped onto my bike, bent low and pedalled for dear life, racing off in a frantic burst of movement.

Luckily, I was cycling downhill and that helped me pedal faster. I was driven by a massive wave of fear since Sethji's reputation preceded him. He was known to possess a fearsome temper and also of being a dead shot, considering the number of big game trophies on his walls. Suddenly, my worst fears came true and I heard a distant 'bang!' in my wake. I was zipping downhill swiftly and the birdshot passed over my head with an amazingly loud whoosh. 'Incoming!' my mind registered from all the war comics I had voraciously consumed. I will never forget the sharp whiplash of the birdshot passing over my head. I cycled five kilometres in a minute and had to lean the bike on my gatepost to collect my scrambled thoughts. God, what a memorable day!

Many days later, when I complained bitterly to Cocko about his father taking a shot at me, he laughed uproariously. I looked at him as if both he and his father had lost the plot. He explained that his father used to handload shotgun cartridges with rock salt for people who came to steal his lychees and mangoes. And though a load of salt in the backside was painful, humiliating and maybe excessive, it did the job well and deterred the thieves from coming back, and it was far from lethal. He asked me curiously what I had done to earn his father's wrath and I quickly changed the subject!

All in all, it was in Dehradun that I learnt some everlasting lessons about forests, birds and animals. It was all about being able to face my fears and perform despite them, excel in the things that interested me, and live with the disappointment of the ones that did not pan out. At that time, people hadn't recognized dyslexia where I lived. Since I came from a family full of doctors and scientists, a disinterest in science and maths meant facing severe disapproval from every quarter. Everyone thought I needed a swift kick up my arse. Much later in life, I realized what dyslexia meant as two of my sons tested for it, and since it's hereditary, and my wife was always a topper in the sciences, everybody pointed to me as the culprit.

That's the first time I came to know the nature of my abilities, or a lack thereof. Children love to excel and they do so in something that they are naturally good at, regardless of our educational system. School is supposed to engage with children who have defined likes and dislikes according to their aptitudes. School is supposed to make the subjects you don't like much more exciting and practical, filled with examples and real-life lessons. However, we have failed miserably at creating such schools. It took a shocker for me even to begin to grapple with the stigma of failure. All through my school life, I struggled with maths, physics and chemistry. Chemistry not so much because I was highly motivated to learn how to make a bomb and blow the school up—that was the level of my frustration.

When everybody's results were put up in seventh grade, my name was missing and I had to report to the class teacher, an unpleasant lady called Mrs Sealy. She was a dumpy, middle-aged, Anglo-Indian lady with freckles on her upper bosom and under her eyes. Whenever she spoke about England, she referred to it as home. When we misbehaved, she often ordered us to stand behind her chair near the blackboard. While she was sitting and addressing the class, we snuck up from behind her and discreetly looked down the front of her dress to see how far her freckles went.

Anyway, Mrs Sealy glared at me for a long moment while I fidgeted and sweated bullets, and then with a smirk she informed me that I had failed and would be kept back in the same class the following term. I went numb with shock. 'Failed!' I whispered hoarsely. I had flunked my annual exam. How would I face my grandparents, mother, uncles, friends and the ignominy of sitting with juniors? I was shattered. My mind went blank, and I found myself a private place to sort my muddled brain and decide on a course of action. It was late evening by the time my numbness had begun to wear off. The biggest issue was how to break it to my family that they had produced a nikamma. I resolved that the last thing I was going to do was go home.

A glimmer of hope kindled in my mind as I thought of appealing for a second chance to Mrs A. I found out where she lived in Clement Town and cycled to her place furiously, talking to myself. I reached her house at suppertime and waited, trying to build up the courage. Finally, I rang the bell, and Mrs A opened the door. She was quite surprised to see me at her home, which was out of bounds unless specially invited. She looked at me coolly and said, 'Yes?' My heart sank—no smile, no welcome, nothing. I blurted out that I had failed my exam and that there was no way I could tell my family. 'Can't it wait till tomorrow, during schooltime?' she asked pointedly. I died inside, even as I mumbled something to further my case. She said, 'I know, but there is nothing I can do about it right now.' I murmured my apologies and shuffled down the steps. She watched for a couple of heartbeats and then gently closed the door.

I collapsed on the steps of the verandah. After a long time, I crept back onto it, curled up on one of the chairs and went into a disturbed sleep, full of shadowy figures, who taunted me for being useless. In the morning, I woke up with a start, startled by the thump of the morning papers that the newspaperman had just delivered. Mrs A came out in her dressing gown to pick them up and almost dropped them in her surprise as she turned and saw me in my crumpled school uniform, shattered by my predicament and nightmares. Even sans make-up, she looked lovely. She was a bit more sympathetic in the morning— gave me a cup of tea and made me ring up my understandably frantic grandparents.

She sat with me, realizing that I was on the brink and threw me a lifeline. She could not and would not promote me, as it would open up a Pandora's box for her. She patiently explained that if I came in the top three of my class for the first three months, she would promote me. Then, she promptly ordered me to go home to my grandparents, who had been about to leave for the police station when I had called. On my way back, I swore to myself that I would study maths, physics and chemistry, and would top the class—and I did.

After that early encounter with failure, it never shattered me again, because what I learnt from that searing experience is that you only fail when you give up learning from your mistakes. So pick yourself up, go at it and don't make the same mistakes again if you can help it. Failing is always a learning experience. I felt grateful to Mrs A again, many years later, at the age of forty-five when I was training to become a scuba-diving instructor on a beautiful island in Lakshadweep. I sat with my scuba-diving instructor, Hugues Vitry, to take an exam on a white sandy beach under coconut trees. I was quizzed on Archimedes' principle on buoyancy and Boyle's Law on the partial pressure of gases and so on, which I remembered studying in school.

It was at Lakshadweep, though, that I truly enjoyed learning the physics of scuba diving because the lab was the ocean and the object of the experiment was my body!

I passed with flying colours in the islands where I had opened India's first scuba-diving school in 1992.

2

Goodbye, Dehradun

My mother, Shashikala Kakar, had separated from my father when my sister, Mandakini, and I were quite young, and so my memories of my father are fleeting. As a single mother, she worked in Delhi to support our education, while we stayed with our grandparents in Dehradun. I remember my father coming to visit us bearing gifts—though for me the most memorable moments were when I was six years old, and he taught me how to ride horses in Delhi. I developed an abiding love for horses from him, which I carry till today. Though she wasn't even a graduate, my mother was a voracious reader. She read and collected all kinds of books: from thrillers and adventures to romances. I inherited my love for books from her.

My mother was a very proud and independent woman, and one day, my grandfather went too far when he pulled her leg about leaving her children with him while she was falooting around in Delhi. This comment did not go down too well with her. The next thing I knew, I was extracted from my grandparents' home and transferred to a strange school somewhere in Punjab called Sainik School, Kunjpura. It was a military school that trained all their cadets to become officers and gentlemen in the Indian Armed Forces. My life had come a full circle. The principal, Colonel Eric J. Simeon (retd), was a friend of my mother's, having served in the same regiment as my father, namely the Signals. When my mother was looking for a boarding school to put me in, he met her at some mutual friend's house and told her, 'Send him to us in Kunjpura! We will put some hair on his chest.'

Suddenly, I was collecting a list of essentials to survive in a military school. I packed my things in a tin trunk with my name stencilled on it, and then went to Delhi by train and on to Karnal by bus, on the Grand Trunk Road, accompanied by my mother. In a matter of days, I had shifted from St Thomas' Dehradun to Sainik School, Kunjpura (SSK), six kilometres from Karnal and in the middle of nowhere. I found myself transported from the Doon valley's verdant forests and greenery to a semi-arid landscape; from green, grassy meadows to a dusty, sprawling school on three hundred acres.

When I arrived it was baking in the midsummer heat, with dust devils whirling in the afternoon. I missed the companionship of girls the most as SSK was an all-boys school. Goodbye, Mrs A. Goodbye, Nalini, Dipika and all the rest, including my best friend, Ian Howard. Goodbye, Dehradun. I was a bit shell-shocked and I went through the motions of admissions like a zombie. I got my kit with my dormitory's details, house and roll number: 415. At that particular moment, it felt like a prison number.

The administrative work took all morning and as I bid farewell to my doting mother, my attention turned to the comments that I could hear. 'Oh, he looks like a bookworm.' 'He is a kagazi pehelwan—ek lagayega, toh baith jayega,' and so on. I reported to the games field as it was that time of the day. My house was Panipat House, and my house master was a tough, grizzled old veteran called Arthur David. He had divided the volunteers for a football match into two teams. When I reported to him, he looked at my gangly frame dismissively and asked, 'Have you played any games at all?'

'Yes, sir,' I replied.

He put me as the goalie, where I would do the least damage to the team I was playing for. To his surprise, I excelled at it. I was agile and athletic, without looking like it, and had done a lot of ground gymnastics with Butlerwhite, so I could throw myself all over the goal without injuring myself—that's very important for a goalie.

He finally decided to test me on penalty shots, which he took on himself. Penalty shots are the most difficult to save. Boxing had taught me to always look at the opponent's eyes because he will give a split-second warning showing where he is about to attack. It's the same with football. The body language does not matter because a penalty-taker always disguises his intentions by using his body like a feint in boxing. It's the eyes. It's always the eyes. I saved the first three shots at the goal and realized that the attitude had swiftly changed from 'Let's see what you can do' to 'I will show the little fucker'.

Mr David's credibility was at stake, and I understood that I needed to befriend my house master rather than antagonize him to survive my school tenure! I let the next three go without making my intentions too obvious. I would dive just short or over the ball, as my desperate fingers clutched thin air, venting about my close miss and thumping the ground in frustration. Now the duel was well and truly on. I saved the next one and let the two after that go. Last of ten, both the teams were quiet and you could cut the tension with a knife. In slow-mo, Mr David trotted up to the ball and stopped mid-kick.

I had already committed myself. I scrambled to the opposite side of the goalpost as Mr David tapped the ball, with a triumphant smile, into the far corner. I changed direction almost in the air, and my fingers just grazed the ball. It veered from its original path and hit the goalpost, still in play. We watched as the ball agonizingly rolled over the line. Everybody expelled their collective breaths, explosively together, and cheered for the closeness of the goal. I became a hero and Mr David looked at me as his go-to boy. I was well on my way to becoming accepted in an all-boys Jat military school!

Sainik Schools were the brainchild of Left-leaning Krishna Menon, the then defence minister of India. He felt that if top public school education was offered to the children of Other Ranks (ORs), they would make first-class officers. The Sainik Schools in India were given the task of grooming, polishing and educating young cadets mostly from rural areas into officer-like material. My school, Sainik School, Kunjpura, was the first to be set up to do this. The biggest hurdle for the young 'rangad' Jats, who came fresh off the farm to school, was to cope with English as that was the medium of instruction, except on the parade ground and the games field. Rangad is a Jat term, meaning uncurried, ungroomed, raw and slightly wild in demeanour. It sort of sums up all of this and more about being a Jat. Here I was, in an almost 95 per cent Jat-dominated school, one of the few who was familiar with *the* foreign language, English. I remember the look of wounded patience my Hindi teacher, the erudite and impressive Mr Budhwar, wore when he asked me to read the poem on the battle of Haldighati during my first day in class.

My face resembled the rainbow as I stumbled my way through this beautiful piece of Hindi poetry and proceeded to massacre it completely. In the stunned silence that ensued in the class, bar a few giggles, he said with great gravitas, 'Angrez chale gaye, aap ko chhod gaye.' Many years later, I heard the same gravitas on BBC Hindi news when a major catastrophe had hit some part of the planet. The BBC had tracked Mr K.N. Budhwar to the boonies of Kunjpura and offered him the position of the head of the Hindi channel. I did not have a gift for languages, and I struggled through my Hindi class and just about scraped through every time, thanks to a little bit of help from my friends.

We had a fascinating mix of teachers at SSK, handpicked by the principal himself. They were from all over the country and initially were very reluctant to come to the boondocks in Punjab. Like the diminutive Mr Marar, who taught us maths. He never raised his voice. Instead, when he found somebody who was not paying attention to his droning, he would walk up behind him and grab the very delicate skin below the upper arm joining the armpit, and pinch it viciously. He migrated to Australia eventually, thank god!

Then there was Chitravanshi, the art teacher. Besides being known for his art, his main claim to fame was a chicken coop full of juicy chickens behind his house. He kept them for their eggs, as if he did not get enough from his rations, supplied by the school for teachers with families. Chitravanshi had five scrawny kids who paled in comparison to his fattened chickens, and we used to wonder whether he was scrimping on feeding his kids and was feeding his chickens instead. I was still a junior in school when I was coopted by the school captain to do a recce of the chicken pen.

I snuck off to the art teacher's chicken pen in the dead of the night. It was strategically located at the back of his bungalow, just behind the kitchen. It was pitch black, and I knew he was a light sleeper and very particular about his chickens. I ninja'd up to the pen and tried to adjust to the gloom to spot the chickens. I found none on the floor of the cage. I looked up and saw them all in a line on a crossbar built for them halfway up the pen. They were sleeping with their heads tucked under their wings.

There was a small gap between the roof and the wall's netting, just enough for a bony arm to reach in. Now I understood why I had been chosen to be the murgi chor. Extreme care had to be taken to grab the bloody bird around the neck and not its backside. It was a matter of dexterity and nimble fingers as shining a torch into the chicken coop in the middle of the night was a no-no. I was the obvious choice to perform the act, since I had a slight build with skinny limbs, but was strong and tensile, thanks to sports and boxing. Having also handled wounded jungli murgis in Dehradun's forests, I was given the task of performing the most delicate and crucial part of the mission.

The problem was finding which wing the chickens had tucked their heads under while sleeping. If you got this essential piece of layout right, then came the next, and extremely crucial, act of grabbing the chicken around its neck to prevent it from squawking and making a racket, as this would disturb the whole roost. You can imagine the noise and panic, both among the chickens and the chors because the repercussions would be immediate and extreme. We did not know whether the art teacher was armed and dangerous—well, he was dangerous definitely, but we assumed the answer after the question mark next to armed was a resounding 'Yes!' The others hung around to keep an eye out and make sure that nobody stumbled on to our nocturnal mission.

We had also learnt from our combat exercises about camouflaging reflective parts of our bodies for night ops. We covered our face and hands with boot polish applied in streaks to look like the night shadows. The whole operation was perilous and fraught with the danger of being caught. But we did it nonetheless—not once, but many times! I think that was the time I really got hooked on to fear and became an adrenaline junkie.

Since I was the junior-most, I was also appointed as the cook and bottle washer. We had duplicated the keys to the school's cold room where all the perishables and goodies were kept, and we compounded our clandestine night missions with regular raids to the cold room for provisions to cook the birds in the dorm. We took butter, cream, onions, potatoes, masalas, bread, jam, and whatever else caught our fancy. The fruits of risking your life are genuinely sweet! We became good at it; so much so that we were never caught! Plus I became a damn skilled cook to boot!

Chitravanshi came to the prefect's lounge one day and complained bitterly that the Nilokheri villagers were stealing his chickens. He told us to do regular rounds at night to catch the thieves. The irony of this whole episode was that now we could be out at night, and if anybody questioned us, we had a perfect alibi. Of course, we were still very cautious!

Our English teacher, Arthur David, grizzled and hard-bitten, was quite vindictive in small ways. I was his blue-eyed boy, not only because my English was impeccable, but also because of the football field incident. He had got the better of me as the ball trickled into the goal after ricocheting off my palms and crossing the line during a penalty shootout. I noticed that he used to pick on a clean-cut, light-eyed boy called Dilip, who spoke excellent English and was good at his studies. It dawned on me after I got to know his surname that he was Colonel and Mrs Jean Simeon's son. Mr David had a bone to pick with the colonel and vindictively took it out on an unsuspecting Dilip. I would have hated to be in his shoes as he was baited and teased mercilessly because of his pedigree.

Dilip and I became terrific friends, as both of us were dismissed as angrez ki aulads. Because of my stream of pretty colourful, vituperative language that I used liberally on the parade ground, the Jat students would say, 'Kakar, jo badi angrezi jhadta hai!' Though I must say, Dilip worked hard to become a part of the Haryanvi crowd. He picked up the choicest of Jat abuses. He was an excellent horseman, and we also got along because of our shared love for horses. Like me, Dilip didn't join the services. He went to St Stephen's College and majored in history. Post-school, we became even closer, as I spent my first year after school in Delhi, trying to get admission to a decent college, without much luck, thanks to my awful grades.

In his third year in college, Dilip Simeon suddenly went UG—the term romantically used by the many groupies and sympathizers of those who had gone underground—and became a Naxalite. He dropped off the map without a trace, and nobody knew where he was.

Dilip used to get along famously with my mother and loved her cooking, as most of my perpetually hungry college friends did. She always made sure to keep her fridge well stocked as a whole platoon of hungry college friends used to land up at odd hours to raid it. So his worried parents finally got in touch with my mother, who seemed to be his only link with his past life. Though my mother's link with Dilip was tenuous at best. He sometimes used to jump over our house's back wall and come in through a conveniently open back door, kept unlatched at night, just in case. He would sneak in at the dead of night, wolf down some food from the fridge, wash the plates, and disappear the same way, drawing a smiley on a torn piece of paper. That was the only way we knew of his comings and goings.

Once he did not come for two months, and we worried and fretted, wondering whether he was okay or not. After two months of no nocturnal activity, the fridge was suddenly wiped clean one night, and we knew Dilip was back. That was when the Naxal movement in West Bengal was at its heights. Indira Gandhi finally decided to break its back and wipe out the hardcore cadres of the Communist Party of India (Marxist–Leninist), whose motto was that political power comes from the barrel of a gun.

By that time, Colonel Simeon had retired from SSK and joined La Martiniere, Calcutta, as the principal. The then governor of West Bengal called Colonel and Mrs Simeon over for tea, and discreetly told them to get a hold of Dilip. He urged them to get him out of the country before the month ended, as he could not be responsible for Dilip's safety. The orders from the powers that be were unequivocal: 'Take no prisoners!'

We always referred to our principal and his wife as 'Pater' and 'Mater' in school, so we left a message for Dilip in the fridge: 'Call Pater! Urgent!' He got the message in time and was whisked away by his parents to England, albeit kicking, biting, screaming, though not too loudly. And the rest is history. West Bengal and Calcutta saw a bloodbath in the following months, and the Congress party never came back to power again.

3

Sainik School, Kunjpura

We had some real characters in our Havildar Majors who taught us at SSK. They were responsible for shaping the Jat cadets' fighting qualities and training the few of us motley types in between, who were desperately trying to belong in order to survive. Tara Singh, the undefeated inter-services, light heavyweight champion, was our boxing coach and drill instructor. He was a pugnacious, ferocious Sardar with a trimmed beard, tough as nails, even though he was pushing fifty. He also knew a bit of English and would miss no opportunity to try it on his hapless cadets.

I remember one cold December morning, the freezing wind had chapped our lips and blew up our shorts, shrivelling our 'whatsits' into oblivion, while we stood at savdhan, with a clunky First World War Lee-Enfield .303 rifle held to our sides, almost welded there. The barrel's metal and the breech were so cold that our skin used to stick to it like a limpet mine, and if we made the mistake of a jerky movement, a whole lot of skin from our palms would peel away, coarsely stuck to the rifle.

Tara Singh was a study in ferocity as he stalked the platoon, glaring at us cadets one by one; our family jewels were freezing, and our palms were burning from the biting cold of the rifle's metal breech. He would suddenly stop and shout in Hindi, 'Squad bayein se tej chal! Squad thumm!' As we took the first marching step forward, we were ordered to halt mid-step, and some of us teetered on the edge of balance, while others lost it, took an extra step, and quickly tried to recover by back-stepping.

Nothing missed his intense, coal-black eyes, and he walked down the formation and stopped by my side. He suddenly bent down, coddled my frozen goolies in his palm, and announced sotto voce like a whiplash which everybody heard across the parade ground, 'Kakar, don't get carried away by the momentum of your balls! Halt means halt, not shifting around to get your balance. Koi shaq!' Sometimes on a winter night, I can still hear him and feel the bloody rifle painfully welded by the cold to my hand, and my knee-jerk reaction is to squeeze my legs together to protect the family jewels.

Tara Singh was also our boxing coach. Having boxed for the army, he had decided that we were a bunch of namby-pambies, so he gave us the works: long runs in the morning going forwards and backwards, hours of practice on the heavy punch bag, skipping and footwork. Most importantly, he trained us like Butlerwhite to watch the opponent's eyes, for he would telegraph his attack a split second early. That was the only warning you got to defend, back-pedal, counterattack and, at all times, remain cool as ice.

Tara Singh used to punish the boys who would lose their tempers and react rather than act. I was one of the few people in school who had boxed before, though he looked at me sceptically. I wished he would find me unfit, so that I could go back to the safety of the football field. No such luck! He decided to put me in the ring with a bigger boy who was game, but untutored, and told us to go two rounds while he and the rest of the cadets watched and cheered, sure that I was in for a thrashing.

My opponent was like a strong and lumbering ox, and I ran circles around him, punching him at will. Not being able to land anything worthwhile, he suddenly lost it and started swinging wildly, and if those roundhouse punches had landed on my face or body, it would have been goodbye! But my inherent fear and Butlerwhite's training kicked in, and I pulverized the poor fellow. I kept looking at Tara Singh to stop the fight, but he kept the stopwatch ticking and let the sparring session continue.

By now, the cheering partisan crowd of boys had become silent, and would wince every time I weaved in and double-tapped him with two straight lefts and set him up for a right cross to the jaw. He was a strong boy, built to endure the punishment. If only he had followed his training and avoided losing his temper, he would have given me a run for my money since he was taller, heavier, and had a longer reach. Tara Singh practically and directly brought home the lesson that losing your temper makes you lose the fight. Period!

The only good thing about being shortlisted for boxing training was the special diet given to the boxers: extra eggs and milk for protein. The rest of the school tiptoed around us, careful to avoid taking an unnecessary panga. For me, it was scary to be in the ring. Whenever I was in it, I always had butterflies in my stomach, and felt nervous and scared. I never got over the fear of being seriously hurt to truly enjoy the sport, even though I boxed right through school and was good at it. I have never forgotten the lessons I learnt and regularly apply them even now to everyday crises. I don't know whether it builds character as all the proponents of the sport claim. But it makes you face naked fear and perform despite it. That's what life is all about, isn't it?

Tara Singh migrated to Canada, and we lost touch with him, unfortunately. For me, he was a much more intense and rougher version of Butlerwhite, and both of them, in their own ways, unwittingly shaped my survival instincts.

―――――――

When I became house captain of Panipat House (Yellow House), I got saddled with a whole lot of responsibility, which I wasn't particularly keen on shouldering. Arthur David set one of the expectations early on. He was very gung-ho about our house being the cock house, which means numero uno in all the disciplines, apart from academics. He had a burning ambition to place Panipat House in the top spot that year and win the best house trophy.

Under normal circumstances, our house didn't stand a chance of a snowball in hell. He hoped that under my leadership and his firm guidance, we could top the charts of the whole gamut of activities. He wanted us to maintain our lead in all the extracurriculars throughout the year: from debating to cross-country running and horse riding, from football, hockey, cricket, to gymnastics like vaulting. It looked a little far-fetched to me as I was much more comfortable taking them one at a time rather than strategizing for all the activities well in advance.

Mr David's eyes had a piercing gaze as he delivered his pep talk. He quoted from some piece of literature, 'Cometh the moment, cometh the man', to which I looked behind my back and found, much to my chagrin, that he was singularly addressing me. He told me that since our school had started in the sixties, Panipat House had never made the number one position. He had to count on me to make sure that we did it this year as, according to his calculations and estimates, if the boys got the right leadership, they would get the josh to perform to their potential! For him, it was a do-or-die situation, and he fixed me with a beady eye, clapped me on my slightly bony shoulders, and asked me, 'Are you ready?'

I coughed and muttered, 'Yes, sir.'

'No,' he said.

'Are you ready?'

I told him, 'Yes, sir,' in a civilized way.

My reply wasn't good enough for him. He looked me in the eye and asked loudly, '*Are you ready?*'

I just wanted to get the hell out of there as the whole thing was getting too intense. I looked him in the eye and said firmly, 'Yes, sir!' He held me by both shoulders, fixed me with a look that made me very uncomfortable and squirmy. However, I kept myself in check knowing what he wanted, and then with great focus, he asked me again, 'Are you ready, son?' 'Yes, sir,' I replied sotto voce and, satisfied, he let me go. I smartly stepped back, wished him goodnight and left, a bit shaken at his vehemence to win at all costs. Now we couldn't be casual about the bloody cock house, having reassured Mr David that either we were going to bloody well win the damn trophy or somebody was going to die in the process.

All our houses were named after battlefields in Punjab: Panipat (Yellow), Kurukshetra (Red), Thaneswar (Blue) and Chillianwala (Green), and the competition between them was nothing short of a battle—with its euphoria and dejection going hand in hand. The whole house, juniors, seniors, staff and their spouses, used to turn up for the action, cheering themselves hoarse from the sidelines. We called for a war council with all the prefects and athletes in attendance, and went into a huddle to figure out a strategy. We looked at our strengths and all our glaring weaknesses!

We desperately needed a second and a third for the debating contest, with me coming in at number one. It just didn't matter if one guy from the team came first. It was all about averages and probabilities. I learnt early on that hoping for the best never works and, instead, planning for the worst works much better. Later, I figured out that this was all a part of Murphy's Law—if anything can go wrong, it will go wrong.

We practised strategy and tactics, both on and off the field. Our coaches did not belong to any particular house and were there for everybody unless it was an inter-school match, which was all about drawing the battle lines. Their main aim was to coach the school team, and they had no affinity with any of the houses. Therefore, all the strategies and tactics based on our strengths and weaknesses had to be planned internally.

We had to counter Harbans Singh, the Green House's scoring machine in football and hockey. He was a brilliant sportsman and, in his time, unstoppable. We had to put three of our best defences to block him at any cost and stop him from running away with the match. During our football match against his team, we managed to distract, block and even foul our arch-rival, Harbans, on the field. We also found out that his house pet name was makhi and he hated it, and we used this to provoke him into losing his shirt and, therefore, the plot. We drew all our matches with the Green House and thrashed everyone else.

We had a few problems with Kurukshetra House as their goalkeeper was Vijay Sawani, a tall, strapping lad who was the school's football goalkeeper. He was also a good boxer and knew the trick about watching the opponent's eyes in anticipation. He was fearless and blocked everything; so it came down to penalty kicks. I had managed to save four on five and so had he. I asked to take the final penalty shot, which nobody wanted, and did an 'Arthur David' on him. I ran up to the ball and stopped mid-stroke, and Vijay committed himself. I had my glasses on. I always wore my glasses when I played games, and while the sun was setting behind him, my glasses caught the glare and he couldn't see my eyes. I casually kicked the ball into the opposite goalpost! He scrambled madly on all fours to try and reach the ball, but no chance; we had five goals to four. Panipat in the lead!

I went back to take on the final penalty. My throat was dry, my eyes intense. Kurukshetra's captain took the kick. He should have given it to Vijay for a chance at revenge, but I got lucky. He ran up to the ball while looking down and then, just before kicking it, he looked up at the spot he intended to kick it in, giving me a split-second warning. I launched myself in the air as he made contact in slow motion; the ball curled away towards the goal's corner. If I had not anticipated correctly, we would have gone into sudden death, and then god alone knows what would have happened! But I had predicted correctly, Butlerwhite and Tara Singh had taught me well. I met the ball, well in time, in mid-air, and punched it out of play, and we won by the skin of our teeth.

Now, two houses were neck and neck for the ultimate trophy, and all that was left was the cross-country race: over twelve kilometres of kutcha roads, fields and thorny bushes. There were a hundred runners, twenty-five from each house, and everybody got points—the first got hundred points, the second got ninety-nine and so on. The runners in the first, second and third place got medals, and their houses collected hundred, ninety-nine and ninety-eight points. The race officials would tally up which house scored the maximum points from its twenty-five runners, depending on how they placed! The cross-country could knock all the calculations and predictions for a six, as it was by far the biggest scoring event in the calendar.

We had DG, a great cross-country runner of all time. He could run ten kilometres without breaking a sweat in full Chindit order. We took DG's 100 points for granted and just concentrated on the next fifteen runners as a fail-safe Plan B. We trained only after lights out so that nobody could find out our modus operandi. DG used to stagger into class, red-eyed and tired, but no one cottoned on. We planned to run the opposition into the ground! Some of our runners would act as pacemakers and set a scorching speed to upset the opposition's rhythm. This tactic would allow the leading runners to conserve their energy and bide their time till the six-kilometre point. Then, they would take over, and the pacemakers would keep up. Everybody else had no stamina left to finish with a flourish except our team.

The big day dawned, and on the day of the cross-country race event, everybody got up just before reveille, which was always announced by an unfortunate bugler on the roof of the dorm at 6.15 a.m. sharp. He got cursed with old drill boots thrown at him for all his troubles. There was a massive banging on my door in the morning. I leapt out of bed thinking it was time for the boys to warm up as the cross-country race was going to kick off at 7.30 a.m. sharp—07.30 hundred hours as we used to call it. I looked at my watch. It was 5.30 a.m. What the shit, I thought to myself as I threw the door open to chew out the unfortunate early riser who had banged on my door. Instead, I found two breathless juniors standing before me, looking distraught.

Before I could say anything, they blurted out, 'Sir, DG ko tragedy ho gayi!' I couldn't believe it, so I asked, 'What happened to him? Diarrhoea? Fever? Did he sprain an ankle?' They looked down at the ground, without volunteering an answer. I was foxed. I looked up and there, in the distance, I saw a tableau of four cadets, two of them supporting the guy in the middle, who seemed to have collapsed into a dher. They had dragged him across the football field, and his toes had cut two lonely furrows in the dirt! The third cadet had a sheet held up like a flag and was trotting along next to them.

You guessed it! The guy in the middle was DG. He had collapsed and was incapable of even standing on his own. I waited, agitatedly, for them to leg it over to me. I was fixated on my champion runner and couldn't believe my eyes. I asked the incapacitated DG, 'What happened?' The junior holding the flag, who had been standing skittishly, suddenly piped up in a dramatic stage whisper, 'Sir, nightfall.' I thought I had heard wrong and for a moment couldn't quite figure out what he meant. Then, I realized the boy was holding up a bedsheet and it had a discoloured patch on it! It then dawned on me that he was referring to a wet dream. I suppose, in the vernacular, as it is a taboo subject, it had come to be known as 'nightfall'.

I suddenly felt relieved and thought to myself that it was not such a big deal. It happens all the time—so, if it's not wanking and deliberate, then it's nightfall and inadvertent. It must have been the result of abstinence. Nothing that a drink of Glucose-D would not solve! So I slapped DG on the back and told him that everything was okay, and he would be fine in time for the cross-country race, which was one-and-a-half hours away. I told him I would bring him a glass of milk with glucose to fix him. DG was mumbling something, and I bent down to hear what he was saying. He was incoherent, and I suppose very embarrassed, coming from a god-fearing middle-class family.

I caught the gist of what he was saying. It was something like this, 'Sir, mein toh barbaad ho gaya. Meri poori takat behe gayi hai! Mein toh khada bhi nahin ho sakta!' He collapsed on the dorm steps, so I thought on my feet and came up with a plausible answer. I told him with great intensity, 'DG, sun meri baat. Teri tanki abhi bhi full hai! Yeh toh overflow hai!' He kept shaking his head and refusing to believe any of my arguments, including my insistence that all of us not-so-good boys wanked our brains out without it ever affecting our on-field performances. I told him since he is a good boy who doesn't ever indulge himself in any such shenanigans, he shouldn't worry. And okay, admittedly, we never had overflows because we regularly emptied our tanks.

No joy. He wouldn't listen and went into a guilt-ridden, zombie-like state! I finally called the school doctor, who arrived on his scooter, looking scrubbed at 6.30 a.m. I have never seen Doc not looking scrubbed. He must have washed his hands twenty times a day. He promptly went to work on DG—he made him lie down, felt his pulse and heartbeat, breathing, etc.—and found no symptoms to explain his state of total physical and mental collapse. He whispered intensely in his ear, 'DG! Stand up! DG, you are fine! DG, get ready to run and warm-up! DG, glory awaits you!' Not a chance. DG was far away in the labyrinths of his fevered mind, in some state of guilt that he had spilled his seed in vain, and had failed himself and his beliefs beyond repair.

We did manage to get him up to attempt a shambling gait and, to our utmost horror and the rival houses' jubilation, DG managed to come last at the cross-country race. But finish he did, with a herculean effort. Nobody had calculated a Plan B. Though we were demoralized by our champion's state, we realized it was a do-or-die situation for us. Egged on by a cheering junior squad, a wild-eyed housemaster and a jack-in-the-box house captain, we somehow did it! We managed to squeak ourselves into a narrow lead with our overall points, and we clinched the trophy to wild celebrations!

Whenever in life, all my calculations have been shattered by one throw of fate's dice, I remember Panipat House's stunning victory, where nobody was willing to back us and our odds were like a snowball in hell. I always keep my hidden joker in the pack: Plan B! It's not the outstanding person who single-handedly wins the long race, but the team where everybody does their little bit and brings home the bacon.

It hassled me to have my champion laid low at the last moment. I decided to get to the bottom of this unusual predicament with a little bit of background work and, after quizzing DG at length, I came to some rough calculations. DG's parents had crossed over from Pakistan as refugees. The trauma of the journey, the experiences en route, and the loss of friends and family had impacted them profoundly and made them a little fearful in their outlook. When DG was six years old, he had been inducted into a social youth club in the neighbourhood, where they had taught him patriotism, discipline, etc. He was there for around four years and was steeped in the Brahmachari philosophy, which taught him that any sexual fantasy and loss of virility was taboo. It results in a loss of character and physical strength, he was told. He had been so thoroughly indoctrinated that DG genuinely believed he was destroyed when he had his wet dream.

He psyched himself into a state of collapse. The indoctrination and belief system was so deeply embedded in him that despite five years of rigorous military training and logic, at the age of sixteen, he had collapsed into a dher. I discovered this form of reality and it was interesting researching it. I found that most fundamental organizations have a direct connection with Pavlov. The Pavlovian concept—where he conditioned his dogs—is still alive and kicking in today's world. Its milder form takes on the art of advertising and propaganda, and, in its much more fundamental avatar, it is the backbone of all the world's extremely conservative organizations.

Apart from our housemaster and English teacher, Arthur David, and our boxing instructor, Tara Singh, another memorable instructor was our riding dafedar, Risal Singh. He was a full-fledged uncurried Jat, who used lots of colourful language in Haryanvi and Italian. Yes, Italian! Risal Singh's regiment had been a part of the Allied invasion of Italy. After the D-Day landing in Normandy, this was supposed to be Europe's soft underbelly. The Italians had gotten fed up with Mussolini's regime by then, so the Indian troops were welcomed with open arms, especially by the ladies.

He quickly realized that the best way into an Italian woman's favours was to woo her with broken Italian and a generous amount of C-rations. In his two years in Italy, he learnt the language and became very popular with the ladies. He would sometimes break into Italian, and wax eloquent about them in moments of weakness and reminiscence. During our riding sessions at school, he would sometimes take us on a cross-country, to impress the village belles with his prowess on the horse while they were busy cutting grass in the fields. He would line us up and pretend to give us a display of his equestrian talents, and they would lower their ghunghats and giggle among themselves.

Risal Singh spent the first week of training in an enclosed corral called the Ring. He had a homegrown theory about horse riding. He felt as long as a student cadet was scared of falling, he could never be completely comfortable on the saddle. The fear of falling off a horse would prevent them from being in sync with the horse. Also, horses—

like all animals—can smell fear, and if a rider is even remotely afraid, the horse will not trust his leadership and will refuse to do as ordered, which makes the situation even worse! Risal Singh had a necessary and straightforward solution to teach horse riding: make the student fall as many times as possible and lose his fear of falling. Most cadets hated riding because of this reason. He would laconically say, 'Kakar, riding seekhni hai toh girna seekh! Aur phir mount ho ja!' (If you want to learn to ride, then you must learn how to fall and get back into the saddle!)

The tricky part of horse riding is that if you are not balanced on the saddle while the horse is moving, regardless of what you do, you will definitely fall. Every amateur rider knows this, but his instinct is to hang on for dear life. Wrong! Never cling to the saddle and the horses in the fond and futile hope of regaining your seat. The danger of clinging to a moving horse is that inevitably you will slide under the animal and fall under his hooves, with a good chance that the animal will step on you and cause serious injury. Instead, it is best if you immediately prepare to jettison yourself sufficiently in advance, pick the position and place of your landing, to cause the least amount of harm. If you're nimble, you will always land on your feet, or your arse. Both are relatively safe spots to land on!

I remember preparing to go for a jump, which I wasn't sure about, and the horse, of course, sensed my reluctance and refused the fence at the last moment, and screeched to a halt with his buttocks touching the ground. Yours truly was poised precariously on the saddle, leaning forward in anticipation, when the bloody horse refused the jump, and I went sailing over his head in a neat somersault and managed a perfect three-point landing on my arse and two feet. I was a bit shaken, but not hurt—just winded!

I was lying on the dusty ground with the reins in my hand. I looked up at the blue sky with its white clouds, and my sheepish horse was looking down at my exit from grace. Old Risal Singh trotted over on his horse, looked down at me, and with a hint of amusement in his eyes, commented, 'Kyun, Kakar-e, kya hua? Moochhon mein pasina aa riya kya? Chal mount ho ja!'

'But, sir,' I stammered, 'I just fell!'

'So?' he said. 'Namak nahi hai kya? Saare din lete rahe ga? Mount ho ja! Abhi!'

Back I climbed on to the saddle and re-attempted the jump until I went over cleanly, aching all over.

That year, a young twenty-two-year-old exchange teacher, Kenneth Smith, had landed up in school from Oxford to do hard labour in the Raj's old penal colonies. His eyes lit up when he found the riding school. He wanted to learn how to ride and landed up at the crack of dawn at the stable with us, only to be given the most ornery and challenging horse, Udhbang. Nobody wanted to ride him because he had a mind of his own with a disjointed canter that met the rider coming down while the horse was going up. He would be met halfway with a sickening crunch.

Seeing Kenneth's reddened face, Risal Singh would quip to the rest of us, 'Angrezon ke chuttra dekhe hain, laal-laal hote hain, bandar ki tarah!' After the ride, we used to see Ken Smith, a bit glassy-eyed, trying to walk with his legs apart as his arse was sore. We thought that would be the last time we would see him, but no! The next morning, he was back again for some more punishment. I watched this for a few weeks and was very impressed by Ken's dogged determination. He actually could stay on the horse, with the correct posture. His grip on the horse was improving faster than ours.

One time, Ken and I were cycling back from the stable across the three-hundred-acre school campus, where the stables were at one corner, at least 2.5 kilometres from the mess. When I told him how impressed we were by his determination, he sheepishly confessed that he had a girlfriend back home who came from manor-born, blue-blooded stock. Her father and sundry other friends looked down on him because Ken was a baker's son.

He hadn't had the privilege to ride, hunt, chase foxes and shoot pheasants, which is what the landed gentry occupied themselves with, while the plebeians worked their arses off! Now, he was determined to ride to show them that he could, and go over the fields and hedges with great aplomb to be accepted. And ride he did! He had become a pretty good equestrian by the time he went back to good old Blighty. Of course, the British had got the Hindi word vilayati arse-wise and, as usual, mispronounced it as Blighty. I was quite surprised at the highly pronounced caste system they still had in good old England. I thought that was only prevalent here. Oh well, you live and learn. I wonder what happened to Selena, his lady love.

Now, I look back at those days of self-discovery, fun and games, and realize that everybody in their right senses should be afraid of a half-bred saddle horse. The horse is sixteen hands at the shoulder, about 6.5–7-feet tall, is 1,500 kilograms of muscle and bone, and has a mind of his own, which needs constant reinforcement that the rider is the boss! He kicks and bites if the mood suits him. It is not as simple as gritting your teeth, leaping into the saddle, and saying, 'Hi-yo, Silver! Away!'—the Lone Ranger's signature farewell. He will probably not budge and will look back at you with an expression of 'Dude? Are you for real?' It all boils down to facing your fears and sending the right signals to your horse. That's when you can look forward to the beginning of a relationship in anticipation, once you are over your state of agitation.

And that is when you start noticing all the joys of riding: the wind on your face and the twitching of the horse's ears as you talk to him! The mood will change as he flattens his ears and rolls his eyes, the rhythm of the trot, the canter, the gallop, and the final awe-inspiring feeling of being a centaur—half horse, half human, one entity! It's all linked to something as raw and primal as fear, and then facing it! That is why I have made horse riding one of the mandatory skills that need to be learnt for the entrepreneurship and advertising class, where the most significant hurdle is fear of failure and risk. Horse riding is not only a test and mould of character, but it is the ultimate partnership between man and horse.

The highlight of Risal Singh's career as a cavalryman was the planning for the Founder's Day celebration and the fact that the chief of staff, General Chaudhary, himself a cavalryman, was to be the guest of honour. The school went into overdrive as the day's activities, followed by a bada khana (feast), were being planned in a frenzy. As far as the school equestrian team was concerned, we were the mounted escort for the chief guest from the parade ground gate. Later in the afternoon, an impressive tent pegging display had been laid on for the chief by my dafedar Risal Singh and the SSK equestrian team.

Tent pegging is a Pathan war sport adapted by the British Army for showing skill and nerve in a combat-like situation. The sport's origins were in the predawn attacks on the campsites of the British troops. It was a display of skill, guts and glory. At the hour, the first wave of riders charged through the sleeping camp, with shrill bolis (battle cries), and removed the wooden tent pegs from the ground with lances, collapsing the tents on the sleeping infantry. Then the second wave of riders galloped through, decapitating the hapless troops with their swords. Thus was born the sport of tent pegging, due to be displayed to the chief of staff by us.

We spent the afternoons practising and were also taught a tent-pegging boli—a challenge, if it may be called so. At the start of his run at the pegs, every rider would stand up in the stirrups, wave the lance around his head and shout out this boli. He would then settle down to a full gallop, leaning down at his galloping horse's side, to align and pierce the wooden peg with his steel-tipped lance. The rider would then disengage backward, under the right shoulder, as the horse thundered past and slowed down at the end of the run to trot back to the starting line! We were supposed to take three pegs for the round, and the rider with the maximum pegs would win. There were four riders, coached under the beady eye of the riding sahib, as it was a matter of great prestige for him to present his acolytes to his chief. All went well in the run-up to D-Day.

The Founder's Day dawned and progressed as per meticulously laid plans, the mounted escort by the guard of honour, and the rest of the formalities went by just tickety-boo. Now came the grand finale and the tent-pegging display. We were full of confidence and strutted around in our riding boots and solar topees. During rehearsals, we hadn't realized that there was no clutter around the chief guests' pandal where the pegs were placed. But, today, there was a lot of stuff around there, the most glaring one being a table full of trophies glittering in the setting sun, just opposite the spot where the pegs were dug into the ground. Horses are very unpredictable and high-spirited animals, and if there is something unexpected or unexplained in their periphery, they will likely react in an entirely high-strung manner.

Well, that's precisely what happened—the glittering trophies spooked them, and being retired polo ponies, they could turn on a dime! The riders shouted their challenge and tore down the track, leaning way out of line for an easy flick of the peg. The horses crossed the table full of shiny trophies and got spooked or bidkooed, and took off at right angles to their predetermined path. The rider continued in his original trajectory, meeting terra firma with a sickening thud, in a perfect three-point landing! I will say this for the riders' training and single-mindedness: they were up in a flash, had chased down a slightly panicky horse, and mounted it again while it bucked and fishtailed, and after controlling it, rode back to the starting point to try again. Risal Singh, his face a picture of consternation, was muttering furiously with his heavy Jat accent, 'Meri naak kat gayi', intermingled with 'Mamma mia!' and something '... puta' in Italian.

The tent-pegging event was in a shambles, with just me and my amazingly calm mare, Shyama, left to retrieve some semblance of what should have been! We cantered up as I talked to her incessantly. Her ears were alert and listening. I touched her with my heel on her side, and she flew into a gallop. I kept the lance hand on her neck, and stood up and let fly my challenge. 'Aaja pyaari mekh, tu hi toh tha Lahore ka launda!' She held her gallop true, and as I leaned out of the saddle to align the peg with my lance tip, I clasped the mare's mane with my left hand, also on the reins, and guided her with my knees. She went straight as an arrow, and except for a little roll of the eyes at the unfamiliar cups, she kept her pace, and I came up with the peg! Risal Singh trotted up to me on the way back and said, 'Izzat bacha di, Kakar, well done!'

General Chaudhary must have seen the consternation on the dafedar's face. He proceeded to make light of the fiasco and diverted our attention by asking us what boli we were using. In the Pathan tradition, each tribe was known by its boli. As taught to us, ours was 'Aaja pyaari mekh, tu hi toh tha Lahore ka launda!' The general sahib laughed uproariously and asked us if we knew the meaning of the boli. Other than the obvious, we had not paid much attention to it, thinking of it as a ritual. He told us about the annual cattle, horse and camel show held in pre-Partition Lahore, which was considered one of the largest cattle and horse shows in the subcontinent at the time. The Pathan and Afghan tribesmen would arrive in the plains to compete for the British Army's substantial prize money, and make the three-day festival highly competitive and entertaining.

Pathan tribesmen would compete with each other by flinging challenges and non-vegetarian jokes. General Chaudhary said that their most frequented brothels were known for their boys, the Pathans' preference. So the bolis were around the beauty and desirability of the boys. 'Either the boys are on me today or come to me, my beloved mekh, I will pierce you like the launda (boy) from Lahore.' While the general laughed, we looked uncomfortably at the ground, pretending not to have understood. Risal Singh, of course, was thunderstruck, as he had not bothered to explain the finer points of the boli to us. To be fair, I don't think he knew about it either, as he spent most of his post-war days in Italy.

The bada khana was something else. The kitchen staff was in their formal best, gloves and all. The principal tapped a glass with a spoon to get everyone's attention, and, in the rapt silence that followed, he raised a toast of water to the president of India. General Chaudhary echoed the toast. 'To the president, gentlemen!' he said, and settled down to a three-course dinner. Many of the cadets didn't realize that the waiters would follow the chief guest's cues and, as soon as he had finished his first course and put his knife and fork together, the waiters would clear the entire school's first course—completed or not! That's how formal dinners go.

On the second course, I was seated next to Mrs Chaudhary and got a tough piece of chicken, which I was trying desperately to saw into when it slipped and skidded, to my horror of horrors, straight on to Mrs Chaudhary's lap. I froze, waiting for the earth to open up and swallow me. Cool as a cucumber, she delicately picked the offending piece of chicken up and placed it back on my plate, and with a wink, she punned, 'Tough old bird.' I have rarely seen such graciousness or savoir faire since!

After dinner, when the staff and prefects retired to the lounge for coffee, I received the best piece of advice of my life—one that saved me from total disaster. General Chaudhary took me aside for a man-to-man and asked me what my plans were. I told him that I dreamt of being a polo player, and since the army was the only institution that could afford horses, I would like to be a cavalry officer. He heard me out, and then told me that he had been talking to Colonel Simeon about me and realized that I was quite individualistic, with definite opinions of my own. He cautioned that since I wore glasses and therefore was a category, I was unlikely to get a regiment of my choice. He laid it to me straight and said, 'Son, if we were not a peacetime army, I am sure you would have made a rapid and exceptional general in a state of war. Since, in 1965, we already gave the Pakistanis a bloody nose, it is unlikely that we will see any major hiccups for the next ten years. In which case, you would get cashiered for insubordination.' Period! He slapped me on the back, laughed and wandered off, impacting my life more than he could ever imagine!

One day the old boy, our principal, Colonel Simeon, decided that the senior boys needed the training to handle life's eventualities with polish. He knew that the boys were a little unsocial with ladies and desperately needed to acquire some social graces. The senior school was abuzz with the news that a busload of girls from Presentation Convent in Old Delhi would visit us soon for a social. The principal and the staff were to prepare us boys and train us on how to behave with girls, so that during the social, we wouldn't go into a shell or a huddle and behave like nincompoops.

I think many of our boys were petrified of attending a social with girls. The entire staff, and the principal and his wife would be there to partake in the festivities. Quite a few of the boys from the boxing team confessed that they would rather face a ferocious opponent in the ring than the girls in a social. There we were, in the prefects' lounge, animatedly discussing the modalities of engagements and combat, when in walks Havildar Major Tara Singh, straight as an arrow and announces that the principal's wife had requested him to teach the boys how to waltz!

'Woh keh hoti hai?' was the reaction of most of the boys. Having learnt the foxtrot in St Thomas's, I wondered how a drill instructor, however competent, could teach us the waltz. But, he did. He put on a scratchy record on the player, cranked up the volume, divided the boys into male and female partners, and instructed us about holding each other as we went about following the waltz's basic steps as if he was on the parade ground! That's how I learnt the waltz to the strains of 'The Blue Danube'.

He called out the timing at savdhan, in attention, 'Gintee se waltz karenge! Ek do teen, ek do teen! Ek!' (Waltz by the numbers 1-2-3-1!) When the boys got into a tangle, he stepped up and demonstrated the steps, describing the dance as 'De chakkar, le chakkar, de chakkar, le chakkar!' I have not forgotten the waltz till today, and as I get into its twirls, I can hear Tara Singh's voice over the flow of 'The Blue Danube': 'Le chakkar, de chakkar. Ek, do, teen, ek, do, teen! Ek!' A drill sergeant taught us the waltz! Bravo!

When the day of the social finally arrived, a busload of giggling schoolgirls got off at the parade ground. Along with the accompanying nuns, the girls were given a guard of honour, which I think was very impressive, with all of us strutting around in all our formal uniforms! We then escorted them to the dining hall, where they and our staff were all seated at the high table. The nuns, of course, wanted to say grace before the meal. A glass was tapped. The hubbub of 350 cadets subsided instantly to pin-drop silence as the Mother Superior led the prayers, while we were surreptitiously checking out the girls.

The boys and girls sat on opposite sides of the hall. The severe-looking nuns supervised the girls, who were waiting for the boys to walk across the daunting twenty-five steps and ask them for a dance. It had been drilled into their heads that good girls don't make the first move with unknown boys. I could see the boys chickening out. Here were a bunch of cadets being trained to walk into any battlefield in the world and even if certain death faced them, they would have willingly done that. Now, in the face of the most desirable and dainty young ladies, they were literally shitting their pants—even avoiding eye contact!

At this critical juncture hung the success or flop of this much-planned social experiment. The principal's wife, the diminutive Mrs Jean Simeon, stepped into the breach and rallied the school forces by announcing a snowball dance. She and Colonel Simeon stepped out to the floor and danced for a few minutes. As the music was paused, they split up and picked new partners from the slightly diffident student lot. By god, were they good dancers and proponents of the 'Le chakkar, de chakkar!' moves. Mrs Simeon picked the school captain, namely me, and Colonel Simeon picked a senior girl from the convent. For a moment, I held my breath, thinking he would ask the Mother Superior, but thank god his sense of humour did not travel down that path!

At the next pause, I had to pick a girl from the convent school, and the girl dancing with the colonel had to pick a boy from the shitting squad. And the colonel would pick another girl, and Mrs Simeon would pick a cadet, and this carried on until everybody was on the floor, with the ice broken. For the boys, a fate worse than death became a lot more enjoyable and an excellent subject for future storytelling.

By this time, the social was rocking, and we had switched from the foxtrot to the twist with Chubby Checker's song 'Let's twist again' playing: 'Come on, let's twist again like we did last summer ...' The floor was full of boys and girls gyrating and contorting in the most extraordinary ways, as the twist was the rage in those days, and the staff watched in horror and amusement. Some of them even tried the twist out, especially the younger ones! Though I do not recommend the twist in a sari for the unaccustomed, as it tends to unravel at the first inopportune moment.

Our foreign exchange teacher, Kenneth Smith, and another exuberant young teacher called Mr Salve were always engaged in repartee. Kenneth Smith, who was six feet, three inches tall, asked Jean Simeon for a dance. She was four feet, eleven inches without her heels, and five feet, two inches with them. The towering Ken Smith bent over Mrs Simeon like a question mark trying to do an awkward foxtrot. He got a bit cramped, so he picked her up right off the ground, and started twirling and whirling her, showing his moves with Mrs Simeon's feet a foot off the ground. Mr Salve couldn't resist calling out to Kenneth Smith across the dance floor, 'Hey, Kenneth, is that the bossa nova you are doing?' Without batting an eyelid or missing a step, Ken Smith replied, 'No, Mr Salve, it's the boss's wife!' All of us collapsed laughing, and Ken Smith went onto become a legend.

———

Spending as much time as I had with the majority of Jats, some of them straight from the village, I got to know them well—well enough to know when to leave them alone and when to push them in the right direction. They are unique people. Almost 90 per cent of them are vegetarians, and they enjoy their buffalo milk. They are a robust and agrarian community with strong, strapping men and women, built of fresh farm produce, with an immense love of milk. It's not surprising that so many of our sports stars come from such a small state. As a regiment, they tend to judge their young officers quickly, and they do not accept or trust them blindly. But when an officer leads from the front, they will follow him into the jaws of hell.

For me, there was one incident that sums up the Jats' love for milk. We used to have a movie evening in school every Saturday. The film was projected on a rickety and rackety sixteen-mm projector, and we had to change the reels and fix breakdowns frequently. It was a big event, where cadets, both junior and senior, staff and their families would turn up for the outing. At this time, some of the senior prefects used to jump over the boundary wall and head to Karnal, where they had a Greens restaurant, which served tandoori chicken and a beer for a princely sum of twelve bucks.

We used to pool in our resources and head for Karnal, on cycles or by the local tempo services, as we knew the staff was busy and there would be no roll call on Saturday. We slipped over the wall and were milling around on the road, waiting for some transport when I noticed another group of four boys had snuck around the bushes. They looked a bit small to be senior cadets, so we called out to them, sternly, as they were in half a mind to leg it back over the wall upon spotting us. Because of their Pavlovian response to the parade ground command, they sheepishly assembled on the road at the call of 'Fall in!'

I checked out this motley bunch of juniors, who had tried to bluff their way out and failed miserably. I singled out a boy I knew from the boxing team—Chikara, roll number fifty-one, a good boxer and an overall good guy. I asked him point-blank as to where the hell they were planning on going. It was taboo for juniors to break bounds. 'Nilokheri,' mumbled a ramrod-straight cadet. I thought I had got it wrong. Nilokheri was the village on the opposite side of Karnal. So, being a suspicious city-born prefect, I immediately presumed that these little blighters were either lying or had organized some local talent. I pointedly put my face six inches from Chikara's sweaty one and barked, 'What's happening in Nilokheri?' Silence. I menacingly spaced my words and asked again. A sweating roll number fifty-one mumbled something in Haryanvi.

I asked again. Out it came, 'Doodh piney ja rahe hain!' I couldn't believe my ears and the audacity of these bloody juniors, who had tried to break bounds and were now telling me that it was all for some milk! I put on my best third-degree voice and warned them to tell me the truth. 'Humnein Nilokheri mein bhains bandh rakhi hai. Humare Papa ne,' Chikara said. I tried to comprehend why they would have a buffalo tied in Nilokheri and told them not to bullshit me as we got plenty of milk in school. To which, Chikara replied in chaste Haryanvi, 'Aap toh glass mein peete hain, hum toh balti mein kuccha doodh peete hain, sir!'

Colonel Eric Simeon and Jean Simeon had started the school in the early sixties from scratch, along with a small group of handpicked staff. They were handed an abandoned property, consisting of a dilapidated haveli being used as a cowshed by the local villagers: three hundred acres of semi-desert, dusty and arid land, in the middle of nowhere. They had to shape it into a school to train and polish the simple village boys of Haryana into some of the finest officers and gentlemen in the Indian armed forces. The boys who had attended the school from the sixties to the early seventies all bore the touch and finish of Colonel Simeon, and the compassionate and kindly touch of Jean Simeon. Our Mater and Pater of the school.

Every single cadet, civilian or serviceman, who was shaped or moulded by this marvellous couple went on to become the best of the best. The number of generals, air vice-marshals, admirals, and successful civilians produced by the school during their tenure was unprecedented. Krishna Menon's unlikely experiment was a huge success. Each state was given a Sainik School to keep a steady stream of leaders, officers and gentlemen supplied year after year to the Indian services. Colonel and Mrs Simeon retired from the school to take over La Martiniere Calcutta, and later, the Doon School, Dehradun, and Cathedral and John Connon School, Mumbai, where they continued to serve exceptionally. However, their heart and soul was always in Kunjpura, the village of the Grey Kunj.

Finally, when the time came to hang up his boots, the colonel's funeral was held in the Delhi Cantonment and was one of the most memorable farewells I have seen in my life. And it was for a remarkable man. A sea of uniforms and shining brass filled the courtyard, with everybody jostling to lend a shoulder to the cortège. Shoulders were changed every four or five steps as so many of us had gathered to bid him goodbye and godspeed on his final journey. They came from all over the world, civilians and officers alike—the gathering of a great clan to put to rest a mighty chief.

4

'Are You Robin Hood, Robin Redbreast or Batman's Sidekick, Robin?'

The class of 1965 from Sainik School, Kunjpura, passed the Services Selection Board and left for the National Defence Academy, Poona, well onto their journey to become officers and gentlemen. In contrast, four of us who had opted to become civilians had to pass the Indian School Certificate (ISC) exam, and were left behind in school sweating bullets while prepping for our exams. I had to slog to get the basics of maths, physics and chemistry out of the way, and was so relieved when the exams got over that a trip to Karnal for a beer and tandoori chicken was a given. The results were going to be announced in a month and a half. We left school for our various home towns in a haze of relief and freedom. My friends in Delhi were in a tizzy, checking out colleges and applications, while I watched smugly, thinking that if I failed the ISC exam I would join the tea gardens for a life of outdoors and adventure. I was already preparing for the worst—Plan B was well in the making!

Of course, my grandmother put a spanner in the works. She categorically stated that I would have to graduate and could do whatever I wanted only after that. I think she had a secret delusion in which she saw me as a diplomat in the Indian Foreign Service. Meanwhile, I just hoped and prayed to pass, and pass I did! Just about. My grades were not good enough for Stephen's, Hindu or any of the Delhi colleges of repute. The chances of getting admission to a decent college in the city seemed remote, and I was left to make the rounds of the lesser colleges at Delhi University. Even there, they looked at me in a sceptical manner and waitlisted me. I had an uncle in Baroda, who was quite fond of me and invited me to check out Maharaja Sayajirao University of Baroda.

I reluctantly packed my bags and headed for the promised M.S. University of Baroda. I had opted for English literature as my major, considering it a safe option since I had a natural inclination for it. I landed in class on the first day of college and found a sprawling campus in the middle of a palace with hundreds of students milling about. All of them were talking in the many dialects of Gujarati. Yes, Gujarat has many regions and each one has a distinct dialect, including the dialect spoken in East Africa. There I was, in this swarming Gujarati melting pot, looking for my English literature class. Nobody had a clue as to where it was supposed to be. I finally found it and, with relief, settled in, waiting for the professor to appear. We were a class of sixty students, ten of whom were boys, and fifty were mostly conservative girls chattering amongst themselves like a spirited flock of parrots. Some of them were bold enough to check out the outnumbered boys.

I found the boys in my class the most disinterested species on the planet! I got the feeling that English literature was the last choice for students who had no other options, and they already looked defeated by the sheer volume of the curriculum. The girls, on the other hand, had a lot more energy but not for English literature. Then, the professor arrived and addressed the class in the most amazingly Gujaratified English I have ever heard. The rest of my classmates had an issue comprehending what he was saying, and soon the professor switched entirely to Gujarati for the rest of the class. I was a bit shell-shocked, to say the least, and extremely unhappy at the medium of instruction.

It must have shown. My uncle, bless his soul, was sympathetic and immediately realized that I would not last in M.S. University of Baroda for too long!

To the rescue came Dr Sonutai Saigal with flags flying, and I shifted to the illustrious Fergusson College in Deccan Gymkhana, Poona—as it was called back then—a whole month after the term had started. Deccan Gymkhana is the abode of a lot of Poona Brahmins, who excelled in academics and education. Their motto was 'simple living and high thinking!' She was thrilled that she had swung my admission into Fergusson College, which had been started by a bunch of eminent Poona Brahmins under the auspices of the Deccan Education Society.

She felt that maybe the culture of the Deccan Brahmins would rub off on me, as she didn't particularly approve of my 'Jatification' in Sainik School, Kunjpura. At least, that's what my grandmother thought for she had finished school in an institution called Huzurpaga Girls School, the oldest Indian-run girls' high school, which was steeped in tradition. Their alumnae consist of luminaries like Irawati Karve, Anandibai Karve, Tarabai Modak (a Padma Bhushan awardee), Rebecca Reuben, Shanta Shelke, Reema Lagoo, Mrinal Kulkarni and many others.

I quite liked the Bhats, as the Brahmins were called, with their collars and cuffs frayed over many scrubbings, and their very superior attitude towards anybody who wasn't a scholar. I found them conservative, though well-informed. They read a lot and patronized a very highly developed Marathi theatre way ahead of its time, in terms of subjects and even highly controversial community behaviour topics. They were known to be stingy and tight-fisted, and were quite proud of the reputation too.

Fergusson College was a roller-coaster ride for me. There was never a dull moment. Of course, I was probably to blame for most of the unconventional nature of the ride, but what the hell! I had been allotted a room in the college hostel in Block 3, the last block on the campus, and realized that Bal Gangadhar Tilak had spent time in this sparse, spartan cubicle—furnished with a steel bed, a thin mattress, a writing table, a chair, and a cupboard. It had a barred window overlooking a basti of Wadarwadis, or stonemasons, from Andhra Pradesh. The college hostel boasted of four mess halls, shared between four different contractors, serving more or less the same terrible vegetarian food.

Even though I am not a very fussy eater—Sainik School had cured me of that—the hostel's food was the pits. I decided to replenish my frugal vegetarian diet with some protein. Armed with a trusty catapult, or gulel, and a willing accomplice with a torch, we would foray after dark to the college's main building, which was infested with pigeons and years of their rock-solid guano piled on to the desks. We were on a mission to decrease the pigeon population. This led to the legendary Kakar's pigeon curry with pav, a local Maharashtrian bread, which we served hot out of Mr Tilak's room in Block 3 of the boys' hostel. Many a diehard and broke non-vegetarian survived on this quite tasty protein, but that's another story altogether!

During the day, I spent a lot of time on the athletics field to make myself useful and to feel like I belonged there, and I met some serious athletes, one of them being Indira Samant, the national discus champion. Everybody was a bit wary of her for she not only possessed a strong throwing arm, but she was rude and blunt to anybody trying to get familiar with her. She was good-looking and fit as hell. It was monsoon time, and I had procured a poncho-style green raincoat for myself. I distinctly remember my first real conversation with Indira was when I complimented her throw with the discus, which was quite spectacular.

She looked at me quizzically—I was scrawny, wore glasses and a green poncho-style raincoat. She decided to pull my leg, so she asked, 'Are you Robin Hood, Robin Redbreast, or Batman's sidekick, Robin?' I was a bit taken aback and decided on 'Robin the Hood' as it was cool! Indira nicknamed me Robin and, in return, I named her Sarge for her bossy behaviour. Everyone called me Robin for the next three years in college and, till today, my Pune friends only know me as Robin.

Indira Samant was the first friend I made at Fergusson College. I also figured that if I were to go wild and sow a few oats during my college days, Robin was convenient as I could happily change my name back to Prahlad Kakar and leave it all behind me! Especially since I wasn't even from Poona. Little did I know that a reputation, especially a notorious one, sticks to your foot like dog shit. Even after washing your shoes many times, the smell lingers on for months! C'est la vie.

I made it to the college football team, not as a goalie but a right wing, and fluked a wet and muddy goal against Wadia College, our rivals from the Poona campus. There was a melee in front of their goalmouth. Everybody was slipping and sliding in the mud. A loose ball came my way, and behind it came a wall of fullbacks with murder in their eyes. I hurriedly tried to get rid of the offending ball by passing it to my closest teammate, lost my balance and kicked the ball straight into the rival goal, totally inadvertently. The rest was lost in a haze of celebration. For a fleeting moment, I was the toast of Deccan Gymkhana! I even made it to a copy of the next day's *Sakal*, the choicest of Poona's newspapers. I made the most of this sudden fame.

Now I became a man among men, a chhati-pe-baal, haath-mein-bandook kind of man, and during this time, I met one of my best friends, Ashok Gune, who came up to me after the mud-splattered match, shook my hand and congratulated me. His father was a colonel, and his aunt was Madhumalti Gune (whom we all fondly called Tai), one of the first lady doctors in Poona. She ran a very successful maternity hospital named Indira Maternity Home, on Jangali Maharaj Road. Indira Maternity Home became a second home for me, not only because of Ashok, but because I managed to get my priorities right and made a beeline for the kitchen, found a distinguished-looking lady cook called Bai and inveigled myself into her good books. She then took over the responsibility of feeding me whenever I used to land up there. My taste for authentic Maharashtrian jevan came from Bai's kitchen. Having sorted out my basic food issues, I now returned with renewed vigour and enthusiasm to college.

Around this time was when my interest in films was cultivated, quite by accident! We were invited as a group from Fergusson College to attend a two-day film-appreciation course at the Film and Television Institute of India (FTII). A few of us from the gang loped off to the institute to check out the girls as FTII had a reputation for their beatnik, bohemian behaviour, from both boys and girls, which was frowned upon by the upstanding citizens of Deccan. This made the proposition even more interesting as all of us were hoping to get lucky!

We arrived at FTII only to find out that they were on their summer break, and only the film archives were functioning. Alas, there were no wild-eyed, pot-smoking, hippie-type people anywhere—neither guys nor any girls! Swallowing our disappointment, we were introduced by Satish Bahadur and P.K. Nair to a two-day film-appreciation session where we saw, dissected and discussed two short-films, which made a massive impact on me. One was *Glass* by Bert Haanstra and the other was a film called *Big City Blues* by Mervyn LeRoy.

Glass is one of the most beautiful short films showing the process of creating hand-blown glass—its artistry and beauty blowing life into the molten glass, transmitted from the rough hands and wise old faces of the glass blowers as the glass becomes an extension of their egos and their dreams. Sheer poetry in motion. Today, glass is commercialized and made on an assembly line by automation. It's like the human race— we've gone from individuals with specific characteristics and flaws to a cookie-cutter type thanks to conditioning and education where we turn out a whole assembly line of mass-produced graduates, MBAs and engineers, who are mostly predictable, malleable, unimaginative and therefore imperfect, even by establishment standards.

The more we discussed *Glass*, the more philosophical the class became. The discussions on the individuality of the human spirit, and the difference between genuine art and mass production, influenced our need to be creative. *Big City Blues*, on the other hand, was a powerful indictment of presumption and Pavlovian preconditioning. In the film, a thirteen-year-old girl is found dead in a building under construction, and the police round up two vagabond wastrels, one 'white' and the other 'black', and incorrectly presume that the black guy is the culprit. It has a beautiful, haunting saxophone track, which plays as an accompaniment to the surprisingly sensitive film.

We came back from FTII, changed as humans—but still virgins— moved by these short films where rarely a word was spoken, which revealed the power of storytelling. Out of the ten of us who attended that class, six of us ended up becoming filmmakers, underlying the impact those films had on us. Our mentors, Satish Bahadur and P.K. Nair, were so deeply committed to their craft and the art of film-making that they left an impression on all of us in the most indelible and profound way.

And so, of course, we decided to start a film-appreciation club in college called Critique—a bit pretentious, but what the hell, it had the first-mover advantage! The four of us musketeers who started the club—Uday Borowke, Ashok Gune, Vijay Paranjape and yours truly—had two objectives. The primary one was to respectably and legitimately recruit all the good-looking girls in college to come and enjoy a Saturday evening with us, watch interesting films and discuss them over cutting chai. It goes without saying that the membership for men was restricted only to the founding members, and we had the pick of the best-looking women in college, a legitimate coup d'état. What-a-fun became, as some of them thought!

———

The Wadarwadi basti, just behind our college hostel, was notorious for its haath bhatti, or country liquor, and its incredibly aggressive and statuesque women. The Wadarwadi community are stonemasons by profession and had migrated from Andhra Pradesh a long time ago. The women are tall, dusky and stunning-looking. They wore colourful cotton saris with the pallu draped across their shoulders and tucked in at the back as they wore no other clothing on their chest. They considered the college their property, and a whole group of them used to take a shortcut from their basti to Deccan right through the middle of our campus at 10.30 a.m. sharp. All the boys used to hang around the main gate to check them out, and nobody but nobody dared to pass a comment or stare too obviously as the counterattack would be immediate and collective. All of us loved watching them discreetly glide past—all lovely, lithe, graceful and high-breasted, with a free-swinging walk that would put most ramp models to shame.

One day, as I was going through the ritual of checking out the statuesque Wadaris, I saw something quite amazing—a guy on a motorcycle, a Royal Enfield Bullet to be specific, whizz through the crowd, yelling something loudly, like a tent-pegging boli. When I got to hear it properly, it went something like this, 'Apro juno, lambe-lambe baal waalon!' Which loosely translates to, 'My people with long hair!' The rider on the bike, standing on the footrests and yelling his boli, skillfully wove through the startled women like a ballet dancer. I was sure this man with a devil-may-care attitude would come a cropper.

But he survived to live another day, despite the ladies recovering from their shock, reaching down to the side of the road and picking up some lethally sized rocks to hurl towards the receding motorcyclist, all the while screaming 'Bhadwe-ya!' The rocks missed his head narrowly even as he laughed at his own audacity. In those days, a helmet was optional. I got to know him later, Shudhoji Rao Tibole—an alumnus of Sherwood College, Nainital, a state champion in swimming and a scion of a landed family from Gwalior—known to his friends as Shudh and to his detractors as Tidda. Shudh was one of the most colourful characters in college. He was well-spoken, with a fabulous swimmer's physique, all of five feet four inches—a bantam-sized Adonis. Shudh's worldview was original and quite scandalous. We used to wonder why a bevy of beady-eyed women had not avalanched Shudh, considering he was well-spoken, loaded, royalty and physically quite perfect.

As I got to know Shudh well, I realized he wasn't interested in any college girls. We speculated that Shudh might be bent, but the truth was even stranger than our speculation! When Shudh turned sixteen, his uncle, who was also a well-to-do royal and the beneficiary of its traditions, decided that his nephew had come of age and should, therefore, have his rite of passage. On Shudh's birthday, he bequeathed him an unlimited credit account with his favourite brothels in Budhwar Peth, Poona. The madams were given the explicit instruction that his nephew's rite of passage should be educational and pleasurable, and that no effort or money was to be spared in the pursuit of the art of pleasure!

Thus, Shudh was the only living person I knew who had a standing credit account with a brothel in his college days. When I met Shudh, he already had a headstart on his education, compared to the rest of us who were still hoping that we would get lucky one day! All of us broke plebeians bunked college to go for a matinee show in Alka Theatre, which ran reruns of old films and charged us one rupee on a first come, first served basis. Meanwhile, His Highness Shudhoji Rao Tibole would retire to the willing arms of his friends with benefits!

In many ways, Shudh was innocent, generous, and never saw any difference between his ladies of the night and other ladies. He had befriended them to such an extent that they considered Shudh part of their family and would do anything for him, which I don't think they would ever do for anybody else—regardless of the pressure or compensation. One day, a friend called Roomly (Ramesh) Shahane was throwing a party on his terrace with the usual suspects. There was always a shortage of girls, which was vital for the success of any do. Everybody was told to BYOG, i.e., bring your own girls. We landed up at 8 p.m. sharp, some with and some without, so an SOS went out to get more girls.

At 8.30 p.m. sharp, Shudh rolled up in a cab and started calling out to Roomly from downstairs. He shouted louder and louder until the whole neighbourhood had woken up. Roomly glanced down from the third-floor terrace and saw Shudh with a car full of girls. Shudh insisted that the host come down and meet his friends. Roomly went down with a whiff of disaster in his nostrils. Lo and behold, Shudh proudly started introducing his lady friends by their professional names—Champa Rani, Gulab Bano, Khatun Bi, Laxmi-e-Bulbul, who was probably named so because she was a singer, and so forth. Roomly took one look at them and shat bricks. His upper-middle-class, prim and proper parents were halfway through dinner, and there was no way to avoid them on the way up to the terrace. The staircase went through the dining room, and then on to the second and third floors.

A horrified Roomly, who had fully understood the delicacy of the situation, took Shudh aside and, with great intensity, told him that there was no way his lady friends could go up to the terrace! Shudh was genuinely perplexed as to why not. He had been asked to bring girls, and he had invited four of his closest friends and couldn't understand the situation. To him, his friends were decent, god-fearing people, whom he could trust with his life, and that's all that mattered. He was utterly untouched by middle-class morality.

Finally, much to Roomly's relief, a very peeved Shudh told the girls loudly that the party had been cancelled and that he was treating them to a movie and dinner. The girls livened up as Shudh drove off with his bevy to the cinema hall in a huff. The party trickled into boredom after that, as there were no women. I still feel that if Shudh had persuaded Roomly to let them come to the party, it would have been a much-needed education for all of us lukkhas. This incident was the highlight of the evening.

Many years later, sometime in my early twenties, I caught up with an old college flame and, in the conversation, while remembering all the characters in college, she asked me if I had run into Shudh recently. I had lost touch with him since I graduated in 1970, and I wondered out loud what had happened to him. She leaned forward and, in a conspiratorial manner, stage-whispered for dramatic effect, 'He has become a famous spiritual leader with a huge following!' I almost fell off my chair, but upon reflection, I realized that he had all the attributes to become a sadhu—a childlike innocence and wonder, belief in the goodness of people and not a malicious bone in his body. He had an enviable, untouched air of detachment, despite his carnal adventures, which protected him from the hypocrisy of our moralistic society—so quick to judge anybody who is different!

Well done, Shudh. I will definitely visit you in your new avatar.

By the end of the first term of college, 'Robin' was notorious and became an object of great curiosity. Two incidents happened, which sort of changed the trajectory of my not-so-normal life on its head.

We used to have quite a few Brahmin boys on scholarship in the college hostel and they had to study Sanskrit by rote. Every day in the hostel verandah, a strange ritual used to be carried out. These boys would collect and spread out their mats, sit on the floor, with these X-shaped stands on which they would place a massive tome in Sanskrit, one of the Vedic scriptures. They would then proceed to rock backward and forward, memorizing the tomes by heart. I knew they were Brahmin by their chotis or shendys, and the college only gave scholarships to deserving Sanskrit students. Watching them, I learnt a thing or two.

At first, I used to think that the choti was a caste indicator of Brahmins and that, other than the belief that it focused the power of the mind, I thought it had no practical use. It is a bit like a Chinese and Japanese queue. I soon realized, though, that it played a huge role in rote discipline. As the students rocked back and forth in the cross-legged position for hours, their chotis were tied to a hook on the wall and allowed for some amount of flexibility in movement. But, the moment any of the students dozed off and his head fell forward, the choti would jerk him awake so that he could continue memorizing the entire tome without a break. I thought it was genius how the choti had been designed to keep the secrets of the ancients only in the minds and hands of the Brahmins. This, in turn, empowered them to hold that knowledge and use it in everything from rituals to statesmanship to quantum physics and maths. The title 'Wrangler' is reserved for those who have gained first-class honours in mathematics. It was considered higher than even a doctorate. We had a smattering of Wranglers among the Brahmin community in the Deccan area of Poona. Thus, the Bhandarkar Trust, the legacy of Wrangler R.P. Paranjape, Wrangler Mahadev Govind Ranade and so on, which my grandmother used to reel off as if she knew these simple-living, high-thinking denizens personally! I only figured out who they were later, because half the roads were named after them.

I started chatting up these boys to find out what made them tick and realized that other than Sanskrit, which was a given, they were dying to learn English. Who else but yours truly was there at the wrong place at the right time for these Brahmin boys. By then, I had already discovered that the best way to teach anyone a language was through song, which increases vocabulary and its usage. Nothing came immediately to mind except a rugby song, which had many non-vegetarian words in it (by the way, the best way to learn a language is to first learn how to abuse in it). So, I gathered this rather unlikely lot and taught them the Blacksmith song's first verse, which went something like this:

Solo: 'The blacksmith told me before he died, don't know whether the bastard lied.'
Chorus: 'Jai! Jai! Bastard lied, bastard lied! Don't know whether the bastard lied!'

I must say they were quick to pick it up, as the tune was reminiscent of a bhajan. Their practice sessions began in earnest. Since the toilet and bathing block was at a distance from the hostel, they would set forth in a phalanx, armed with soap, towels and toothbrushes, singing heartily every morning, on their way to the bathroom and back to the hostel. In the beginning, it attracted a bit of attention, but not too many understood the words as their enunciation wasn't that great. For many days, they got away with it.

One day, our economics professor overheard them and perked up, as he was a sharp young cookie. Initially, he thought that they were singing a garbled English version of a bhajan and became curious. He stopped the bhajan mandali mid-sentence and asked them to sing it to him, which they did with great enthusiasm. His eyeballs almost popped out when he understood the words. He, very politely, asked them whether they knew the meaning of what they were singing. They, of course, had no clue. Then, equally politely, he asked them: Who, pray, had taught them this English bhajan?

To which, innocently and proudly, they proclaimed, 'Robin!' He asked for my real name, and nobody knew, so he decided to do some jasoosi of his own, and of course figured it out. But I will say this for him, he never let on in class. It was only at the end of the term that I received a polite letter from the bursar, who was the gentleman in charge of the hostel. He wrote to say I was no longer welcome in the hostel as I had been held responsible for corrupting the morals of the

Brahmin boys! Farewell to Mr Tilak's room, the awful food, Robin's pigeon curry and pav, and the Brahmin boys. Life sucked.

———〜———

At the beginning of my late arrival at Fergusson College, I was confused by the array of subjects on offer. I had to choose from history, psychology, economics, statistics, English literature, political science, and so forth. To be very honest, I was confused, and only knew immediately I would opt for English literature. I was determined to stay away from maths, physics and chemistry, and was left with the arts subjects. In those days, arts was chosen by the girls and by the lame-duck boys, who either weren't ambitious enough or just incompetent, as they would never become doctors and engineers—the choice of all parents for their doppelgänger children. All the others were wasting the best years of their lives in labs or extra classes, while all of us duffers in the arts lived it up and had a blast in the three years of college.

Everybody pushed me towards economics, telling me that it was an excellent subject to get a job later in life. I was sceptical, but reluctantly took it. And then I got a massive break, which changed my life—then and more so now. I found out that Poona University offered a unique subject for undergraduates. It was military studies. The history of war, tactics, strategy and economics. Wow! I just jumped at it.

The head of the department was a Major General Paranjape with a Sandhurst English accent. He even spoke Marathi like a Sandhurst man. He used to pat his coat's top pocket searching for his pipe. He would say in chaste Marathi with a clipped British accent, 'Majhe pipe kuthey gaylee?' (Where the fuck is my pipe?) He used to inadvertently pat his pocket even when looking for the wife at home, with the same action and accent, 'Majhe baiko kuthey gaylee?' (Where the fuck is my wife?)

The beauty of the class was that half of the sessions were held at Fergusson in the Deccan Gymkhana side, and the rest were held in Wadia College in the Poona Cantonment area. All of us Deccan Tantias (after Tantia Tope, I presume) were dying to go and check out Wadia College, as the cream of the cantonment girls studied there. Moreover, socially, it was a couple of hundred years ahead of Fergusson. The girls wore miniskirts and tank tops to college, and it was the happening place.

I leapt into military studies with gusto. There were only twenty of us in class—six bored, nondescript girls, and the rest boys, half from Fergusson and half from Wadia. It was an incredible experience. Other than learning the inside stories of the battles and wars fought, we learnt strategy, tactics, the factor of luck and Murphy's Law. We learnt about Napoleon, Wellington, Cornwallis, Clive and about some key battles and wars, which changed the destinies of countries. We learnt about emperors, heroes and despots.

The general was a fantastic teacher. He was eloquent, eccentric, knowledgeable and transported us mentally to the battlefield, in the thick of the decision-making that so precariously balanced the fate of empires and nations. We also went on field trips to Ahmednagar for the Armoured Corps tank exercises and Deolali for the artillery exercises. I don't know about the others, but I loved every moment of it. The best part was, after our Wadia College class ended, we could hang out officially at the college canteen and check out the girls. Outsiders weren't allowed on the campus. I also made some great friends at Wadia College, even though we were fierce rival colleges!

When people ask me how I teach branding without ever having done an MBA, I laugh and think to myself: I did the mother of all MBAs. I studied the art of war, where the destinies of countries, cultures and people were decided, not just some little brand whose failure you can brush off and start again. In the theatre of war, mistakes could mean mass destruction and death, and some armies, like Genghis Khan's, took no prisoners and built pyramids of their defeated enemies' skulls, while their women were used as currency.

The margin for error is small and the window of opportunity fleeting. War prepares you to survive in situations where you have to be lean and mean; it requires a tremendous amount of anticipation and the talent for springing a surprise. For that, you throw the manual out of the window, for even the enemy has studied it and can anticipate your moves and counter them with drastic results. In my branching and advertising class, the recommended reading for our students is the *Arthashastra*, the Gita, *The Art of War* by Sun Tzu and *The Book of Five Rings* by Miyamoto Musashi. Together, they take the pants off any MBA curriculum.

————

Two very eccentric professors took my English literature classes. Professor Dhavale was straightlaced, able, knowledgeable and severe. He was a slightly built man with no excess flesh on his face, his skin tightly drawn over his skull. His favourite phrase was, 'Now, for a touch of pathos', as he pointed his index finger dramatically towards the ceiling—that was also the only time there would be a flicker of expression on his face.

The other professor was someone who knocked the class out, not only because she came from a family known for its strong-willed and intelligent women, but because she was a famous poet and writer in her own right, and had travelled across the globe with her many husbands. She refused to dress anything like the Deccan Gymkhana type. She was statuesque at five foot nine and had an exceptionally well-endowed figure. She showed it off to great impact and chagrin from the other professors by wearing tight, long-sleeve sweaters and beautifully tailored slacks. She was awesome, not only because she was great-looking, but also because of her in-depth knowledge of the English classics. Her name was Professor Gauri Deshpande.

In her first class, we were twenty-five students and I don't think any of us boys registered a single word that she spoke. We hung on to every expression on her face, mesmerized, while our ears shut down. She was a riot on the campus as she shocked the knickerbockers off the fuddy-duddy professors—male and female—and nobody had the guts to tell her otherwise. A week later, her next class had 150 attendees, some not even from our college! That was the impact Professor Gauri Deshpande made on a staid, cobwebby institution of higher learning. By god! I loved her. Without even knowing that I existed, she became my role model. After her classes, I never attempted to fit in. I just became comfortable in my skin and never tried to make excuses or apologize for being me. Thank you, Professor Gauri Deshpande!

A brilliant teacher, with her knowledge of the classics, she introduced us to the world of English poetry. She encouraged us to write love poems to the young ladies we wanted to impress. I remember her saying that nothing can beat the impact of poetry—not chocolates, not flowers, not even being serenaded by besura, but dedicated voices. However, as puerile as it may sound, there is nothing like a poem to make a lasting impression on the object of one's desire.

By the end of the first semester, I discovered more people like me, and though I stuck out like a sore thumb on campus, I had been accepted, warts and all. I had found my groove. It was around this time I noticed a tall, leggy young lady, very shy and conservative. She was a frontbencher in my economics class and always under the radar, which I realized, much later, was deliberate. She intrigued me because she was intelligent and extremely private. Her name was Manjushree. Yes! A true-blue Bong in Tantia land.

Manjushree had an elder sister who also attended our college and was more outgoing, though cut from the same cloth: Attractive, definitely not nondescript. But she was nosy as hell and extremely protective about her younger sister. She looked upon me with extreme disfavour and gave me a massive break by warning her sister about Lotharios like me. This immediately gave me the kind of reputation and a devil-may-care air that I did not necessarily possess. Sometimes, it's good to have a reputation as it provides you with colour—of being dashing, romantic and a cut above the ordinary. When I showed interest in getting to know the young lady concerned, she didn't reciprocate the slightest inclination. That is, not until her sister got into the act and made me out to be an exciting villain.

In hindsight, I can tell you that most prim and proper women are always attracted to bad boys—and our case was no different. As an opener, we smiled at each other, snatched a few words in here and other, and then nothing else initially as her sister decided to babysit her, much to her chagrin. In pure defiance, she agreed to go out with me for dinner. I was over the moon. The harder it was to negotiate a middle ground, the more involved I became, partly in real but mostly in fantasy, especially with my lucid dreaming, where fantasy and reality unwittingly merged. Manjushree insisted on bringing along her best friend for respectability. Those were the days of innocence, before Tinder!

Off we went for dinner to a fancy restaurant, which I had arranged by dipping into my scant life savings. I spent the evening trying to impress her best friend, while Manjushree watched bemusedly. It was a coup. As usual, the whole college was talking about it the next day. Her sister was seething and biding her time. On my birthday, Manjushree presented me with a book that surprised me by its timing and subject. It was *The Razor's Edge* by Somerset Maugham.

The term ended and we all left for our homes. Mine was in Delhi. Surprisingly, Manjushree was also going to be in Delhi as her family had been vacationing there with her uncle. We promised to stay in touch. Those were the days of postcards and discreet phone calls. In the hurly-burly of the holidays, I tried her landline a couple of times, found a strange male voice on the other end and gave up, thinking I will catch up with her when the college reopens.

Two incidents happened before I joined the next term. I received a formal, nondescript brown paper envelope that looked like a government summons informing me that I was unwelcome in the college hostel because of the episode with the bhajan mandali. The second was my selection to the college athletic team as a 110-metre hurdler. The first one was a downer, and I wondered where I would find affordable digs in Poona. I asked Ashok Gune if I could stay at his place temporarily.

He said he would have to ask his aunt, Dr Madhumalti Gune, and since he wanted to avoid doing that, he went into overdrive looking for cheap and cheerful digs around college. And bingo! Above a law college professor's house, he found a barsati room for me—a one-room apartment on the terrace—available on a sharing basis with another boy from the law college. It was close to college and affordable. The only problem was it had a tin roof and was hot as Hades.

After term started, the first day of college was pretty hectic, catching up with friends and colleagues. I looked for Manjushree and couldn't find her, so I asked around some more. Finally, her bestie, who had become good friends with me by then, handed me an envelope and watched with a placid expression as I opened it and out fell a wedding card! I read it with a sinking feeling. Manjushree was getting married in fifteen days. Shit, I was in shock.

It seemed the whole college knew about it, except me. I looked around to see a smirking elder sister laughing with her friends at my expense, and at that moment, I knew that she had something to do with it. I was right. She had sneaked to her ultra-conservative Bong parents, and told them how her younger sibling was out of control and hanging out with people of ill repute, like yours truly, and painted a lurid portrait of me. I looked forlornly at the wedding card and saw a scribble at the back in Manjushree's handwriting. It was a brief accusatory line: 'Why did you not get in touch with me? I couldn't handle the pressure. Sorry!'

I was seemingly nonchalant, but shattered inside. To boot, a friend came up and whispered that my name was up on the wall at the back of the ladies' hostel. I hurried to see what the hullabaloo was all about and found that someone had scrawled in large, whitewashed letters: 'Lock up your daughters, Robin's in town.' That was all that I needed. I was sure Shudh had pranked me. If I hadn't been so upset about Manjushree's impending marriage and the reinforcement of my notorious reputation, I would have found it very funny. It was quite hilarious. However, the college staff did not think so.

I brooded over the next three days and imagined Manjushree had been forced into marrying some lout by her sister—the villain-in-chief—her brainwashed parents and other sundry relatives. I convinced myself that poor Manjushree, all alone and outnumbered, had looked out for me to support her and then, in the absence of my support, had finally succumbed to the relentless pressure. Impulsively, I decided to head back to Delhi (that was where the wedding was) to gallop to her rescue, bugles blaring, pennants flying, like young Lochinvar. I got so carried away by my fantasy that I was determined to leap to her rescue, to the refrain of 'Lochinvar'[2] triumphantly playing in my head, which built my resolve to do the impossible.

> O young Lochinvar is come out of the west,
> Through all the wide Border his steed was the best;
> And save his good broadsword he weapons had none,
> He rode all unarm'd, and he rode all alone.
> So faithful in love, and so dauntless in war,
> There never was knight like the young Lochinvar.

I was encouraged by my friends, the romantic Sikri sisters who were army brats from Dhaula Kuan in Delhi, and was promised to be accompanied for moral support. Along with my trusty friend Shashi Dalal, who was known for his choice of clothing, namely a lungi, and thus nicknamed 'Luungs'. An unlikely squad, we hitched a ride to Bombay to catch a train for New Delhi. The Sikri sisters could afford a sleeper, but both Luungs and I were broke; as I had just paid my rent at the new digs, we decided to WT (without ticket) it. Thus began our ill-fated adventure. We spent most of the time in the toilet avoiding the TC (ticket collector), kept dodging from one compartment to the other, and made it to Delhi in one piece, though a little shop-soiled. The girls left for Dhaula Kuan, and Luungs and I went to Defence Colony to my mother's flat.

My mother took one look at us and almost had a cardiac arrest. She was sure I had been expelled. Well, almost. I sat her down and explained that we were on a mission to rescue a damsel in distress who I would carry away!

My poor, suffering mother asked, 'And then?'

I said, 'Then what?'

She patiently explained that if we were going to whisk her away from the marriage mandap, somebody would have to marry her, right? That hadn't occurred to me till then. We sobered up and went into a huddle, much to my mother's amusement.

'Okay, I would have to marry her! Cool, but what about our education?'

My mother humoured us and said she would pay for both of us.

Yay! Problem solved.

The next morning, the four of us set off to Talkatora Gardens to Manjushree's uncle's house where they were putting up. The Sikri sisters were crucial at this point as they lent respectability to the toli. When we were refused an entry initially, the Sikri sisters pulled their weight by declaring firmly that we had come from Poona and we were not going to budge. To avoid a scene, we were reluctantly allowed to enter. We discovered, much to our dismay, that the young lady was isolated in a haldi ritual and nobody could see her. We went into another huddle and decided that it was now or never as the marriage would happen the next day. By that time, her sister had spotted me. After a lot of backstage discussion with her sister and her family, we were unwillingly led to an outhouse where they had ensconced the young lady.

After much knocking and calling out her name, she opened the door, and I saw an apparition coated in yellow haldi from head to toe. Her eyes widened on seeing me, and I quickly slipped into the room while my friends kept guard. She was clearly hassled—partly because she didn't expect me to land up in the middle of her nuptials. She asked me why I hadn't called her and told me how the family, led by her sister, had gotten on to her case for a month and a half, and slowly worn her down as she had no support! I heard her out and then told her about the plan to escape, take her back to college to finish our education, and get engaged to legitimize our relationship. She looked a bit askance because, in her wildest imagination, she hadn't factored that young Lochinvar would land up, disrupt the proceedings and whisk away the bride, leaving behind a shocked and breast-beating family and a wannabe groom.

She baulked at the idea as, whatever said and done, she was from a close-knit family, and they would be shattered and shamed. I immediately understood that she wasn't ready to escape, and had reconciled herself to a delusional 'unhappily ever after'! It took me an instant to realize that it wouldn't work as she was afraid that her family would excommunicate her forever. With a heavy heart, I held her hand and reassured her that it was okay, and I would not create any further problems for her and her family. I wished her the best for a happily married life and left—much to her relief, I think.

On the way out, a smiling sister accosted us and, just to rub salt in our wounds, insisted that we come for the wedding-cum-reception the next evening. We mumbled our excuses and fled. It didn't end here. We went home in a disappointed huddle and, unfortunately, decided to attend the wedding and not slink off with our tails between our legs, to let them know that our intentions were noble and honourable. We thought it was empty bravado, but we did it anyway.

I asked my relieved mother for a piece of jewellery that she didn't need, to give Manjushree as a present.

She told me where to find her jewellery box, and I found a pretty silver necklace with semiprecious stones. I thought it was perfect for the occasion and packed it neatly in gift-wrapping paper. The next evening, we stepped out in our best—the Sikri sisters in sequined saris, Luungs in a clean shirt and ironed trousers, and yours truly in a resplendent white sharkskin dinner jacket and black trousers. The dinner jacket had regimental silver buttons and had been purloined from my father's uniform trunk, and since I did not own a dress shirt, I wore my favourite maroon shirt with a Texas string tie. Armed with the brightly packaged gift, we set off for Talkatora Gardens. When we arrived at the venue, there was a buzz as the entire family had figured out that I was the young Lothario from whom they were trying to protect their innocent daughter.

The ceremony began, and groom and bride were carried to the women, ululating away as per tradition. Then came the meet-and-greet on the dais. I self-consciously walked up to the couple— closely watched by all her relatives, who were holding their breath. I congratulated them and handed her the present. She very excitedly opened it up right there and then. She took out the necklace and held it up for all to see, and there was an audible gasp from the gathering along with a lot of tittering.

The Sikri sisters, who were just behind me, nudged me sharply in the ribs and hustled me off the stage and out of the venue. My last look at my lost love was of her looking at me adoringly, or so I imagined, still clutching the necklace. On the road, I stopped to catch my breath and asked my friends why they were in such a hurry for us to get away and even skip dinner.

Veena Sikri looked at me and said accusingly, 'You idiot, why did you give her a mangalsutra? And that also in front of everybody! You really have guts!'

I looked perplexed and asked, 'What's that? What's a mangalsutra? I gave her a necklace I found in my mother's jewellery box!'

She patiently explained to me that a mangalsutra is given only by a husband to his wife. It's a sign of marriage. Oh, shit, I thought, and hurried the hell out of there, imagining a bevy of irate relatives and guests ready to beat us up. And that's how that sorry episode ended. I have often wondered what my life would have been if she had had the guts to run away with me. However, in the safety of our college, the four of us were treated like the winning team and not the losers that we were. Somehow, the story of the mangalsutra had gotten around, and everybody thought it was gutsy and deliberate. The motto of the story—it's better to have loved and lost than never to have loved at all!

5

'Ob-La-Di, Ob-La-Da, Life Goes On!'

Back in college, I went about settling into my spacious new digs. It was winter, so the room's temperature was bearable. My roomie was from Sholapur and travelled a lot as he ran a side business while studying law. We very rarely came into contact with our landlord. We used to see him watering his plants occasionally. He had two college-going daughters and he was overprotective of them. He had even warned us to have zero contact with them!

Around this time, a young American exchange scholar came to stay with her Indian host family, who lived a little distance away from us. I met her in college because she stood out like a sore thumb, very much like I did, and we soon got chatting. I discovered that she was a sociology student, and her choice of research during her stint in Poona was the dynamics of the ladies in the red-light area of Budhwar Peth. All cities in the world have their own red-light areas. Everyone discusses them in hushed tones as if it's all a big secret.

This young lady was having problems accessing individual brothels to talk to the women inside. The owners and madams were very reluctant because most of the girls had been coerced or sold into the trade illegally. Of course, my go-to person was Shudh, who was extremely helpful and escorted her there personally to introduce her to his favourite lot, who then passed her on to the rest. As long as she was interviewing the girls during the day, it was all hunky-dory, but the moment she professed the need to see the action for herself after hours was when her problems started.

She lived with a very conservative Maharashtrian family, who insisted that she be back home by 6.30 p.m., a respectable curfew for young ladies from good homes. There could be no argument about that as someone had to stay up and open the door to let her in otherwise. Now, let's call the young American lady Jacquie—short for Jacqueline. Jacquie was a bit frustrated by the house rules as it prevented her from her nocturnal research. She asked me to escort her to Budhwar Peth one night, as it wasn't safe for single young ladies to be traipsing around that area after hours. Being an honourable and helpful type, I agreed to escort her there. And so it went that we were double-seated on my bicycle en route to 'BP', as it was called. It was my first time there, regardless of Shudh's many invitations that I had avoided.

At 10.30 p.m., it was fully lit and buzzing with the ladies of the night hanging off balconies and in barred doorways, chatting with each other and potential clients. The street was full of slightly inebriated men checking out the display of all shapes, sizes and colours, who were speaking a dozen different languages and dialects. The women had been procured from all over the country and beyond—from Nepal and Bangladesh. Their madams could be recognized by their multiple rings encasing their fingers. All of them wore garish make-up and shiny, synthetic saris. They were sitting in doorways on khatiyas with a paandan in front, chopping suparis into thin slivers with a supari-cutter, while soliciting business from likely customers. I was gobsmacked by the festive atmosphere in the alley. Hindi film music wafted out of its various nooks and crannies, and men who were eyeing the customers in a predatory fashion hung around here and there. I realized they were pimps and acted as suppliers to the various houses run by the madams.

Jacquie and I were an item of great amusement and curiosity. Since Shudh and his ladies had highly recommended us, everybody left us alone—other than the occasional loud, funny comment, which Jacquie did not understand. She was far too busy taking photographs and recording interviews. As I was hanging around at a loose end, I became the butt of all the jokes and comments. By the first evening, I was named 'Dhapnyea', or four eyes, because of my glasses, and Jacquie, of course, was 'Gori Chitti', which means fair and lovely.

The night flew by in a kaleidoscope of colour and sound, a very Fellini-esque experience much like Satyricon. We headed back by 2 a.m., with Jacquie fretting about waking up her Indian host's household at that unearthly hour and dreaded the quizzing that was sure to follow. She innocently asked whether she could stay at my place. My roomie was out of town, so I hemmed and hawed before reluctantly agreeing. We tiptoed up the stairs, and she crashed on the spare bed.

The next day, I left for college. When I got back, by god, I was in for a shock. She was still sleeping there! I asked her why she hadn't gone home. Bleary-eyed, she told me that she had. She had explained to her Indian hosts that she was staying with a colleague till her research was complete, as it involved late hours. They were not pleased and had immediately lodged a written complaint to her college. The letter claimed that her hours were unacceptable to them and stated that she was no longer their responsibility since she had found another accommodation. I looked at her, both horrified and concerned at the same time.

What was she going to do now? She blinked her big, blue eyes and said, 'I can stay here if it's not a problem.' I thought about it for a moment. Anyway, I was going to escort her to BP during the week, after which she would be going back to America. At first, I tried to wriggle out of this predicament, but lost hands down because her eyes and cute button nose defeated my instinct for self-preservation. Young Jacquie had moved in fully. I did not mention this to my landlord since

I knew he would never agree, and my roomie would be overjoyed to have Jacquie hanging around. There it was: a recipe for disaster.

Everything went well for a week, and my name Dhapnyea became well established in the red-light area of Poona, thanks to Jacquie's nocturnal research. Everything was tickety-boo, until one day, I came back from college to find one of my landlord's daughters agitatedly waiting for me at the gate. She said her father wanted to see me immediately. I looked up to the terrace and all seemed peaceful. I straightened up and entered the professor's inner sanctum to see a bizarre sight. The sixty-year-old professor was lying on his couch in a fevered, agitated state, florid face and all. He could barely speak while his wife and second daughter alternately fanned him and tried to give him water. Upon seeing me, the younger daughter broke into a wild, accusatory narration of what happened to the old boy. He had been happily watering his prized roses in the afternoon, as usual, until he looked up at the terrace and almost had a cardiac arrest.

On the terrace lay a blue-eyed, blonde-haired woman, butt naked barring two minuscule strips of cloth, or what we usually refer to as a bikini. One barely covered her top and the other flimsy piece, the bottom. A generously applied thin film of oil all over, she lay glistening in the sun on the parapet. At this point, he looked away for a moment in disbelief and then looked back again, pinching himself. She was still there! And, in fact, she waved out to him. He dropped the watering can and rushed indoors in a state of great agitation.

He keeled over in his study on the couch and loudly summoned everyone in the house, including the deities in the puja room, to list his last will and testament as he was sure he was dying of a heart attack. After many glasses of water and frantic fanning by his wife and daughters, he managed to blurt out his experience to his concerned family. And that was how I found him, still not quite recovered. He could only speak half sentences between gulps of water and my presence seemed to make his blood pressure spike.

His wife took over and admonished me soundly in Hindi and Marathi, saying that I kept women in the barsati and that too shameless ones who hung around without any clothes on. This was a massive blot on the family, more so since their innocent daughters were of marriageable age. It was a disaster of unmitigated proportions. My nefarious activities were utterly unacceptable and I must immediately vacate the premises with my blonde girlfriend. I couldn't even get in a word edgewise during this tirade, so I just said, 'I am sorry!' and left to brood over my fate, thinking, 'Ab mera kya hoga, Kalia?' As it turned out, the young lady concerned was scheduled to leave for America and had decided to get a last-minute tan. I will say this for her—she helped me pack!

Wringing my hands, I went back to Ashok Gune for a solution. He looked at me accusingly as if it was entirely my fault. But, by some luck, our friend Vijay Paranjape piped up and declared that his parents were moving to some hill station, and I could stay at his place as long as I paid. I hugged him in relief and moved to his home. His mother was still there for a week, while his father had gone ahead to scope out the cooler climes. She stood, arms akimbo, and looked disapprovingly at my motley belongings and me.

In the next week, I tried to be on my best behaviour in front of her and reiterated that I too was a quarter Konkanastha Chitpavan. To no avail, she just stared and snorted her disapproval. Vijay pacified me and told me his mother was a bit difficult and had a thing about cleanliness. I am sure she suffered from some form of OCD. Anyway, to my great relief, she finally left, muttering a parting shot and calling me gadhav mulga (idiot boy) in Marathi, which she mistakenly thought I would not understand.

Being free of scrutiny after so many years was so relaxing that I started enjoying the space the house offered. For the first time, I noticed the house cleaner (katkewali bai). She was young, about seventeen or eighteen, tall by the average standard for women, about five feet, seven inches, wore the traditional Marathi navari sari. She was slim, long-legged, and high-breasted with an expressive, attractive face and she carried herself with great confidence. She was a phenomenal worker and super-efficient, cleaning the entire house, laundry, dishes and all, in an hour and a half—a feat considering there were now three untidy people living there—leaving the house looking shiny and new.

Out of curiosity, I began watching her as she went about doing her work methodically. It was like watching a professional. It helped that she was quite easy on the eyes. I tried to engage her in small talk, but she would have nothing of it, moving through the house like a buzz saw.

Every morning, when she would arrive, I managed to greet her and she flashed an attractive smile in return. I would always wonder where she would hurry to by 10.30 a.m. I later learnt that she did three more households before lunch and earned about Rs 2,000 from grateful homes, giving her a take-home salary of eight grand—a royal sum in 1968. At that time, MBA management trainees got about that much from multinationals, with tax deductions.

So, young 'Shamma', as we will call her, would work like a beaver and go home singing like a lark. She had a huge fan base. There were many households waiting, just in case somebody dropped dead, they could grab hold of her as she only worked in four households at any point in time, period. I wanted to get to know Shamma a little better in the one and a half hours of attention she gave our house, so I started bunking college and hung around the house pretending to 'study', while watching young Shamma going about her routine, waiting to catch her eye.

A month passed, then—oh joy—one day, in the middle of her routine, Shamma stopped casually near the bed I was lying on and pretending to study. Leaning against the door with her arms crossed over her chest, she asked me if I liked her. I almost fell off the bed. Startled, I gulped some air and pretended not to have heard and mustered 'Pardon, kya bola aapne?' She looked me straight in the eye and said in Marathi, 'You heard me. So?' I was flustered. This was the first time a woman had propositioned me and it hit me for a six.

I quickly took the patli gali and protested feebly, 'No, no, it's nothing like that! I just think you are a nice person.'

Not missing a beat, she replied, 'So, why do you bunk college and watch me all the time?'

'I was studying for the exams,' I responded swiftly.

She took a step forward as I cowered backwards. 'In fourteen days, you have not turned a page in that book.' She was correct, of course. She gave me a final withering look, leaving me totally shattered.

I spent a sleepless night talking to myself. Neither Vijay nor Fuldruk, another student who joined us later, were around. I cursed myself for the complete lack of courage I had manifested and the hundreds of clever lines I had practised in the hope that I would catch such a break, all to no avail. The destruction of my ego and self-esteem was so complete that I paced up and down muttering about it to myself. As dawn was breaking, with its fingers of light and hope uncurling, I decided I would wait for Shamma to arrive. She came right on time without looking in my direction and carried on with her work as if nothing had happened.

I followed her with my eyes, waiting for some eye contact, which never came. As she was about to leave, I confronted her. 'I want to talk to you.'

'About what?' she replied. I cleared my throat and told her that I wanted to discuss what she had asked yesterday, and blurted out that I did like her and bunked college just to watch her and then ... Silence. Shamma looked at me in a strange manner and said matter-of-factly, 'That was yesterday; raat gayi baat gayi. I have work to do so please get out of my way.'

She calmly left me in a worse state than the day before. I avoided her like the plague for about a week, but my curiosity and her flat, outright rejection drove me to talk to her again. It never occurred to me that she was a house cleaner and I was as different from her as 'aasmaan zameen'. I was just a glutton for punishment.

It took me a month of gentle cajoling to get Shamma to talk to me and then we became friends. It was then that I discovered that at eighteen, she had two children: a girl and a boy. This really threw me. After a long pause, I asked her when she had gotten married, to which she nonchalantly told me that she wasn't. I choked and spluttered, and asked in shock, 'So, who is the father?' Shamma carried on as if she had not heard me, and then told me later that she didn't know and it didn't matter to her. It took me a day to digest that googly.

The next day, I told her that she must have some idea about who the father of her children must be. She stopped katka-ing the floor, looked at me in the eye and said that she had three partners and the children could be from any of them. But they were her children and would carry her name. Shamma saw my shocked expression and I saw her trying to smother a grin at my expense. The craziness and coolness with which she told me about her situation was unacceptable to my middle-class sense of morality and it really disturbed me.

After some soul-searching, I asked her the next day why she didn't pick the best of her three partners and marry one of them to give the children some sense of permanence. Shamma looked at me quizzically for a long moment, and suddenly changed the subject and asked me how long I had studied and what it cost my parents. I hemmed and hawed, and told her that I had been studying for about seventeen years and it would have cost my parents a good couple of lakhs, if not more. She laughed in a spontaneous, open manner and it really pissed me off as I was sure it was at my expense. And sure enough, it was. She looked at me gravely with the light of laughter still in her eyes and asserted, 'What a waste of an education. They have taught you nothing about life.'

Miffed, I said, 'What is it that you know and I don't?'

She gaily explained the equation: her partners were always on their best behaviour because they ate at her house, willingly contributed for the food and the education of the children, and accepted them as their own and took the responsibility for looking after them when needed. The house belonged to her and so did the children, and her partners were privileged guests if they contributed and behaved themselves. She was the glue which held all of them together. 'Now, supposing, I followed your educated advice and married who I thought was the best of the lot, then suddenly from a privileged guest he would become the co-owner or hakdaar, and would slowly exercise his authority over me and the children.'

So much so, she went on to explain, that he would question his fatherhood and believe the children were not his, but from the other two, and so he would start drinking to drown his doubts and unhappiness. Soon, he would chuck his job, and start living and drinking off her as he was now a hakdaar, and had become a complete liability. To vent his frustrations, he would ill-treat the children and probably beat her, and it would completely disturb her perfect life. It would also mean going through painful legalities to get rid of the bugger.

She explained the facts of life to me in twenty minutes—things I hadn't learnt in my seventeen years of privileged education. It was so clear and visual that I could see it unfolding in front of my eyes. I was stunned into silence, but, in my conditioned middle-classness, it took me a long time to come to terms with how she lived her life. I even tried the line of social acceptance and how cruel children in school could be to her kids. She had an answer for all my conditioned responses. She told me that all the people who looked down on her and gossiped were just jealous of how she handled herself and her life with such strength and dignity.

She asked me: if something happened to her or she needed help or money or just moral support, would any of her critics come forward to help? Wasn't it more likely that they would just watch smugly as she was hurt? Why should she live by their rules when she didn't need them or care about their opinions? I kept in touch with her for many years after leaving Pune, amazed that nothing had changed. Her children received an English education, and got decent jobs and life partners. The men retired and moved into her house, and their pensions were enough for them to live comfortably. They still worship the ground she walks on at the age of seventy-five. I have not met or seen a happier extended family. What I really learnt from her, in all humility, was that there are no perfect men. Yes, ladies. Three imperfect men make one perfect man—you just have to potty-train them.

———

After Vijay's mother's departure, peace and quiet reigned for a while, and we were joined by a Thai student, a sweet fellow named Fuldruk, who, other than being a good cook, was also a musician and played the guitar. Now, Vijay, our host, had his eye on a young lady who stayed in the building right across the road. He would hang around the gate when she used to leave for college, and again in the late afternoon, when she returned. Unfortunately, with very little luck. I suggested that we serenade her, with Vijay as the lead singer and guitarist, and us accompanying him on the drums and flute.

Vijay loved the idea and, before we knew it, we became a full-fledged band with Vijay on the guitar and vocals, Fuldruk on the flute and yours truly on the drums. Every afternoon, around 4 p.m., we would pretend to practise on the front lawn, in the hope that the young lady would be impressed by our cacophony disguised as a love serenade. We carried on with this for about a week, until, one fine morning, a distinguished-looking elderly gentleman rang the bell at our house.

I let him in and he asked to see all of us. The three of us lined up to hear him out. He introduced himself as the young lady's grandfather and came to the point straight away. He was distressed by the quality of music we were dishing out, especially during his teatime when he sat on the balcony to relax. 'Could you please just desist?' he asked politely. Dead silence from all of us.

He had also figured out that the noise was meant solely to attract his granddaughter's attention and, to this end, he had a proposal. We waited in anticipation. He said that if we stopped the awful racket, he would personally introduce us to his granddaughter. Bingo! We had cracked it. A formal introduction by her grandpa would be perfect for Vijay. We stopped playing and Vijay started hanging out with the young lady, and eventually, to his mother's eternal dismay, married her.

A year later, when we were in our third year, the gentleman summoned me to his balcony for tea. I was a bit perplexed, but I quickly spruced myself up and went across. He sat me down and I quickly realized that he had a fabulous view of the neighbourhood, and of course, our house. If interested, he could watch all the goings-on in our pad. We sat down for tea and without further ado, he handed me a newspaper cutting, saying, 'I think this is just up your alley. Check it out!'

Later, I read the advertisement carefully. It was from an advertising company called JWT and they wanted some creative misfits who thought differently from everybody else. And the old boy could think of nobody else but me! At that time, I thought he was joking, but by god, was he correct in his observations about me. Misfit! I even went for an interview during my holidays; however, they turned me down. They wanted creative misfits, not a raving lunatic!

———

We had a late entrant into college during our third year—a Swedish boy called Bjorn, whose father worked for Larsen and Toubro. He was a happy-go-lucky Nordic boy. He was a bit stocky, but otherwise quite presentable. He used to hang out with us and attend some of our parties.

One day, I found Bjorn looking long in the tooth and slightly low. After a bit of cajoling, he came right out with it. 'Indian girls no like Bjorn,' he said dejectedly. All of us rallied to his side and assured him that wasn't the case. He was blonde and good-looking, with an impressive physique. Sure, his English needed some brushing up, but that wasn't such a big concern.

He kept quiet for a bit and then said, 'Indian girls avoid me.' I asked him what exactly had transpired. He looked morose and said, 'I said, hello, we fork. And they run away!' He was genuinely hurt and perplexed. I patiently explained to him that in India, we don't shake hands and 'fork'. We hang out together, get to know each other, get married perhaps, and then, and only then, you might get to 'fork'. Not before that! He was foxed and said, 'In Sweden, we meet, then fork and, if it's good, we invest in making friends. Otherwise, what's the point?' I couldn't have agreed with him more, but I told him to try making friends first as things stood. He shook his head, trying to figure that one out. I must say he wasn't the brightest eighteen-year-old I had met.

Some days later, Bjorn arrived at Roomly's place and announced, 'Birgitta, my seester, she come!' We all perked up with one single-minded thought—if Bjorn 'forked', then Birgitta 'forked' too. I casually asked him about his sister's age and what she did. He said that she was two years older than him and lived with her boyfriend. I asked him what she did when she was not living with her boyfriend. He patiently explained that she then lived with her other boyfriend, who resided in a nearby town. We sat quietly and digested this information.

Birgitta was twenty, Swedish, single, and ready to mingle and even fork. Wow! With all our hormones jumping, we went into a fevered fantasy of blue-eyed, blonde-haired Nordic beauties throwing themselves at us. We planned the mother of all parties to be held at Deepak Vaidya's house. He was the son of an industrialist and immediately volunteered his home, thinking he would get first preference as the host. The date was set and all of us lukkhas were waiting with bated breath to dude up.

The party was scheduled at 8 p.m., and Deepak informed us that his parents were out of town. Whoopee! Now we were straining at the leash. The D-day arrived, and I bathed, shaved and doused myself with my previously rationed aftershave. It was bloody expensive, especially for a college-going kid. I left early to check out the setup. As I was halfway there, I realized I had a flat. Shit on a stick! I tried to find a nearby cycle-puncture repair shop. No such luck. They had closed their shops and were probably partying too.

I dhugged the cycle for the next kilometre and arrived at 8.30 p.m. I could hear the music and the party was in full swing. Sweating profusely, I cursed my luck. I was sure I had missed the bus with Birgitta. Continuing to curse my luck, I went up the stairs to the first-floor party room, which had a wooden floor. It was dark, the music was on full blast and a Beatles album was playing. The dance floor was jammed with gyrating bodies. I peered into the gloom, hoping to catch a glimpse of a blonde head. After some time, I gave up and wandered off to the fridge to get a drink. What the hell, I thought, having legged it all the way, the least I could do was to get smashed to the Beatles belting out 'Ob-la-di, ob-la-da, life goes on!'

As I opened the fridge door, in its fluorescent light, I saw a fleeting image of a bobbing blonde head in the corner where the cushions were stacked on the floor. I grabbed a beer and closed the door. Then it struck me that I had seen a blonde head. I opened the fridge door again to make sure I wasn't hallucinating. There it was, a blonde head bobbing to the beat. Somebody shouted, 'Close the fucking fridge door!' I quickly shut it and leapt to the corner, hoping not to stumble on any bodies on the ground. And there she was. I thanked god for the opportunity, thinking her escort must have gone to the loo or something. I breathlessly asked her, 'Birgitta, is that you?' She nodded and said, 'Ja! Ja!' in a German or Swedish kind of way.

I asked her for a dance and she immediately accepted. She passed me somewhere on the halfway point and kept going. I looked at her in awe. In the backlight, she was about six foot one to my diminutive five foot six. I was looking up at a true Norse warrior princess, and she was built like a tank meant for war, not love! My heart quailed and now I realized why she was all alone in a khopcha. I tentatively invited her on the dance floor, keeping a healthy distance. We danced—at least, she did; I just waited in fearful amazement. She took two small jumps forward and a massive leap backward. I watched her move for thirty seconds and felt the floor emptying of other bodies. I quickly indicated that we do the foxtrot. I must say she was more than willing! The Beatles were belting out 'Life goes on!'

I held out my arms to keep a healthy distance between us before we launched into a foxtrot and Birgitta lurched towards me. She enveloped me into her ample bosom. Suddenly, I went from hearing the Beatles singing 'Ob-la-di, ob-la-da, life goes on!' to nothing except a loud thudding heartbeat—thump-a-thump-a—accompanied by a lingering smell of lavender talc. After a while of stumbling around in the dark, I thought, this is the way my pathetic life will end, suffocated in the bosom of a Nordic warrior princess with the smell of lavender talc in my nostrils.

I went into slow motion, the voice of my swimming coach reverberated in my frantic brain: 'Turn your head under the armpit to your right and, as your mouth breaks the water, breathe, and go back, one, two, three, four, breathe, and back.' I followed my instructor and turned my head, and as my right ear and mouth broke the surface, 'Life goes on!' sang the Beatles. I gulped in some air and went back to the heartbeat. Thump-a-thump-a, three, four, breathe. Miraculously, after two minutes, I was still alive. God bless my swimming instructor, who thought I would never learn the crawl. And here I was doing just fine. He would have been proud of me. Thump-a-thump-a, and the lavender talc again and back to 'La-la, life goes on.' And then, thump-a-thump-a, and the lingering smell of lavender, while the Beatles sang, 'And if you want some fun, take Ob-la-di, ob-la-da.'

Finally, the song ended and while Deepak was trying to change the music, Birgitta loosened her vice-like grip on me. I quickly gave her the universal sign of 'number one', holding up my little pinkie, and escaped to the loo. By god, saved by my hapless swimming coach. Till today, whenever I hear the Beatles' 'Ob-la-di, ob-la-da', I can immediately smell lavender talc. That was the end of my infatuation with enormous, heaving bosoms. I became a leg man forever.

6

The Handy Twins

Being dyed-in-the-wool non-vegetarians, members of my tribe and I went to great lengths to procure a good meaty meal, especially because of the horrid vegetarian fare dished out to us at Fergusson College. It was only natural that when a dear friend of mine hand-delivered a bottle of bataer, or quail, pickle, all the way from Rajasthan, I quickly hid the bottle and waited for an opportune moment to devour it while nobody was around. After an excruciating wait, one quiet afternoon, when I was on my own, I hauled out the bottle of the quail pickle from its hiding place and decided to have at it with a loaf of bread. When I opened the bottle, the contents were spilling out; it looked as if the quails were trying to climb out on their own! I had to force it back in and lean on the lid to close it.

Now, I have found in human nature—well, mainly among men—that greed and lust make us lose our perspective and sense of self-preservation. I opened the bottle again and the high-octane smell of the pickle was masked by the generous amounts of fragrant masalas in it. Without further ado, I piled on to the rare dish and managed to demolish most of it in one go. After I finished, I burped in satisfaction.

The aftertaste of that first burp gave me a hint of impending disaster, but I quelled my uneasy conscience and put it back in its hiding place.

During the wee hours of the morning, around 3 a.m., I realized with full force that exercising discretion over greed would have been advisable. I doubled up with acute gripes and nausea, and I didn't have the heart or the sense to wake anybody up. I lay groaning on the bed. After what felt like hours, I just about managed to hobble to the loo, in great pain, and threw up, in rapid gushes, into the commode. I flushed the remains of my late lunch, rinsed my mouth to get rid of the bile and started to limp back to my room, still doubled up with pain when the pressure on my sphincter became unbearable. I made a swift U-turn and plonked myself on the potty only to spend the rest of the early morning hours as a permanent tenant of the toilet, purging my intestines, and the morning sun saw me clinging to whatever was left of me.

I somehow managed to wake Vijay up, who took one look at me and almost died of shock. He later told me that I looked like 'death warmed up'. He wanted to call up a doctor he knew, but I insisted on seeing Dr Madhumalti Gune. After many phone calls, interrupted by a flurry of visits to the loo, a car turned up with Ashok Gune at the wheel. I hung on to what remained of my sphincter, and we made it to Indira Maternity Home in the nick of time. That's right—a maternity home.

Dr Madhumalti Gune, whom we affectionately referred to as Tai, quickly examined whatever was left of my shattered insides and muttered, 'Acute food poisoning.' She proceeded to give me some medicines that knocked me out and then put me on a drip. For the next six days, I was in a ward full of expectant or new mothers with lots of their relatives coming and going, and then there was me—the only male lying in a maternity ward on a drip! Through my haze of pain and weakness, I realized that I was as much a subject of curiosity as the newborn babies. I was waiting for a portly grandmother to come up to my cot and make clucking sounds to comfort me, and stick a pacifier into my mouth. Alas, the nurses treated me professionally, like any other regular patient.

Even though I had returned from the valley of the shadow of death, I got none of the royal treatment that was meted out to expectant mothers or their babies, who were received with squeals of pleasure. Secretly, I felt that I had gone through my own 'motions' of labour, and deserved all the clucking and comforting that the mothers and their babies were receiving. Tai occasionally made the rounds to check on all her patients. She would look at my progress approvingly. And it seemed Tai, with her Maharashtrian sense of humour, had deliberately put me in the middle of a maternity ward because she felt I deserved it for being greedy.

I slowly recovered from being a caricature of a human to an actual one. Tai later told me I was lucky Ashok had got me to the hospital because I was so ill that I looked like a 'hima gajar', or dehydrated carrot, and had almost croaked. Phew—saved by a sphincter!

I made some great friends in Poona Camp, thanks to my military studies classes in Wadia College. I befriended a young scion, Hoppy Mohite, of some royal family. He lived with his brother in a sizeable, rambling bungalow somewhere near Bund Gardens, Poona Camp. Since there seemed to be no curious adults around, it became a place for much partying. I had also become close to a young lady called Claire, who was positively delicious-looking and part of the stylish Wadia College crowd. She used to attend all of Hoppy's parties.

Hoppy's parties were legendary, exclusive, and quite wild. He was also very popular with the jet set in Fergusson College and some of the better-looking women, including the handy twins, Famida and Shahida, who were the toast of the college and had a large entourage of admirers. Once, I had gone on a trek to Sinhagad Fort, one of strongholds, with the twins. It was drizzling in typical Poona fashion, so the going was tricky and slippery. On the way down, we were all having trouble, and the twins and I ended up helping each other down. At the bottom of the mountain were a whole bunch of aashiqs, waiting to catch a glimpse of the twins. They were a bit cheesed off seeing me with the sisters. A friend of mine, Premal Malhotra, also an aashiq, sidled up to me and asked sarcastically, 'So did you have a good time?' Without batting an eyelid, I shot back, 'I don't know about a good time, but it was slippery and wherever I slipped, I grabbed anything handy.' That shut him up pronto!

The twins, Shahida and Famida, looked so alike that—especially when they dressed similarly—very few people could tell them apart, and we would sometimes use a common name for both, Hamida! I had not met Famida in a while since she had gone on an exchange programme to the US for a year. In her absence, we had cleverly recruited her twin, Shahida, into the film society, Critique, for some play-reading which we wanted to perform, I think it was *Blithe Spirit* by Noël Coward. When we learnt that Famida was returning to Poona from the US of A, the college was agog. So, of course, a party was planned in her honour at Hoppy Mohite's house and all the regular suspects were invited.

I togged up and cycled to Poona Camp for the party. People had already arrived and Hoppy was on the music, and it was rocking! I saw some familiar faces and then spotted Shahida in a kurti and jeans looking lovely. Next to her was a glamorous version of her in a dress, with a mane of ringlets framing her face. I stared as Shahida brought her sister over and introduced her. Famida was identical to Shahida. Still, America had done something to her which made her different, something in her body language and assurance that she was an independent, mature woman, while her twin sister was still trying to find her identity.

She was hugely attractive, and I was gobsmacked and awkward. She shook my hand and then held on to it, saying, 'So, you're Robin! I have heard so much about you from Shahida.' I blushed a beetroot red and mumbled something. Just then, a whole lot of people arrived and surrounded her. Obviously, they were her old friends. So I extricated myself and slunk off thinking, by god, what a woman. Totally out of my league!

I loitered about, meeting the regulars—everyone stunned by the new and improved, back from the US of A, Famida. I was standing next to the potted plants, nursing a beer, when I first smelt the perfume. It was heady and intoxicating, and yet fun. Famida came and stood next to me, not saying anything, while my heart was doing cartwheels and my hormones were totally out of control. There I was, standing next to the toast of Poona Camp, trying desperately to be cool and matter of fact. The pregnant silence was uncomfortable and yet full of a kind of glow. She finally spoke up and said, 'Sorry I had to rush off before, there are so many friends, all trying to speak at the same time.' I nodded dumbly as the proverbial cat had got my tongue. She looked at me sideways, held my arm, said, 'Let's dance,' and led me to the floor.

Thank god no 'Ob-la-di, ob-la-da' this time! We danced to a disco number, where the music was fast and you moved your body and its extremities to the beat, and did what you wanted and could. I loosened up and was having a great time, when the wicked Hoppy dimmed the lights and put on 'Unchained melody', or something equally slow and romantic. I held out my arms to accept a civilized foxtrot with a foot of distance between us. She smiled, looked at me, and came straight into my arms in a close clinch. My heart leapt out of its socket and started hopping around uncontrollably.

I held my breath so as not to disturb this memorable, magical moment. And in between my hammering heart, I could hear hers— steady, reliable, no panic. I could not believe that this celestial creature was dancing with me, and so closely at that. I could smell her perfume, I remember the colour of her dress and in the three minutes that the number lasted, I was in another zone, waiting to exhale. The music ended and, for a moment, nothing moved, and then she deftly disengaged herself, smiled and said 'See you around', and floated away.

I was a bit dizzy, probably because of the lack of oxygen from holding my breath. I went out into the garden with the heady smell of her perfume lingering on. Later, I found out that it was the rage among teenage girls worldwide—a flowery fragrance called 'Charlie'. Those three minutes changed my life; very subtly, but radically. To Famida, after her US experience, it was just another dance, but to me, it was as seismic as the shifting of the earth's tectonic plates. It changed me from the inside.

As life carried on, almost forty years later, I saw a familiar silhouette on the Colaba Causeway and raced to overtake her. It was a fantastic reunion. We stopped for coffee, caught up with each other's lives and jabbered away about all the trivia in the world. Finally, she had to leave and I had to tell her, so I did—of how she was responsible for my coming of age. She remembered the party and meeting me, but nothing of any earth-shattering consequence. I knew that, but had to tell her, nonetheless. Both the sisters are doctors now and have settled down in Canada. I have kept in touch with them ever since, to the degree that many years later, Famida sent her lovely daughter to apprentice with us at Genesis during her two-month summer break.

7

The Lukkhas

Life in college was careening along between hanging out with the twins, rehearsing our adaptation of *Blithe Spirit*—the comic play written by Noël Coward—Gauri Deshpande's eclectic lectures and gleefully bunking classes to watch *King Solomon's Mines* at Alka Theatre. The movie featured the toast of the season—a nude Ursula Andress who would emerge from the flames of eternal life. All the college boys who watched the film for the umpteenth time waited with bated breath for Miss Andress to emerge from the pillar of flames wearing nothing more than her birthday suit. In the silence punctuated by heavy breathing, some wag would inevitably call out, 'Cross your legs, boys! Here she comes!'

The gang had also found a fabulous secret hangout in Uday Borowke's grape farm, behind Empress Gardens. Every weekend, our lot used to congregate to swim in the boughdi, or open well, eat grapes, and have a lunch of teekha, chilli-hot village-style pitla bakhri. This spicy gram flour curry is the typical Maharashtrian village fare. After our swim, we would be famished and wouldn't mind the fact that it was really spicy. Once we devoured it, we would sweat from every possible orifice, topped by a runny nose. The day always ended with a bullock cart ride to the bus stop on the highway. I still hunger over pitla bakhri and never give up an opportunity to get invited to a Maharashtrian home to eat it.

In the middle of our college routine, during long breaks, the military studies class would go for a field exercise to Deolali and Ahmednagar, or 'Nagar', as the armoured corps called it, to observe battle inoculation training for both regiments. In Deolali, we learned the term 'battle inoculation', where raw troops are put through intense conditions of real battle with live ammo to harden the soldiers and officers.

The men were in a trench while a battery of twenty-five pounders laid a creeping barrage, the shells exploding on an advancing matrix up to the entrenchment, and then over it to go behind them. This bombing gave the jawans an idea of what a patterned explosive concussion does to a defending force by softening them up with artillery. Even if there are no direct hits on the foxhole or trench, the detonations itself disorient, confuse and put the fear of god into them.

The troops also learn how to distinguish between an incoming artillery round and an outgoing one. An incoming shell is fired at you by an enemy battery. An outgoing round is fired by friendly artillery from behind your lines towards the enemy position. Knowing how to identify the subtle difference in the sound of the round passing over your head or coming straight at you can save your life! The word 'shell-shocked' describes the suffering of the aftermath of an artillery barrage.

Our trips to Nagar were a lot of fun as the cavalry officers were a jolly lot and poked fun at the poor bloody 'pongos', or infantry, who had to walk hundreds of miles during ops. In contrast, the cavalry traditionally drove their tanks into battle. They would stand hip-shot at the bar, like the horsemen that they were. The armoured corps' motto was on the top of the bar: 'When in doubt, only drink beer; don't touch the water, fish fornicate in it!'

Since my time in school, I had always wanted to join the 61st Cavalry as they were one of the only regiments in the world who still ride horses—be it for ceremonial reasons now. The 61st Cavalry are still horse-riding, polo-playing officer gentlemen who escort the president's carriage with pomp and glory. They get their pick of the best horses from the breeding facility at Saharanpur, run by the RVC (Remount and Veterinary Corps).

Apart from this, the final year of college was a blur of activity, and the institution's canteen had been abandoned for a place called Vaishali, which was near our college gate—a cheap and cheerful Udupi type of place. That's where all the action was. Another hangout was Good Luck Café, an Iranian joint, which served cutting chai till 1.30 a.m. to all the midnight oil burners and people suffering from exam fever. The tea was milky, sweet and addictive, and we all suspected the owner 'ghollowed', or dissolved, a touch of opium in it to get us hooked because the café's cash cow was the chai—but then again, who cared? The chai was fabulous and a lifesaver during exams.

What seemed like one regular day after college changed my life dramatically. I was at an Alliance Française do one evening, where most of the Deccan intellectuals assembled to discuss, philosophize and network, and us lukkhas arrived for the free food and the occasional glass of wine. A lot of earnest and seemingly strait-laced women attended the dos as well. I have learnt the hard way in life that you can never predict a woman's behaviour by your first impression of her. That night, I met this much-awarded, gold-medallist scholar, all of five feet, two inches, wearing glasses behind which her twinkling, wicked eyes sparkled. On her shoulder hung a cloth jhola. All my instincts told me to run. But being young and foolish, I followed her with my eyes because I could make out that even though she wore a khadi sari and Kolhapuri chappals, she moved like a gazelle.

She caught me staring at her, and brazenly and confidently walked up to me and asked, 'Are you an Aries?'

'Yes,' I replied.

She smiled impishly and said, 'I thought as much,' and nonchalantly walked away, throwing me off balance and leaving me with my mouth agape. I waited for her to circulate the crowd and come within hailing distance, before blocking her. Feeling quite cocky, I said, 'You meant as aggressive and horny as a ram, right?' She looked me straight in the eye and, clearly suppressing a glee that came with baiting a trap and seeing it snap shut successfully, she said, 'No, just sheepish!'

She traipsed away and for once in my life, I had no comeback!

From then on, I kept running into Suniti at all sorts of forums. She was the gold standard for the Fergusson College professors—a 100 per cent Chitpavan Brahmin, brilliant in her scholastics. She was attending college on a Maharashtra government–sponsored scholarship because of which her parents did not have to pay a penny for her college fees. She was a closet poet, to boot. And here I was, the college's bad boy—more an outsider than an insider, despite my grandmother's credentials. However, Naniji also shared a rebellious streak, evident from the fact that she had run away with my grandfather.

I found Suniti intellectually challenging, smug and superior, and pursued her quite single-mindedly. Once, I surprised her by asking her out on a date to watch the sunset. She looked at me innocently and said, 'Sure, but it has to be a special location.' She had put me to the test. Now, I had to find an exceptional location. A friend told me about a spot at Pashan Lake, which was off limits as it came under the municipal water works department and was guarded by a barbed-wire fence. He also told me about a hole in the fence through which I could climb in. Finally, plans for my date had started gathering momentum.

Bai from Dr Madhumalti Gune's kitchen contributed a flask of hot chocolate and jam sandwiches, and I set off armed with a book of T.S. Eliot's poems, after dousing myself with my heavily rationed aftershave. I picked up Suniti on my trusty bicycle, which lacked a passenger carrier. We met discreetly, some distance away from college to avoid unnecessary gossip, and headed towards Pashan, which was a good eight kilometres away. As we passed the Poona University gate, she kept asking where we were going. I turned on to the NDA Road, which went past Pashan Lake, but refused to give the surprise away.

Huffing and puffing, we reached the lake, skirted to the gap in the barbed wire and slipped through it with our hearts in our mouths. There is nothing like a healthy dose of fear to kindle romantic illusions.

We walked along the lake to a dilapidated and rotting wooden jetty and underneath it, we found an old boat just like my friend had promised me we would. Suniti was gobsmacked by the location and the elaborate arrangements I had made, and the present and clear danger that discovery would involve. We settled into the boat, opened the flask of hot chocolate, unwrapped the jam sandwiches and waited for the sun to set, turning the lake into a sheet of gold. What could be a better backdrop than this for a touch of Eliot.[3]

> Let us go then, you and I,
> When the evening is spread out against the sky.

It was truly magical and when we rode back, it was a profoundly comfortable silence that enveloped us, with her head resting on my shoulder. I tried to desperately control my huffing and puffing resulting from the exertions of double-seating on a bicycle. Luckily, most of the way back was downhill, so I just coasted along, bathed in the afterglow of the spectacular sunset.

Many days later, Suniti casually told me, 'I didn't think you were intelligent, but you managed to surprise me pleasantly.'

I was chuffed and felt like I was walking on air. My efforts at courting her were slow, but steady. One weekend, she finally invited me home to the National Defence Academy (NDA), where her father was the maths professor for the young cadets who were being polished. I turned up in my Sunday best and met the old boy, who was a cool, affable gentleman, and I immediately took to him.

The mother was a different kettle of fish. She took one look at me and instant dislike bloomed across her face. She disappeared into the kitchen, muttering under her breath all along. Suniti quickly stepped in to rescue me and took me out for a walk to look at the Khadakwasla Lake from a grassy knoll. We sat amidst the golden grass and looked down at the beautiful lake stretched out in all of its glory for a distance of eight kilometres. We sat in silence, gazing upon this fabulous vista, as she gently put her head on my shoulder and held my hand, apologizing for her mother's reaction to me. She seemed to think it was normal and something of a litmus test, because she only wanted to pick guys her mother detested. Wow!

It was late afternoon, the sun was low in the sky and a gentle wind rustled the grassy knoll. She turned her face towards me, waiting to be kissed. I immediately went into flashback mode and thought about my first date with Nalini in Dehradun and how my attempts to kiss her had only ended in disaster. Now, many years later, I was older, but none the wiser, having practised kissing only on the back of my hand. I tentatively kissed her rather chastely.

There was a pause as each of us digested my inadequate attempt at the kiss. Suniti looked at me quizzically, and my delicate, intellectual sati savitri turned into a tigress and proceeded to teach a novice like me the art of kissing. I, of course, was a more-than-willing student. The next two hours flashed by in a blur of long, sensual kissing, with us coming up for air in between. I have, till today, not met a better kisser. She had made it into an art form, complete in itself. We had to abort the most intense experience of my life as the sun had set and it was time for me to catch the bus to Poona, and for her to go back for dinner and face her mother.

I was in seventh heaven, with a silly, annoying grin pasted on my face, and all was good with the world. I was deeply, totally, head over heels in love with a dyed-in-the-wool Brahmin girl who could turn from a studious and intellectual scholar into a minx. My Sunday afternoons transformed from lazy, time-pass days to highly anticipated lessons in a much-needed art form. I believe that kissing is a complete art in itself, and one can remain immersed in it for hours without it getting repetitive or boring. And boy, was I an ardent student of hers.

We finally put up the play *Blithe Spirit*. It took so long because I kept fluffing my lines, and the girls refused to go on stage with me trying to ad-lib. The original play is hilarious and timing is everything. With me moving the goalpost all the time, we couldn't get the comic timing right. As the term drew to a close, I finally managed to tear away from my kissing classes to learn my lines. During the intervals between acts, we planned to have a band perform—led by none other than my friend Ashok Gune—to keep the audience from leaving while we changed our costumes and the sets onstage. The reviews were less than flattering, and it was noted that the musical interlude stopped being 'musical' very quickly and it was a relief to have the actors on stage, even though they hammered their way through the proceedings. So much for our valiant attempt to put up an English play in Fergusson College for the first time ever!

Meanwhile, Suniti and I stole every chance to hold hands surreptitiously all over the campus in plain sight—by crossing our arms over our stomachs and holding hands, which we hid below our elbows. We did so while sitting on the steps to the main hall, at bus stands, waiting for the NDA bus or even behind the shrubbery of the botanical gardens that the college boasted of having on campus. The terms flew by, at an incredible speed, to bring us to the moment of truth: exam time!

Most of the revision sessions were held in Vijay Paranjpye's house with the entire gang of lukkhas landing up, and Uday Borowke was the only one amongst us who possessed a complete set of textbooks and some notes. He was the most responsible out of all of us. For a month, we mugged non-stop, with me reading aloud from a solitary set of textbooks while the others lolled around, listening and making useless notes. We went into the exam on a wing and a prayer. I wasn't worried about my military studies exam, as I was on top of my game and had read and absorbed so much more than just the syllabus. The subject fascinated me. However, my economics exam was touch and go.

We finished our papers with a sigh of relief and had a few days to kill before parting forever from the people who had become such an essential part of our lives. I went into a huddle with my friends to discuss some unfinished business—namely what Suniti and I were to do now. She had two more years of college left, as she was doing an MA while I was heading off to Delhi to look for a job. We decided that Uday Borowke, the most respectable of the lot, would escort me to meet Suniti's father and help me formally ask for his permission to be engaged to his brilliant daughter.

On a bright, sunny Saturday morning, Uday borrowed his brother's car and brought his fiancée, Neelima Girme, along for moral support. The three of us drove to the National Defence Academy staff quarters for my tryst with destiny. We were greeted by Suniti's leggy, younger sister, all agog with the proceedings. The mother, slightly truculent, disappeared into the kitchen after greeting Uday and Neelima. I was studiously ignored. The father appeared, affable and smiling, with his slightly Bugs Bunny–like teeth. We had a cup of tea and got down to business.

Uday explained what we had planned to him, while a hovering Suniti disappeared into the kitchen. I piped up and said, with great bravado, that by the time she finished her MA, I would be earning fifteen-hundred rupees a month and we could get married. Her father looked at all of us hopefuls and, very softly and gently, told me that he had no problem with what us youngsters wanted to do. With a twinkle in his eyes, he added that it would be an excellent time to get engaged when I started earning twelve hundred a month. Dead silence from the ranks.

To save face, Uday slapped me on the back and said, 'What a good idea!'

I thought that Suniti's father did not believe that I could earn that much in two years and was all set to argue. Fifteen hundred rupees in the 1970s was a whole lot of money—after fifteen years of service, her father was probably getting two thousand in hand. Of course, with perks thrown in! He probably believed that I was a cheeky young whippersnapper to think that I would earn fifteen hundred in two years. Hah! Let's put him to the test, he must have thought. So there we were, checkmated by a smart old professor. Since Uday had already grabbed the exit line by agreeing to the suggestion, we trooped out—not destroyed, but disappointed.

However, all was not lost. I noticed an antique Lambretta scooter parked in the verandah. It was a 1956 model in excellent condition. Suniti's father saw me looking at it and said, 'It's for sale.'

I boldly mustered the courage to ask, 'How much?'

He said, 'Around fifteen hundred rupees,' which was the exact sum of my imagined income two years hence. I offered twelve hundred in twelve instalments of a hundred rupees each. He looked at me and my dejected body language, stuck his hand out and said, 'Deal.' I looked pointedly at Uday, and he fished out a crisp hundred-rupee note and handed it over to me. 'That's my first instalment,' I said, and we left.

That scooter was a lifesaver. Much later, in Bombay, as it was called then, it became famous with all my friends and a part of the traffic constabulary. That afternoon, however, though we were a bit disappointed, we consoled ourselves with the fact that the old boy hadn't listened to his wife and thrown us out on our bums. There was still hope.

8

'Ladka Sattle Ho Gaya, Ki Nahin?'

With our exams behind us, it felt like a huge burden had been lifted off me. However, that delightful feeling was short-lived because, immediately after that, I was faced with another equally daunting task ahead. It was called looking for a job. The peer and familial pressure to perform well is colossal, regardless of how emancipated the family is. The ultimate question posed to a North Indian family is always 'Ladka sattle ho gaya, ki nahin?' In reply, the family would say, with long-held suffering smiles firmly in place, 'Dhoond raha hai. Mil jayegi.' Though they were secretly thinking, 'What the hell is this idiot going to do with a degree in military studies when he is a civilian out of choice! He should do an MBA.' Without even realizing it, they passed on their fears and trepidations to their idiot child—namely me!

I took a week's break to go to Bombay before heading back to Delhi, to make endless résumés and fill in applications for appointments—back then, it was the standard way of job-seeking for a non-MBA who didn't have the luxury of campus placements. 'A BA in military studies ...' I started to scribble on one form. Oops! Scratch that. I wrote down BA (Hons) in economics instead. Sounds better, right?

Apart from dropping off my résumés, I wanted to spend some time in Bombay because I was fascinated by water, especially the ocean. I had lived in landlocked areas until then. This fascination began in Dehradun when I spent many hours of my childhood along banks of meandering rivers. In Bombay, hours would go by in a flash as I contemplated my future, watching the constant ebb and flow of the ocean's waves and tides.

One day, I was strolling down Flora Fountain when I saw a banner for a walk-in interview with a multinational bank. I marched into the institution's staid and intimidating portals. I was ushered into a holding area for hopefuls in their jackets, ties and suits, paired with pointy and shiny shoes. All of them stared and sniggered at my street-friendly attire—jeans and, luckily, a tee with a collar, along with my favourite suede desert shoes. I had heard of walk-in interviews for maids, drivers, peons and singers, but never for a management trainee at a multinational bank. After glancing at the suited and booted lot, I plonked myself down in a straight-backed chair and pulled out a book by my favourite author—a Western by Louis L'Amour—and started to get into it when a liveried peon announced my name.

I was led into the inner sanctum, which was wood-panelled and foreboding, only to find that, seated behind an impressive desk, was a cool dude dressed exactly like me—jeans, sneakers, tee. My interviewer was a guy named Mike, a firangi. He was leaning back in a swivel chair and was going through résumés in a desultory manner. He looked at me and brightened up seeing a fellow dude—or so I thought. Thus began my interview, which lasted an hour and a half while everyone else was dismissed in ten minutes flat. I laid my cards out fair and square, and told him outright that I had just finished my exams and was going to be lucky if I scraped through, except for military studies and English literature, in which I was sure I would do well. Though I had to admit that the economics part looked dicey. He was amused and we talked about everything under the sun, other than banking. He was an ardent surfer and scuba diver, and I was a lover of oceans and forests. We swapped stories and adventures, and finally, he laid it down that even if I got a second class in my exams, I could come back for a final interview. Unless there were any hiccups, I would get the job.

Holy shit! I had landed myself a plum job as a management trainee in a multinational bank. Now, for the bloody results. I was cock-a-hoop and spent hours talking to the ocean after the interview. I also stupidly and casually told my family in Delhi about the interview, not realizing the extent to which they had given up on me. Their reaction was unnaturally hysterical, as if a miracle had occurred, an answer to their incessant prayers. I was extremely embarrassed by this unseemly outpouring of joy.

After the dust had settled, I decided to scope out where the trainees had to work till their confirmation one year later. I toodled off to Flora Fountain, reached their office and politely enquired about the trainee centre. I was reluctantly escorted down two flights of stairs into the basement area, where I saw lines of young trainees seated in straight-backed chairs with heavy-duty calculators in front of them, balancing giant tomes of ledgers. This was well before the digital age and everything had to be done manually. The trainees were recording, for posterity, the business of the day.

The room was brightly lit and the walls were a dull greyish green with no embellishments except a large clock. The trainees were more or less dressed in the same formal office clothes, and reminded me of Aldous Huxley's *Brave New World* and George Orwell's *1984*—where you couldn't differentiate the men from the women. All of them, in their neat little rows, were bent over their calculators, desperately trying to beat the 6.30 p.m. deadline. There was not a single window in sight and, as it was below the level of the main road, I could feel the tremors of a passing bus overhead. There was absolutely no sunlight coming in. My heart quailed and I felt acutely claustrophobic. I turned around and fled this Kafkaesque scenario. Back on the street, I took a deep breath of the slightly polluted air and looked at the sun, as though I was seeing it for the first time. One always takes the simple things in life for granted until one is faced with life in a corporate dungeon! I ran for my life.

I did end up getting a reasonable second class in my BA, and sure enough, I topped the military studies class. I went back to Delhi with my tail between my legs and no amount of cajoling in the form of threats or emotional blackmail could make me go back to Bombay to join the multinational bank. I remembered the lines from the movie *Deewar*, 'Mere paas gaadi hai, bungla hai, Miss Mangala hai, aur tere paas kya hai? Kya hai tere paas?' And the answer: 'Mere paas azadi hai, hawa hai, jungle hai, samudra hai. Aur kya chahiye?'

My Plan B was to work in the tea gardens of Northeast India. After all, the Assam agitation had just started and it had become like a war zone. So, naturally, there was a dearth of assistant managers to work in the plantations. I knew I could waltz into a tea job, as there would be very few takers for that position. Delhi was a pain as, day after day, I woke up to breast-beating litanies of what an ass I was. To find respite, I started taking long walks in the Jor Bagh area. It was green and relatively quiet, and Humayun's Tomb became my sanctuary.

One day, while walking down a beautiful side road called Ratandon Road, I stumbled upon a bunch of laughing, attractive young people. They were colourfully dressed and sat on the lawns of a bungalow on that lovely winter afternoon, enjoying the sun as they shared lunch. I knew they belonged to some company because there was a sign nearby saying, 'Advertising and Sales Promotion Co.', or ASP. I liked the name ASP—reminiscent of the asp nestled in Cleopatra's bosom—and loved the staff's happy, sunny disposition.

I started quizzing them about what they did and all of that. That was the second time I realized that advertising was a profession and there were other companies, like JWT, that did this for a living. Seeing how well they were doing impressed me. It seemed like fun work, so I asked to talk to someone about a job and they sent me to the receptionist. I went through the porch and found her behind the PBX telephone exchange. Farida Pandey was a statuesque, pretty young lady, about five feet, eight inches tall, and wore a miniskirt, which revealed the best pair of legs I had ever seen in Delhi.

Not only did it take guts to dress like that in Delhi in the 1970s, but she carried it off with great aplomb—though I was sure she carried a can of mace in her handbag. I later realized that Miss Farida Pandey was tough as nails and didn't need to carry mace on her. Anyway, I was well and truly blown away by Miss Farida Pandey, so I tried chatting her up and she responded to my queries in between phone calls. In addition to her other responsibilities, she handled all the incoming and outgoing calls, and I was soon to find out that she was fondly referred to as the 'deep, throaty voice of ASP'.

She was forthcoming and explained a lot about the work that they did. I asked her if I could meet the boss, a man called Jog Chatterjee. She told me that he was in the middle of lunch. In a conspiratorial whisper, she warned me about the foul mood he was in and suggested that I come back in a few days. Since I was already there, I decided to take my chances and asked her to see if I could get ten minutes with him. She didn't say much to that, but after half an hour, she got up and knocked on a large door on the foyer's right side and called out to him by his first name, 'Jog, it's Farida.' She marched right in. I realized that she must be the boss's favourite and that's how she was on a first-name basis with him.

Maybe it was my lucky day. She came out and told me that the boss would see me for ten minutes, but warned me again about his foul mood. I went in with my heart in my mouth. Jog Chatterjee sat on an informal sofa-set arrangement and I noticed a working desk in the corner. He was fifty-five-ish, balding, stout and wore a pinstriped shirt with trousers held up by very fancy suspenders. He was frowning deeply as he motioned me to sit down and kept staring unhappily at the newspaper he held, which had a full-page colour ad in it. He finally put it down and turned to me brusquely, asking me why I was interested in joining the advertising field. I honestly told him that I knew nothing of the profession, but got interested in it after meeting some of the staff in the garden. It seemed much more exciting than working for a bank or a multinational company. He glared at me from beneath a pair of beetling eyebrows and then he snorted derisively.

Once I finished my spiel, I waited in anticipation. Mr Chatterjee handed me the newspaper and asked me what I thought of the ads. I opened it to see a full-page colour ad for Liberty Shirts. The visuals were striking and the copy was provocative. The ad had a photograph depicting the back of a man in a plaid checked shirt, of black and red checks, and facing the onlooker was the pert visage of a good-looking woman with her eyes peering over the man's shoulder. She had her hands around his neck and was holding a pair of stilettos in them.

The photograph was risqué. The positioning of her hands, which were around his neck with her stilettos dangling from them, immediately signalled that she was barefoot, which was hugely intimate—much more than even the way she was holding on to him. The copy was stunning in its suggestion. It read, 'We met at a boring party. One thing led to another and we ended up at his place. I loved his shirt, so I started with the top button. Tinker, tailor, soldier, sailor, oops, no more buttons.' And then the 'hero', which is adspeak for a product—'Liberty Shirts! Anything can happen!'

I knew Mr Chatterjee hated the ad, but I loved it. It was so amazing— the layout, the suggestion, the copy, the colours. Wow! Now came the test of truth and dare. Mr Chatterjee cleared his throat ominously and asked, 'So, what do you think?' Should I side with him or my sensibility, my brain raced—the job hung by a thread in a delicate balance. I took a deep breath and told him that I loved it unequivocally. He looked thunderstruck and said, 'It's vulgar, immoral and unethical! Why do you like it?' I swallowed my consternation and told him as calmly as I could that the ad was meant for twenty-year-olds and he was the wrong age to appreciate its finer points. If he had liked it, it would have failed as a campaign along with its positioning.

I also pointed out that he wouldn't be seen dead in a shirt like that. He harrumphed derisively again, and lost interest in me and the ad. After a while, he called Farida in and told her to show me around the office. His parting shot to me was, 'I am going to pay you the same amount as my peons. The royal sum of Rs 350 per month.'

I was ecstatic as a beaming Farida took me around the office and showed me my desk, right next to the men's toilet. I had landed my first job—in an advertising agency just as Anjali Sonalkar's grandfather had predicted I would when I was in college in Poona.

9

Pharida Phibe Times

My first six months in ASP flew by in a kaleidoscope of activities, learning and being treated like the dogsbody I was. I learned the ropes of advertising bottom up.

The first independent responsibility I was given was to proofread and oversee the production of the State Trading Corporation (STC) annual report at Caxton Press, Jhandewalan Extension, behind Karol Bagh. It was printed on a Heidelberg cylinder, a flatbed printing machine, which was state of the art in the early seventies. I can never forget the addictive smell of fresh printing ink. I spent long nights at the press, struggling to sleep on a narrow wooden bench, while waiting for the proofs to come out.

One of the main reasons I had to babysit this task with hawk-eyed scrutiny was that the Heidelberg was in short supply, so the jobs had piled up in the dozens for their turn to be printed. Now, typically, Delhi jugaad has to be learned first-hand and nothing less. The other guys hanging around, waiting their turn, would get impatient and slip a few hundred rupees to the machine operator. When the operator thought I was fast asleep or not paying attention, he would switch the job to somebody else's and I would lose a couple of hours in the process. I had to sleep as light as a cat and the moment the machine stopped, I would leap up and check whether the operator had switched jobs. By god, never a dull moment!

I was put under the second in command at ASP, a veteran, Sumedh Shah, who in turn put me under an account executive who was a young nawab (or nawbob as the British pronounced it) from near UP. He was tall, good-looking and professed to be a poet—he certainly looked the part with his dreamy demeanour. He was soft-spoken and his Urdu was lajawab. All the women in the office were quite lattoo over him. He owned a vintage Jaguar, which was the envy of the entire office, including Jog Chatterjee. He was married (aren't they all?) to an ambitious young socialite, who was extremely well connected and was promoting the hell out of him among the embassy crowd as a renowned painter.

Here I was with Nawbob, handling a client called Sylvania and Laxman—one of the world's top lighting companies that had a dyed-in-the-wool Jat marketing manager, whom we nicknamed 'Twenty-Five' because that's how he pronounced it. Now Mr Twenty-Five Singh was a tough, no-nonsense type and wasn't particularly impressed by our Nawbob or his vintage Jag. He was giving Nawbob a hard time about delivering a campaign for his world-beating product. Whatever the art department put together was summarily bounced by Mr Twenty-Five with extreme prejudice, and a few behn and ma ki gaalis thrown in, which did nothing for Nawbob's delicate persona. He would sit behind his desk in a gloomy mood, with his head in his hands and become incommunicado—much to my dismay and chagrin, as I was just a trainee and had a hard time getting anyone to notice me on a good day.

One day, we received a letter from Mr Twenty-Five, which stated that if we did not present a viable campaign in the next forty-eight hours, we would be sacked as an agency. The letter was opened, read, and quickly crumpled and thrown away—and now we were in a full-fledged crisis. Nawbob paced up and down his room furiously, with me watching him with great foreboding. The clock ticked on, and our resident royalty wore out the already threadbare rug with his pacing and muttering. Then, as the clock struck one, he picked up his car keys and vanished, leaving a stricken trainee in his wake. Bloody hell, now what? I had precisely thirty hours left before my career in advertising came to an inglorious end.

I scampered to the art department where all the senior graphic artists, illustrators and visualizers sat, but my bleats for help were soundly ignored. In desperation, I coopted the company of a fellow trainee, Moina, an attractive, leggy graphic designer who had joined ASP at the same time as me. I shared my woes with her and we decided to have a go at it ourselves.

I remembered a publication called **SPAN**, published by the American Consulate, in which I had seen a stunning photograph of Earth taken from space at the time of moon-landing. It showed the blue planet, with half of it covered in darkness. Together, we cooked up a headline which said, 'At any given time, half the planet is lit by Sylvania and Laxman.' Now, the only thing left was to get a hold of the damn photograph. Luckily, Moina had a connection at the consulate; so off we went to try and get them to give it to us. After much cajoling and pleading, the publicity officer parted with a photograph in black and white. We rushed back to the office and worked furiously through the night to present the layout to Mr Twenty-Five the next day by noon. He loved it. Whew! Saved by the moon-landing.

The advertisement was sent into artwork and then a block, and in the next two days, a quarter-page ad appeared in the *Hindustan Times*. The whole office was agog and, finally, people started taking notice of Moina and me. Even Mr Scowly Chatterjee smiled at us! Three days later, His Highness, the Nawbob of Kucch Nahin arrived as if nothing had happened and was congratulated for saving the account. And so it became an accepted pattern—he would have a crisis, take off in his Jag, leaving the crestfallen trainees in his wake holding a crock of shit.

As an aside to this episode, I learnt many years later that the Nawbob's first wife's father had run off with the then army chief's wife. In a fit of rage, he had put into the rules of conduct of officers and gentleman that 'Stealing the affections of a brother officer's wife' is a court-martial offence!

———

There were some amazing, hugely talented people in ASP, Delhi, and I got to interact with all of them. There was Mickey Patel, the incredible illustrator, cartoonist and designer, who was India's answer to Feiffer, the American cartoonist and social commentator. Mickey also had a wicked sense of humour and his take on ordinary people was extraordinary. There was Saeed Mirza, a copywriter, who later moved to Bombay to make outstanding films on the city and its various communities—not the glitzy movies of Bollywood, but hard-hitting, exceptionally insightful films on the marginalized communities in the City of Dreams!

There was a Bong mafia who ran the studio and art department and would continuously spar with Farida for not getting them on their requested phone calls in a hurry. They could hold everybody else to ransom, but not Farida Pandey. No, siree. I would hear this litany every day, 'Pharida, phibe times I am telling you the number and you are not listening!' So much so that we finally started calling her 'Pharida Phibe Times'. We had some hugely talented ladies like Benazir, who came from Hyderabad and was an exceptional writer. She looked like Cindy Crawford because of the very edible-looking mole at the corner of her mouth.

Slowly, the itch of wanting to specialize in films became an obsession of mine. Especially after having started Critique, the film club at Fergusson College, I had realized, over the years, that my calling was in Bombay, with the various possible avenues the city offers to get into film-making. Finally, something snapped within me when I came face to face with the unpleasant underbelly of Delhi and I decided it was high time I left the city.

It all started when the second group of Comex students was due to arrive in the city. Comex was an overland Commonwealth Exchange Students' Programme. There was a buzz around town that Comex 2 was about to come to Delhi University any day. Several Greyhound buses had started their journey in England and it was going to culminate in Delhi University. The buses had 250 students from England, out of which 200 were girls and 50 were boys. They would traverse half the world by road and then return to England, taking some students back with them along the way.

A friend of my sister in Lady Shri Ram (LSR) College had managed to get a seat going back with the Comex lot to spend a year in London on an exchange programme. Her name was Irene and she hailed from Goa. So, I was, of course, coopted to drive her to Buddha Jayanti Park on a rat-fatty motorcycle borrowed from a friend. Buddha Jayanti Park was where the university bigwigs would be receiving the bus passengers with garlands and high tea.

Comex 1 had arrived pretty quietly a year earlier and had gone back without much incident. But the stories of their stay had spread like wildfire: of wild parties, lots of willing and able international students, and what a great time the boys from Stephen's and Hindu had had. With each retelling, the stories got wilder and wilder until even trans-Yamuna held its collective breath, waiting for Comex 2 to arrive. I should have warned Irene because I could sense the feeding frenzy building with every local mawali girding his loins and coming to the park so as not to miss the party.

The fateful day arrived. The buses had been held up at Wagah border and were running late. We reached Buddha Jayanti Park in the afternoon. A small group of professors and student office-bearers were walking around skittishly as a sea of rough-and-ready types from all over Delhi had thronged to the venue and were getting restless. The few women there were huddled around the receiving tables, looking nervously at the mob, which was inching closer. No one had called the cops yet as it was a strictly university-only reception and nobody had anticipated the power of rumour. Alarmed, I told Irene to stick close to me and be ready to run if necessary, as I didn't like the look of things at all.

The buses finally arrived two hours late, covered in a film of dust, and came to a stop with the wheezing of their hydraulic brakes.

The crowd surged forward, swamping the receiving party and their furniture like a tidal wave. Nothing happened for a heart-stopping thirty seconds. Then, the door opened and a young student sporting a pair of John Lennon–style spectacles appeared and stood blinking in the late afternoon light. A low growl from the surging crowd startled him and he stepped down, only to be swept aside immediately! A girl appeared—blonde, blue-eyed, freckled—with a big smile, which disappeared when she saw the mob. Hands reached out to grab her. She quickly jumped back as many vernacular voices shouted, 'Sister, come I show you Dilli!', 'Abey oye! Baju ho ja, meri hai, I take you in my rickshaw!'

The atmosphere was explosive. I grabbed Irene and ran for my life before it didn't matter any more whether it was an Indian girl or a foreigner who was within the mob's grasp. We made it out by the skin of our teeth. The next morning's headlines screamed something to the tune of 'Lathi charge at Buddha Jayanti Park! Unruly crowd mobbed international students and disrupted the university reception. Students ran for their lives!' For the next week, no woman in Delhi was safe. It didn't matter whether they were Indian or not. Everybody and anybody female had been accosted and propositioned, even aunties. The fate of Comex 3 was sealed—they never came back.

It was as clear as day. Delhi was not my city. I had to get the hell out of there. I needed to be in Bombay to make films and remain within shouting distance of Suniti, who was still very much on the cards. Though, I have to say, anybody who tells you that distance makes your heart grow fonder is talking shit. I needed the Delhi office to support my trip to Bombay as the snooty office there would resent my arrival, since I was a Dilliwala. I had to do a balancing act to smoothen the process. Suck up to Bombay and tell Delhi that they needed a trained film executive as television had massive potential in the future.

10

The Reluctant Guru

My break to go to Bombay came inadvertently; it almost felt like an act of god. It was fuelled by a growing, scary realization in the advertising industry that the next big thing after ice cream was going to be television. And this meant a whole new set of disciplines had to be learnt to address this idiot box with an enormous appetite for content—fed and furnaced by advertising revenue. The television felt like an ever-hungry octopus, its tentacles spreading to every nook and cranny of this hugely diverse country. Never before in the history of this nation had there been such an opportunity to capture and brainwash so many diverse, sweating millions with the switch of a button. The government was putting its full might behind linking the country with relay stations.

The turning point, for me, was a surprise visit to the Delhi office by Shyam Benegal, senior executive and one of the pioneers in the industry for making breakthrough ad films for cinema. He was a legend in the advertising circles. I, somehow, inveigled myself into a quick chat with him and professed my immense love for cinema. He was a bit dismissive of my genuflection at first. I thought it was because I was from Delhi. Even in those days, Delhi was known for its jugaad.

But I did manage to impress on Mr Scowly Chatterjee that someone from the Delhi office needed to head off to the Bay to learn the ropes of this TV thing. Since I was totally dispensable, who better than me to learn from a reluctant mentor like Shyam Benegal? Mr Chatterjee bit the bait and paved the way for a three-month training trip with Mr Benegal in Bombay. Yay! After the euphoria had died down, I learnt that I was expected to survive in Bombay on my measly salary of 350 bucks. Holy cow!

——————

I arrived in the city on the Rajdhani train, lugging my essentials in a haversack, and was met by my patron and lifesaver, Larry Grant. We had an old Dehradun connection. His mother had been my infirmary in-charge at SSK, and his aunt was my dentist there. How small the world is! Larry Grant was a bit of a legend in his time—brilliant, eccentric, truculent at times, with a wicked, sarcastic sense of humour. He was a football fanatic and a permanent fixture at the Cooperage Ground during matches. I figured out his professional reputation only after I started working at ASP, Bombay.

Larry took me to Colaba, behind the Taj Mahal Hotel, to his digs in an old building called Umrigar Building on Ormiston Road. After climbing four flights of very large stairs, we reached the flat, with me huffing and puffing behind him. It belonged to a Parsi lady called Mrs Meherhomji, all of seventy years of age. She was a bundle of latent energy, bustling about, organizing things for the Parsi community, doing social work and whatnot. I was presented to her as the occupant of Larry's room for three months, while he was away on a sabbatical. It was a beautiful, large, airy room with a view of the rooftops of all the buildings behind as they were only three storeys high. A room with a view! Mrs Meherhomji reluctantly allowed me the use of her kitchen to warm my food whenever necessary, after which she ensconced herself in her drawing room on her favourite rocker, from where she used to hold court.

Larry Grant played a vital role in my introduction to the city. Not only did he give me his digs to stay in, but he also took me around the locality and showed me the real back alleys of Colaba. What a warren of pulsating life that the mohalla of Colaba had, and still has—from eating joints to beer bars to seedy dives that sell anything and everything. Colaba has a very serene and respectable façade. One end of it props up the pride of the Tata group and Bombay—the Taj Mahal Hotel, reputed to have been built backwards with the back end facing the bay—and the other end has the Causeway, which offers a shop-till-you-drop experience.

In between was a beehive of illicit activity, from haathbattiwalas (country hooch sellers) to kerbside prostitutes, to vendors of Bombay Black—a terrible concoction of ganja, boot polish and god alone knows what. Colaba has also been home to some fantastic eateries, which open on the streets after ten in the night and stay open till four in the morning. Also, what made Colaba so popular back then were the aunties serving booze by the quarter illegally in their own places as prohibition, thanks to Morarji Desai. It was the mainstay for all illegal income churned out in Bombay. All the aunties' joints had a large photo of Morarji bhai, festooned with a sandalwood garland. What a time for the idealist, who fled Delhi, the city of jugaad, to come to Bombay, which was like an electric shock to a relatively innocent army brat. And I took to it like a duck to water.

I realized very quickly that over here nobody bothered about which part of this boisterous city you lived in; the only thing that mattered was the value you brought to the table. Black money was so common that every street urchin was a potential entrepreneur or tycoon. The city was only interested in the value that you created and therefore owned. Only having money was 'passe'. The nouveau riche flashed it around and old money stayed coolly distanced and aloof—only opening the doors for the truly talented and brilliant young professionals, who flocked to the city of dreams to prove that they had arrived.

In the middle of all of this were the desperate survivors, who defined the city's subculture. The mick on the make, the bootlegger, the ageing prostitutes with large hearts, the pimps who sold anything from women, men and struggling actors to stolen goods. The Muslim quarter where everything goes—from made in Bombay to antique furniture, to kebabs to bheja ghotala, to second-hand clothes and shoes. What a melting pot this city was! Not much has changed from then till now. It attracts the best and the worst in the country, with a police force that is probably the topmost in the country, though crippled by corrupt politicians and a complete lack of reforms.

Colaba became my haunt and after Larry Grant took me on a guided tour, I explored every nook and cranny of this teeming suburb. The lane parallel to the Taj was where the action was after-hours and I was fascinated by the wildlife I found there. Bagdadi Restaurant, one of the oldest in Colaba, was run by an ageing Muslim gentleman and catered to an eclectic set of customers, from off-duty cabbies and prostitutes to the last of the flower people passing through to Goa.

There was something for everybody on the menu—keema pao to fried fish and chips. The owner had an impressive collection of miniature airline cheeses, which I loved. They were stacked on the counter and sold by avaricious international crew members. The going rate was a mere two bucks a pop. I even found a case of Stolichnaya vodka sold by Russian sailors, trying to make a quick buck in exchange for lipsticks, which were in great demand back home in Mother Russia.

I met some real characters in my stint at Colaba—like this ageing lady of the night, who used to hang out under a lamp post on the corner of Ormiston Road, behind the Taj Mahal Hotel. One day, she disappeared and the word spread by local street urchins was that she had fallen ill. On the third day of her absence, another contender to the throne arrived and occupied the prized location.

A few days later, our original lady of the night arrived and found, much to her chagrin, that a usurper had plonked herself under the prized lamp post. After a few not-so-pleasant opening salvos, it became a heated catfight, with a swelling partisan crowd of the regular street types cheering on their favourites, who were exchanging choice expletives. Finally, the usurper lost support and decided to go back to her own beat, but not without a parting shot. She walked a few steps and turned around for a final repartee; but at a loss for anything new to hurl, she said, 'You ... You prostitute!' and left in a huff. I almost fell off the fourth-floor balcony rolling with laughter.

———

In the meantime, I had been seconded to a filmmaker called Kantilal Rathod, who had just made a festival film in Gujarati called *Kanku*. Shyam Benegal had found a reluctant guardian for me. Mr Benegal sent me to my new mentor's office on Nepean Sea Road. Mr Rathod lived in Baroda and worked in Bombay. While I was with him for two and a half months, he was mostly absent. I was left twiddling my thumbs in the company of his trusty photographer, Dayaram Chawda, a laconic paan-chewing man with a shock of unruly grey hair, which had never succumbed to a comb.

He had the run of the office and shot nudes there in his spare time. I always wondered how he got the girls to agree to be photographed. They came in droves, from college girls to homemakers to socialites. I must say, he was a thorough professional and an unlikely gentleman. His speciality was to make them hold an object like a fruit or an object d'art in the foreground, which was in focus, with the nude lady in the background, appearing slightly hazy. They loved it, as it gave them a vicarious thrill without their identity being revealed. And Dayaram was a thorough gentleman, never one to kiss and tell. He never revealed the identity of the ladies concerned to anyone. Ever.

When there was no work, which was most of the time, I used to cross the road to the sea, sit on the rocks and watch the ocean with great fascination. It was powerful—sometimes turbulent, sometimes deceptively gentle, but always moody and unpredictable. To this day, I find the sea mesmerizing, with its immense power to reduce even the most arrogant and proud human being to abject humility.

11

'Chirpy, Not Tippy, Stupid!'

As my return to Delhi came closer, I started getting restless and desperate. My three months in Bombay had whizzed by too quickly. I hadn't even learnt all that much in that time. Somehow, Bombay felt much more like home than Delhi ever had—especially because of its traits of professionalism, efficient time management and a relentless pursuit of excellence. These were followed not because it was necessary, but for the sheer exhilaration of proving that one could hack it with the best of the best—be recognized and sometimes even rewarded for it.

I wrote to the Delhi office, who had by then started bleating for me to return. I requested them for some more time to make a short film of my choice to prove that my time in Bombay was well spent and that I was ready for serious responsibility. Pat came the reply: I had been sanctioned the royal sum of Rs 450 to make a coherent film, to showcase my talent and learning. Four hundred and fifty measly bucks to make a two-and-a-half-minute film with a month to write, cast, shoot, edit and finish the post-production. The gauntlet had been thrown, and I had no choice but to pick it up and then make a go of it.

It was a life-defining moment for me—damned if I do and damned if I don't.

It was at this time that I met two people who influenced and honed my enthusiasm into a discipline, such that I was prepared to attempt something as challenging as making a film. The first was A.K. Bir, a cinematography graduate from FTII. He promised to help me between his commitments. My other mentor was one of the most brilliant, self-effacing professionals in our business—the father of animation in India, Ram Mohan. I had met him quite by chance during the screening of a documentary at Films Division, which Dayaram Chawda had dragged me to attend.

Ram Mohan sat patiently with me the next day to chalk out an innovative way to shoot my subject. We decided we would shoot sequential, still photographs, process the black-and-white negatives and blow them up and animate them on his costly Oxberry animation table. Following this method essentially meant that we would have to shoot the stills in a predetermined pattern to stimulate movement.

His idea to animate stills was a breakthrough not only because it was unusual then, but it was also something I had never even considered. And the best part was that it would be within my budget. All that I had to buy was processing chemicals and photographic printing paper as everybody else's services and equipment were being borrowed for free. The most expensive piece of equipment was my camera—an Asahi Pentax that I owned (whew!). Other than the camera, the costliest machine was the Oxberry animation table offered to me magnanimously by Ram Mohan. In my great enthusiasm, I never realized the sheer number of photographs Bir and I would have to develop and process in the pursuit of this magnum opus.

Now came the business of finding a suitable subject or story for my film. As luck would have it, I had written a poem, pompously titled 'Reflections'. I had penned it on the train from Bombay to Delhi, after leaving the love of my life, Suniti P. behind in Poona. The poem was a semi-abstract piece that traced the highlights of a boy and girl falling in love. It portrayed their expressions cast against the backdrop of the landscape whizzing past the window of a train.

The poem captured the clickety-clack of wheels hitting the joints of the rails, which turned to a deep, booming roar when the train sped over bridges and through tunnels, only to go back to the rhythmic click-clack of the swaying carriage as it passed through the ever-changing countryside. The images were vivid and nostalgic, capturing the humour and laughter on the girl's face to sudden bursts of intensity and longing as their romantic relationship progressed towards the intertwining of souls and, finally, the painful realization of love (so deep!).

How on earth were we going to capture that progression on film, or, rather, still photographs? If I had chosen a simple 'once upon a time to happily ever after' subject, life would have been much easier for me. But, no! I had to go for broke and choose a poem amateurly written on the impossible subject of a flashback about falling in love. God, that was dumb! First off, I had to find a girl who would spend many weekends with me, trying to awkwardly negotiate the treacherous waters of glorious, bittersweet love, of a romance made in heaven. The hunt to cast the protagonist was on and it brought with it its own dilemmas: Do we find a professional actress? How much would she charge? Would professional actresses be interested at all? Should we go for a rank non-actor and play it by ear instead?

I was trying hard to find the perfect person for my movie, but couldn't seem to find anyone. I knew my deadline was approaching and we had to get down to work soon. In my experience, if you want something deeply, the universe conspires with you. One day, I was sitting with some friends in Samovar. I would usually sit with my back to the entrance to allow my friend Vikram from the Times of India (ToI) to sit facing the door because whenever a likely young lady passed by, he was like a good hunting dog.

His eyes would go 'boinggg'! They would jump out of their sockets and follow her, which is why we had nicknamed him 'Banana Eyes'. Right on cue, Banana Eyes went 'boinggg', and I turned around to see a doe-eyed young lady in a cotton dhakai sari with a startled look on her face, like a gazelle, frozen on the edge of flight. Until she spotted a familiar face and then a smile of nervous relief lit her up. I was riveted by her ready-for-flight body language and attractive elfin-like face. I had found my muse.

I realized in those first few moments of intense observation that she was new to Bombay and had very few friends. She was not quite used to the hurly-burly of a metropolis. She came from a sheltered background—probably Calcutta—and this was her first taste of independence. Whoa! I was running away with my imagination. As it turned out, I was so damn right. I recognized some ToI colleagues she was with, and went across and introduced myself. Now came the tricky part: to convince her to be my muse in the film. I very tentatively told her about the project after a brief exchange of background information, and she perked up. She was all eyes and ears as I told her about how important it was for my future and how stressed I was about the whole project.

I even explained how I was going to animate still photographs. She understood everything, including the fact that I could only shoot over weekends and in available light as we were on a shoestring budget. I didn't dare tell her that she would be the object of desire in the film. 'Stupid, chicken-shit idiot,' I muttered to myself, but managed to get her to agree to meet me the next evening for chai and pakoras at Sam's (Samovar).

The next day, I duded up in my only ironed buttoned-up shirt and a clean pair of jeans, ditched the chappals for shoes, slicked my hair back and applied a liberal splash of my rationed aftershave. I met a very distracted young lady in a newly starched cotton sari with minimal make-up on, looking delectable. It took me a little while to calm down and get her full attention as some goings-on at her office were bothering her. When I finally got her attention to listen to the poem, I baulked and mumbled something about needing some help in the running around. Would she be my assistant dogsbody?

A long heartbeat later, she squealed with delight and said, 'I'd love to, but I have no clue about making a film.' I wanted to tell her that nor did I, but kept very quiet. I introduced her to A.K. Bir, the strong and silent director of photography (DOP), and he was also charmed by her. Her pet name was Chirpy but I preferred Tippy. She immediately corrected me, 'Chirpy, not Tippy, stupid!' So I held my peace and wagged my tail like a 'good doggy'. There was too much at stake for me to offend her now.

For the next two days, since it was the weekend, the three of us sallied forth to engage with the fickle winds of fate and destiny. We looked for locations and the quality of light at different times of the day. Luckily, as it was the winter, the sun never went toppish. We brainstormed about setting the mood and the colour of the clothes to underline the emotions, while always pretending to be on the lookout for the right girl. I had warned Bir to follow my lead and keep his trap shut. He looked at me most disapprovingly, but followed suit. He couldn't understand the need for this elaborate hoopla.

Anyway, after the first two exhausting days, we had managed to purloin the black-and-white negatives from the leftover film, which we handloaded into cassettes in a dark room. Bir was superbly adept at this. We also discovered that the artist Akbar Padamsee had received a Nehru Fellowship grant and had set up an inter-art Vision Exchange Workshop (VIEW), which had a darkroom with an enlarger and the works.

Akbar allowed destitute photographers into the dilapidated flat on Nepean Sea Road to use the darkroom. We met with him and he gave us the nod to develop our negatives there—such a sweet, gifted, brilliant man. But there was still no leading lady in sight! I hesitatingly broached the subject to Chirpy about her bailing me out, saving my job and paving a future for me, all with a woebegone face.

She looked at me with her startled doe eyes and, in a small voice, said that she would have considered it if she had an iota of talent. One, two, three heart-stopping seconds later, I leapt into the breach, thinking that it was now or never. The lines from the 'Charge of the Light Brigade'[4] ran in my mind:

Theirs not to make reply,
Theirs not to reason why,
Theirs but to do and die,
Into the valley of Death,
Rode the six hundred.

Cannon to right of them,
Cannon to left of them,
Cannon in front of them,
    Volleyed and thundered ...

It was just my heart pounding and not real cannons, of course, but the feeling was evocative of the poem. I sprang to her side to tell her that she was perfect for it and she needn't worry about how well or poorly she performed. The camera loved her and that was all that mattered. She looked very uncertain, so I kicked Bir under the table to pitch in and thank god he did, in his quiet, confident way. I could see that she was on the backfoot, desperately trying to find a way out of this extremely tricky situation. She finally gave in and, in a tremulous voice, said, 'Okay, but if you find someone else in the meantime, please let me off the hook.'

I wanted to hug her in relief, but desisted because she might have judged me as being too forward and changed her mind. Whew! Saved by A.K. Bir.

In all my meetings with Chirpy I had made sure that she only saw me with the Pentax around my neck. Even while talking to her, I used to speak to her through the camera. This way, she got used to me and the camera as one entity, and wasn't self-conscious when I started shooting her. It was as if the camera had become invisible and she would respond only to me spontaneously. It helped tremendously in her performance, which was then neutral, transparent, spontaneous and authentic.

We would work out scenarios, talk, laugh, provoke each other for reactions, and capture them in the same magnification, in a rapid-fire sequence. Bir was critical to this whole exercise, for the right compositions, quality of light, and to add a healthy dose of sanity and gravitas to the entire proceeding. The more comfortable we were with the process, the more ambitious we became, and the more edgy and intense the film, despite the occasional leg-pulling, laughter and fun. We used to shoot on Saturdays and Sundays, and process and print all the usable sequences over the week, as Chirpy had to work then.

I could see her confidence developing. She was growing into herself, transforming from a girl to a woman in front of my eyes— or should I say lens? This was the uniqueness in shooting over a comfortable span of time. No matter how accomplished, no actress could transition from a girl to a fully grown woman on camera unless it happened organically. Chirpy had an elfin face and a devastatingly attractive persona, and both Bir and I could see the transition. Chirpy and I were hugely attracted to each other, and the chemistry was palpable, especially to Bir, who tried broaching the subject delicately with me a couple of times. I was too single-minded about the shape the film was taking and ignored him.

By the time we were into the third week of production, both of us were hopelessly involved in the movie and each other. It must have been obvious to a very concerned A.K. Bir, who, in his wisdom, realized that this was a recipe for disaster. He knew that I had a Suniti P. standing by in Poona, and Chirpy was hugely naïve and vulnerable, and possibly didn't know what she was getting into. I think Bir's concerns were mainly for Chirpy and not me, as he thought I was bulletproof and had been around the block a couple of times. Little did he know that nobody is bulletproof in these circumstances.

There is an intensity about anything that starts with an expiry date. The feeling of inevitability makes everything seem real and intense— the film would end and our relationship would change. The glue of the film-making experience that was holding us together would disappear. We would have to stand in the glare of each other's scrutiny after that. Without the passion and commitment to making the film, the personal relationship we shared was in for a nasty surprise. And that's how it unfolded.

We completed the film after many hours in the darkroom. We were running around, trying to put the soundtrack of a train and a music track to suit the picture. In those days, there was no digital technology. We had to edit the images separately and then match the sound on an optical track afterwards, run it on a doubleheader projector and marry the sound to the picture only when completely satisfied. (In a doubleheader, sound and picture played separately, but in sync with each other.) If there were any corrections in hindsight, you were right royally screwed as you would have to go back to the beginning of the edit and start all over again. Because there was no dialogue in the film, it was simpler to execute the train's sounds and music as the audio overlay, and hopefully create visual poetry.

Chirpy had come through with flying colours and the camera indeed loved her as I had predicted it would, and, finally, the film was ready. All of us nervously wanted to see it on a big screen, but had no funds to book a preview theatre. We brainstormed, trying to figure out where to run it. And bingo! I knew of an in-house projector that Lintas had in their old office, so off we went to try our luck. Fortunately for us, we bumped into Mubi Ismail, the film executive at Lintas, and Gerson da Cunha, the big daddy of them all.

With great trepidation, I asked Mubi if we could screen an experimental film in the theatre. She perked up and looked at the three of us—two scruffy-looking fellows and Chirpy, who was looking as pretty as ever. Mubi turned to Gerson and, on his nod, we all toodled off to the theatre. I hadn't expected an audience for our first screening and had serious butterflies in my stomach—so much so that I felt weak with nervous anticipation.

We ran the film twice and I was so numb that other than some close-ups of Chirpy, I couldn't focus on anything else. Two and a half minutes seemed to fly by. Afterwards, Gerson cleared his throat and all of us looked at him as he smiled widely, but then he always smiles that way. He said, 'Very nice film; now tell us what it means?' That's how we figured out what the title of our film would be—*Very Nice! Now Tell Us What It Means?* Jokes apart, Mubi was so impressed by our effort that she gave us our first official film from Lintas for Britannia Marie when I started my own ad-film production house six years later.

Now came the big test: to screen the film for Shyam Benegal, who was such a reluctant mentor. Shyam babu had just arrived from out of town and was editing a movie in the Blaze Minuet in Colaba. I was in such a blue funk that poor Chirpy came along for moral support. Shyam looked at me quizzically and told the editor, Bhanu, to load the doubleheader on the Steinbeck editing machine, which had a pretty large screen. We held our collective breaths while he and Bhanu watched it a couple of times. He then looked at Chirpy and said, 'So that's you in the film, is it?' Chirpy blushed and nodded, while he turned to me and said, 'Not bad! Who did the animation?' I told him that Ram Mohan had helped. He nodded sagely and said, 'I will see you in the office tomorrow.'

I exhaled deeply—it felt like I'd been holding my breath forever. And that was how I managed to stay on in Bombay by the skin of my teeth. Shyam babu managed to ward off the Delhi office, despite their many protests. Usha Katrak, who was running the Bombay office and was a mother hen to all of us homeless waifs, settled me in nicely.

Meanwhile, back at the ranch, we were coming to terms with the vacuum that the finished film had left us in. Chirpy and I met every day after office because we desperately wanted to see each other. Both of us were tiptoeing around the elephant in the room, until one fine day we took a long walk down Marine Drive. It was a blustery December evening and unusually cold for Bombay, with the wind picking up as we strolled the promenade. It was my usual route back to Colaba from Kemp's Corner. Chirpy was amazed at the number of people I knew hanging around Marine Drive.

From the fishermen casting for singara—a kind of catfish—to the old gentlemen and their wives taking an after-dinner stroll, and the chowkidars huddling over small fires in dustbins warming their hands. Since Chirpy was feeling quite frozen in the biting wind, we shared one chowkidar's waste-bin fire, and swapped stories and experiences with him. He even offered us some rotis, which he had in a dabba.

Chirpy was charmed and snuggled up to me, either to ward off the cold or because she had felt an urge to do so. We walked back hand in hand to Olympia Restaurant on Colaba Causeway and ordered some cutting chai. Both of us were quiet and pensive, 'sipping' delicately around the issue on hand, until I finally reached across, held her hand

and asked, 'Now what?' That was the tipping point, and it all came out in a gush during the next week. We were inseparable.

I had managed to hang on in Bombay, make my first film and fall in love. I was in love with two women simultaneously. I felt a twinge of guilt, but had to live with it because I couldn't choose between Suniti and Chirpy. I loved them both totally and completely. Tough luck, I thought to myself. What was eating me up from the inside was the dilemma of coming clean with them and losing them both, when, as usual, fate took a hand.

Chirpy had a local guardian, a youngish and balding corporate type. I think he had a bit of a crush on her and was very concerned that she had disappeared from his life for a whole month. She usually spent her weekends with him, so he cornered her one fine day to quiz her about her whereabouts. He filled her head with all kinds of things about my *type*. God alone knows what that meant. He chided her about how her parents would be horrified at such irresponsible conduct.

The next day, Chirpy arrived—face loaded with gravitas—and told me that she couldn't, nay, wouldn't see me any more. It caught me off guard and I tried to reason with her, to no avail. The damage had been done. She stopped seeing me. It took me weeks of talking to myself on long and lonely walks along Marine Drive to finally accept the inevitable and move on. Thank god for Suniti, I told myself. Little did I know what the universe had planned for me!

12

The Tenets of the Slaves

I started working with Shyam Benegal in 1972 at ASP, Bombay. The ASP office was on Dinshaw Vacha Road, right next to the Oval Maidan in Bombay. We were on the fifth floor with Ogilvy & Mather (O&M) on the second floor. That's how I fleetingly met the fantastic Frank Simoes, the creator of the Liberty Shirts campaign, which almost cost me my first job in advertising. I met him in the lift when he was on his way to O&M. He was then the copy chief of that excellent agency. Meanwhile, ASP gave everybody a run for their money with superb campaigns for Amul Butter, Lakmé, Finley Fabrics, Anacin and Kolynos toothpaste for Geoffrey Manners.

ASP was a mid-sized agency and was forever a beehive of activity, albeit in a very systematic way. In Bombay, I could feel the urgency, but never heard a raised voice or any kind of bedlam like what I was used to in Delhi. Here, it was like a well-oiled machine—though it sometimes went off the rails in a spectacular display of pyrotechnics, which was then quietly underplayed even when we lost an account that made a significant dent in the agency's exchequer.

For the first few months, I was like a fly on the wall—observing everybody and everything, and happy being entirely invisible and ignored most of the time. The film department consisted of two people, an old veteran called Thimmaya and me. We sat in a little cubbyhole that had a table with an underlit milky glass panel to check film prints, over which spilled cans with loose reels rolled into circles. Although, in the beginning, I ended up spending very little time there, and instead wandered around the office chatting up people, getting the feel and lay of the land. It was a large-ish office with the senior executives in frosted glass cabins, the secretarial pool at one end, and the art department and creatives at the other end, with the pantry somewhere in the middle. The accounts department was across the road in another building.

The heads of ASP, Bombay, were Usha Katrak (she was the wife of the legendary Kersy Katrak of MCM), K. Kurien, Shyam Benegal and Eustace Fernandes. There was also Marie Pinto in the art department and Radha Khambadkone in copy. I loved Usha Katrak, whose management style was protective and motherly, but she could also be hard-boiled when she wanted to be. Mr Kurien was a serious advertising professional and had a great eye, which would immediately catch an excellent, creative ad. He would back it unconditionally, even if that sometimes meant going up against a client. He was formidable, and I was alert and cautious around him. Eustace Fernandes was the one who created the famous Amul girl and boy. He was an outstanding art director who churned out great ads and visuals with Radha at the copy department's helm. Marie Pinto was a full-blown Goan lady at fifty, tough and talented as hell, with a soft mushy heart. I had to find my way around and build equations with all of them to survive in Bombay.

The first thing that struck me was that the personal assistants at the office ensured the smoothness of day-to-day operations. Three ladies—Audrey, Mrs Katrak's assistant; Roshan, Mr Kurien's assistant; and Mohini, the receptionist and telephone operator—quietly and efficiently ran the office. The funny thing was that each of the secretaries and personal assistants took on their respective bosses' persona. I wonder why is it that in the olden days, the telephone operator was such a key person in an office's invisible working processes.

All these ladies decided to adopt me—the Orphan Annie from
Delhi—along with Shyam babu's excellent personal secretary, Silvia
D'sa, who was like a young mother hen and always covered for me.
Between Mohini and Silvia, I was saved many a time from disaster—
both personal and professional!

———

I began attending a couple of shoots with Shyam babu and felt rather
lost since I had no clue about what was happening and why. His
venerated cameraman and go-to person was Kamath mama, a strict,
no-nonsense, old-school spry gentleman of about seventy years of
age. He had this massive energy about him when he was on the set.
I found out that in his spare time, he loved to paint and was rather
talented at it.

Kamath mama was among the first camera professionals to use
colour film as the norm. In the early days, most of the classics, like
Satyajit Ray's films, were in black and white. Watching Kamath mama,
I realized that as a painter–cameraman, or DoP, as we call them now,
he was painting with light! He would stand in the middle of a set
(without a light meter, which is unheard of nowadays) and orchestrate
the lighting like a Michelangelo—feeling the light on the palm of his
hand. All the light boys on the tarapa, or lighting platforms, perched
high on the roof of the studio, and ran from light to light and adjusted
them to Kamath mama's orchestration. Everybody on the set respected
and feared him.

Kamath mama saw me—an awkward North Indian buffoon trying
desperately to stay invisible while also trying to belong—and decided,
for god alone knows what reason, to take me under his wing. He talked
to me as a thinking adult and not as a nincompoop slave who was only
getting in everyone's way and asking imbecile questions in the middle
of a shot. He was patient on most days and, when his patience ran out,
he would often give me a playful tappli, a light whack on my head. My
first shoot was for a Burnol film, a yellow burn relief cream in a tube,

and I got my first tappli from Kamath mama for looking vague and lost. I struggled, initially, to make myself useful around the set.

Kamath mama taught me about framing and lensing, and how a story can be told without a word spoken, provided the composition and frame are correct. Especially for master shots, which are usually ten–twenty seconds long, in commercials that are time-bound, and in which the talent were often models and not necessarily film stars. The actors, production crew, lighting crew and slaves had to know the sequence's continuity—the movements, screen direction (left or right of the camera from the point of view of the audience), looks and the lighting. When we broke up the sequence with master shots, close-ups and mid-shots for heightening the moment, the editor and director would then have multiple choices for speeding up the action or slowing it down, which reduces from real time to compressed time for the viewer.

Thus began my real training on shoots, as slave number five. I realized many years later that it's relatively easy for a director to cover up their shortcomings, but there's never any place for an assistant to hide on a set if they are clueless. Another great insight was that as a slave, if you sit during a shoot, it takes you just that much more time to react to a problem; so by the time you scramble to solve it like a headless chicken, the damage has already been done and you end up with egg on your face.

The name of the game is anticipation and not reaction. And if you haven't anticipated the problems, the least you can do is react with great alacrity and be there before anybody else so as to minimize the damage. At Genesis, Joel Fonseca, as a production hand, had this remarkable ability to be there first and contain the damage quickly, which is why he is today considered one of the most valuable production people in the business.

According to Shyam Benegal, the bible for all of us slaves was basic with simple lessons to be learnt and enshrined till death. First, there is only one god and he has only one commandment. His name is Murphy and his commandment is, 'If anything can go wrong, it

will go wrong!' That means don't hope for the best, but prepare for
the worst. Murphy always screws you differently every time and only
repeats himself if you haven't learnt your lesson or are stupid.

The first chapter of Shyam babu's bible lays out the terms of
engagement:

1. Slaves cannot run away (in fear of the pain of death).
2. Slaves cannot ask 'When can I go home?'
3. Slaves cannot ask for a raise.
4. Slaves do not ask 'Why?' Slaves only ask 'How high?'
5. Slaves do not sit on a shoot. It makes them lazy.
6. Slaves have their brains in their asses, and the only way to activate
   the brain is to get a swift kick up the ass, which galvanizes the brain
   into activity (this is probably where the term 'kick-started' comes
   from!).
7. Slaves cannot resign. They can only be sold!

The slog was on and, luckily, ASP's film department was hugely
busy as Shyam Benegal had created a unique system. Ad films were
directed in-house and only their production was farmed out to the
production houses—this meant massive responsibility and exposure
for us slaves. We had to be involved in everything from the creative
process of ideating with the copywriters to getting the concept approved
from the clients (according to the brand promise and positioning
values), getting a quotation from the production house and then
having it rubber-stamped. We had to get the job commissioned by
hustling and getting an advance, while ticking off and meeting all
the production requirements and getting the set design approved by
Shyam babu. Whew!

The entire load of the detailing and mounting of the films became
the responsibility of the slaves and god forbid if there was a major
fuck-up because of a lack of diligence, common sense or sheer sloth.
Shyam babu's diktat was unwavering. Everybody on the slave side had

to take complete responsibility for the entire job—regardless of who it had been delegated to. All the slaves had to know every minute detail of the job collectively or be sold to any of the syphilitic Arabs who frequented Colaba Causeway.

Today, when I look back at who shaped my cinematic future, the credit goes to Kamath mama for teaching me framing, lensing and lighting, to my many editors for making sense of the rubbish I shot, and Shyam Benegal for teaching me the art of storytelling and how to capture it on celluloid. And also to Shama Habibullah, who stood in for Shyam babu when he was out of town on projects. She taught me that the god is in the detail and film-making could be fun—not a chore of a job, but a way of life. And that's how I made a stuttering start in my long journey in advertising.

13

No Pain, No Gain!

At work, Murphy struck—again and again, and all plans and predictions turned to dust. I was somehow surviving by the seat of my pants, literally, and with some help from Lady Luck. I managed to escape from being sold not to a syphilitic Arab, but to a man of taste and talent with a proclivity for young boys. Once, I screwed up right royally (thanks to Murphy) and I was promptly told to report to the said gentleman. I was sent with a ribbon around my neck and a note that said, 'With the compliments of Shyam Benegal for the duration of the evening.'

I rang the doorbell of a tastefully done wooden door and it was opened by a fey, youthful servant, who told me to await His Lordship in the opulent drawing room. The room boasted of an upright piano, with an overweight tabby cat draped over its top, dutifully neutered. The gentleman, His Lordship, arrived, in a cloud of aftershave, gave me a once-over, wrinkled his nose in distaste and proceeded to dial my boss. When Shyam answered his call, he plaintively complained, 'Shyam, the young man in question is too hairy for me!' Whew! Saved by a hirsute genetic line of North Indians; read: Punjabis.

Life was an ever-changing kaleidoscope with never a dull moment or time to stop and stare—I careened between pre-production for shoots, coordinating with the production house, and shooting and editing. I was a busy lackey—observing, fetching and carrying. I kept my trap firmly shut, so that I didn't put my foot into it and land up at His Lordship's door again—this time, duly defoliated.

One evening, I was hanging around Raj Kamal Sound Studio, with cans of film and unmixed sound, waiting with half the industry for the real star to arrive. His name was Mangesh Desai, the sound engineer par excellence, who had an aura and a temper to match. Mangesh was legendary and his entourage consisted of the industry's who's who—directors, editors, ad filmmakers like Shyam Benegal, to art film types like Satyajit Ray. And, of course, yours truly, shitting in his pants as slave number five. I tried to merge with the landscape as much as possible and make myself invisible—the industry term for it was 'soomdi mai komdi' (ducking responsibility furtively).

My education in sound design as a fly on the wall in Raj Kamal Sound Studio with Mangesh Desai was, at the very least, life-changing. The interweaving of sounds, dialogue, sound effects, music and ambient sound, when done by a master like Mangesh Desai, was magical, and changed the destinies of films and their makers. No wonder he was considered a god and not meant for the faint-hearted or for those who did not appreciate detail. And Mangesh Desai could tear a second asshole into those who took his work for granted. Usually, the sound editor, the assistant director and, finally, the director himself would be lined up at the shooting range. Anybody who ever attended a sound mixing by Mangesh Desai was always treated to a masterclass in film sensibility and sound design. We were so privileged.

Sitting with Bhanu, the editor, was another kind of education in film language, storytelling (or the lack of it), pace and its importance, and timing to keep an audience on their toes. Many a night was spent abusing the ADs (assistant directors) for lack of continuity and jumps in the narrative. Sometimes, there was a complete lack of coherence in how the films were being shot. The editing team would be tearing their hair out because of the direction team's lapses. Then, they would try to retrofit the pieces of the story together by turning the film on its head to stay within the brief.

The best education anyone can ever get on all the facets of film-making is to sit in on the edit. That is where the cumulative shit hits the fan. Every possible mistake in the writing, screenplay, performances, camera angles, movement, dress and set continuity, irregular and lousy lighting, and camerawork shows up as glaring red flags during the edit. And, for a novice like me, it was a god-sent opportunity to attend the graveyard shift, when all the edits usually took place in the quiet.

This was a life lesson on how things can go terribly wrong in a film. Long live Murphy! The most intense learning happened during the countless hours we burnt the midnight oil on various edits, brainstorming solutions to save the narrative. The film-making process and a gradual understanding of its finer details were indelible learnings for me, stamped on my impressionable mind for the rest of my life.

As a child, I always saw stories in pictures—rather than as word descriptions—and comics of any kind had a profound impact on my storytelling. Since I was a voracious reader of pulp fiction and comics, even as a youngster I had a considerable repertoire of visuals, cartoons and photographs in my head. And later, thanks to *MAD* magazine, all kinds of advertising films and feature films were stored in my right brain. Though I was a reticent child, I had a vivid imagination. When necessary, I articulated my thoughts in a language of my own, interspersed with original sounds to share the visuals in sequence with the uninitiated.

Even today, when I read a script, I can close my eyes and translate it into moving visuals with sounds—and that's how the direction of the film becomes clear as day to me. I usually refuse a job if I read the written script and can't see the movie in my mind's eye. This is because I'd then have to eventually resort to copy–pasting the visual narrative from a reference resource, which immediately puts me on the back foot in terms of fluidity and tactility. Not only do I have to see and hear the scenes, but I also have to smell them. To me, that is the essence of a film.

———

Soon, I had entrenched myself relatively firmly into the film department and was given a lot of autonomy in its functioning, especially when Shyam babu was travelling all over the country for his documentaries. On one such occasion, he let me handle the Anacin films, which we did every year, as Geoffrey Manners was one of our major clients. The Anacin films were formula based—they followed a pattern, only the language and the cast would change and, therefore, the locations of every ad. We usually travelled to ten states and cities to find equivalent professions and actors who could become characters in our ads.

After about six months of being part of the film department, Shyam had to travel to shoot the Hindustan Steel films. His next in line, Shama Habibullah, was committed to shoot the Fanta Orange films at the same time. Thus, the onerous task of shooting the Anacin ad film fell on me. Shyam babu fixed me with a beady eye and asked whether I was up to it. I gulped and, with a tiny, high-pitched squeak, I whispered, 'Yes.' My heart was in my mouth.

'What?' asked Shyam babu with his voice rising in irritation. 'Why are you mumbling, you imbecile? Are you up to it?'

'Yes,' I said, after clearing my throat.

'Good!' he said and walked away; my bladder suddenly felt very full. My career as a director was off to a shaky start and the question that remained unanswered was—could I add value to a bunch of formulaic films, or was I going to copy–paste, or, worse still, fall flat on my face?

I spent many a night taming the butterflies in my stomach as I tried to figure out how to own the films I was about to shoot. Ownership of a job, I discovered, is the key to stamping your signature on it. Now, how on earth could I improve ad films that were moulded by the hands of the master himself and had proven themselves time and again? Being better is an illusion as it is always relative—the trick was to be different; change the casting and activity to push the envelope constantly. I knew I was taking a huge risk. It could all just as easily blow up in my face with tragic results, specifically for a slave who thought he could fly!

I watched the existing films hundreds of times to understand how to make them different without ending my fledgling career as a film-maker. There was no way I could risk my life for a paltry difference, which nobody might notice, and bounce the films and me along with them. I reluctantly took the bit in my quivering jaws and went for it. I recast the ads with unique characters and professions, from dance masters of Bharatanatyam to small-time printing press owners where headaches or 'thalaivalis' were not only from the noise around them, but also from stress and deadlines, with proof lines blurring and rhythms going awry.

We shot in the back alleys of small towns in the South to the dusty streets of the North, from rice mills to grain mandis. We travelled across the country by train and even shot a ticket collector with a headache. Finally, we canned, edited and sound-mixed twelve one-minute films, and waited with bated breath for the final reckoning. The client side consisted of a Mr Noorani and another Mr Benegal, with no relation to Shyam Benegal. They arrived and genially greeted everybody. K. Kurien, Usha Katrak and Shyam Benegal, who had flown in especially for the presentation, were also there that day. That was how important the whole deal was. Nobody was fooled by Mr Noorani's smile. He was known in the agency as 'Mack the Knife', a smiling executioner. The wider he smiled during a screening, the more vicious he was in its aftermath, lashing out on the hapless architects of the job in question.

The tune of the song 'Mack the Knife', sung in Ella Fitzgerald's silky voice, kept playing in my mind, as I watched Mr Noorani settling himself in to watch the films. The lyrics go something like this:

Oh, the shark, babe, has such teeth, dear
And it shows them pearly white ...
You know when that shark bites with his teeth, babe,
Scarlet billows start to spread.

Everybody was on tenterhooks, especially the fresh lamb for the slaughter: namely me. We settled down and held our collective breaths as the films were screened as doubleheaders (sound and picture are run in sync but separately). There was dead silence. I know I was holding my breath, but the others seemed relatively nonchalant. 'May we see them again?' asked Mack the Knife, with a flicker of a smile. We reran them. By this time, I could see Shyam babu visibly relaxing, which was a good sign. Soon, the second screening came to an end.

A long couple of heartbeats later, Mack the Knife breathed out with a whoosh, devoid of any trace of his shark-like smile. With a big, sloppy grin pasted on his face, he said, 'Not bad.' Following his lead, our tense body language transformed and the entire room relaxed. The rest was a blur of relief as I quickly exited the venue, did a speedy cartwheel and landed straight into the midst of the warm typing pool—Audrey, Silvia, Roshan, Mohini, and others, who were my buddies and support system at work.

The Anacin films were where I cut my teeth, and built my repertoire and reputation. I also realized that the saying 'No pain, no gain' resonates deeply with me. That's one of my biggest learnings as an entrepreneur, as well. It's all about the acumen and instinct to take calculated risks.

14

Madame G

By this time, projects were flying thick and fast to the film department in ASP. Shyam was caught between his mammoth documentaries for Hindustan Steel and a feature film he was trying to write. So, under Shama Habibullah's guidance, I supervised ad films for LIC and other clients. Shama was a British-educated chain-smoker of enormous talent and she was obsessive about production details. She was the daughter of Sonny Habibullah, who came from a royal lineage and was a thoroughbred horse breeder of repute, and the beautiful Attia Hosain, from old-school Lucknow known for its culture and tehzeeb. Attia was considered one of the twelve best-looking women in the world at her time in a list that included Maharani Gayatri Devi.

During an eventful trip to Indore to shoot the LIC documentary, Shama got chased by a large bull in one of the lanes and escaped by a whisker—or should I say, nostril? But what took the cake during that trip was an incident with Mr Patki, a gentleman from LIC, who represented the august institution and had supposedly come along for the ride. I could not see any purpose for him being with the crew. He was interested neither in the film nor in the proceedings. His only contribution was to choose where we should eat, preferably at a five-star hotel, and he refused to go slumming with us. Since there were no five-star hotels in Indore at that time, we ended up in a slightly tacky wannabe restaurant that boasted of air conditioning.

As we waited for the food to be served, the waiter arrived with a complimentary green salad of tomatoes, cucumbers, sliced onions and green chillies. In the centre of the dish, to embellish the ordinary starter, the chef had placed a pièce de résistance of brightly coloured plastic flowers. I saw a peckish Mr Patki eyeing the salad. Since nobody had touched it yet, he leaned across and plucked a plastic flower off the dish. Even before I could warn him of its synthetic nature, he had shoved in the whole thing into his mouth. Just like a spoilt birthday boy, who can't wait for everyone to start singing 'Happy birthday' and plucks the marzipan rose off his birthday cake, popping it smugly into his mouth, grubby fingers and all.

We watched—both horrified and fascinated—as Mr Patki chomped down the plastic decoration. For a flicker of a second, his expression changed when he realized the true antecedents of what was in his mouth. But he saw that the entire table was waiting for him to react to his faux pas and his expression hardened to resolve. He chewed on the plastic flower as if it were a praline, smiling and nodding to whoever caught his eye. After an alarming minute of chewing, he swallowed the offending object and drank a glass of water to wash it down as if it was the most natural thing to do.

We were aghast. Mr Patki was so full of himself that he didn't want to admit his mistake and just carried on simply to keep up appearances. Suddenly, his aura of superiority dimmed and he became an object of great amusement. We immediately nicknamed him Col Dundee. Though I must admit, on that particular occasion, he lost his large and voracious appetite, which had always prompted him to grab his favourite dishes first and polish them off while we looked on in mild resentment. The plastic flower did him in.

My days spent with Shama Habibullah were full of little nuggets of learning and though she built a formidable reputation for herself as a director, I felt she also excelled in film production. No amount of production detail was ever good enough for her. She was the most anal production person I have ever met! Shama was working on Sir Richard Attenborough's *Gandhi* as a second unit-in-charge. They were supposed to shoot landscape shots of the Mahatma's tour of rural India across UP upon returning to India from South Africa. Shama started her prep with great gusto and did a thorough recce of the location with photographers, taking shots of sunrises, sunsets, etc.

In one set of research material, I came across a whole report on how many Western toilets existed en route to the locations in people's homes. It contained their names and exact addresses, and written permission from the owners for the use of their toilets! I was curious about this particular detail and asked her about it. She replied with great intensity, 'Though this is a second-unit shoot, there is always the possibility of Sir Richard turning up to see how things are shaping up. And so, supposing he does, and suppose, god forbid, he gets an attack of the loosies, then the production crew would have a detailed Plan B on where they could rush a cramping Sir Richard to a nearby Western toilet.'

Whew! The sheer level of anticipation blew me away. Those were the days when vanity vans had not yet come to India for shoots. Thank god, Sir Richard never did turn up and left the second-unit shoot in the capable hands of Shama Habibullah. That was when I realized the importance of Mr Murphy and the fact that the name of the game is anticipation. Always prepare for the worst instead of hoping for the best.

One day, I found Shyam babu in Bombay halfway through his Hindustan Steel schedule, looking hassled and irritable. I discovered that none other than Indira Gandhi, the prime minister of India, had summoned him. In her infinite wisdom, she had taken a narrow victory in elections, and rendered it null and void. She then plunged the country into a mid-term election in a bid to get an absolute majority in parliament and ram through the issues that were plaguing the nation. She gambled it all on a 'double or quits' move by going back to the people to decide.

To make this gamble a reality and to reach out to the sweaty millions to communicate the issues at hand, she had summoned Shyam Benegal, communicator extraordinaire. She wanted us to carry the message home, in a series of films, underlying the promises she had made, and how vested interests and politicians were opposing her from delivering those, as she did not have an absolute majority to be able to do so.

Yours truly was coopted into this amazing exercise, purely because there was no one else available. I had to go to Delhi for the shoot and carry the rushes back to Bombay, then edit the material and take it back to Delhi for approval; all this while keeping Shyam babu, who was somewhere in Bhilai, in the loop. We were already running on an impossible deadline. A lowly slave like me usually would have to slog it by train or bus or a donkey caravan to reach the location, but because of the crazy schedule, I had the privilege of travelling by air with the big boys for the first time in my life.

We landed up for the shoot at 7, Race Course Road, at Mrs G's official residence on a wing and a prayer, as there was no actual script. We met on the lawn of the imposing building, with the usual suspects in tow accompanied by Mrs G's meagre security detail, which was nothing like what it is nowadays, bustling with Black Cats, safari suits and officious busybodies. There sat an imperious Mrs G, and Ike, i.e., Inder Gujral, then the minister of information and broadcasting. Her secretary, Mr Dhawan, was also present, along with a few other motleys. She looked at Shyam babu and smiled, saying, 'So, Shyam, what do you think?'

Shyam babu, who had been furiously trying to wrangle some sense out of the brief on the flight, decided that being subtle was not going to work. He immediately grabbed the bull by its horns and settled on the best strategy—brutal honesty. Shyam babu felt it was a gamble to call for a re-election and, therefore, it deserved a straight-from-the-heart appeal by the lady, with no holds barred. There was stunned silence from the cohorts as the last thing a seasoned politician does with their vote bank is to lay their cards on the table.

Mrs Gandhi heard Shyam babu out without a flicker of expression and turned to poor Ike, who was visibly squirming. He wanted to hedge his bets; it was clear he was extremely uncomfortable allowing Madame G to take the bit in her mouth and go hell for leather after the opposition and the so-called vested interests. Ike knew if the shit hit the fan, he would be in the dead centre of damage control and would probably be the fall guy. He shifted his weight uncomfortably and muttered something inaudibly, trying to buy time and come up with a less do-or-die plan.

She fixed him with a baleful glare and said, 'C'mon, Ike, by the time you make up your mind, the elections will be over. Should we or shouldn't we?' Poor Ike still didn't want to commit himself to a path of no return. So Madame G impatiently and imperiously took the call, and said with a smile at Shyam babu, 'I like it! Let's put the lily-livered spineless opposition, including the fence-sitters in my party, to the sword. Let's do it. Shyam, tell me what you want.'

Thus unfolded one of the most powerful appeals by a sitting prime minister. She urged the nation to give her the mandate to push through for reforms or remove her from office. Now or never, all or nothing!

But, in execution, it wasn't as simple. Shyam babu wrote the appeal with Madame G and shot it from multiple angles with close-ups. It was all done on film, as there was no video in those days. I was packed off to Bombay to process, edit and sound slap the commercials, and fly back with the rough cut for approval nine times in one week. And so it went. I would fly to Delhi, show the rough cut, fly back to Bombay to make the tweaks and changes, edit all night and return the following day to Delhi. Finally, the film was ready, but I didn't know whether I was coming or going any more. I was jet-lagged travelling between Bombay and Delhi.

We made five thousand prints and released it in theatres all over the country, and the nation woke up to an unprecedented gamble by a politician and was fired up by it. Every citizen felt it was their duty to cast their ballot and make a difference. Indira Gandhi won a resounding victory, which put her firmly in the driver's seat. She was hugely charismatic and her timing was impeccable.

Shyam went off to complete *The Pulsating Giant*, a massive film on the steel-making capacity of India, and I retired, jet-lagged and exhausted, to the position of a favoured son. While Shyam babu was editing the movie, I was left to my own devices to stay busy with ad films. Soon, I got my break to see through a high-end textile film—from script to execution, all on my own. Shyam babu gave me his blessings and support, and everybody in-house toed the line.

It was a huge deal for me. The product was Finlay Fabrics and was, at that time, a top-end sari and fabric brand. The film was going to be a Durga Khote Productions. In those days, modelling wasn't such a bling thing. The only models were ramp and press ad models—such as the likes of Persis Khambatta, Naqi Jehan, Leela Chitnis, and so forth. Most of the casting for ad films had to be done by the production house or the director. There was no such animal as a casting director at the time.

As our office overlooked the Oval Maidan, I spent a lot of time checking out the girls who walked or jogged on the ground, especially one lovely young lady with long legs and an upturned nose. I made it a point to be there when she started her jog at 5.30 p.m. sharp. It took a lot of gumption to go up to her and ask her if she would feature in my ad film. She examined me quizzically and said she would have to ask her parents. So off we toodled to a building called Oval View and I formally asked her parents for their go-ahead—it almost felt like a marriage proposal. I sat nervously at the edge of a sofa, batting the questions thrown at me. Why, when, for what, for how long, etc. Finally, they reluctantly agreed.

Her name was Neela and, on closer examination, she had a minute scar on her upper lip. Very sexy, but still a bit worrying as far as the agency and the client went. Advertising has its stupid standards of perfection. I have always found perfection and beauty in imperfection, for the ideal is always relative. Only against flaws does beauty reflect itself. Perfect physicality always leaves one feeling cold and distant. So I dug my heels in and fought for Neela. Luckily, Shyam babu supported me. Off we went to Alibaug to shoot in the mustard fields with Neela in different saris, looking stunning, scar et al.

We became terrific friends and the film turned out to be quite dreamy in a romantic kind of way. Neela was engaged to a young doctor, so that was that. But I have always felt that if a film director can find a muse in the leading lady, it adds an exciting patina to the whole process of creation. Vanraj Bhatia composed the music and he found a new, husky-voiced singer for the ad film. She turned out to be Usha Uthup's sister, Maya Sami. We alaaped our way through the jingle, and it was a wee bit off-key but quite lovely altogether. Shyam liked it. I was off to a flying start.

The whole business of ad films is quite tricky. The main thing is to get noticed. The best way to gain recognition is to have a film that has unusual, funny or spectacular elements. The worst way is if the film, even by advertising standards, is atrocious, poorly cast, badly shot and put together. Then the maker is immediately booted on to the train of no return. Luckily for me, Finlay Fabrics passed the acid test, and people started talking to me and not over me.

~

Shyam babu finished the 'Pulsating Giant' films and immediately started prepping for his first feature film, *Ankur* (1974), a story he had nursed since his college days. Most of it was true and involved a college friend of his, who came from a wealthy landed family.

Shyam babu and his college film club members in Hyderabad had a common wet dream while growing up, and her name was Waheeda Rehman. The entire story of *Ankur* was based on an attractive farmworker who gets involved with a young Lothario zamindar. He is banished to the farm after plugging in his exams and spends his time loafing around, drinking and creating mayhem. Now, finally for Shyam babu, after many years of fantasizing, the moment was nigh and the Blaze advertising people, who had a monopoly on the distribution and screening of ad films in theatres, were going to fund the feature.

When Shyam babu finally met Waheeda Rehman and offered her the role, she was a bit diffident as she was now a big star in Bollywood. She also wasn't ready to go back to regionalized art films with a director, who, as far as the industry was concerned, was a newbie with unproven credentials. She refused, albeit gracefully, to do the part; so it was back to the drawing board for us.

One day, a young lady arrived in the office and asked to meet Shyam babu. Her name was Shabana Azmi and she had just graduated from FTII's actors' batch. There was something mesmerizing about her. Her features might have been plain—a noble nose like her mother's, a set of coconut scrapers for incisors and long, shapely feet—but she was gorgeous. All the slaves were agog at her arrival and dying to eavesdrop on Shyam babu's conversation with Shabana, but had no such luck. After she left, smiling to herself, we hung around waiting to see if he was as smitten as all of us. Two hours later, he summoned some of us into his room and kept us fidgeting while he signed endless stacks of papers.

I couldn't contain myself and blurted out, 'She is perfect, sir. Don't you think so?' He looked up, inscrutable as ever, and said, 'It's my job to think, not yours. Your job is to follow instructions; so kindly shut up while I finish my work!' Those ten minutes of waiting without knowing were frustrating. Finally, Shyam babu looked up, made a call and then eventually turned to us. 'So,' he said, 'liked her, did you?' We all nodded frantically. 'Bit young for the part, don't you think?' he asked blandly. We collectively swallowed and were about to reiterate how perfect she was for the role, when he put his palm forward and said, 'We will see.' Shyam babu finally made the necessary changes in the script, and nineteen-year-old Shabana Azmi was signed on.

While Shyam babu was knee-deep in casting and prepping for *Ankur*, I was left to handle the new Gold Spot films. Gold Spot and I had an interesting history. When I first started working with Shyam babu, the campaign featuring a young Rekha was among the most crucial film shoots that I attended as slave number five. She was fresh off the boat from Chennai and, though a relatively successful star in the South, was starting her career in Bollywood. She had agreed to do the Gold Spot campaign, thinking that it would give her a great platform, and it did. Rekha had a face, and a mouth, to launch a million crates of Gold Spot.

We shot the film in Juhu beach and it's a series of close-ups of Rekha going down on the bottle, with a sublime expression, intercut with fresh oranges. The mole on her lip was the sexiest thing I have seen. It inspired me for future references of the perfect mouth. When the legendary Kersy Katrak of MCM fame happened to see the rushes, he immediately coined the catchphrase, 'Live a little hot! Sip a Gold Spot!' Purrrfect!

So it was only natural that when I was asked to do the Gold Spot films I went into a Rekha fantasy mode. To my dismay, the exercise we had to communicate was the fresh taste of the 'New Gold Spot'. The FDA, the perpetual spoilsport, claimed that allegedly the synthetic orange tastemaker used in the product was vaguely carcinogenic and banned it with immediate effect. Parle, the company that owned the brand, went into a huddle to find an alternative.

The only acceptable option had affected a subtle change in the taste of the drink. They could either let it be or make it a product plus point. Mr Kurien of ASP suggested going all out for it, like a product relaunch. The creative department came up with the line 'Have you tasted the New Gold Spot?' The film department came up with the idea of popping the question at a critical moment to dramatize it.

Suhaag raat: 'Ghunghat uthane ke pehle, yeh bataiye, kya aapne naya Gold Spot taste kiya hai?'

College graduation: 'Before I give you the certificate, tell me, have you tasted the new Gold Spot?'

And so forth.

This project landed squarely in my lap and I had the heebie-jeebies. This, I have realized, makes you shoot-ready and ensures you take nothing for granted because the more deceptively simple the script looks, the more nightmarish the production. We had to shoot five separate commercials with five situations and they were supposed to be funny. But, in my gut, I felt they were just predictable—especially after watching them once or twice. I realized, with a lurch, that it doesn't matter what you have done in this profession or how much potential you have. You're only as good as your last film.

I fretted right through the shoot, even though it went off smoothly. That was another red flag. If there is no sign of Murphy on a shoot, then beware. He is not on a holiday, but just waiting to screw you during client presentations. I agonized my way through the shoot knowing that the films were not funny—just predictable and forgettable. We were shooting the final film in a college canteen, where a guy is asking a girl on a date and, of course, she asks the formulaic question. I couldn't take it any more, so I called for a break and paced up and down, trying to crack it.

Suddenly the idea came to me and it needed a nerdy-looking character. So I sent for one of our account executives from the office, a Parsi fellow named Dara Acidwalla. Beetling eyebrows, thick soda bottle–like glasses and the innocent, dreamy expression of a happy pot smoker. Dara arrived looking nonplussed, while I briefed a bright young lady. It was time to film the take. The party was on and Dara emerged from under a table, looked around slightly dazed, and said with a zonked expression, 'May I have a Limca?'

The film screeched to a halt as everybody stared at him in pregnant silence. This cute, perky girl then pipes up, 'Shut up, stupid! This is a Gold Spot film!' The reaction of the cast and crew was fabulous, and we knew it worked. Humour is something that catches you by surprise. You should not be able to anticipate the punchline. In the Gold Spot film, no one could have imagined that he would ask for a bottle of Limca and be told this is an ad for Gold Spot.

Now came the final hurdle—the client presentation. Off we went with the rough cuts of all the films to a preview theatre in Andheri with the entire brass of ASP in attendance. Parle's owners, Ramesh and Prakash Chauhan, their brand managers and their marketing head, a Mr Menon, were on the client side. Mr Menon had a very smug expression on his face and was carrying a hand-drawn storyboard with him to ensure we had stuck to the brief.

The screening kicked off and we laboriously went through each film. They were approved with a few tweaks here and there. Our turn to screen the final canteen film had come, and we held our collective breaths. Mr Kurien had already seen and vetted the film. In his gruff, disapproving way, he had loved the ad film. The doubleheader rolled out and the line was delivered.

Mr Menon gravely cleared his throat and said, 'Nice job. Now show us the real film!' We shuffled around, not making eye contact. Mr Kurien stepped into the breach and loudly proclaimed, 'I love it!' as if he was seeing it for the first time. Everybody visibly relaxed, except Mr Menon. 'But it's selling Limca,' he complained. Mr Kurien looked at him and said, 'So what? That's also your product! And it's very clearly a Gold Spot film with a twist.' Mr Menon, not ready to give up easily, made his final argument: 'But nobody has done this before!'

Mr Kurien, bless his soul, just fixed him with a steely look and we left for the office. The campaign ran and was a great hit. The canteen film changed how humour worked in advertising. I had found my groove. It reinforced my irreverent sense of humour and my capacity to laugh at myself, which helped me never take myself too seriously— an infectious disease very common in advertising.

Dara Acidwalla became an overnight star and his ten seconds of fame made people stop him on the road, in trains, in meetings and parties, where they all looked at him and asked, 'Aren't you the idiot who asked for a Limca in a Gold Spot film?'

⌒

Meanwhile, my train-latkoing weekend trips to Pune came to an abrupt halt. Every weekend, I'd head to Pune to spend quality time with Suniti after going through the entire working week thinking about her. I'd land up in the city as a highly demanding paramour, not realizing that however much she cared for me, she had lots of commitments of her own, from her MA course in English to her tight-knit family living on the NDA campus. She spent most of Saturday with me and, sometimes, on Sunday mornings, I'd trudge to the NDA campus. There were times when she was committed to family functions on Sundays which left me fretting and fuming that I wasn't the centre of her universe like she was for me. These dark moods carried over to the next week and ruined the Saturdays we spent together as well.

After a few disastrous weekends, she sat me down on the grassy knoll where she had taught me how to kiss for the first time. She looked me straight in the eye. 'You are just too intense and hyper, and it is affecting my studies and my relationship with my family. Your behaviour makes me very tense,' she told me.

I was baffled and said, 'I thought being intense was a good thing.'

'Yes, it is, but not 24/7! You have to learn to allow the relationship to breathe. So we should give it a break; a cooling-off period.'

I was shattered and numb, and nothing that I said to make it better seemed to change her mind. She had clearly given it a lot of thought.

I had left for Pune on a high with a Gold Spot film under my belt only to return with my tail between my legs, chastened and upset. It took me a long time of brooding and many lingering walks along the sea face on Marine Drive to come to terms with it. Suddenly, I had lots of weekends ahead of me with not much to do. But before I could drown in self-pity, I was rescued by being included in the spanking new unit of *Ankur* as slave number four; promoted by a count!

15

PPPK

Shyam babu was neck-deep in pre-production and the film department at ASP was now the epicentre of all the activity. Even those who had very little to do with the writing and mounting of a full-length feature film were all agog, and kept stopping by for updates. I was wondering if I was going to be left out of the film to handle the department, as usual, in Shyam babu's absence. Halfway through the prep, he summoned me to his chambers and nonchalantly asked, 'Do you want to come to Hyderabad for the shooting of the film?'

I almost leapt on him in excitement and gratitude. He fixed me with a beady eye and warned, 'It's going to be relentless hard work with no breaks. The film has to be completed on location, on a forty-five-day schedule; so there will be a lot of attrition. Especially at the fag end of the shoot, people will be dropping like flies because of exhaustion. So don't cave in on me!' I, of course, was too excited to pay attention and could not wait to be on location.

We finally embarked on our long-awaited trip to Hyderabad. As slaves, we had to travel by train. The sheer excitement was too much for us to even sleep that night. We arrived at Nampally station, bleary-eyed and bedraggled, only to be carted off to our pure-vegetarian hotel, where most of the unit was put up, except the lighting and camera crew. Since I had already travelled to the South for the Anacin films, I had a rough idea about the region's cuisine. However, I hadn't had the good fortune to taste the famed Hyderabadi non-vegetarian fare. And here we were—stuck in a pure-vegetarian two-star hotel, with no time to partake in traditional Hyderabadi delights. What a bummer!

We spent the first couple of days whizzing around and prepping the location, an hour away from the hotel, in a village called Yellareddyguda. That's where Suryam's farm still stood, pretty much in the same condition since Shyam's college days. We had to organize a local caterer to feed the crew during the shoot and select a cast from local theatre groups, friends, family and other animals. That done, we went into the shoot with all the gusto of the ill-informed.

Ankur was a huge learning experience for us all, as most of us slaves had no idea about what it takes to shoot an entire two-hour film in one stretch and that too in a remote village. The only exception was the amazing Kamath mama, who had shot many features in his time. He was a godsend, and the go-to person for anything to do with cinematography and lighting. There was, of course, Govind Nihalani, the main DOP (director of photography), who is now well reputed, but it was his first feature film too.

Meanwhile, us slaves were responsible for keeping the shoot humming along smoothly. It started with the art of giving the sound clap at the beginning of every shot so that, later, the film editor could make some sense of the material we had shot and its sequencing. We had to be 100 per cent alert to anything that could derail the shooting. We organized everything from transport to food to the makeovers of sets and locations to cyclostyling call sheets. We looked into the nitty-gritty of everything. Every day, we gave the entire unit details of the shoot, location, scene, costume continuity and what time everybody needed to be there.

Shyam, Govind and Kamath mama had decided to shoot most of the scenes with a humongous studio camera called a Mitchell, which weighed at around 25 kilos or more, and was highly unwieldy compared to the Arriflex II C. But we chose the Mitchell because of the superiority of its picture quality due to the fantastic film gate design with its double pin registration, which made the shots filmed rock steady compared to the Arriflex-single pin/claw function.

The main problem was that the Mitchell used an ancient parallax viewfinder placed parallel to the camera body. In comparison, we could view the Arriflex II C frame while we shot it through the lens. In layman's terms, this meant that if the Mitchell was moving on a trolley or a crane, we could never be sure that the characters in the frame were composed correctly. We had to wait till we got the rushes three days later to verify the composition as the parallax viewfinder was never 100 per cent accurate. After that, the lab in Bombay would process the film and send the rushes back by train, for us to review.

One night, we were watching the rushes and, to our horror, we came across an outdoor sequence where the sky was overcast. We had lit the scene with reflectors to get detail on the faces, as the ambient light was dull because of the overcast sky. While watching the rushes, we were shocked to see that the paddy fields were bright green, the sky grey and the faces pitch black. There was a stunned silence until the assistant cameraman piped up and said that his readings were accurate and didn't know why the faces were underexposed.

After watching the drama ensue for a few minutes, Kamath mama gently reminded us that even though the sky was overcast, it was at least four stops over the ambient light. This interfered with the reading on the faces unless we blocked the sky, and only exposed for the faces and let the sky get overexposed. And so it was. We had to reshoot the scene. Since all of us were relative newbies, it took the experience and sagacity of Kamath mama to be the problem solver.

As Shyam babu had warned, the pace of the shoot was killing. Our wake-up call was at six in the morning, with barely enough time to grab a quick breakfast before heading off to the location, just so we could reach by 8 a.m. During this shoot, we learnt how to save five minutes for some more sleep in the morning. To snatch some much-needed shut-eye, the crew simply began growing beards over the forty-five days and night schedule. It didn't happen overnight, mind you. But as the days grew longer, we started skipping shaving and endured the furious itching for five more minutes of sleep. Newly developed stubble can be damn itchy. So, except for Kamath mama, who was old school and clean-shaven every morning, everybody else started looking like the bad guys in the *Magnificent Seven*!

I had been given the task of waking up the cast at 6 a.m. I especially took great pleasure in waking up Shabana. By then, all of us had a massive crush on her! So I would call her at 6 a.m. sharp, and she would answer after a few rings, sounding groggy, sexy and husky. She would plead for five more minutes of sleep and I would magnanimously give her ten minutes, and then call her again with my signature, 'G'morning, sleepyhead! Time to rise and shine!' It was the highlight of my day. Since she was the one young and attractive woman in the forty-man unit, everybody—yes, every single male—was competing for her attention. Naturally, Shyam babu won hands down. So, of course, flunky number four had as much of a chance as a snowball in hell! But he who bides his time and waits patiently gets another throw of the dice.

During a shot, one day, Shabana stubbed her second toe badly and I leapt at the chance to rush to her aid. I stopped the bleeding with a first-aid kit and some TLC (tender loving care) and dressed the wound. Then on, every morning, after I reached the location, I would diligently change the dressing very possessively and hover around like a mother hen, much to the amusement of Shyam babu and the rest of the crew. That's how Shabana's dominating second toe on her right foot came to be known as PPPK (the Private Property of Prahlad Kakar) as I was its caretaker while it healed. And for long after, Shabana's second toe was known as PPPK.

Shyam babu has always maintained a particular tradition in his shoots. The entire cast had to report to the location at call time in full costume, as the clothes needed to be worn in and aged. They had to come even if they were not required for the day and had to make themselves busy by helping in whatever way they could. This was a very unusual practice as, typically, the cast not needed for the shoot that day would goof-off and pretend to study the script, while they slept late or went shopping or whatever suited their fancy. But not on Shyam babu's film schedule. No, sir! They would arrive, bright-eyed and bushy-tailed, and loiter about looking busy. It was a cherished tradition and the uniqueness of a Shyam Benegal shoot.

Halfway through, I understood the method in the madness. When the film's main cast reported on set, along with everybody else, it helped in the performances since everyone was in character all the time. It facilitated a deeper understanding of the dynamics between the rest of the cast and a rough idea of the narrative's momentum. It also helped bond the unit into a streamlined entity as we worked, ate and toiled together as one large, unhappy family! This was not too difficult to accomplish during *Ankur*, because, luckily, the actors had not yet morphed into the so-called 'stars' species with their trailing entourage of chamchas.

The other fabulous tradition in a Shyam Benegal unit was that the heads of departments and the cast ate dinner together after pack-up. We would do a postmortem of the day gone by, and plan to thwart Murphy with anticipation and foresight for the days to follow. This was finally how I finally tasted the much-vaunted Hyderabadi cuisine. The driver, who had the task of driving Shyam babu to the location every day, was a dyed-in-the-wool Hyderabadi from the old city. When he discovered that Shyam babu was also a mulki from his beloved city, he immediately coopted his wife, an excellent cook, to prepare a dabba of the finest home-cooked delectables. Not for us, the standard fare of Hyderabad biryani—which is meant for tourists.

At dinner time, the smells emanating from the tiffin left us weak with anticipation. Baig Sahib, the driver, became our bringer of delectable delights. The shoot transformed into a parade of home-cooked Hyderabadi food, never to be found in any restaurant. Every evening was a feast and during Ramadan, even more so. The niharis, haleems, kormas, shikampuri kebab, even the famous vegetarian baghare baingan, khatti dal and mirchi ka salan were to die for. The only other time that I had a similar quality of food was when Mohammed Khan, advertising doyen of Enterprise fame, sent across his favourite Hyderabadi caterers for my wedding to Mitali. Oh, what a feast! More about that later, though.

Before the shoot, Shyam babu was diagnosed with an aggravated peptic ulcer and he refused to be hospitalized or take bed rest or eat the diet advised. Instead, he carried his list of medicines and a strict timetable of food intake, which he had in a thick shake made with Complan to alkalize his system. One day, Nira Benegal, his wife, summoned us slaves before we departed for Hyderabad. She briefed us on his regimen, the timetable for his meds and the Complan shake, leaving the responsibility of her husband's well-being in our quivering hands.

So, other than the planning, fetching and carrying, we also had to take turns to prepare the shake and meds and follow Shyam babu around till we caught his attention, so that he could gulp it all down. The making of the shake was a fine art, as the bloody Complan had this tendency to become lumpy and Shyam babu hated lumpy. Finally, we figured out the proper water temperature to whisk the damn powder into a smoothie. It had to be thick enough to be tasty and thin enough to go down the hatch quickly. We kept at it till we got it down to a T and were able to keep the juggernaut of a shoot running smoothly. Notwithstanding a few hiccups, of course.

I remember we had scanned Hyderabad for a working antique Morris Minor and found one in a decrepit haveli, covered in a canvas sheet. The owner swore that it was in working condition. He even got out the old crank handle and started the car, which, after a bit of wheezing and backfiring, settled into a sporadic rhythm, coughing up large quantities of black smoke. The owner promised us that by the time we needed to shoot the scene, she would be 'tickety boo', à la Danny Kaye. I wasn't convinced, but had no choice as Shyam babu had mentioned he wanted this particular model and make, and there weren't too many around.

On the day of the shoot, Surya—the hero/villain of the film—was supposed to make a grand entry into the farm in his hand-me-down Morris Minor, with his luggage in tow, and move into the spartan living quarters of the farm. The problem was that the bloody car, which we had driven from Charminar, had decided that she had had enough of an outing and packed up on us. And despite our cajoling and cursing as we turned the car's starting handle furiously, she just sat there near the gate like a pile of junk (which she was).

After a reasonable pause, Shyam babu lined all of us slaves up and read us the riot act for not ensuring a working car for the shoot. If you ever get to see *Ankur* and come to the scene of Surya's grand entry, you will, if you look carefully, see the car trundling along cheerfully. But under the car on the far side, four pairs of dwarf feet are running alongside it! We puffed and panted as we dhugged the piece of junk with all our might, taking care to stay on the leeward side of the car to avoid getting caught on camera. Take after take, Shyam babu and the camera crew exhorted us slaves to run at greater speeds. 'Faster, faster!' they would cheer, while we were bent over double, so as not to be seen, running our lungs out to get a usable shot for the film. Murphy was alive and well, thank you!

———

Shyam babu has built a massive reputation as an actor's director, someone who can squeeze a scintillating performance out of a piece of wood. In my years of associating with him, I saw ample proof of precisely this ability. He has always been a great believer in method acting, and the first time I saw what he was capable of was when we were doing a critical scene between Sadhu Meher (playing Kishtayya) and Shabana Azmi (Lakshmi). We filmed the single-shot scene in a hovel. There was just about enough space for the actors and the camera on a trolley.

In the film, Lakshmi, a simple servant, has an affair with Surya, the young Lothario zamindar. Things come to a head when Surya's wife, Saru—wedded to him in the age-old tradition of child marriage— arrives at the farm to stay with him. Saru is aware of Surya's affair with Lakshmi and immediately lets Surya know that she is uncomfortable with Lakshmi living in the house with them. The next day, Saru finds out that Lakshmi is ill and informs Surya. He steals away to ask about Lakshmi's health and she reveals that she is pregnant with his child. Later, an unsuspecting Saru advises Lakshmi to work in the fields due to her ill health and live in the hut there. A few months later, we see a pregnant Lakshmi wake up in her hovel to discover Kishtayya, her husband, lying next to her. Kishtayya is a dumb and mute labourer. Accused of stealing from the big house, he was drummed out of the village, with his head shaved and riding backwards on a donkey.

She wakes up with a start to see him next to her, and her first instinct is to protect herself and her unborn child. So she crawls as far as she can go in the hovel, and looks at him in fear, guilt and apprehension. When he wakes up and finally notices that she is pregnant, he is overjoyed that god has blessed them with a child after many years of barrenness. He can't contain his happiness and blubbers away in his attempt to communicate his joy. Lakshmi realizes that he does not intend to harm her or the child, and all the shame, loneliness and social stigma come bubbling out in her relief at her husband's return and his total acceptance of her state. She breaks down completely, opening the floodgates of her trauma, and weeps copiously. It's the pivotal point of the film.

We rehearsed the scene a few times, but Shabana was nervous. She wasn't sure if she could pull off something so intense and visceral in one take, and so Shyam babu took her for a walk while we held our breaths. About fifteen minutes later, he returned with a very subdued Shabana, who refused to look at anybody, taking her position and just nodding to Shyam babu and Govind to film the shot. Then, in a hush, with no words spoken, the camera rolled and the scene unfolded. Thinking about Shabana's performance in that scene gives me goosebumps even today, just like it did when we shot it.

It took precisely four and a half minutes to shoot it and, by the end of the scene, Shabana had lost all semblance of self. She became one with the character. As Lakshmi, she wept her heart out, with no sense of decorum or control, long wires of saliva streaming from her distraught mouth, and she wept and wept till long after the camera stopped rolling. Finally, Shyam babu took her away, heaving and bawling uncontrollably. There was a sense of sombre triumph in the crew that day. The intensity of the performance had shaken us all.

We returned to Bombay and started assembling the film in post-production with Bhanu, our film editor, when Vanraj Bhatia was called in to begin discussing the structure of the film and the kind of music it required. He was Shyam babu's go-to person when it came to music and, as the movie started taking shape visually, we sat like church mice while Shyam babu briefed Vanraj and argued, fought over and discussed his ideas. Vanraj was a hugely knowledgeable music director who had insights on all genres of music—Western classical, Indian classical, pop, rock and even Bollywood-ishtyle music, which he hated as it had no pedigree. The only other music director as talented as him is Ilaiyaraaja from the South. During his time, no one else had a comparable background that could rival his deep understanding of the many forms of music.

Vanraj was stubborn as hell and fought for his space, unlike all the other commercial music directors who either copied or changed their tune to suit the whims and fancies of the filmmakers. This might explain why he wasn't too popular. He was far too intimidating to get the credit he deserved for the enormous knowledge he possessed. He always stood his ground and made his point. Though *Ankur* had no song sequences, it was the first feature film for which he would be composing background music. Despite Shyam babu's run-ins with Vanraj and their constant arguments, he produced a haunting background score for the film.

Much later, I asked Shyam babu what he had said to Shabana to elicit such an intense performance from her in that one scene. He looked into the distance to get the feel of the moment and said that he had asked her to think of the most important person in her life. When she nodded, he told her, 'Now imagine somebody has brought you the devastating news that this person has died.' She digested his brief, choked up, signalled that she was ready and the rest is history. Shabana got a standing ovation at the 24th Berlin International Film Festival and they couldn't get enough of her. A star was born!

16

The Chhattisgarhis

*A*nkur got rave reviews in the international film circuit, and it was one of the few arthouse films to recover its cost when released. For all of us slaves, it was a baptism by fire. Experiencing the making of a full feature-length film had rearranged our grandiose illusions of how we could shoot better films than the ones being churned out by mainstream Bollywood. A healthy, if grudging, respect had crept into us—not necessarily for the content of these movies, but as an acknowledgement of the sheer logistics, organization, planning and dogged hard work that film-making involves, day after day after day.

Ankur did its rounds of previews at the Blaze Minuet, the plush preview theatre owned by the producers Mohan Bijlani and Freni Variava. There was a feeling of disquiet manifested by them that the film was too arty-farty for a regular Hindi movie audience. Despite the crème de la crème going gaga over it, this feeling persisted as the preview audiences were predictably hypocritical, only criticizing the film behind your back and never to your face. However, most of them wouldn't be seen dead watching a mainstream Hindi movie with the hoi polloi. We decided to put the film to the acid test.

Blaze, at that time, was toying with the idea of running a car rental company, like Hertz, and had about forty drivers hanging about the premises. We rounded them up to watch the film. I don't think they had ever watched a movie in such plush luxury like the Blaze Minuet. They sat transfixed as the film played out to its hugely dramatic climax, and the lights came on to pin-drop silence. Nobody said anything derogatory about the film, so we pushed the audience to give us an honest opinion.

One of the more outspoken drivers finally blurted out, 'It's a terrific film, no doubt, and we loved it. But *Ankur* is meant to be watched by classy people like us and not meant for the masses. They might not understand it.' All of them nodded in unison. This had us in splits, because for all our efforts, they were the masses! We knew then that we had a winner on our hands.

After *Ankur*, Shyam babu pushed off to Chhattisgarh to shoot *Charandas Chor* (1975) on location with Habib Tanvir's troupe. They were a fantastic bunch of folk artistes who had started their careers by performing for village and small-town audiences, and later toured the world. Their audience would surround the stage from all sides, demanding an encore of their favourite songs and scenes. To their credit, the actors succeeded at reprising their roles to surprise the audience with something new every time to keep them on their toes. The performances would go on from anywhere between four hours to ten hours—it was non-stop rollicking entertainment, from burlesque to extempore to slapstick. There was no form in theatre that they couldn't perform and they knew how to improvise when in doubt. The sheer energy and euphoria of their non-stop performance were astounding.

Shyam babu and Habib Tanvir decided to film a folk movie based on a folk tale called *Charandas Chor*. It was one hell of a task, as the live performance would have to be reduced to ninety minutes and adapted for the screen. The leading characters' roles could not be cast from the troupe itself, since the main lead was a bit over the hill. The business of casting the queen and the main protagonist, Charandas, had to be done in Bombay. A young dusky newsreader in the Marathi bulletin from Pune had caught our attention.

She had developed a massive fan following because of her delivery style and attractiveness, which shone through even on a black-and-white television screen. When somebody suggested her name to Shyam babu, he said he was open to approaching her. She was none other than the young and charismatic Smita Patil. We were all charmed and lattoo over our Marathi mulgi. Smita was terrific in her screen test—the camera loved her. She was cast to play the queen, and Lalu Ram, from Habib Tanvir's troupe of artistes, played the main character of Charandas. His sidekick and the rest of the cast were also from the village troupe.

I could not be a part of *Charandas Chor* as I had to hold down the fort at ASP. So I missed all the fun and games, and had to hear about it from everyone else after the shoot. The one thing that came out of the exercise was that Shyam babu had found yet another talented film star, Smita Patil, who soon became a part of his extended family-cum-unit. The other major discovery the crew made was a leather sandal—after the fashion of the ancient Roman sandals—used in this rice-growing region of Chhattisgarh. The locals had adopted this thonged Roman sandal to use while planting paddy as during the planting season, the rice fields are flooded in knee-deep water and full of keechad. The villagers would sink into this wet, oozing mud and water, to plant rice. As they took their feet out, their footwear would be lost forever to the mud, whether it was their chappals or their prized plastic slip-ons. To remedy this, an old mochi had resurrected the ancient art of tying the thonged sandals, which had an ankle strap and a fastener on the top of the instep to prevent the sandal from coming off. Keechad or not!

The beauty of these sandals was twofold. Firstly, it did not have a single metal or cotton part in its construction, and the sole was very similar to that of the Kolhapuri chappal, stitched entirely out of leather. Secondly, the sandal was highly customized and the mochi would do the first fitting on the customer's foot. A single eight-foot-long leather thong was wound and woven around the foot through four connecting leather flaps with slits to accommodate the thong. This made it the most comfortable, durable piece of footwear that fit the foot like a glove while allowing it to breathe freely. It took the ninety-odd-year-old mochi twenty minutes to tie it on each foot, and the entire unit came back from the shoot sporting a pair of Chhattisgarhis. That's what we named them. The villagers dismissed them as paddy-planting footwear meant only for the fields and much preferred their brightly coloured plastic footwear for more regular use.

The city slickers, led by Shyam babu, leapt at the chance to collect the sandals and started living in them. I was green with envy as the crew sporting their Chhattisgarhis was the cynosure of all gatherings. Then came luck by chance and the tables were turned. After the assembly of the film's rushes, Shyam babu realized that some small links needed to be shot. The troupe members had to be brought to Bombay for the shooting, instead of taking a crew to the village. In hindsight, I'm sure this whole business of shooting patchwork was a cover to get the aged mochi to come to Bombay as the film crew was petrified of running out of their prized Chhattisgarhis.

The fundamental objective was to ensconce the aged mochi in a seedy hotel on Grant Road to get as many Chhattisgarhis out of him as possible. All of us realized that he was the last of his line and, if something happened to him, it would spell the end of the Chhattisgarhis. Only he knew how to tie the intricate knots that held the sandal together. The old mochi arrived by train with the rest of the troupe and was received by yours truly. I had volunteered to escort him to his digs since I was desperate to get a pair from him. They had become the signature style of Shyam babu's crew.

He was a fascinating old gentleman, a bit taciturn and highly industrious. He had carried the stitched soles and its earflaps from Chhattisgarh because he was not sure if we had the karigars to make them in Bombay. He had never heard of Kolhapuris or Kolhapur, where the technique of stitching chappals in leather was very similar. I spent one week with him because I wanted to be sure that I got my sandals. I hung around the whole day asking questions, to which he responded with inarticulate grunts while he worked. Eventually, I got him to teach me about the knots, their dynamics, and the finer points of the aesthetics and balance of the sandals. I was amazed by the concentration and effort it took to make each sandal. He was a true artist and, if marketed correctly, could have become an Indian Jimmy Choo.

Every evening, I took him to Chowpatty Beach for an outing and some fresh air. The ocean fascinated him and we spent some quality time together, counting waves as we sat on the shore. By the end of the week, he had warmed up to me enough to let me tie the sandals he was making. But, of course, he would unravel them immediately afterwards, maintaining that my sandals weren't quite good enough yet. So I hung in there, picking up something new every day, until the veteran mochi from Chhattisgarh said he was feeling homesick and wanted to go back to his village, regardless of the money he was making. Almost Rs 450 per day, with no expenses! He was pretty adamant and claimed that he had run out of soles as well.

There was a mad last-minute scramble among the crew for Chhattisgarhis and we bid the old maestro farewell, knowing that we would never see him again—the last of his dying breed. The Chhattisgarhi episode does not end here at all, but culminates many years later in London. Meanwhile, back at the ranch, we were all sporting our new Chhattisgarhis and wondering if we would ever get hold of a new pair. I reflected on meeting the elderly gentleman who would never give up on his craft and the detailing of his product. It was a humbling experience to be acquainted with this simple man from a far-off village who showed us the true meaning of the god is in the details because, for him, his work was worship.

Meanwhile, since I loved the sandals so much, I sourced soles from Kolhapur, sent cardboard cut-out dummies for local mochis to follow and finally managed to get a working model together, after many trials and errors. I soon became the go-to person for Bombay-made Chhattisgarhis for anyone who wanted to curry favour with me. Oh, the power of a skilled monopoly!

17

David vs Goliath

While *Charandas Chor* was in the post-production stage, Shyam babu's latest discovery, Smita Patil, was written into a supporting role in his next feature, *Nishant*. It is a powerful story of inequality—set in a village in Telangana, the zamindars exploit their landless labourers with impunity. Things come to a head when the zamindar's brother kidnaps and rapes the new schoolteacher's wife. In despair, the teacher, in cahoots with the local pujari, galvanizes the village to rise in revolt. It is a stark and brutal film that reflects the social issues of its times. The film stars Girish Karnad and Shabana Azmi. A towering Amrish Puri played the oldest brother and head of the zamindari family, with Mohan Agashe, Anant Nag and Naseeruddin Shah cast as his siblings. Smita Patil plays the young wife of Naseeruddin. What an ensemble cast that came together for this film!

Shyam babu, Govind and the crew went back to Andhra Pradesh to shoot *Nishant,* and left me holding down the fort again. However, I didn't mind it so much any more because I had grown into the role. I was able to handle the film department and its many aspects quite adeptly. I had settled into this major responsibility in two years. By then, the team had reconciled themselves to dealing with me in Shyam babu's absence. I made critical decisions, wrote treatment notes and directed films. It would have taken me four years of hard labour to achieve this. Even then, I might never have been allowed to work with the pick of the litter. I was fortunate.

And so I went at it like David taking on Goliath. In my principal, Col Simeon's words, 'There is no man in the world who is not afraid to die in battle. Courage and character is the ability to face and overcome that fear, despite wanting to run and hide to protect your ass at the cost of others. Courage is the capacity to do the right thing, especially when people depend on you.'

I was hugely influenced by *MAD* magazine, and its satirical takes on the institutions of academia and life in general. It poked fun at everything the Establishment chose to take very seriously—be it the movies, politics or the goings-on of high society at the time. That's how the seeds of my irreverent style of functioning were planted and irrigated while growing up. I looked at the world and its institutions from the outside in. Everybody told me that the empire would strike back and I would always be at the risk of being screwed over for my beliefs. School had taught me how to blend into the woodwork when necessary. But, later in life, I failed at it miserably. I was never happy being conventional, and always managed to act, look and behave differently. So it came as no surprise that when I started visualizing and writing scripts for ad films, they all turned out quirky and different. I had a tough time selling them to the powers that be!

Much later, I became infamous for stating an inconvenient truth that the to find the best ideas in an agency is in the dustbin. The dustbin is the graveyard where most great ideas go to die, because nobody dares to rock the boat of mediocrity, and stand up to take both brickbats and victory laps on the chin. During the early days of Genesis, I remember dealing with a client in Boots, a pharmaceutical company headed by Anil Kapoor, who was ex-MCM (Mass Communication and Marketing).

He was large, florid and aggressive, and enjoyed reducing his agency's creative team to tears. Trikaya, one of India's more creative and original agencies, was handling a small account of Boots for a product of theirs—a sugar substitute called Sweetex. In those days, people considered sugar substitutes an elitist product and they had not penetrated the Indian middle-class market to any success. Sweetex was a small account with not too much ad spend. Still, Trikaya had bagged the client based on its original work for Thums Up and a few other leading domestic brands.

Trikaya had an excellent team of creative people who had been brutalized by the client, affectionately known by a few as Billy the Kapoor. His basic philosophy was to put the agency's creative pitch to the sword. Then, if he found that they couldn't defend it to the hilt, he told them to go back to the drawing board. The creative team at Trikaya was shattered by his slash-and-burn approach. At this point, just when the team was about to throw in the towel and migrate to another country in despair, I was called in on the client's recommendation for he wanted a cheap and cheerful film.

I spent two days in the agency, rummaging through the rejected ideas to no avail until I looked into the dustbin and, lo and behold, found a gem lying there, all crumpled and forgotten. It was a line that said, 'No squeeze, no wheeze, no sugar in my coffee, please', authored by a newbie called Uttam Sirur. I found it hugely catchy and visual, and promptly went back to the client and re-presented it. He, of course, said, 'I have already rejected this. So?' So, we told him we would shoot it, regardless of what he thought and he could pay us after the event if he chose to. He was most disgruntled, and huffed and puffed, but we went ahead and made the ad anyway.

After a preview of the rough cut, Billy the Kapoor reluctantly admitted to loving it, but he had no money to back the campaign, so it fizzled out. But, in a stroke of luck, their London office chanced upon it, as Mr Kapoor had proudly lugged it all the way there to show them the India office's work. They liked it so much that they snapped it up, paid for the cost of production, which was minuscule, and ran it with great success in the UK!

Meanwhile, Shyam babu returned from a gruelling shoot for *Nishant* and decided to move full-time into feature-film-making, and I was left holding the baby. At that time, ASP was the only agency specializing in the whole business of making ad films—from visualizing, casting and directing to the editing in-house. Shyam babu, Shama Habibullah or yours truly directed all of the films. So, for once, I was at the right place at the right time! I spent six years at ASP—the first four as Shyam babu's slave in the film department. For the next two, I was independently in charge. However, I was still Shyam babu's slave when he needed me for any work he was involved in, independent of the agency. Remember, slaves cannot leave. They can only be sold!

Nishant turned out to be a spectacular film, much ahead of its time. It held up a mirror to the brutal truths of casteism, providing an insight into the uprising against the zamindari system in Andhra Pradesh, with some fantastic performances by a brilliant cast. But, unfortunately, the crew and cast collapsed into a heap because of the relentless, non-stop schedule of the film because, as you know, there is no rest for the wicked. We had been summoned to Anand, Gujarat, by Dr Verghese Kurien to be briefed on an ambitious film showcasing the just-completed first phase of Operation Flood.

Dr Kurien, the Amul team, and the National Dairy Development Board (NDDB) had miraculously linked the country's major metropolitan cities—Delhi, Bombay, Calcutta and Madras—with the Amul model of cooperative milk collection. It was a first-of-its-kind, end-to-end cold chain system that processed and marketed the milk, and its products were financed by the sale of skimmed milk powder and butter oil gifted by the European Economic Community (EEC) through the World Food Programme.

To successfully conclude the first phase of this wildly ambitious project and convert a massively milk-starved country to a milk-surplus country was indeed a White Revolution! Dr Kurien had announced a worldwide gathering of milk farmers in Delhi. In his words, we were going to have farmers from Montana checking out farmers from Ludhiana. So, Dr Kurien summoned Shyam babu and his slaves to Anand, where he himself briefed us. I was officially involved since ASP was handling a part of the Amul account. I was so excited to meet the legendary man who spawned the idea of Amul with Tribhuvandas Patel and then implemented it against all odds. They had engaged in a turf war with existing middlemen and a big company like Polson, famous for its tinned butter. No quarter was given or asked, especially when it turned violent and political, causing massive social churn (manthan).

Dr Kurien was a diminutive Malayali with a wicked sense of humour and a simple, unassuming manner. He had no airs or frills about him as he narrated a fantastic series of incidents building up to Operation Flood. It started with how Tribhuvandas Patel enticed a young graduate, about to join Unilever, to work with a few marginalized farmers in Gujarat, who were exploited mercilessly by middlemen and prominent companies to supply milk and milk products to starved cities in India.

The youngster chucked his offer with the multinational company to tramp around the Gujarat villages, convincing farmers to buck the status quo and start a milk cooperative of their own! Dr Kurien regaled us with stories about the kind of pitched battles they had to fight and guard against, enthralling us with anecdotes of sabotage and vicious physical attacks by paid goons. Finally, emerging victorious, they started the milk cooperative called Amul, which stands for Anand Milk Union Limited.

Taking things one step ahead, Tribhuvandas Patel had insisted that any office-bearer who wanted to hold political office should resign from the cooperative first. There would be no exceptions to this rule which they set in stone in the cooperative's constitution. They established this rule because of Maharashtra's sugar cooperative, which had served as a cautionary tale—taken over by politicians and run into the ground. The sugar cooperative had become sick and bankrupt because it involved so many farmer groups that politicians saw a huge opportunity to create vote banks. Therefore, they wanted to insulate the milk cooperative from any political involvement. Thanks to this bold step, the milk cooperatives flourished, unlike the sugar cooperatives.

Dr Kurien also laughingly narrated how he managed to hijack the Rs 100 crore tranche from falling into the hot, greedy hands of the agriculture ministry and disappearing forever into its maws. He had spoken directly to Indira Gandhi herself and pleaded his case to have the funds transferred directly to the NDDB instead of being routed through the agriculture ministry. Mrs Gandhi had hemmed and hawed as this would be a step against accepted protocol.

What saved the day was a gentle reminder that the agriculture minister had conveniently not paid his income tax for ten years, and when asked about it, he had replied, 'I forgot.' And so, she had agreed to divert the funds directly to the NDDB. Sure enough, with the resounding success of Operation Flood, India became a milk-surplus country!

We went back to Bombay to set forth on our Bharat Darshan, courtesy of the NDDB, to deliver the film in time for the International Milk Producers Congress in Delhi. We travelled the country's length and breadth, wherever Dr Kurien's teams were busy organizing milk cooperative societies on the Amul model, which was unique in itself. They had managed to discourage the universal malpractice of adding water or other substances to increase the volume of milk artificially.

The Amul model tested every litre of milk given by a farmer for its fat content, and then the payment was calculated on that and that alone. Buffalo milk usually has a fat content of 8 per cent upwards and cow milk has about 4 per cent fat content. For this reason, buffalo milk in the subcontinent is more costly than cow milk, even though the latter is considered healthier. Moreover, today, people have figured out that the indigenous breed of Indian cows has A2 protein in its milk, which has become premium.

We filmed first-hand the kind of problems the team leaders had with the villagers in implementing the scheme. Everybody thought Operation Flood sounded great on paper, but they hugely sceptical of its implementation by any quasi-government body because of their past experiences. Dr Kurien had anticipated this very issue and had given carte blanche powers to the team leaders to invite the village sarpanches to come to Anand and see the scheme's working without window dressing. The NDDB even went to the extent of covering their expenses and transport. They were given a car to go anywhere in

Anand. They could ask any questions to the locals about the working of the milk cooperative without supervision. Such was the confidence and pride of the entire Amul team.

And so it came to pass—while it took a few years to crack it, crack it they did! The biggest hurdle was bringing the state of Haryana onboard, which, along with Punjab, contributed and supplied 90 per cent of the milk sold in Delhi. The Jats of Haryana are a breed apart and their thinking is not just out of the box, it's off the wall! I should know because I spent so much time in school with them. I had tried to anticipate how they would think and react at school, and failed countless times.

I remember a telling incident at the interstate bus terminus in Delhi. Buses from all over the country arrived and departed through the day, carrying passengers to Delhi on an hourly schedule. Unfortunately, a couple of us schoolkids had missed the school transport after the holidays and we had to make our way back by the state roadways. Upon arrival at the enormous bus terminus, we found the Haryana Roadways adda. To our amusement, we realized that while all the other state buses departed on a strict timetable, it was not so with Haryana Roadways.

I found out later that this was because the Haryana government had conveniently handed over the entire operations to some relative of the then chief minister, running the departure schedule based on how many passengers had boarded the bus. If the bus was three-quarters full, then and only then, would the conductor allow the bus to depart—damn the schedule! I am sure that the conductor also got a commission based on the passenger load.

We started looking for a bus to Karnal, and there was one displaying the sign 'Panipat', which was being readied for departure. Since Panipat was en route to Karnal, we decided to board the bus. However, the conductor was on the footboard shouting, 'Rohtak! Rohtak! Rohtak!' We were all foxed as the board on the bus clearly stated Panipat. A very spry, oldish ex-army gent, with a tin trunk, went round to the front to countercheck and, sure enough, the board said Panipat. He came back and tried to ask where the bus was going.

The conductor ignored the old gent and carried on shouting, 'Rohtak! Rohtak! Rohtak!' Back went the old boy, checked the board and returned to pluck at the conductor's pyjama leg as he stood on the footboard. The conductor stopped mid-announcement and cast a withering look at the old gent, who politely told him, 'Board par toh Panipat likha hai!' The conductor casually replied, 'Toh board par chadh ja!' and went back to announcing, 'Rohtak! Rohtak! Rohtak!' That's a Jat for you.

So, when the Amul team made a presentation to a group of Jat sarpanches on the benefits of starting a milk cooperative in their district, they went into a huddle, and then a sarpanch came back with just one question: 'What are you getting out of this?' The South Indian team leader replied, 'Nothing, I am doing my job.' They refused to relent until the poor TamBrahm was flummoxed and had to call the headquarters. They told him to bundle up the Jats into a bus and bring them to Anand, so they could see everything for themselves, all on the house. And only then did Haryana agree to be a part of the milk cooperative movement. Whew!

Operation Flood—the White Revolution—opened in Vigyan Bhavan to thunderous applause, from 1,500 milk farmers from all over the world, who got together, language no barrier, for three days to exchange technology, folklore and cattle feed. The American and European milk farmers, who produced a minimum of thousand litres a day each, had to wrap their heads around the logistics of collecting an average of just five litres of milk twice a day from six lakh farmers, who were paid every day. And this was just in Anand alone, to make the whole Amul model viable. It just boggled their minds!

While making the film, I managed to see the country from north to south and east to west. We got to experience things unique to each part—saffron in Kashmir, spices to a four-foot-long paper dosa in Erode, Tamil Nadu, where the chef was called a dosa master! We discovered the difference between an ilish maach and a pomfret.

However, my real education was yet to come, after the dust had settled and all the doodhwalas from Montana and Ludhiana had gone back home. Shyam babu casually mentioned to Dr Kurien that we had collected such a treasure trove of stories and incidences that we could make a full-length feature film, depicting the trials and tribulations of starting this revolutionary Amul journey. Dr Kurien, being Dr Kurien, perked up and asked, 'Really? When?' He hadn't even bothered asking us about the whys and the hows. Just, 'When?'

We were taken aback, especially Shyam babu, who told him that we would need some time to compile the script. He mentioned that it would cost about Rs 12–13 lakh, which was a large sum in those days. Shyam babu probably thought that was the end of that. Even a magician like Dr Kurien would have a hard time rustling up that amount, especially if he had to justify it first to a government audit body. Little did we know what was in store for us! We left him, making all the right noises about the script, and Dr Kurien promised to try and raise the money. Exactly five days later, Shyam babu got a call from Anand.

'I have the money,' Dr Kurien said. 'Where is my script?' We were in a state of shock. Where the hell did he manage to get that kind of money so fast? We suspected that he might have robbed a bank. However, what he had done was even more remarkable! He had set in motion the first crowdfunded project in India. He had told the milk collectors to inform every farmer that he was taking an advance of Rs 2 from each of them for a movie ticket.

In a year, they could go to any theatre in Gujarat to watch a film on Amul and the farmers of the state. Since they had earned this money from the milk they had sold to Amul, they were more than willing to part with it for such a worthy cause. He had collected Rs 12 lakh in one shot and was now baying for the script, and justifiably so. A year later, when the film *Manthan* was ready for release, it carried the legend on the posters, trailer and movie that read: 'Five hundred thousand farmers of Gujarat present *Manthan*!'

18

The Churning

Manthan threw the entire unit into a tizzy. For the first time, the funding for the film was ready, but the script, cast and location were nowhere on the horizon. This was the first and last time Shyam babu attempted to shoot with a script in progress. We had all been put to the sword, especially the scriptwriters—Shama Zaidi and her team. It's just that there was so much material from the *Operation Flood* documentary that poor Shama Zaidi hadn't had the time to put it down coherently in the form of a script. However, we had a broad idea of the narrative and storyline, and the line-up of the main characters had been put in place. But I remember we went into the shoot with no bound script—Shama Zaidi trailing along furiously filling in the gaps the day before.

Meanwhile, the slave pen was busy scouting for locations in Gujarat and Saurashtra because that was where the milk cooperative had started. We lucked out as Girivar Singhji, manager of the Opera House in Bombay owned by the Gondal royal family, was a great admirer of Shyam babu and casually offered us his kothi in Sanganva village, Saurashtra, as a location, free of charge. Off we went to check out the place, located thirty kilometres outside Rajkot. While it was unsuitable as a location for our film, the picturesque village of Sanganva proved perfect. Shyam babu and the production slaves decided to use the house as a staging area and production base for hair, make-up and food. We prepared and served meals for the unit there, and the cast used it for rest and recreation.

The village Sanganva was a perfect location for the film—clean, neat and properly leppoed (patted by hand with a mixture of cow dung and clay). Sanganva's villagers were a tall, good-looking lot. The women wore colourful ghararas with odhnis. While the menfolk wore lots of silver jewellery, paired with off-white kurtas nipped at the waist, and riding breeches–like pyjamas flaring from the waist to the thighs, then narrowing down to tight churidars at the ankles. Saurashtra was also the home of the 'Bhavni Bhavai', a spectacular folk dance form that was vigorous and acrobatic.

The story of *Manthan* is about a spearhead team that goes to a village in Saurashtra during the early days of Amul to start a milk cooperative there. The launch of the cooperative soon opens up a Pandora's box of issues. It sparks a war between the landlords and the landless, and the rich and the poor. In the meantime, the spearhead team's leader falls in love with a not-so-simple village belle, played superbly by Smita Patil.

The film is based on several real-life stories. It depicts the beginnings of a game-changing milk cooperative, which acted as a social catalyst to alter the rural landscape of India and its regressive traditional society. Only by churning cream from milk can you get butter, which is why the film and its recording of social upheavals was called *Manthan*.

We set off for Rajkot, where the bulk of the unit would be spending their nights. Rajkot was closest to the village and a decent hotel there was booked to put the team up. Every morning, we travelled one and a half hours across bumpy roads to the location in Sanganva village. The slaves had their hands full with the sheer logistics of the shoot.

We had decided to cart an entire catering staff to the location to provide hot meals to the crew—breakfast, lunch and early dinner. The onerous responsibility of arranging all of this fell squarely on my shoulders, as I was the only slave who showed any interest in cooking. I planned the menu for an army of hungry and finicky technicians, who woke up regularly at 6 a.m. to travel from Rajkot with just a cup of tea in their empty stomachs. They would arrive shaken but not stirred from a bone-jarring journey, in a relatively foul mood, to be greeted by a breakfast for champions that prepared them for the challenging day ahead. We laid it on, as I have always believed that the most important meal of the day for a working crew is breakfast. If you could pull that off without too many hiccups, they would really perk up and go at it with a gung-ho attitude.

So, besides my responsibilities as an assistant director, I organized the daily feeding of a sixty-five-man unit plus cast. We provided everyone with three square meals and an endless supply of tea and nimbu pani during the mind-numbing sixty-day schedule. We set up a massive kitchen from scratch. We had to hire and lug all the utensils, crockery and cutlery along with glassware from Bombay, as the locals were all vegetarians and refused to part with their cookware to prepare meat.

We had a designated storeroom for dry rations and a makeshift cold room for perishables. The supply chain had to be clear for all the provisions—from vegetables, meat and eggs to milk, as running out of any basic food was utterly unacceptable. It would have led to considerable rumblings in the ranks, among other things. We had to billet the kitchen staff in the village to avoid ferrying them to and fro, which was both impractical and avoidable.

The biggest problem was that there were no loos, except in the main haveli reserved for the cast and heads of departments. So everybody had to get used to going into the fields before sunrise, and be back lighter in mind and body by dawn. I decided to stay in the village with my colleague, Ravi Uppoor. We found ourselves a nice room at the edge of the town, leppoed to cool the place down. In Saurashtra, all the beds hang suspended from the main beam of the house, much like a swing. It took a week for me to get used to the sensation of rocking in my sleep. In the beginning, I was seasick as hell in the swing bed because the slightest movement would make it rock and make me dizzy. Though, I must say, once I got my sea legs, I slept like a baby.

It took a week of hits and misses for us to finally get the kitchen running smoothly, which was a huge relief. We started experimenting with the menu and, believe me, we churned out some incredible food! I had to dig deep to prepare the occasional delicacy, like partridge, for the direction crew's lunch. I would head out to the fields before sunrise to avoid getting caught with my pants down—literally since the whole village was up and about at the crack of dawn. I had managed to purloin an old hammer-type twelve-gauge shotgun, which belonged to Girivar Singhji, and carried it with me during my predawn sojourns.

On my way back, as the sun rose higher in the sky, I used to pot a few partridges for a delicious repast. Both Ravi Uppoor and I became damn good shots, and even managed some lefts and rights on the fly after flushing the birds from the fields (for the unacquainted, left and right means to bring down two birds on the wing—one with the left barrel and one with the right barrel, a pretty handy achievement).

One day, I woke up a tad late. I found a clear spot close to the village and hunkered down in my hurry to get on with it. Halfway through, I saw the first light of dawn beginning to tinge the horizon. Then, to my utter horror, I heard the tinkling of cowbells, the creaking of ungreased axles and the bright chatter of young voices. In the cold light of the dawn, I realized that my chosen spot was plum in the middle of the village road, with a bullock cart swiftly approaching, to boot. I put my head down and pretended that crapping in the middle of the road was the most natural thing to do in the world.

The cart stopped and peals of laughter emanated from its general direction. I looked up to see a cart full of enthusiastic young schoolchildren pointing and laughing at me! Shit! Shit! Shit! Unable to do anything about it, I brazened it out, waved and smiled through my acute embarrassment. I carried on as I had no other choice. The school cart full of giggling children remained rooted to its spot as I was squatting smack in the middle of a single rutted track, and there was no space available for them to overtake me. I finally finished, washed up and stood aside sheepishly, while the schoolkids trundled off on their very educative day.

In a moment of weakness, I mentioned the incident to Shyam babu, who immediately summoned an amused Shama Zaidi and instructed her to write it into the script. It showed a bunch of city slickers in the spearhead team acclimatizing to the conditions of the village. In the film, Anant Nag's character does a similar number. He heads to the kheth and ends up in the way of a group of giggling village belles. They follow him wherever he goes and he is unable to take a dump in peace. Until he gets so desperate that he confronts them about it only to find that they were all on their way to the well to fill water and he was always in their way!

Shyam babu insisted the entire cast turn up every day in full costume and I, once again, understood why he did this. Not only did they manage to age their clothes, but they also learnt the habits of the locals and blended into the landscape. I remember, one day, we had visitors from the neighbouring village. The sarpanch and his wife had specially dressed up to check out the Bollywood stars shooting on location. They hung around for a bit and were disappointed that they couldn't spot any Bombay-type glamorous people on the set—all they could see were the local villagers playing themselves. They were shocked to see two village belles squatting on the ground and surreptitiously smoking beedis.

They complained to the sarpanch of Sanganva, saying something to the effect of 'What a shameless bunch of hussies your village girls are, openly smoking in public!' The sarpanch of Sanganva laughed uproariously and pointed out that the girls weren't locals at all but actresses from Bombay. It was Smita Patil and Anjali Paigankar, quietly smoking beedis! The visiting dignitaries left in a huff as they thought that they were being fobbed off. I realized how much our cast had succeeded in blending in with the locals—even the villagers didn't give them a second glance.

Naseeruddin Shah took the whole business of authenticity to another level. He realized that since he was playing the village firebrand, he would be required on set from day one. Therefore, unfortunately, he didn't have the latitude to wear his clothes in. So, he walked up to the most tattered-looking villager and swapped clothes with him. Voila! A malodorous Naseer emerged from the bushes, totally transformed, with a beedi tucked behind his ear, smelling to high heavens.

The weather changed from a nippy late winter to a hot summer during the shoot and brought with it swarms of flies that dropped the visibility in the verandah to ten feet. We had to light dung cakes with neem leaves to smoke them out. It was quite the sight: Girish Karnad sneaking power naps in between takes on a chair, his head covered in a chunni to keep the bloody flies out.

The shoot had been trotting along at a tidy pace with no major hiccups and all of us slaves were happily patting ourselves on the back for having done a great job. Then came the night-attack sequence, which depicted a bunch of landlords who had decided to teach the lower caste landless lot a lesson. The landlords felt that they were getting uppity because the milk cooperatives had democratized the village into a one-person, one-vote system, regardless of how much land you owned or cattle you ran. This system made the landowners and the majority of the landless lower caste population equal on all counts in the 'seesoty', as they called it.

It led to an outbreak of violence in the movie, and a gang of upper caste goons attack and burn down a lowercaste basti at night. We were all set for this hugely dramatic sequence. We built the basti from scratch, doused it in kerosene, and rehearsed there with the actors and villagers. We started filming the master shot of the inferno, with people running in the foreground as the basti burnt. Everybody was in a self-congratulatory mood until Shyam babu called for a retake. Panic! Whatever was left of the set was still burning. We had never thought of a Plan B or built smaller, controlled areas to do close-ups or cutaways. We had to go back to square one and rebuild parts of the set for the reshoot the next night, and the night after that, until Shyam babu was satisfied.

For sixty days, us slaves never got a day off. It was work as usual at five in the morning—we attended to the call of nature and at 5.30 the sun rose on a pile of steaming turds. (Have you ever wondered why fresh turds, human or animal, steam in the early morning light?) At six, we knocked over some partridges and then work began for the day. Never a break, just relentless, by god. Finally, we finished the film, or at least we thought we had.

We packed up the kitchen and support staff. I must say the kitchen staff did a superb job under hugely trying circumstances. They kept the crew's morale consistently high with great food and never made any fuss about unreasonable demands. We staggered back to Bombay and practically collapsed, only to jump into post-production, editing, music, background score and sound recording.

Vanraj Bhatia rose to the challenge once again and produced some of the most memorable music for the film. His score was adopted by Amul as its anthem and can be heard even today in commercials! The film was released with great fanfare and the opening sequence mentioned how the farmers presented the movie. One week later, cities in Gujarat were thronged by bullock carts, tractors and all other kinds of rural transport. The 5 lakh farmers of the state had landed up to camp outside cinema halls and encash their precious, long-held tickets to watch their movie. It was pretty spectacular.

19

The Drive of a Lifetime

The best thing about working with Shyam babu was that he already had his next project planned, even before completing the previous one. Barely had we got into the post-production stage of *Manthan*, and he was already working on his next film, *Bhumika*. Someone had presented Shyam babu with a slim, scandalous book in Marathi on the life and times of Hansa Wadkar, a famous Marathi film actress in the 1930s and 1940s.

After retiring from the industry, Hansa's memoir in Marathi spoke about the exploitative nature of the male-dominated industry, chronicling the systemic abuse of female leads, in particular, those who struggled for their brief place in the sun. They could never feel secure without a male protector and mentor, who in turn also demanded his pound of flesh—quite literally. The book *Sangte Aika* was a scathing take on the Marathi film industry, and Hansa spared no one, however big or small they were. Not even herself!

When word got around that she had written her tell-all memoir and named villains and heroes, the entire industry collectively shat their pants and scrambled to get the book banned. They tried every dirty trick in the book and then some, but she stood isolated and adamant through it all. One by one, the big-name publishers buckled under the pressure. Until alone, desperate and destitute, she found a small-scale publisher, who happened to be an ardent admirer of hers. He agreed to publish a soft copy of the book on the fly at great peril to himself. It might have never seen the light of day even then, as the powers that be had managed to frighten away the distributors and advertisers.

Finally, the book was released in minuscule quantities and sold on the footpath, available only to the Marathi-reading public. It promptly disappeared without any trace since no reprints were published. It must have been the first 'Me Too' book ever, as far as I know. Gutsy and honest, Hansa had shared lots of gory details about her life in the industry. I've never figured out how Shyam babu got hold of a copy and had it translated to English, but once he did, he was hell-bent on making it into a film. Of course, it was duly sanitized because of our archaic and Victorian censor laws.

If we had been faithful to all the goings-on with names and places mentioned in the book, we would have ended up in jail. The film would have been buried in the vaults of the Censor Board. As we put the finishing touches on *Manthan*, the writing of *Bhumika* was progressing furiously. I spent my days at the office's film department and my nights at the editing table with Bhanu for *Manthan*.

Meanwhile, there was a lot of ad-film work piling up and, by this time, I was the trusted go-to person within the agency. I had my hands full. The first job that I handled alone was for Kinetic Pune, in which we had to shoot a moped ad. I managed to get Smita Patil to agree to play the brand ambassador for the two-wheeler as Maharashtra, especially Pune, probably had the largest number of lady two-wheeler riders in India, if not the world. We shot the Kinetic film in different locations across South Bombay, with most of the shots taken near Worli Sea Face. As we were doing a retake of a tracking shot, I almost had a heart attack when Smita and her sister were turning around to go to the start mark to begin filming the retake because an idiot coming out of the gate blindsided us.

While gawking at the camera crew, he ploughed straight into Smita's younger sister, Manya. For a heart-stopping moment, I wondered what I would tell her mother. To my utter relief, the trooper of a girl scrambled up from under the damaged moped. Other than a few bruises, she seemed okay and sportingly volunteered to carry on with the shoot. It was only later that I saw the cuts and welts she had suffered in the line of duty. I recently ran into her again, and she reminded me of the incident, showing me the battle scars that she carries till today.

At the time, ASP was also handling the account of CEAT Tyres. I heard that a new campaign was being planned for it. The agency was all agog about the possibilities of creating a breakthrough campaign for the car tyre brand. Shyam babu summoned me to the editing room and asked me to work on the script for the brand. I was hugely chuffed at being given this responsibility and was trying to crack an idea that was original and nothing like other car tyre advertising campaigns.

We put up a soft board in the conference room, with all the competitive brand advertising pinned to it. We blanked out all the brand names. The idea was to see if any of them stood out on the big-picture idea or on originality. Remarkably, very few of them passed the test. They all said the same thing—highlighting the brand's comfort, safety, braking power, durability and toughness to take in all conditions of roads. Later, as we followed this method for other brands to separate the professionals from the amateurs, we found that for most brand categories, everybody ends up making the same claims, in the same way. This included a lot of our earlier campaigns, as well. The only difference that remained was the brand name or legend.

If a brand had the first-mover advantage in its category or the client had deep pockets, the ad films could cement their brand leadership. The customers then followed the bhed chaal and the advertisers succeeded. Since everybody claimed the same advantages in the brand category and people had no way to differentiate one brand's claims from another's, they would end up saying, 'Let's go with the brand leader; at least, they are not fly-by-night.' I have seen this peculiar phenomenon happen in Indian advertising quite a bit.

So, here we were, struggling to innovate for a leading brand of car tyres. Yet, we could not afford to be too out of the box, either.

Otherwise, the client would chicken out and go back to safe old mediocrity. As on many occasions, my inspiration finally came from the irrepressibly irreverent *MAD* magazine. Its motto was to engage the readers with a dynamic line and hold the punchline until the end, so that they could never guess much about the product until it was delivered. I have always believed that the impact of such communication is indelible.

We came up with a film idea. We envisioned taking a close-up of a driver's face at the steering wheel. He is focused on driving the car around hairpin bends and winding roads, much like a car chase. We captured the concentration on his face as he spun the steering wheel, the look of intent, relief, joy and near misses as he drove. The backdrop moved and spun frantically as he wove his way through all kinds of road conditions and traffic.

We intercut it with close-up shots of him changing gears, leaning on the gas pedal, etc. For this, we needed a great actor with a phenomenal sense of timing, as his face would need to reflect every possible emotion in the book. We added the squealing of the tyres as a background soundtrack. I went to Shyam babu, presented him with the idea and pitched Jalal Agha as the leading actor.

I remember Shyam babu looking at me quizzically, rubbing his jaw and contemplating the idea. I'm sure he was playing the film back in his head. Then, he said, 'Good. I think it will work.' After which, he asked me the million-dollar question: 'And how does it end? Where is the packshot?' (The packshot is the shot of the product, also known as the hero shot.) In my excitement, I had forgotten the most crucial part of the script. The product punchline!

So we decided that right at the end Jalal careens around a blind corner, opens his eyes in horror and slams his brake to a screeching halt to the waft of burning rubber. We pull out to show him sitting on a packing crate in a factory-delivered chassis, with the engine, the wheel, the foot pedal, the gear *and* a gaggle of schoolchildren crossing the road ahead hand in hand. The legend then read, 'It doesn't matter what car you are driving. What matters is the tyres you are on. CEAT tyres—the drive of a lifetime.'

Shyam babu backed the film and the client bought into it. We made the film and I loved the process of being in charge of a film shoot—especially solving the technical problems of the shoot. In this case, the driver's face mirrored the drama in the film, while the car sped through its manoeuvres and the constant changing of the backdrop showing the performance of the tyres. We tried mounting the camera on the vehicle and shooting Jalal driving around Bombay. However, it didn't work as driving a car on its own is neither dynamic nor action-packed, but a bit boring.

Instead, we mounted the car on a truck with a low bed that transported containers from the docks. We got Jalal to drive around Malabar Hill early in the morning before any traffic or cops arrived. He mimicked the truck's motion in a highly exaggerated manner, but in perfect sync, as he wrestled with the wheel around hairpin bends, slopes and climbs. It would have never worked without Jalal and the pick-up truck. I realized then and forever that most times advertising is the art of exaggeration. It's not about telling lies; it is about pushing the truth, because, in the director's mind is a massive encapsulation and compression of time, during which you have to take the audience on a seamless rollercoaster ride visually. They should feel the entire experience and not merely watch it onscreen.

To understand this, a film student must study cartoon animation films in 2D or 3D to see the exaggeration of the motion control. Then, they must try and replicate this larger-than-life experience with real actors and sets on which gravity rules. The trick here is to defy gravity, as cartoon characters do. Then, and only then, do you get a hugely compressed but highly impactful visual, enhanced by sound and music.

It's not easy and sometimes you have to actually rig up your talent to wires to make the action look larger than life—the death-defying leaps over buildings or moving traffic, the use of slow motion to enhance the movement. For instance, the simple act of a hand coming out of a doorway to grab a character by his collar and yank him into an alley is hugely complicated. In a cartoon, the character first becomes horizontal to the ground and then disappears into the alleyway; in live action, he tilts into the exit and his feet never leave the ground. To follow a cartoon character's departure from the frame requires an entire wire-stunt team if you want the detail correct and the impact memorable.

These little nuggets of learning first-hand on the rigours of shooting a film, with no holds barred, have stayed with me for life. I always tell young slaves that you don't just read a script. You must see it in your mind's eye in all its glorious, gory detail, and only then can you venture out tentatively to replicate that vision—not before that, never before that. Very few non-filmmakers understand this process of assimilation. 'What's the big deal?' they wonder. 'You have a bound script; so go out and shoot the damn thing.'

I wish life were that simple. The introduction of state-of-the-art technology in India has made the life of filmmakers much simpler. But unfortunately, it has also meant that the young kids on the block haven't been through the process, i.e., the mill, the meat grinder—the heartbreak, the perseverance, and the sheer obstinate doggedness of not wanting to compromise their vision and going the distance to make things happen. They get so carried away with the technology available to them that a lot of today's work looks glossy and fabulous, but lacks a great idea and, more importantly, a heart. The thought process they follow is to resort to incredible pyrotechnics without a great story at the heart of it. While visiting a set, I have found teams muddling through a shot, uninterested in making sure it's near perfect. Instead, they use a tired line on the agency and client by saying, 'We will fix it in post-production.' In my book, that sets a bad precedent and smacks of 'jugaad'.

Therefore, I am not surprised that the cutting edge of film-making—advertising films, in particular—have not grown in Delhi, the land of jugaad. They've grown instead in Bombay, Chennai and Bangalore, where professionals don't follow the motto of 'Thook laga ke haisha!' or 'Jor se bolo haisha!' Yet, some of the best advertising professionals in Bombay migrated from Delhi—as I did. All of us from 'Dilli twon' (Delhi town) had one overriding characteristic, though: the hunger to succeed. Bombay taught us how to be professional, unlearn jugaad and learn how to do things correctly. Along the road of hard knocks, we also learnt to say no, regardless of how prestigious a brand was or how large the film's budget was. We learnt to say no if we couldn't see the film intuitively. We learnt to say no if we couldn't deliver it in time. And we learnt to say no if we weren't given the trust and latitude to innovate by the agency or the clients.

Remember, it is all hunky-dory if the film is well-received. God forbid it turns out to be a turkey, nobody will stand by you—not the agency, which had all the answers before the shoot, not the client, who wanted to change the main model because his wife didn't like him or her the night before the shoot. The most important lesson for us to learn is that once you accept the job, you do it to the best of your ability, come hell or high water. You don't compromise the vision, the detail or the execution. Damn the return on investment (RoI). The real RoI is the quality of the job because you don't do it—you own it. Remember, this lesson does not change regardless of the ease of technology. You are only as good as your last job.

You should never leave a shoot you are not happy with and never get into a shoot which you are unclear about. But, as I was saying before, the problem with young filmmakers is that they are far too reliant on technology and far too little on storytelling. As exceptions to the rule, there are a few great storytellers even today, and they stand out from the herd, like Amit Sharma, Rumaan Kidwai, Shujaat Saudagar, Uzer Khan and Vinil Matthew. Yes, the films must have good production value, but that means very little without great content or an outstanding idea. It comes as no surprise then that many commercials we see on TV or social media today have lots of sizzle but no steak!

20

Kakar's Leap

Just before we started shooting *Bhumika*, I stayed with a family of retired naval officers in Pilot Bunder, Colaba. Their younger son was dating a girl from his college. One day, at a casual get-together, she introduced me to her elder sister, a teacher. I spent the evening chatting with the elder sister, whom we shall refer to as SS. She was a bright, very centred young lady with a strong spiritual bent of mind, as her family members were followers of Swami Chinmayananda. She was not a ravishing beauty, nor was she the slightly upwardly mobile, flighty type who was tuned into the Big Apple's latest fashion and music trends, like some of the other young ladies I used to meet.

We got along famously and laughed a lot at the priorities and idiosyncrasies of the world. I genuinely liked her. I was attracted to her decency and my hormones, which were usually leaping about out of control, were unusually coy and subdued with her. She was very different from everyone else I knew. We became good friends and would have remained so, if only people around us had left us alone. But they didn't.

Her mother took two spoons of instant dislike towards me and swallowed it with a warm glass of water. The youngest sister, who was dating my landlady's son, liked me, but her middle sister decided the mother was right. The more unreasonable the family members got, the more stubborn and headstrong SS became. Now it was a question of honour; it was us versus the world.

She kept seeing me and her courage helped me grow a spine, and I hung in there, more as a support system for her than as a boyfriend. I watched as she transitioned from a gentle, docile, spiritual being to a rebellious, doggedly stubborn young lady. The main contribution came from the fact that we were the proverbial 'just good friends'. Still, we slipped into a close bond because of the unreasonable and biased opposition we were facing. That intimacy would probably have never happened if we had been left alone!

Due to her abnormal defiance, her family put her under the surveillance of a moustachioed ex-army driver. He would escort her to her teacher's training college in Marine Lines and back home, with strict instructions to see that she never met any accidental Lotharios— namely me. She was kept home and always watched, especially when she used the landline phone. Remember, there were no mobile phones back then. SS, of course, passed little notes to me through her friends in the teacher's training college with instructions to pass by her building at 1.30 a.m. on my khatara scooter (courtesy of Suniti's dad). She would give me the all-clear by keeping her bathroom lights on as a signal and leaving the front door ajar.

I was shitting bricks when I received her notes but was committed to the cause, and cursed myself and fate for getting into such an impossibly messy situation. I imagined going past the watchman nodding off in his chair in the foyer like they all do, creeping up the staircase, pushing the door open with a loud 'cr-ee-aa-k'. I would then be faced with an irate parent armed with a shotgun, who wouldn't accept the explanation of 'Oops, sorry, I've got the wrong house. I lost my way!' With these thoughts buzzing in my head, and no chance of chickening out, I sallied forth with a fervent prayer to Ganpati Bappa, 'Iss time bacha le, mein kuchh bhi karunga, kuchh bhi!'

There was no way I could now chicken out of this dire, angst-ridden rendezvous. It became a matter of prestige! Screwed if you do, screwed if you don't. How did I always manage to get into scrapes straight out of the movies without even trying? Anyway, I cruised past the building at 12.30 a.m. and was relieved to see no lights were on in the flat. So, I went past to the President Hotel, for a late-night coffee to wait till 1.30 a.m., hoping against hope that everybody had passed out by then. No such luck! As I cruised past the darkened edifice, I saw the light was on only in the first-floor bathroom window.

My heart quailed and leapt about frantically, and my pulse jumped to unheard of counts. The fear of being caught drove a tremendous amount of adrenaline into my quivering body, bracing it for the inevitable raid into enemy territory. I knew now how the troops felt on D-Day—waiting for the ramps of the landing craft to fall on the beaches of Normandy. Ready to leap into machine-gun fire, on a wing and a prayer. 'It was not to question why. It was to do or die!' But question the stupid crazy situation I did at that moment.

I parked the scooter by leaning it against the curb as it did not have a stand, slid past the watchman ninja style and tippy-toed up the staircase, holding my breath. I finally exhaled at the front door as I found it slightly ajar and, with my heart beating an erratic tattoo, which I was sure could be heard for miles, I slipped into the darkened flat. Going past the master bedroom of her sleeping parents, I crept into SS's room, faintly lit by the bathroom light. Jesus Christ! What the hell was I doing here? my mind demanded. Yes, encouraged my wildly beating heart, as I saw her sitting up in her bed, a flash of her teeth as her face broke into a smile and my fear retreated by just a fraction, enough for me to smile back. Before my legs could collapse with sheer fright, I sat down on the edge of the bed and grabbed her hand.

We sat for what I thought was ages, clutching each other's slightly sweaty hands, just listening, waiting for a sound. The injection of adrenaline into my system had expanded my mind to five times its average functioning size. I was suddenly acutely aware of the street sounds, the groaning of a building contracting in the cool of the night. I could even feel the flaws in the weave of the bed sheet and, most of all, I could hear the uneven breathing of her parents lying down next door. The bed creaked as her mother turned in her sleep and the moment her breathing pattern broke, I knew she was awake. She lay quietly in her bed trying to figure out what had woken her. She sat up on its edge and stood up, paused for an eternity, listening, then shuffled to the toilet.

Both of us held our breath for what felt like forever. Finally, the flush was pulled and her mother shuffled out, before stopping again to listen, trying to figure out what was it that had disturbed her sleep. She stood forever outside, with her head cocked to one side. Then she lay down again and started breathing evenly. Whew! How intuitive was she, by god! I hung about for a bit longer. My neck and shoulder muscles started cramping from the tension of being there. After what seemed like ages, I said goodbye and ninjaed out of the flat down the staircase, exiting the gate. I pushed my trusty khatara for half a mile so as not to disturb the neighbourhood, then I revved it up and fled!

When I reached the office a little later in the morning, the aftershocks were setting in. I developed a jumping pulse on my forehead and a funny twitch near my mouth. I was wasted and behaved like a zombie through the rest of the day. I had thought that was that, but then on, every time I found the light on in the first-floor bathroom, I was committed to making that suicidal run to SS's room. Until I realized that I was hooked to the fear of the moment and I had become an adrenaline junkie! Zombie by day, ninja by night.

One ordinary afternoon, I got a call at the office from SS. She excitedly told me to land up at her home at 5.30 in the evening as her parents and siblings were headed to Powai for a family dinner. She had feigned a headache, so she was home alone and awaiting me with bated breath. Thus, young Lochinvar, true to his salt, leapt on his steed (the khatara) and backfired his way to his tryst with destiny. For once, it was daylight, and I boldly parked the steed and leapt up the stairs, two at a time, rang the bell, with a touch of drama, I was admitted in and made my way to the hallowed bedroom. I had carried a cassette of Harindranath Chattopadhyay's 'The Curd Seller' to play to her, in lieu of a poem by T.S. Eliot, my go-to poet.

Time flew by this time. I wasn't shitting my pants and hyperventilating. Instead, I was quite relaxed, listening to 'The Curd Seller', when, around 7 p.m., the doorbell rang. SS blanched and her eyeballs looked like they would pop out. I realized that something was very amiss and asked her, 'What?' She whispered, 'My father is back ahead of time for some reason!' Trapped between the father and no place to hide, adrenaline kicked in and everything went into slow motion—at least 500 frames per second. I had three options: hide under the bed until the coast was clear (god alone knew when that would be), hide in the toilet, or go over the balcony, with a prayer!

The most logical way out was the balcony, but, as they say, there is many a slip between the cup and the lip. Lying stretched across the door jamb was a wretched mongrel recently purloined by the mother, whose instincts had told her something was up nocturnally in her daughter's room. Now, this mongrel, true to his nose and the mother's instinct, had developed a lingering dislike of yours truly. He would have loved to get his chompers on my delicate nether regions and was only prevented from doing so several times in the past on SS's severe reprimand.

So, there he was, stretched across my only escape route, salivating in his doggie dreams. In my adrenaline-induced desperation to escape, I chanced the canine's bite. Then, in slow motion, I jumped over the mongrel and, before he knew what had happened, I had one hand on the balustrade of the balcony. While I was in the process of vaulting over, I happened to glance down and almost froze mid-air. Fifteen feet below, the watchman stood facing the gate, with his back towards me, picking his nose with great concentration. I imagined I was going to land with a thump, a few feet behind him, and he would collar me on landing and frog-hop me up the steps to confront the old man (who, by the way, did own a shotgun). Screwed!

Back to reality: I sailed over the balcony towards our nose-picking chowkidar, thinking furiously. In my final year in school, I had topped the ground gymnastics course, which involved floor exercises and learning the parachute roll, or the shoulder roll. In this, one tucks their face into their right shoulder, crooks their elbow to protect it and lets the momentum of the fall flow into a perfect shoulder roll, coming up instantly on one's feet in a flash, totally in balance. And that is precisely what I did, as I landed with a thump, having executed a 10/10 shoulder roll. I stood up straight as the watchman turned around upon hearing the thump from my landing.

He turned towards me and I turned to look behind me, in perfect sync. I looked around, then back at him and said, 'Kucch gira hai!' He nodded and ran around the building while I ran out of the gate to freedom. I got on to my trusty steed and went straight to Olympia Café on Colaba Causeway to order a cutting chai, pani kum! When the tea arrived, I noticed my adrenaline wearing off. My hand was shaking so furiously that I couldn't lift the cup to my mouth and had to dip my head to the teacup, like an alcoholic. What a close call!

In the meantime, SS had been put under full lockdown with no choice of communication—by phone, friend or pigeon post. I was fretting and fuming, and getting a bit desperate. I wanted to storm the bastion with some friends and rescue the fair maiden from her cruel family. But before I could do something idiotic, I got a call in my office from her younger sister. I was about to ask her how SS was when she handed the phone to her mother!

In measured tones, she informed me that SS had gone on a hunger strike, and had been refusing all food and drink until she was allowed to meet me. And, much against her mother's will and better sense, I was invited to the house for tea. However, I had been ordered not to get my hopes up at all. They were hell-bent on marrying her off to some gentleman of their choice and were only humouring her to ensure she didn't harm herself. I was told that if I genuinely cared for her, I should advise her to stop acting silly and listen to her parents.

That was when I decided to shave my beard for the first time in three years and dressed up in my Sunday best. I turned up to a very hostile reception from the family and was uncomfortably placed at the edge of the sofa waiting for SS to arrive. She wafted into the room in a pale green sari, smelling deliciously of a gajra of mogras. I got up to ask how she was. She smiled radiantly and enquired how I was handling the situation, so I proclaimed sotto voce, 'Let's run away!' To which she laughed delightfully, but sobered up immediately after and said she couldn't as her mother had convinced her that if she did, her father would die of a heart attack, and she loved her father too much to be the cause of that. I knew that. They were quite close.

So I had my tea and reassured SS that I would survive, wished her the best in her life and left! All to the sound of a single bird crying in the wasteland of my soul. Long after we went our separate ways, try as I might, I couldn't hold a normal relationship together because it all felt dull and meaningless. Then I realized, to my horror, that I actually missed the fear-induced high of our relationship. That made the most innocuous moments into hyper-special, earth-shattering occasions, indelibly imprinted in my fevered mind. Now, when I look back at my slightly colourful life, I wonder if, in memoriam, the Brihanmumbai Municipal Corporation (BMC) will name the corner of the building on Cuffe Parade: 'Kakar's Leap'! Tan-ta-tara!

21

The Electrician, the Flunkey, the Pig and the Ghost

*B*humika was a fantastic experience. I had graduated from a slave to a gofer (go for this and go for that). The dictum was that slaves could be seen, not heard, but gofers could speak up too. Therefore, my involvement in *Bhumika* was not only physical (in the fetch and carry sense), but I could also contribute to the narrative and character development. I could be heard out patiently before I was summarily dismissed!

In terms of cinematic learning, *Bhumika* was a tremendous experience. As I mentioned earlier, it was based on the life of Hansa Wadkar, with the only difference that Shyam babu had sanitized the script and named the lead actor Usha. The schedule revolved around three major locations: Goa, Pune and Bombay. Hansa Wadkar grew up in the Konkan area in Sawantwadi and lived in a traditional Maharashtrian joint family in a wada, a structure found in Maharashtra.

For the shoot, Kamath mama's ancestral home near Vasco, in Goa, turned out to be the perfect location. It was a classic Maharashtrian wada, with a massive aangan in the centre that had a tulsi plant and a well called a bauwdi. We spent the first leg of the schedule in Goa, where we shot with Smita Patil, who was playing Usha, a young, pretty thirteen-year-old with two braids looped in a circle, as was the fashion in those days. She could sing and dance beautifully, and her much older cousin uncle convinced her to join the movie world and go to the big, bad city of Bombay with him.

Feature films are very rarely shot sequentially. We would keep jumping timelines in the lead character's life, depending on the availability of the location and cast. While in Goa, we were also scheduled to shoot a married Usha at the ripe age of twenty-four, with her growing-up years to be continued in Bombay. Guess whose job it was to keep tabs on the continuity for clothes, hairstyles, make-up and jewellery? Of course, it was assigned to all of us gofers, and there were three of us—the late Girish Ghanekar, Ravi Uppoor and yours truly. In those days, there were no phones or digital cameras, to help us take photos to ensure continuity.

We had to write copious notes in great detail, make sketches of the look and feel, and take photographs on film, which had to be processed and developed. These were then printed and filed with the notes to help jog our exhaustion-sodden memories when they ultimately failed us. Keeping continuity on a Shyam Benegal set was a nail-biting experience as he was a stickler for detail, with the memory of an elephant. God help the flunkey or slave who overlooked a continuity detail.

Off we went to Pernem in North Goa to shoot Usha's tryst with marriage. She was twenty-four at that time and had become a relatively successful star in the world of Marathi cinema, but she yearned to become a wife and a mother too. She met this wealthy, suave gent, who was a landowner and a man of the world. He swept Hansa off her feet and proposed marriage to her. She is charmed and decides to marry him as he seems to be the perfect man, urbane, sophisticated, and well-to-do. Unfortunately, the moment she does, he turns into an ogre. He becomes high-handed, bigoted, narrow-minded and turns out to be a wife-beater. She suffers near bondage and violence in her marriage until she escapes to the film industry's familiar exploitation.

We had been offered a beautiful location in Pernem by a Mr Deshprabhu, who held the title 'Visconde de Pernem', given to him by the Portuguese. He offered Shyam babu his old wooden ballroom as the location for this episode of Hansa Wadkar's life. It was a beautiful two-storeyed structure, which had housed over 500 guests in its heyday, with a live band and a wraparound balcony skirting the dance floor, for oglers.

We converted it very cleverly into Usha and her husband's main house. It was a two-hour drive from Panjim to Pernem, and we had to cross two rivers by ferry to reach it. The disgruntled unit had to rise at 5 a.m., start their journey to the location by six, get there by eight, have a decent breakfast and be ready to shoot by nine. I tried it for two days, gave up and decided to stay on location all by myself.

I convinced the one-eyed major domo of the property to lay a camp cot in the middle of the ballroom for me. He filled a porcelain jug of water and retired to his quarters. The first night of my stay, there was a full moon in the sky, and the ballroom was bathed in a surreal glow coming in from the huge French windows, with muslin curtains billowing in the breeze. It was pretty magical, except for my fertile imagination and fevered mind.

Instead of enjoying the view, I kept getting up and peering into the dark corners of the far end of the wooden ballroom, where the moonlight didn't reach, imagining formless beings floating around, dancing to the devil's own tune. I also started hearing creaking and groaning sounds from the wooden structure itself, in a mad symphony, which frightened the shit out of me as I had heard that the ballroom was haunted. I curled into the foetal position, covered my head with the pillow to block the sounds and visions, and tried to sleep. But to no avail!

I woke up to a welcome dawn, quite shattered, to find the major domo standing with a cup of steaming hot tea. With great trepidation, I broached the subject of the noises at night and ghosts to the one-eyed Jack. He laughed uproariously, much to my chagrin. He explained that wooden structures expanded in sunlight during the day and contract at night because of the cold. Therefore, they made all manner of noises.

The visual fantasy of dancing couples was spun entirely by my own hyperactive mind. Despite my palpitating heart and wild imagination, I stuck it out in the middle of the ballroom for the rest of the schedule, albeit armed with a flashlight. I would peer myopically into the dark recesses of the room, only to find a pair of dancing curtains in the wind. What a mind fuck!

But it wasn't only me who seemed to be spirit-struck. Since the crew had to get up at the crack of dawn to travel to the location, kept alive by a single cup of tea, not everybody was lucky enough to find the time for their morning ablutions. As the few available toilets on the location had been usurped by the cast and heads of department, everybody else was left to fend for themselves.

I have never been able to understand why production people never factor in the anal health of the ordinary crew and why the available toilet became such an essential part of territorial real estate. Anyway, to cut back to the chase, we had a new electrician on location, and, like most of us, he was a first-timer in Goa. He was a North Indian with the most disagreeable character—ill-tempered and truculent, especially when he was a bit drunk, which was most of the time. He would wake up in the morning in a foul mood and it would carry over to the rest of the day. Though, I have to say, he was a competent electrician. He was tolerated on set, barely.

Every morning, he was required to reach the location and connect the generator to the main lighting board before heading for breakfast with the rest of the crew. One fine day, we all finished our breakfast and landed up on the set to start the shoot, but the lights hadn't been turned on. So the slaves and gofers headed off in different directions to find out what was wrong, egged on by a few choice expletives from the camera department, furious that nobody had connected the generator to the lighting board.

We started looking for our unsavoury electrician and he seemed to have vanished into thin air. There was consternation on the set by this time, and we divided ourselves into hunting parties to find him. We first searched in the immediate vicinity with no luck, so we fanned out into the surrounding paddy fields, further and further away from the location. I had a niggardly suspicion that he had gone off to answer the call of nature. But, for the love of Mike, why did he have to go so far? Then, just when my hunting party was about to give up and return to base, I heard a plaintive cry, 'Bachao! Bachao!'

The voice had an edge of hysteria to it. We followed the sound and stumbled upon an unbelievable scene. In the distance was a lone raintree, magnificent in its spread of branches, and halfway up the tree, squatting on the fork of its branches, was our electrician with his trousers around his ankles and his hairy derriere exposed to the elements. His pasty face was contorted into a look of abject terror. All the while, he kept looking down between his legs and screaming, 'Bachao! Bachao!'

Our disbelieving eyes panned down to the object of his terror, and we saw a large, old sow. She was looking up at our treed gent with a patient gleam in her piggy eyes, occasionally licking her chops. As we drew closer, our friend, the electrician, spotted us and hope leaped into his distended eyes, and he screamed incoherently at us. 'Mujhe bachao iss bhoot se, yeh mere peechhe pad gayi hai! Aur chhod nahin rahi hai! Yeh shaitan hai, mujhe kha jayegi!' Finally, after shooing the old sow away from her potential breakfast, we managed to get our hysterical electrician down. We convinced him to draw his pants up and listened to his babbling to piece together the sorry sequence of events.

He had hung back on the set and, feeling the need to take a dump in the morning, had grabbed a pail of water and headed into the khet. After finding a decently hidden spot in the bushes, he lowered his trousers to contemplate his hairy navel, when he was startled to see a sow had approached his exposed bum and had started drooling gently in anticipation. He was so frightened that he got up and scurried to a new location, hurling the choicest expletives and a few stones at the offensive pig.

All to no avail, she had decided he was her object of desire. She was stuck to his arse like a limpet mine, and however far or fast he scurried, she was right there in a flash. Being new to Goa, he hadn't realized that the reason for the state's pristine beaches and the environment was its army of shit-eating pigs, who would go to any lengths to not be denied their snack. So it went, the further and faster he scuttled, she was right there, up close in anticipation and drooling until he was convinced that his late ex-wife's bhoot had possessed the pig and was now taking revenge for all his kartoots and the abuse he had once heaped on her.

Eventually, in desperation, he had climbed up the tree, thinking he had shaken her off only to realize by looking between his legs that there she was, waiting. At which stage, he lost the plot. We hauled him back to the location to an irate Shyam babu. But, by then, he was totally beyond any measure or hope of sanity. He had become a twitching wreck and had to be evacuated to Bombay for treatment. We finally found a local electrician who did the job just fine, and the shooting resumed much to everybody's relief. The filming of *Bhumika* continued in Bombay and finally in Pune.

But Goa had left such an impression on me that I decided that if I had to have a house anywhere in India, it would be in Goa. I loved the happy-go-lucky, musically inclined people, the food, the ocean and how effortlessly it embraced orphan Annies like me. I had found a home, and so it was that I bought my first house in Goa thirty-eight years ago, on the banks of the Mandovi river, right opposite Panjim, in a small hamlet called Betim. I paid for it in instalments while it was under construction. It took me two years to pay for it. Viva la Goa!

22

The Genesis of Genesis

Back in Bombay, *Bhumika* was well into post-production when the three musketeers—Mandeep Kakkar, Ravi Uppoor and yours truly—decided to start a moonlighting operation to shoot ad films for small clients. All of us were Shyam Benegal's slaves and had learned the ropes the hard way. Our reputation had started rippling out by then, and we offered to do cheap and cheerful films that none of the established filmmakers were willing to touch. We decided what the hell, what goes of my father? (Mere baap ka kya jaata hai?) As long as we didn't lose any money, we could test the waters. After all, we had stable jobs to fall back on.

The three of us, plus Smita Patil, who, by then, was very much a part of the gang, went into a huddle and Smee (as we called her) suggested that we name the company 'Genesis'. This was inspired by a graduation film made by an FTII direction student, Rahul Dasgupta, which she thought was brilliant. So, Genesis, it was! Since we were pretty broke and lukkha, we decided to design our own letterhead. We went to a printer to select an unusual typeface for the main legend, 'Genesis Film Production'. After going through all the usual suspects, we came across a bold and not oft-used typeface, which was quite awful and not at all biblical. We chose it temporarily because we had to urgently send a quotation to a prospective client and thought we could always change the awful logo later.

Never judge a book by its cover, a king by his clothes, or a company by its logo! The first exceptional film that we did was for Air India. Firdausi Jussawalla, who was the understudy of the legendary Bobby Kooka of Air India, called me one day and asked if we could do an experimental film on flight destinations based on the Air India posters of the Maharaja. He warned us that there was very little money involved and no advance. We were a bit flummoxed. How could one make a moving film on still posters, however interesting they were? Cut to my secret saviour and genius animator, Ram Mohan!

We sat with him like little raggedy orphan Annies, and he not only gave us his invaluable time but cracked the storyline for us as well. Starting with a poster of the Maharaja as a bioscope vendor, he helped us track the movement on paper until it made a coherent story in thirty seconds. Now we had to superimpose our commentary on it so that Ram Mohan could time the narrative with the help of his amazing Oxberry animation table. We went back to the drawing board to write a piece of commentary in the cadence and style of bioscope vendors of yore.

I had just heard the recording of Harindranath Chattopadhyay reciting his poem 'The Curd Seller'. The rise and fall of the cadence in his raspy voice was divine and I was hooked. The strains of the bioscope vendor's call from the halcyon days of my childhood echoed in my mind. We started writing 'Dekho dekho, duniya dekho'. The original line used by the vendors was, 'Chhattis maund ki dhoban dekho', which, of course, we could not use. Nevertheless, the rhythm and boli of 'The Curd Seller' rang in my ears as we crafted our narrative in a couple of hours. Though, notwithstanding a few hiccups. We needed someone with a distinct voice to be our narrator. We didn't want a professional and slick voice, but wanted one reminiscent of the village mela.

The hunt was on and we went looking for some qawwali-walas, who had the required vocal range, but, since coming to Bombay, they had gotten very pricey and were out of our league. While we were frantically looking for the right voice, we kept playing 'The Curd Seller' on a cassette player to give the recordists an idea of what we wanted and, bingo, one of them came up with the solution. He said, 'Why don't you ask Harindranath Chattopadhyay himself?'

'But where do we find him?' we asked.

Remember, there was no Google in those days. He casually dismissed our query by answering, 'He is usually sitting on the Worli Sea Face at this time.' Good grief, what a windfall, sirji! Off we went to Worli Sea Face on our rattfatiya two-wheeler. I was still driving Suniti's father's 1966 Lambretta, which had seen better days and was without brakes. We reached our destination to find a spry old gentleman, with a shock of white hair, beetling eyebrows and a wizened elfin face, who was quite mobile and wholly absorbed in ordering a platoon of street kids into a marching squad. 'Left, right, left, right,' he instructed them. We went up to him and he brought the gaggle of urchins to a halt, and said, 'Squad, dismiss!'

He heard me out patiently and immediately said, 'I don't do commentary.' I reminded him of his rendition of 'The Curd Seller'. He frowned at me through his thick eyebrows, but his eyes were alive with mischief. 'So,' he said, 'you have heard "The Curd Seller"? Good. Are you going to pay me?'

'Yes, sir! We have a budget of twelve-hundred rupees,' I replied nervously, thinking that he would say 'Dismiss' to us as he had to the urchins. But he got up abruptly and said, 'Let's go! Where are we recording?' We hopped on to my Lamby. And off we clunked and clattered to Film Centre in Tardeo, where a friend was doing a background music recording.

The other two musketeers and I begged and pleaded with my friend, and he gave us half an hour to finish our work. Mr Chattopadhyay, at this stage, looked at the Hindi script and announced that he couldn't read the language. Screwed! Now what? We scrambled to write the boli in Roman Hindi, i.e., Hindi written in English. He couldn't take breaks, so he rehearsed by speaking the words fluently and tried not to break the rhythm by breathing in the middle. It took quite a few takes, but once he got the bit in his teeth, there was no stopping him. He was committed to earning his twelve hundred rupees, come hell or high water, and finally, he did it in style and brilliantly at that.

Thanks to Ram Mohan, we finished the animation and presented the doubleheader to Firdausi. He hopped around in glee and said, 'I never imagined it would turn out so delightful!' The film was released in Sterling, in town, to a very appreciative Bombay audience—even though it was recited in Hindi at an English movie theatre. The film ended up winning many awards that year in the annual advertising club jamboree. However, that wasn't the end of the story.

When we went back to Firdausi for the balance payment—he had only given us a miserly advance—he said Air India hadn't budgeted for the film, which meant that the balance could only be paid in tickets depending on where we wanted to go. I had a girlfriend in those days who was flying for Air India, and she was posted in London for a few months to operate the London–New York leg. I decided to use the free ticket to visit her.

After calculating many permutations and combinations, I was handed an economy class ticket to Amsterdam on an Air India Express flight. When I told them, with consternation, that I wanted to go to London, not Amsterdam, they told me that the money owed to me only got me as far as Amsterdam. I would have to make my way to London from there, so I could 'Take it or leave it'. I took it and paid a hefty sum to get to London from there.

The whole episode reminded me of the waiter in an Irani restaurant I visited announcing loudly after I had asked for a glass of water and dropped the glass by mistake, 'Kuchh khaya nahin, kuchh piya nahin; ek glass toda, paanch rupay!'

One fine day, I walked into the office, and my friend and protector, Mohini Rege—the telephone operator and receptionist, told me in hushed whispers that the whole office was in an emergency lockdown and was huddled in the conference room. Something serious was going down. As it transpired, Usha Katrak had discovered that large amounts of cash had been transferred out of the company's accounts with the connivance of the chief accountant, and that the promoters of the company had something to do with it. So, the next day, our beloved ASP agency split. Most of us—Usha Katrak, K. Kurien, Eustace Fernandes, Shyam Benegal and a motley collection of us juniors—formed a new company called Radeus.

We moved to an office in the back alleys of Colaba, in the annexe of the Artistic Building. At this time, Larry Grant returned to reclaim his apartment from me. I was looking for a place to sleep and asked if I could stay the night at the office with my friend Mandeep Kakar. They reluctantly allowed us to do so. Since our salary amounted to a measly sum, we eventually moved into the new Radeus office, which we referred to as Khatmal Niwas. Hundreds of bedbugs used to crawl out at night from the wooden rafters, attracted by the salty smell of our sweaty bodies.

We took to putting a line of DDT powder around our mattresses like a Lakshman rekha to prevent the bugs from getting to us. But, somehow, we still ended up being bitten. I just couldn't figure out how this was possible! The mystery was solved one night when I was awake and reading, and Mandeep was trying to sleep. I suddenly noticed a bug on his bare back, then another and another. They appeared in quick succession, one after the other. The Lakshman rekha was intact, so how was this happening? That's when I looked up and, lo and behold! I noticed that they had impatiently queued up on the white wooden beam above and were merrily skydiving on to his back. Splat! Another one landed. I couldn't believe it! They had bypassed the DDT and were launching themselves off the roof, by god! Necessity is the mother of innovation.

———

The Air India film got us noticed in the advertising fraternity and we received a few desultory enquiries. But the breakthrough came when we got a call from Mubi Ismail, the film chief of Lintas, who had been keeping an eye on me ever since she had seen my debut film with Chirpy. Mubi wanted to know whether we could produce and direct a film for Britannia Marie biscuits for Lintas. We leapt at the opportunity and had a few meetings with their creative team. Mubi played mother hen to all the wild ideas I was throwing at them.

The basic script was that there were guests over for tea and we had to bring out the Marie biscuits to serve them. The film had little sequences of different guests enjoying Britannia Marie biscuits, set to a jingle. It was pretty straightforward until I started adding my two bits to the proceedings. We added things like a guest spotting a pack of Marie biscuits lying next to a tiger skin and when he surreptitiously tries to snatch the packet up, the tiger skin growls at him. He drops it immediately and jerks his hand away, looking startled and guilty at the same time.

I got carried away and suggested many more sequences—one with a kid and a funny-looking uncle, who conjures up packets of biscuits for him. Now, all of these sequences would require top-level actors and not models as had been visualized earlier. This led to a bit of heartburn. The original script and the budget had already been approved by the client, a Mr Sunil Alagh. The agency's creative team was reluctant to go back to him with new ideas and ask for a higher budget since he was reputed to be quite hard-boiled. Mubi then rallied around us as she loved my suggestions and said we could discuss them with Mr Alagh as long as we stuck to the original budget. We readily agreed to this demand.

We managed to convince Kulbhushan Kharbanda to play the role of the guest. We also cast a gentleman called Joginder Singh (Jogi), whom I had met at a party. He was an incredible mime and all-around funny, stand-up guy. And, lastly, we enlisted the reigning child star, Jugal Hansraj—a fair, light-eyed, beautiful child—to be a part of the shoot. After confirming our cast, we toodled off to the Britannia office with Mubi to present our ideas to Mr Sunil Alagh, whose reputation for being direct and abrasive preceded him.

He heard us out patiently and immediately got to the point, asking us how much more the film would cost with these new additions. We nervously shuffled around and Mubi answered, 'Not a penny more!' To which, Mr Alagh arched an eyebrow and said, 'Really?' We nodded in unison. That was when he smiled like the cat that got the cream and said, 'Great! Let's do it.' All of us sighed in relief and, before we proceeded to shuffle out, I cleared my throat and ventured meekly, 'Sir, can we also sort of copy the tune of "Rule, Britannia" for the jingle?'

Mr Alagh glowered at us while Mubi was shooting daggers at me. Then, after a pregnant pause, he said, 'As long as we don't get sued, you can go ahead. Otherwise, you have to redo it at your cost.'

'Yes, sir!' I agreed meekly. This was a big deal at that time because very few clients appreciated humour then and it was virtually unheard of to add twists to an otherwise uncomplicated film that the client had already approved. Little did we know what a different kettle of fish Sunil Alagh was!

He had already given the go-ahead earlier for a Britannia glucose bestseller biscuit to do a clever take on the famed *Sholay* episode where Gabbar is quizzing Kalia about his failure to threaten the village into surrendering. The ad reframed the scene, cast with the original actors, delivering hilarious takes on the dialogues from the original screenplay. The lines for the ad film were penned by none other than the legendary Javed Akhtar. Shot by Kailash Surendranath, the ad was called 'Gabbar ki asli pasand'. It ended up with a sizeable cult following of its own, almost comparable to that of the original *Sholay* film!

Meanwhile, back at the ranch, frenzied preparations for the Marie ad's shoot were under way, and final decisions regarding the cast, crew and an eye-catching location had to be taken, considering we didn't have a budget to build a set. We were frantically calling up friends, family and all sorts of other animals to find an upmarket home with a high ceiling to help with the lighting. Finally, Usha Katrak and her husband, Kercy, were our saviours. They offered us their beautiful seaside home, across Nepean Sea Road, in an old-style building with high ceilings.

The house was as pretty as a picture, and I don't think Mr Katrak was quite prepared for the invasion and disruption of his home that ensued during our two-day shoot. That is the first time we at Genesis learnt the first lesson of being different. You never treat a home location as a studio. The crew wore gloves, so as not to leave greasy stains on the walls and, after pack-up, we fit everything back in its original place, no matter what it took or how long. That way, when the inhabitants returned to their abode in the evening, they would not feel like their beloved house had been vandalized.

After much searching, we found a tiger skin with the head intact. We came early to set up the shooting areas, especially prepared with a hint of the brand colours. We did this on the spot without a brief from the client or agency. We wanted to add value to the look and feel of the film. We had already recorded the jingle with the doyen and legend Vanraj Bhatia, and we were very chuffed by his take on the British patriotic song. The ad's slogan went something like this: 'Guests for tea, bring out Marie! Britannia, Britannia, Britannia Marie!'

Kamath mama was our cameraman on the shoot. In those days, cameramen hadn't taken on the director of photography (DOP) title yet and were quite humble, despite their extensive experience and seniority. The cast and crew arrived an hour early for lighting and make-up. We decided to first take the shot with Kulbhushan and the tiger since we had to return the skin at the earliest to its worried owner. The star kid arrived, meanwhile, with an entourage in tow, which surprised us. There was a harrowed-looking mom and dad, and one fussy ayah. I didn't pay much attention to them because, by then, I was busy with Kulbhushan and the tiger skin. However, I could hear the hubbub of a disconcerting commotion brewing in the make-up room.

Meanwhile, the pack of Marie biscuits had been placed casually in the open tiger's mouth and a furtive Kulbhushan was trying to grab it on the sly. The moment his hand touches the pack of biscuits, the tiger growls. Kulbhushan is shown pulling his hand back with a yelp and looking around sheepishly, before he ventures gingerly to make another attempt, but with the same result. Finally, he looks at the tiger skin with a sense of astonishment that reflects on his face almost as if to say, 'You are dead and dusted! Why are you getting possessive about the damn biscuit?'

Kulbhushan was an excellent theatre artiste and gave us exactly what we wanted, and more. We finished shooting his sequence and it was now time for us to film the child actor's sequence. I knew that a five-year-old's attention span lasts for about half an hour on a good day and that we would have to film as much as we could in that window. However, this kid was another can of worms altogether, cute and angelic as he looked. Little did we know that he was hiding the mind of a terror, ready to wreak havoc.

He refused to get the little make-up that was needed done and was in the middle of a massive tantrum when I walked in. I bent down with a big smile and asked, 'Ready?'

'No!' he shouted and rolled on the floor, all the while yelling at his distraught parents, who were desperately trying to coax him by doling out lollipops, chocolates and other treats. Many years later, I would come to accept that when the main lead is a badly behaved five-year-old, and he gives early signs of trouble, just drop him like a hot potato and find another kid, pronto. It doesn't matter how much the client or agency is in love with him. He has the capacity of totally derailing and hijacking an ad film.

This was our very first shoot and we couldn't afford to take that risk, so we soldiered on—much to the relief of a worried Mubi Ismail, whose hand he had spat on when she had offered him a placatory toffee. We managed to shoot a few scenes with him, when he suddenly shifted his laser-like focus on to Kamath mama and loudly proclaimed, 'I don't like that buddha uncle!' And so it was, he had added a new demand on the table. As long as the 'buddha' uncle was on the set, he would refuse to shoot. We had reached an impasse!

Kamath mama and I retreated to another room while the nervous parents took over with a worried Mubi hovering on the fringes. An hour passed, and he was still screaming and shouting and rolling on the floor with no chance of a respite. So, we broke for lunch, hoping that a decent meal would calm the little fucker down. No such luck. He was full of sugar and junk food, and was hyper-energized like the Duracell Bunny. After waiting for a few hours to allow the parents and Mubi to try and persuade him, I suddenly realized that I could no longer let this child hijack our first major shoot.

We took a few desultory pack shots, desperately wishing the commotion would die down, but it didn't. The rest of the cast and sequences were scheduled for the next day, so that was it! We had to shoot his sequences today. Finally, at about four in the evening, I just made up my mind and decided to do a kamikaze (a do-or-die kind of thing). I barged into the make-up room, took in the complete carnage with a glare, as the little bugger had thrown his food all over the place, and quietly said, 'Enough.'

In the heartbeat of silence, before he kicked up a ruckus again, I very calmly told his parents and ayah to please go home and asked the production team to escort them out. They were flabbergasted and started arguing about who was going to handle their impossible child. I replied that I would do the needful, or else we would have to cancel his contract and send him home. His parents and ayah left reluctantly, all the while casting fearful looks over their shoulders. By this time, the little monster had taken cover under the bed. Everyone traipsed out, including Mubi, as they knew this was the icy calm before a storm.

Now there was just the kid and me in the room, and I sat down in a friendly manner next to him, while smiling wolfishly. He wasn't fooled one bit and watched me warily out of the corner of his eye. I tried to explain to him rationally that if he continued behaving in this unreasonable manner, we would have to cancel the shoot; I would lose a lot of money and it would destroy my shaky future. He didn't say anything. Then I proceeded to tell him how I did not want to cancel the shoot and lose lots of money, but, on the other hand, I was dying to cancel the shoot so that I would be free to punish him in whatever way I wanted since there was nobody to stop me. He observed me like a chicken watching a python. I smiled and told him very nicely that everything now depended on him. Either he continued with the shoot or, better still, if he was not going to cooperate, I would be more than thrilled to cancel the shoot and deal with him!

You know, I have always believed that we underestimate kids—we think they don't understand what we're saying, but oh, they do! And know very well when they have pushed the limits of manipulation too far. He stared at me for a long time while I smiled at him, savouring the idea of spanking his cherubic little dimpled bottom. He knew I meant it, so with a sigh, he nodded his head and said he would do the shoot without any histrionics.

With a reluctant and disappointed look, I called for the shoot to be resumed and it went off smooth as butter. Not a cheep out of him—he was good as gold. Mubi asked me many times what had transpired behind the closed doors, but I never told anybody. Anyway, here it is, in case anybody remembers or is interested. Jugal Hansraj was then offered Shekhar Kapur's first film, *Masoom*, based on his performance in the Britannia Marie ad film. I wonder how Shekhar managed to handle him for the entire duration of a feature film. That deserves an interview of its own. Or perhaps, by that time, young Jugal, clever as he was, had figured out when to avoid taking pangas! Twenty years later, I had to deal with my impish three-year-old son Anhjin, cast in a Britannia campaign. But, by then, I was well versed in the art of dealing with bratty kids.

Air India and Britannia Marie had truly launched both Genesis and my career as an ad film director. The grapevine was agog and hungry, so it wasn't long before I was summoned to K. Kurien's office in Radeus. He immediately came to the point and, with a scowl, said, 'I believe you have been moonlighting.' I shifted weight from foot to foot and mumbled, 'Yes, sir! As there is not enough work in Radeus, I thought I should get some experience.' (What a lame one!) 'Harrumph,' he snorted before saying, 'Young man, you have a decision to make. Either you work here, with us, or you can freelance. You cannot do both.'

It was Hobson's choice, and I just took the bit in my mouth and said, 'Thank you for everything, sir, but I think I will quit.' I blurted it out before the insecurities of being on my own overtook my brain and I chickened out. So now, there I was—one-third partner in Genesis and scared shitless as to where my meals or rent would come from.

Many people have asked me since about how much planning it took to leave a secure job and freelance, and I keep telling them that, in truth, there was no planning whatsoever! One day, I had a job and the next day, I had a share in a company with an investment of Rs 250 of my hard-earned salary—no office, no phone and no regular postal address. When the three of us talked to Shyam babu, he guffawed loudly and said he had been wondering how long it would take for me to get sacked from Radeus for moonlighting.

He gave us his blessings and told us one thing: once a slave, always a slave. So whenever he needed any or all of us, we would have to drop everything and come running. And it holds true even today. We moved our office to Mandeep's digs in a large paying guest (PG) accommodation in Nepean Sea Road and even had an editing flatbed (editing table) with our trusty editor, Ramnik Patel. We got really lucky. We never had to chase work and we were always afloat financially. And we never did change our logo as we jumped headlong into the topsy-turvy world of advertising. It remains the same to date!

23

Khatmal Niwas

As a young bachelor in Bombay with very little extra cash, you are always on the lookout for a cheap place to stay and have to change locations quite frequently. I got to see a lot of the seedier parts of South Bombay and Colaba; I stayed for varying lengths of time at places like Khatmal Niwas and spent some really desperate spells in PGs in Colaba. In one, I had to share a toilet with a family of six; I left in a hurry when, one fine morning, I went to the loo and sitting on the commode, claiming its right to territory, was a large cockroach, glowering at me from its perch with its antennae feeling the air for fear or aggression—the two strong emotions that large cockroaches elicit *from* most people!

After my initial shock and disgust, I loosened my footwear and launched it at the offending creature, only to see it scurrying off into a crevice in the bathroom tiles; my slipper, thrown with venom and speed, ricocheted off the edge of the pot, careened off the cover and dropped into the bowels of the pot. It lay there on its back, floating gently in a turbid pool of filthy water. Shit, shit and shit again! I gingerly fished out my precious footwear, washed it in the basin and performed, hovering six inches above the commode so as to not touch it with any part of my anatomy—shit again.

I got the hell out of there and luckily found a place at Kemps Corner, with threadbare furnishing, opposite Allah Beli, a restaurant of dubious antecedents. The apartment belonged to the famous Alkazi theatre family. Ebrahim Alkazi was the head of the National Institute of Drama (NID), Delhi. The flat had been given to Suraj Rai, a prominent ad filmmaker. It had only one iron cot, which he immediately occupied, and housed two other lukkhas, who were both struggling filmmakers. Robin Dharmaraj slept on a mattress on the floor, while I found a whole lot of empty film cans that I stacked five deep to form four posts and balanced some wooden planks crisscrossed over the cans to form my bed. Robin was popularly known as 'ek gol, ek lamba', because he wore a pair of spectacles that had one circular lens and one rectangular lens (not what you all thought). We had some interesting encounters with the neighbours, especially the katkewali bai as Robin usually slept in the buff and would open the door clad in a loosely flung bedsheet. This meant that she refused to come to our flat and we had to cart the garbage down to the dump.

Finally, I got a really lucky break, as a family living in a posh flat on Marine Drive had a two-year posting abroad and needed a caretaker for the flat. Their neighbour, a lovely Gujarati lady who was a friend of the family's, recommended my name. I was shown this three-bedroom apartment on the third floor of a building called Chateau Marine. The family had locked two of the bedrooms and I was presented with one bedroom, a small sitting room and a kitchen with a servants' quarter attached.

For me, it was a godsend—I did not have to pay rent, only the electricity and water bills! Everything was perfect, except the fact that occupying the servants' room was a seventy-year-old family retainer, whom everyone called Bai. She had looked after two generations of the family. She was like their kith and kin. The short-sighted, squint-eyed, suspicious and severe lady was there to protect the place. She resembled a small and shrivelled, but fierce, female warrior in a nine-yard sari. She followed me around the house like a bloodhound and watched everything I did with a cataract-shadowed beady eye—rather like a ferret. It took a month of great patience for me to convince Bai that I wasn't going to sell the furniture or the premises!

Since a whole stream of friends would pour into the house, Bai would park herself at the door, leaning at the jamb and would scrutinize the proceedings. She was extremely inquisitive and rather irritating. She acted as though she owned the property, while my friends and I were mere interlopers. One day, I got a call from my sister in Austria, who said her best friend's sister had just got a job as an air hostess with Air India and had to come to Bombay for training. Could she crash at my place since she had no other accommodation?

Why me? I thought angrily. I had to slum it too, so why not her? Anyway, the icing on the imaginary cake was that she might bring back lots of imported goodies when she started flying. But, first, to cross the beady-eyed Bai. I decided not to inform her and carried on, as if it were completely normal to have a young air hostess crash at your place.

Suman moved in, looking around and crinkling her pert little nose in mild disapproval. Little did she know about slumming it out in Bombay. She was very pretty, with a very Indian face—large dark eyes, sharp nose and a long neck. She was neatly put together at five foot, three inches. But her feet were wrong for her—in retrospect, I should've heeded my instinct! We all live and learn; or at least some of us do. From a very wary and stilted beginning, we sort of drifted into a relationship, which became very intense very quickly—watched, of course, by a very disapproving Bai.

The remarkable thing about Bai was that she had her own take on life. She was seventy years old and, having been widowed at sixteen, she had spent her life in the service of my landlords, the Ghatges, looking after two generations of children whom she considered her own. Once Bai got over her initial inhibitions, she became very fond of me. I nursed her through a serious illness, even cooked and fed her when she was too weak to get up. I was also petrified of her dying on me. Meanwhile, Bai tried to wrap her head around the fact that

Suman would go off on her flights, for a week at a time, and come back jet-lagged and crotchety. Being very protective of me, one day, she confronted Suman and asked her in her own blunt, forthright manner what her long-term plans were. Was she going to stay the distance or was this just a pit stop for her?

They got talking and Suman explained the job of an air hostess—in those days, it was highly coveted because of the opportunity one had to travel the world while being paid handsomely. She also explained the rules that the airlines followed back then. Once you got married, you would have to resign from flying. Bai digested this news slowly, mulled over it and pottered off. The next time Suman was preparing for a flight, Bai gave her an amazing speech. She was completely uneducated in the formal sense, but a great observer of life around her. Bai's logic went far beyond accepted ritual and behaviour.

However protective and concerned she was of my interests, she told Suman, 'Never give up your job for marriage. It is the only independence and respect that a woman gets because of her financial independence. Regardless of how educated a woman might be, marriage involves sacrifice, the suppression of one's dreams and bondage into a patriarchal system. Giving up financial independence is completely unacceptable!' Suman was a bit stunned by this observation from a wise village woman who had watched the world from her porch through rheumy eyes.

By this time, unfortunately, both Suman and I had started finding fault lines in our relationship. When she returned home from a long flight, she was really strung out and jet-lagged; anything and everything would set her off. I didn't help much, although I tiptoed around her. She resented the fact that my work always took precedence over her. And, over a period of time, our relationship became cumulatively toxic—anything could set off a bitter argument and even send us into a deep, brooding depression. Both being relatively sensitive to each other's moods, even the smallest hint of anything untoward would spark an acrimonious, bitter, long and drawn-out verbal confrontation, with words forming missiles of extreme hurt and exploding over long-term open wounds. We were both at our wits' end as to how we could resolve this seemingly insurmountable chasm. And yet, we loved each other hopelessly!

In the meantime, my mother decided to sell our house in Defence Colony and rent a place instead. She wanted to divide the money between my sister and me, leaving a small corpus for her to put in a fixed deposit to tide her over as well. I found myself a one-bedroom flat on Nepean Sea Road, a really fancy address, in a building called Om Dariya Mahal, which seemed like an afterthought and was probably illegal, though regularized. This was huge! I finally had my own digs in Bombay; no nosy landlord, no sharing the loo with joint families and cockroaches—the lord and master of all I surveyed. I was doing cartwheels! For a while, anyway.

Suman and I moved into a bare flat with no furniture, no kitchen utensils and no bed. There were only fans and an old-fashioned geyser in the toilet. Hot water in the shower, what a luxury! We got down to trying to make the flat liveable in the cheapest and most innovative way possible. We procured mango-packing crates made of jungle wood from Crawford Market and, by throwing some cushions donated by friends on them, we turned them into chairs. The dining table—the only table in the house—was a long sheet of glass, which we found lying in the building's front yard, propped up on a corrugated cardboard packing case. The bed was merely a large mattress on the floor. For guests, there was a moth-eaten single mattress in the living room.

We lived together for a year and fought bitterly in every possible public location. Our capacity to fight till exhaustion, make up, recover and fight again was spectacular. It felt like my life had split in two. When Suman was in town, between flights, I felt withdrawn, distressed, antisocial and wary. Even if I as much as looked at another woman, Suman would pick up on it and our conversation would quickly become unreasonable. When she did go off on a trip, my sense of relief and freedom led to a pretty wild kind of behaviour. I can't even lay the blame on her because I was equally complicit.

We were both committed to destroying each other and there was no escape, as the relationship was built on love and guilt, and had survived five years of pressure-cooker intensity. My go-to song for the entire period was 'The End' by The Doors, in which Jim Morrison croons, 'This is the end, my only friend'—I just couldn't get it out of my head! I still managed to balance my work with this relationship, despite the desperation of those years. One day, while Suman was out on a flight, I woke up from a terrifying nightmare where, in a cataclysmic war, Suman and I had destroyed each other. Perhaps in the hopes of finding some relief from a never-ending spiral of cumulative bitterness and desolation!

I finally decided to end it one way or another. When she returned, I told her I was leaving and that she could keep the flat. She refused. Now the key to my imagined guilt was her accepting the flat, because, to me, when a destructive relationship has to end, the aftermath for the woman to heal properly is the capacity for her to shut out the world and grieve in privacy. Having her own space would make that possible, I thought, especially in an overcrowded place like Bombay.

I knew that she was a desperately private person, and when hurting and devastated would need the privacy of a house, not a PG. It was of paramount importance to me to have her accept the flat, and set me and my conscience free. It took endless days and nights to convince her that there was no going back. Only then did she relent and give in to my decision—to my tremendous relief (and my mother's dismay, as she had gone to great lengths to personally supervise our Defence Colony bungalow's construction whose sale aided me in buying the Nepean Sea Road flat). I walked away with a small suitcase and my prized riding boots. It took us both a long time to recover, but I doubt we ever fully did. She eventually chucked her job and joined an ashram as a sanyasi!

24

'General Bundelino of the People's
Republic of Marijuano'

In between leaping out of balconies and suchlike, the company Genesis was rocking. Soon, we had managed to rent an office in a large dilapidated building called Navjivan Society behind Bombay Central railway station. We finally had our very own phone line, too. The first time the phone rang, we all jumped up in surprise. It had a loud, raucous sound, and we picked up the phone to find an excited Mubi Ismail on the other end, telling us that she had an exciting script in hand for a boot polish.

We immediately headed off to have a preliminary meeting with Mubi and her team. They shared a cute, simple script in which the story is about two characters wooing the same girl, one character is wearing shiny shoes, and the other character has dirty shoes. Many doors opened for Mr Shiny Shoes, and many were shut firmly in the face of Mr Dirty Shoes, who is basically given a hard time and eventually loses the girl. All this had to be shot to a line conjured up by none other than *the* Alyque Padamsee (*god* himself), and it went like this, 'Something special is coming your way! Did you Cherry

Blossom your shoes today?' Though it's a catchy line, I felt it was a tad too long.

In the meantime, the Lintas language department was in a bit of a furore over the punchline. It took us a while to figure out what had caused the commotion. It seemed the client was insisting, and rightly so, that they wanted a Hindi translation of God's line, which they loved! And the head of Hindi copy, a gentle and hugely talented soul, called Mr Balwant Tandon, was refusing to translate the line verbatim as he claimed it was not translatable. Having taken the bit between their teeth, the account executives insisted that God didn't want a single word of his copy changed or mutilated! Usually, a very reasonable and cooperative gent, Tandon Sahib, had suddenly dug his heels in over this and refused to translate the impossible line. He became sullen and truculent, much to the surprise of the servicing crowd. The servicing suits were trying to ride roughshod over the language department. A placatory Mubi had understood the reason behind Tandon Sahib's reluctance. She knew that the line could not be translated verbatim to any proper acceptable standard in Hindi. Finally, the diminutive Mr Tandon got up and left in a huff and took his home phone off the hook, much to the chagrin and annoyance of the servicing suits as God himself was riding their backs for a translation.

A week had elapsed with no sign of the translation or Mr Tandon, who was still sitting and sulking at home. By now, we had realized that Tandon Sahib was no accidental Hindi writer but a maestro in his own right. He had written poetry and lyrics for many Hindi movies before retiring to what he thought was a cushy mindless job in a top advertising agency. So, he had decided enough was enough, and he did not want to work for English *falooting* and dreaming popinjays, for love or money, and had gone incommunicado! Meanwhile, the Calcutta-based clients were getting frantic as the upcoming Pujo festival was the most crucial season for their product's sales. They were good boxwala Bongs (Bengalis) who hadn't lost touch with their vernacular side and were not embarrassed by it, unlike their counterparts in Bombay, who considered the vernacular as downmarket! In the middle of this ego tussle was a defiant Mr Tandon. He had barricaded himself at home and was immune to all the pleading and threats of a desperate servicing team that needed to answer to God himself.

The servicing team prostrated themselves before Tandon Sahib's door. They used the classic Hindi movie line (probably written by Tandon Sahib), 'Hamari naukri ka sawaal hai, sir, humare pet par laat mat maro!' So, a reluctant Mr Tandon let them in and gave them a piece of paper torn from his notebook. In it he had handwritten the legend: 'Chalte chalte, kismat chamke!' Wow, we were all gobsmacked at the simplicity and genius of the line. Even God was silent in his acknowledgement. And now came the task of actually translating this on to celluloid. We took a page from the conception of the legend, and realizing that less is more, we suggested that the film be shot with extreme close-ups taken below the knees and focusing on the feet, as the centre of attention was the shoes.

At first, there was stony silence from the creative group. Then, Mubi, pre-empting the beginnings of a fatal fallout, quickly jumped into the breach and said, 'Fascinating idea! Let's break it down for the flow!' So, we did precisely that and realized that to communicate the competition between Twinkle Toes and Sloppy Joe (the two characters) we would need dancers who were adept at body language as a discipline. We found Mr Sam Aaron, a brilliant sixty-year-old Western dance teacher, who ran a Western tap dance school in Colaba. We got him to play Twinkle Toes and trained our go-to actor, Dalip Tahil, to play a bumbling Sloppy Joe!

The entire film was planned in movement, with long tracking shots of Twinkle Toes and Sloppy Joe, dancing their way to glory. The much-lusted-after damsel not only had to be coy and flirtatious, but she also needed to have her beautiful feet clad in a pair of strappy red stilettos. I have always realized when there is a need to be visually classy, and if there is even the slightest doubt, always go for stilettos, as they never fail to deliver posture, elegance and style! So, we cast the delicious Monica Dutta as the prize for polishing your shoes (as beautiful as she was, you didn't get to see her face in the ad). Though, her feet were perfect. Everything was working like a bomb, except that we needed Twinkle Toes to gleam and wink and didn't want to do special effects during post-production as the quality was abysmal and rudimentary. However, it had to be filmed in camera. Back to the drawing board, and I dug deep into my military school days of spit and polish and polished the toe caps of Twinkle Toes' shoes to a high gloss, but no cigar!

That's when the childlike curiosity and innovation of a seventy-year-old cameraman, namely Kamath mama, came into play, and he took the problem home. The next day, he went to the office, put a pair of black formal shoes on the table, focused the camera with a star filter over the lens, and asked me to look through the eyepiece. I peeped through it and found nothing out of the ordinary in the frame except just the clean, shining shoes, so I looked at him quizzically and asked, 'What?' He grinned impishly, adjusted the light, and asked me to look again. As I glanced through the eyepiece, he twisted the star filter from the twelve o'clock position to the three o'clock position. Within a split second, the toes of the shoes winked at me and went back to being a pair of ordinary gleaming shoes.

Kamath mama had become a miracle man, and I couldn't for the love of me figure out what he had done, even after looking at the shoes closely. Then, with a chuckle, he explained that he had taken a small shiny orb from the decorations of a Christmas tree, and after smashing it to pieces, he had taken a sliver of glass and stuck it on the tips of the pair of shoes, with a bit of saliva. It immediately became invisible to the naked eye, but as he adjusted a top light on the shoes, they flashed a naughty wink that then subsided. So, with that, we had our Twinkle Toes and his twinkling shoes! The film was such fun in the making, as everybody got into the act to innovate and polish the narrative: cast, crew, agency, et al. All thanks to the brilliance of a seventy-year-old childlike cameraman with a mischievous sense of humour.

The line 'Chalte chalte, kismat chamke' epitomizes the spirit of Cherry Blossom, as never before, and is remembered even today by professionals and consumers alike! As students of cinema, we learnt from that one shining example, set by a diminutive writer, Tandon Sir, that you never need to be literal in your translation of an idea from English to the vernacular. Instead, you have to find that magical essence in the communication and write it in the rhythm and cadence

of the language itself. Thank you, Tandon Sir, for holding your ground
and teaching us the basics of rhythm and poetry!

———

Television had just been introduced in black and white to the sweating
millions on the subcontinent. The penetration of television sets
was concentrated mainly in the metros, with Doordarshan (DD)
monopolizing the content. Even so, a huge number of people had
started regularly tuning in to watch shows on their television sets.
If a household proudly owned a television by chance, their home
would inadvertently become a mini movie hall, with neighbours,
reacquainted relatives and casual friends, all crowding in on Sundays
when the prime-time serial *Mahabharat* was being telecast. '*Main
samay hoon ...*' the familiar narrative voice of the show's sūtra-dhāra
would begin.

By and large, the advertising industry could see the writing on the
wall but hadn't made an effort to read it just yet. Among one of the first
agencies that woke up to smell the coffee was Rediffusion, led by the
amazing Arun Nanda, who, as a gold medallist from IIM Ahmedabad,
was furiously headhunted by every multinational worth their salt. He
chose advertising as his first choice and joined Kercy Katrak's MCM
to grapple with the hands-on hurly-burly and hustle of advertising. He
quickly learnt that the truth lay at the heart of the 'sizzle'. A client's
trust is hard-won and can only be earned after a lot of heartburn by
communicating with honesty and transparency.

So, he started his own company called Rediffusion, which made
waves from day one, mainly because their creative team was outstanding
and the management, led by Arun Nanda, backed them one hundred
per cent. Arun Nanda was a born entrepreneur and risk-taker once
he was thoroughly convinced by a creative idea pitched to him. If the
client wasn't convinced even after ten or fifteen repeated attempts, he
would put his money where his mouth was and back the campaign to
the hilt, much to the dismay of the waffling, difficult client. When the
client went so far as to dare to ask for options, regardless of how much

billing was involved, Arun would quietly get up and walk away, saying, 'We don't do options!' Rediffusion had one such difficult client called Jenson and Nicholson, for whom they had done a fabulous print and outdoor campaign with the tagline—'Whenever you see colour, think of us.'

Now Arun Nanda had proposed to his client, Arun Nehru, to try the fledgling TV medium for the paint campaign. To which, Mr Arun Nehru had guffawed and said, 'How are you going to sell colour in black and white?' In turn, Arun Nanda had taken it up as a challenge after returning from the Delhi meeting. He gathered the faithful around and briefed the creative team led by the redoubtable Kamlesh Pandey, known in advertising lore as one of the pioneers of bilingualism in advertising. He could dream in two languages fluently: English and Hindi. This quality set him apart from the rest of his tribe of creative people who mainly dreamt and wrote in English, only for it to be awkwardly translated into the vernacular later. Kamlesh Pandey had the unique ability to write original ideas in both languages following the same brief and concept. So now Kamlesh and his team had to come up with an answer to the million-dollar question—how do you sell colour in black and white?

Kamlesh called me in to be a part of the project. We managed to list out the various avatars of its attributes.

1. It was durable and long-lasting.
2. Anyone could clean dirt off the surface of the coat of paint easily by wiping it.
3. You could choose from a hundred and twenty shades.

Kamlesh came up with a brilliant idea. Instead of cramming all three attributes into a single ad film, we would do three individual films for each one of them with a sign-off line, saying, 'Also available in a hundred and twenty shades from Jenson and Nicholson.'

In a first-of-its-kind communication, he had proposed three different concepts in these separate ads when the whole world was trying to cram all claims into a single overburdened ad to save costs for the client. The challenge was to simplify the execution into three hard-hitting but still entertaining 30 seconders to grab the consumer's attention. In his typical understated manner, Kamlesh rolled off six excellent scripts for the client, of which the client could choose three ideas. He put them past Arun Nanda, who immediately realized that the concepts were so original and tongue-in-cheek that there was a great possibility of the client rejecting them because of their uniqueness. Most clients are very comfortable with a mediocre tried-and-tested method as it is familiar. They become uptight and risk-averse if you give them something that is way out of their comfort zone. So, all of us got into a huddle to figure out how to present each script idea as simply and clearly as it was when conceived.

We realized that the best way to present the script was to shoot the scratch films and then show them to the client. But how? Forget digital photography; even handycams hadn't entered the market still and whatever was available had terrible quality. Shooting the scratches on a film roll was out of the question as the whole exercise was too expensive and time-consuming, and we had neither the time nor the money. Then I had a lucky brainwave: Sophia College's media department had just been gifted a three-camera studio setup, and I had been invited to come and check it out. So, I hared off to meet the nuns in charge of the studio and found the setup to be exceptionally professional. The cameras were mounted on tripods, wheels and all, and the college had an audio recording studio to boot.

I looked suitably impressed, and with great gravitas, told the nuns that we had a project to shoot some scratch films and would test out their equipment, and as a bonus, we would allow their media students to attend the shoot and help in the production as a part of their course. The nuns were delighted, and we got our studio setup for free, so next, we had to plan out simple sets and lighting for the scratches. I managed to coopt an assistant cameraperson to help us for a pittance as he was curious about the studio cameras made by Sony. Finally, we were ready to roll. Now, all we needed was a cast. We had a burglar who climbs into a house from a window and leaves his fingerprints on the windowsill, panics, takes out a handkerchief and rubs off the incriminating prints easily, looks into the camera, and says, 'Thank god, it's Robbialac.' The lights come on, and he is nabbed. The voice-over (VO) states: '120 shades of Robbialac Emulsion Paint', and the logo of Jenson and Nicholson flashes on the screen.

The second film shows a husband returning home late after a night out with the boys. He has forgotten to tell his wife he would be late, and she has cooked an elaborate meal for him. He sneaks into a darkened flat with his shoes in his hand, thinking he will get away with it. The lights come on, and an irate wife starts throwing the dinner at him, plates and all, and he ducks some of them, apologizing furiously while the dishes crash into the wall behind him. In the concluding shot, she tells him to clean the walls. He does so quite easily, looks into the camera sheepishly, and says, 'Thank god, it's Robbialac.' Cut to the packshot and legend: '120 shades of above Robbialac Emulsion Paint' with the Jenson and Nicholson logo.

The third script was about a husband and wife in a maternity hospital. She is visibly pregnant, and they are arguing about the colour of the nursery walls. 'Pink,' says the wife. 'Blue,' the husband retorts. A nurse comes out and leads the wife away. As a parting shot, she says, 'Pink if it's a girl and blue for a boy.' The husband is sitting and waiting at the reception with an ashtray overflowing with half-smoked cigarette stubs denoting the passage of time when the nurse comes out and says, 'Congratulations!' The husband interjects, 'Pink or blue? I mean, is it a girl or a boy?' The nurse smiles and replies, 'Twins, a girl and a boy!' A funny expression crosses the husband's face as if he doesn't know whether to laugh or cry. The VO cuts in, 'Pink, blue, and 120 shades of Robbialac Emulsion from Jenson and Nicholson.'

The fourth script was about a Banana Republic dictator on a podium in a military uniform. Having won a fixed election, a super introduces him as 'General Bundelino of People's Republic of Marijuano'. This was purely an in-house joke, and we were sure somebody would catch it and make us change it. Fortunately, nobody noticed it, and so it remained. His speech was very telling. 'The paint on the walls of my country has lasted longer than the last regime! It was Robbialac Emulsion Paint! And I promise you a government that will last at least as long as Robbialac.' He fires a shot in the air with his pistol to establish his authority. Then, he gives a Hitler-like salute to resounding cheers and the legend: 'Long Lasting Robbialac Emulsion Paint form Jenson and Nicholson'.

The last film starts with a son lighting an agarbatti in front of his deceased father's photograph on the wall. The father suddenly comes alive and calls out to his surprised progeny. 'Hold it, son, I have been dead for five years, and nobody has bothered to change the paint on the walls around me!' The son looks a little taken aback and replies, 'But, Dad, the paint looks so fresh and newly painted even after five years!' The father looks around and agrees, 'It must be Robbialac!' The son, now satisfied, says, 'You are dead, right, Dad?' And the father goes back to being dead. We end with the legend: 'Robbialac Emulsion Paint from Jenson and Nicholson'.

We were casting the scratches when we decided to use the same actor in all the films as the main lead character and only change the supporting cast. So, we did precisely that. We cast Dalip Tahil as the burglar, the late-latif husband, the slightly balding general and the husband-cum-expectant father. We changed the actors only in the sequence with the father and son duo. It featured Kulbhushan Kharbanda as the father. We shot the scratches at Sophia College's studio, much to the delight of the nuns and students who were helping out. Kamlesh Pandey was there to make the relevant changes, just in case any of the scripts were not panning out as planned!

All went well, and the scratches turned out to be good! We turned the cameras to the black-and-white mode to see the contrast and check the other parameters. The scratches turned out to be fabulous. By the time we edited and got the scratches ready for Arun Nanda's viewing, we were running out of time. So, Mr Nanda, who loved the scratches, decided that he would make *all* the films in his own unyielding and uncompromising way. He would try and find the budget to do so, and because he believed in the work so much, we could go straight into the shoot, much to the dismay of our aforementioned difficult client.

Within two days, we shot all six commercials in a studio with basic sets for each scenario. They were dialogue-heavy and featured set pieces, which was very unusual as advertising was sworn to jingles at that time (when in doubt, don't say it, sing it was the mantra on everyone's lips). Finally, we just about made the deadline and skidded them into the portals of Doordarshan, 24 hours before the telecast day! Arun Nanda swore by the uniqueness and the originality of the commercials, though secretly, I have always thought the scratch films were much better as they were spontaneous, flexible, and the actors were in the zone.

When we went into the shoot, we already had a working format, so a lot of the spontaneity had evaporated. But now that we had access to both exercises, we could compare the two, and I favoured the ones where we had fun and experimented with form and narrative! Soon, we had a worried, angst-ridden client on our hands, who kept asking Arun when he would see the films for his approval. I will never forget Arun Nanda's reply to Arun Nehru. He promised him that he would see all the ads at 6 p.m. the next day! In a state of great agitation, Arun Nehru did a double-take and then exclaimed: wasn't that the time we had booked the slots on DD? So, Mr Nanda, completely straight-faced, told Mr Nehru that he was right about the telecast time of the film and could watch them from the comfort of his home on his very own TV set.

There was dead silence for a few heartbeats, and then Mr Nehru came back and, with great seriousness, said, 'Suppose I don't like them!' Equally seriously, two heartbeats later, Mr Nanda replied, 'Then don't pay for them!' End of conversation. Now that's a true legend! Right on cue, the following evening, the ad films burst out on the small black-and-white television screens and took everyone by surprise. Mr Arun Nehru loved them, as did the audience. Even the advertising fraternity fell in love with them, and the TV campaign for Jenson and Nicholson won most of the ad club awards that year.

25

Khatak!

One day, we were asked to meet the creative team of a medium-sized boutique agency called Sista's—named after its founder, Bobby Sista, a very respected, old-school advertising professional and a thorough gentleman, rare even in those days. So off we went to Worli, where they had an office in Poonam Chambers. We were introduced to their young and enthusiastic team headed by an exceptional creative director, Jean Durante. Jean was a Goan lady, who had settled down in Bombay. Her delicate, bird-like physicality belied a tough, determined and, sometimes obstinate, professional core. Nevertheless, she managed to bully even the most hard-boiled creative professionals into going way beyond their beliefs and known capabilities. Jean was very 'propah' and initially a bit formal until she understood how much value we could add to an idea.

Once she realized that a director, photographer or producer took ownership of her ideas, she would relax and allow you however long a rope you needed to take the idea to its limit as long as it was within the budget. And yes, when she found that the director was exceeding the limits and turning from the sublime to the ridiculous, she would gently but firmly dig her heels in and refuse to budge. We, at Genesis, loved

Jean as we realized very early on in our long-standing relationship that for her the end product was everything and she rose above everybody's egos—including her own—to achieve that.

She used every trick in the book to ensure you never deviated from delivering a quality product based on a solid and straightforward idea. Bobby Sista and his wife, Sheila, knew how important a person like Jean Durante was to an advertising agency, and were hugely protective of her; although it was not like she needed anyone's protection. She was a tough cookie on the outside with a soft marshmallow coating on the inside. We, at Genesis, were, of course, the 'Bad Boys of Advertising'. We were bold, in your face and irreverent; we didn't care for all the rules and niceties of the 1980s. Initially, quite a few suits from Sista's hovered around protectively in case we, or rather I, became obnoxious and behaved inappropriately with the gentle and oh-so-propah Miss Durante. Little did they know that we would get along like a house on fire from day one.

On that particular day, Jean and her team pulled out a small plastic use-and-throw camera from a cardboard box labelled 'Hot Shot'. We were briefed about the camera as a convenient, no fuss, point-and-shoot camera, which took 35 mm film in colour. So anybody, anytime, anywhere could point and shoot with it. It even had a built-in flash. I fiddled around with the camera and found it easy to use, but it had one huge flaw that nobody had noticed. I aimed the camera at Jean, who hated being photographed, and immediately covered her face. I pressed the button and it went 'khichik' very silently. The button didn't make a sound. The shutter was inaudible, except for an unsatisfactory 'khichik'. So I tried again and again. Khichik! Khichik! Khichik! No joy.

I looked at Jean, slightly disappointed. She had stopped mid-sentence as I pointed the damn thing at her, and she looked at me quizzically now. What was I trying to spell out? 'It's a bit of a flop,' I told her. She immediately flew to its defence, and listed all its conveniences and features. I cut in rudely, 'It's got no *d-u-mm*! You know, guts.' She looked at me like I had lost it. 'Nonsense,' she exclaimed. 'It's perfect, and it will be a hit.' I remembered the Rolling Stones who sang, 'I can't get no satisfaction …'

Jean disagreed violently—that is, the minuscule amount of violence she was capable of. I told her, 'Why can't they put a "khatak" sound in the camera's shutter? Then at least people would bask in the momentousness of the occasion. That's just not happening with this silent movie sound right now.'

Everybody stared at me like I was playing the looney tunes. So, I demonstrated. 'See,' I said. 'First, try taking a photograph with the present camera. "Khichik!" "Khichik!" "Khichik!" it goes. Now suppose it went "khatak"?'

I looked around. 'Every photograph comes with a sense of achievement.' They all stared at me, including Jean, who found it all very funny and desperately tried to keep a straight face.

Feeling inspired, I told everyone to say 'Khatak!' when they used the point-and-shoot camera. 'It will work because, in their mind's eye, they will feel the thump of a satisfying "Khatak".' QED. Jean stared at me for a couple of nanoseconds and said, 'Fine, that is how we will shoot it.'

And the rest is history as Hot Shot became one of the most successful product launches of its time. People started saying 'Khatak!' while taking photographs to the extent that some thought that the product was named Khatak!

The campaign had many fifteen-second teasers, where the most unlikely people were effortlessly pointing and shooting, and then looking into the camera and saying, 'Hot Shot: Point and shoot. Khatak!' The master film had six-year-old Anjori Alagh, Sunil and Maya Alagh's daughter, pretending to be a model and posing for a calendar shoot with an eight-year-old boy dressed up like a fashion photographer (à la Atul Kasbekar doing a photo shoot for a Kingfisher calendar). Anjori Alagh became a child star and our go-to model for kiddy shoots.

The client loved Jean for the fabulous campaign she had given them. We carried on shooting the Hot Shot films for many seasons until the advent of digital photography laid low the entire film-based industry—including the fall from grace of the biggest of them all, Kodak. They had refused to adapt quickly enough. Fading sounds of the refrain 'Jack be nimble, Jack be quick' sung to the single call of a bugle playing the strains of 'Last Post'. Fade to black.

After the success of Hot Shot, we became the go-to production house for Sista's and Jean loved the effortless way we added value to her scripts. We were having a blast because her scripts had so much potential. We did some fantastic work for Sista's—from VIP suitcases with a jingle reminiscent of Cliff Richard's 'Travellin' light'. We even did a Hindi version with the lyrics 'Ud ud jaye, dil mera ud ud jaye'.

26

Prithvi Café

I moved around and crashed at friends' places, never long enough to have outstayed my welcome, as you can feel the warmth turning into the unspoken question, 'When are you leaving?' Finally, I met an old friend, Suresh Bajaj, at Prithvi Café in Juhu and he offered his place for me to stay on Linking Road, Khar. I immediately leapt on the offer and was ready with my now tattered suitcase. What he didn't tell me was that his two-bedroom flat was a commune for the 'Children of God' movement, and his house was a crash pad for about twelve couples plus fourteen children. The flat was threadbare, as everybody carried their own sleeping bags and came to the flat only in the evening.

The only part of the flat that was elaborately appointed was the kitchen. The children were the collective responsibility of the commune and were home-tutored by someone or the other from the community. The rest of the commune left early in the morning to distribute pamphlets and other literature to collect funds and find new recruits.

The children's playroom was magnanimously given to me. It was as bare as the rest of the house, except for a bed which I immediately converted into an open cupboard and decanted all my worldly belongings on it. I was the only occupant of the room at night. What I didn't anticipate was that the children were up and about at 7 a.m., dying to reoccupy their classroom. They had been strictly instructed to avoid waking me up as I worked very hard for a living and needed my sleep.

So, they would sit on the edge of the bed and around it, staring at my sleeping body, wishing that I'd wake up soon. Invariably, when I opened my eyes, they would run through the house in a frenzy, shouting, 'Palash is awake! Palash is awake!' (That's what they called me.) They would then gleefully occupy their classroom. I stayed there for nearly a year, and they treated me with great kindness and generosity, even though I was not of their faith or in agreement with their philosophy.

While I lived in the commune in Khar, with its ever-changing inmates, I met Jennifer Kapoor, née Kendal—Shashi Kapoor's vivacious and lovely wife—at Prithvi Theatre. She had got him interested in theatre during their courtship as Jennifer, her sister, Felicity, and the rest of the Kendals were part of a travelling theatre called 'Shakespeareana'. They crisscrossed India in their pursuit of promoting Shakespeare in schools and institutions. Shashi Kapoor was so smitten by Jennifer that he happily joined them in their theatrical adventures.

Prithvi Theatre was the couple's pet project. They wanted to convert Prithviraj Kapoor's legacy—a sort of ramshackle theatre in Juhu that also housed his bungalow—into a fabulous performing arts hub that was both convenient and affordable to the growing theatre scene in Bombay. So, they funded and built Prithvi Theatre, and subsidized it with a corpus. Prithvi is an experimental theatre that seats 200 people. Every known actor worth their salt has cut their teeth there as they struggled to make a mark.

I met Jennifer Kapoor after a performance when Prithvi had just opened its doors to young enthusiasts, both on the stage and for people wanting to watch good theatre. It also housed a beautiful little art gallery, and a small tea and vada–samosa canteen. I was completely bowled over by her energy and passion for her baby, the theatre! I casually mentioned that we should do a 'Joe Allen' in the canteen space, which was essentially a counter and a garden area with nine concrete chairs and tables. She perked up and asked, 'So you've been to Joe Allen in London?'

I nodded with great enthusiasm as the American chain of theatre restaurants had really impressed me in London. It was typically American in a very British locality. Situated in a basement with sawdust floors, it had tables with checked tablecloths and a long, wooden Western saloon–type bar! And, unlike British pubs, the bottles were all in a counter behind the bar with peg measures and liquor had to be hand poured. The local pubs had the regular poison on a backet facing down with a lever—the barman could, with one hand, press a handle with the rim of a glass and a 60 ml peg would decant into the glass. This made the job of the bartender very easy as he also had to pull the English version of flat beer, called bitters, from a pressurized keg.

Joe Allen served cocktails with straight drinks, and had beer that was fizzy and not flat, with a menu that was also typically American: spare ribs, buffalo wings and some amazing salads, like blue cheese and walnut. It used to be as dead as a doornail during the performances, but the moment the plays would end, it would be packed to the gills with theatre audiences, actors, crew and the occasional gobsmacked Indian. It was, and remains, an institution.

I let my imagination run wild and explained to Jennifer how we could convert a sleepy canteen into a happening theatre experience before, after and during performances. She smiled at me indulgently and asked me where I was going to find the time. I vehemently told her that I would make time from my film-making schedule. She thought about it for a moment and, obviously my enthusiasm had got to her, said, 'Okay, your rent will be seven hundred and fifty rupees but I will take four hundred until you have found your feet.'

She showed me a garage in the old bungalow across the road that I could use as a kitchen and, before I knew it, I had to start planning a full-fledged café called Prithvi Café, which would open at 6 p.m. and close when the patrons of the theatre had dined after watching a play.

Like everything else in my life, I found myself in the thick of it before I could properly plan it. It's always mauke pe chauka. Never regret, never look back; if it interests you and you can learn something from it, go for it. The experience itself will be worth all the blood, sweat and tears. And imagine the number of lives you get to touch along the way.

I set about trying to find a compatible chef, as I considered myself a self-taught cook—partly for passion and partly for survival. I had realized that my face was not going to be my fortune and looking into the mirror with great concentration wasn't going to change my face even a fraction. I had to do something pretty spectacular for young ladies to notice me. So, cooking it was, and I was inspired by my mother, who was a phenomenal cook and ran her kitchen entirely on intuition. For me, my calling as a cook was inspired by the game that I stalked, shot and cleaned myself. I refused to let anybody else prepare the meat dishes, purely because of the enormous effort it took and the hours spent in all kinds of weather, to get within range and sight of the game—be it partridge, junglefowl or an occasional rabbit or duck which I was lucky enough to bag.

I would spend hours in the kitchen, trying to do justice to the effort put into procuring the meat. Cooking had thus become a relatively important part of my creative fantasies. And, much later, in the chequered life I have led, I could safely believe, 'Men who cook get laid far more often than men who pump iron.' Therefore, finding a compatible chef was as important as finding a compatible wife, especially when it came to running a restaurant.

I devised a test for potential continental (conti) chefs: they had to cook two seemingly simple dishes, scrambled eggs and soufflé omelette. These are some of the trickiest dishes, as the eggs cook really fast and have to be cooked on a medium-to-low flame so as not to overcook them and ruin the dish. Scrambled eggs have to be soft and melty with a hint of cheese and a dash of pepper at the end. To prep it properly, you have to add half a cup of milk to two whipped eggs, then salt it just right and throw in a generous handful of grated cheddar. Then you heat a heavy-bottomed frying pan and mix in a dollop of butter, keeping the flame on medium. Swirl the pan around to spread the butter evenly on the bottom. Add the egg mixture to the pan and swirl the pan again to spread the eggs over the entire bottom of the pan. Wait a heartbeat. Then reduce the flame to low. Run the spatula through to one end of the pan to curl the egg. Continue curling the semi-cooked eggs to one corner of the pan and keep exposing the liquid egg mixture to the heated bottom to solidify just so.

To prevent turning the eggs into a bhurji, you have to control the pan and not the flame, by constantly lifting the pan off the heat and testing the egg's softness, lightness and creaminess. A good chef always controls the pan and not the flame, regardless of what you cook in a frying pan. The eggs turn out perfect if they are light, creamy, curled and not minced, no runniness, firm but soft. Now you can garnish the eggs with whatever you choose—bacon crumble, pepper, olives. Most bad cooks don't know how to handle the pan and tend to use a high flame, since they are in a hurry.

Soufflé omelettes are also a piece of art—the trick is to cook the skin on a dancing pan until the skin is golden, firm and even, while the centre is still runny and fluffy. The art is in turning the omelette while still partially raw, without breaking it in two and serving it beautifully golden with a hint of brown—fluffy, light and perfect with a runny centre. Voila! Again, the expertise is in handling the pan and not the flame. To turn two ends of a half-cooked omelette without breaking it requires extreme skill, judgement, courage, timing and commitment. Remember, the eggs have to be whipped to a stiff foam so that the omelette is light and fluffy when decanted on to a plate.

The whole exercise takes eight minutes, including whipping the eggs into a frenzy, and, if done well, is a delight to behold. We, at Prithvi, made the best soufflé omelettes in India, by far. But, coming back to my test, all the 'conti cooks' flunked and left me in a bit of a tizzy. Then, young Jenny Pinto from the Genesis office looked at my dejected face and piped up, 'My mom is a great cook!' Yeah, yeah, we hear that all the time. 'My mommy is the best,' 'My mommy wears the pants!' I must have looked sceptical, because she invited me over for dinner the next day, and I went. Mrs Pinto knocked me over with the quality of food that she served.

She was a short lady, mother of four hungry and demanding children and one short, demanding husband (a fifth child). The whole family came pocket-sized and, boy, did they know how to eat! Mrs Pinto had a beautiful round face and she sported a huge bindi on her forehead. When she smiled, the sun would burst out of the clouds and bathe everyone in her warmth and her delicious food. She was Mangalorean and had quite a deft, but delicate, touch to her. I loved what she cooked, specifically the seafood. We got along like a house on fire. She became the actual face of Prithvi Café. And though she was shy and rarely came out of the kitchen to meet the guests, they all took the trouble to trek to the kitchen, where she held sway, and congratulated her for the amazing food she served.

We shared recipes and she immortalized my smoked leg of ham with a honey glaze. Our most popular dishes were her pomfrets stuffed with pickled prawns, her fish and crab curries and delicious cheesecakes. Her assistant, Bala, had the potential to be a great cook, and I trained him to make soufflé omelettes behind the counter on a single burner. He got it right from the word go, when all the qualified continental chefs had floundered and failed miserably. Bala perfected the art of handling the pan and turning the still-runny eggs, and, with a little practice, he turned out beautifully cooked eggs every time. Whenever he got a compliment, he would puff out his chest and start owning the space.

A large, fluffy omelette, golden brown, with coleslaw and potato wedges for six bucks was a steal anywhere in the world. One day, there was a huge rush for omelettes and Bala was getting overwhelmed. I, as his guru, stepped up to the counter, got hold of another stove and started helping him out. He looked at me gratefully and we both went at it. What took the longest time was beating the eggs to a fine, frothy foam. So, armed with a hand-operated egg beater, we went at it in a frenzy and turned out some fabulous soufflé omelettes that day.

I was temporarily distracted by a lovely-looking young lady, who seemed to be a little lost. I took my eyes off the pan for a few seconds and a small, goddamn dark-brown patch quickly spread on the omelette. It was perfect, except for the brown blemish. But because there was such a rush, I folded the patch under the omelette, so it wouldn't be visible, quickly put it on the counter and summoned the waiting customer to collect it. When I looked up from my next omelette, it had disappeared and I presumed that it had been collected and devoured by a lucky guest. I had presumed wrong, as after about ten minutes, an irate guest showed up at the counter to enquire about his omelette. I told him it had been ready ten minutes ago and had been collected. He stood his ground and insisted that he hadn't received it. I started looking for the lost omelette. It was nowhere to be seen! After about five minutes of frantic searching, Bala said, sotto voce, 'Sir, usko phenk diya.'

'What!' I exclaimed, raising my voice. 'What do you mean you chucked it? Where?' He sheepishly pointed to the waste bin and there it was—my poor omelette lying on its back, displaying the brown patch with its legs in the air, quite dead. I whirled around and, gritting my teeth, shouted at Bala, 'How dare you chuck my omelette in the bloody bin? How could you?' He looked quite chastened and said, 'Sir, hamara naam kharab ho jata.' The sheer audacity of the man! I stomped off and left the bugger to handle the rush alone. Much later, after cooling down, I realized that Bala actually owned the job and wasn't simply doing it for the sake of it. The next day, I assembled the kitchen staff and Bala, who was expecting to be dressed down or sacked in front of everyone. I grandly announced that I was promoting Bala to be the manager of the café for his courage and commitment to our uncompromising standards of quality. Years later, Bala went on to become a great chef in the Middle East.

We also served an Irish coffee with a healthy splash of brandy, and it ended up becoming the item of the year at Prithvi. People used to travel for miles to get an after-dinner Irish coffee for six or seven bucks at the café. The trick was to serve the coffee and brandy piping hot and to pour chilled cream over the back of a tablespoon so that we got two clean layers, one of dark, strong coffee topped by a layer of cold cream floating in a wine glass—for style. It is still served at Prithvi Café thirty years later and, of course, they don't give me credit for it.

Looking back, Prithvi Café was such a roller-coaster ride and the number of interesting people I met was amazing. I even managed to get a lot of work done at Genesis at this time. As everybody realized, though my timings were very unpredictable during a working day, I would be available at Prithvi Café at 6.30 p.m. sharp, come hell or high water. So, that's when they would make a beeline for the café if they wanted something urgently. They would get an Irish coffee and corner me for a quick meeting.

We had a cautionary note scrawled on the blackboard menu, which never changed for the two years we ran the café. It stated, 'The management reserves the rights to kiss all the pretty girls on the premises.' Of course, I was the management and it became a tradition for me to do the rounds, kissing all the girls, without favour or bias, on their cheek in my parrot-green tracksuit (with their consent, of course). We also had the best-looking, if not the most efficient, service in town, as all the single girls who came to the café were coopted to help me serve tables. Now, being totally unused to it, they could barely take an order accurately, let alone calculate the bill. However, they were very popular and really helped in relieving some of the pressure.

We also started a unique honour system, where we told all our clients that they would have to bill themselves by remembering what they ate and drank. We asked them to jot it down on a piece of paper and their bill would be totalled up. It was so easy to cheat us that nobody bothered and just paid what they owed. Sometimes, they were even a couple of weeks late, as they would get home, burp and remember a dish they had consumed.

One day, a very pretty young lady called Amrita came running to me in a flap, and said her table was acting funny and not paying. I went over and realized I didn't recognize any of them; it seemed they had come over on the recommendation of one of our regulars. I joked with them for a while thinking they were just fooling around and then understood that they weren't. They were actually being extremely obnoxious. I smiled my Cheshire cat smile and asked them if they had enjoyed their meal, and they nodded vigorously. I then thanked them for their presence and told them not to worry as the meal was on the house. They all looked victorious, until I cut in coldly and told them never to come back, and walked away.

Their temporary victory turned to acute chagrin as, by this time, the whole café was looking at them disapprovingly. One of them sheepishly came up to the counter and offered to pay, but I would have none of it, and I rubbed it in by ignoring him and placating the poor girl who was really upset by the behaviour of the table. We made a note of it and called whoever had recommended them the next day, and told them not to send their riff-raff friends to the café again. We never had a second bad experience. I met some incredible people in our time at Prithvi and we loved playing host to all of them.

The Kapoors adored Mrs Pinto and our food. Sanjana, Shashi Kapoor and Jennifer's daughter, even helped us serve tables occasionally. We started a system of feeding strugglers a thali for five bucks and, if they helped serve tables, the meal was on the house. At that time, I met a stunning young actress from Delhi, who had just arrived in Bombay. She looked a bit lost and was sitting at the café having tea. She flipped through our menu, and then glanced at the cautionary note about the management kissing all the pretty girls and broke into a broad smile.

She looked at me and asked whether she could choose who could kiss her. I emphatically told her no, in jest! We became very good friends and remain so till today. She was a vegetarian and decided to teach all our Malayali cooks the fine points of North Indian vegetarian cooking. Mrs Pinto and I practically adopted her. And she became a fixture at the café in the evenings, helping out with the service and whatever else was needed. We named the baingan ka bharta after her: 'Neena Gupta's Baingan ka Bharta'!

Prithvi Café quickly became a gathering spot for foodies, writers, poets, out-of-work actors, theatre folk—even Alyque Padamsee turned up one day! Our regulars were couples who met clandestinely, like Protima Bedi (Kabir Bedi's ex-wife and Pooja Bedi's mother) and her bigwig politician boyfriend, whom she was very secretive about. Then there was the Kapoor khandaan, and, of course, our angel and benefactor, Jennifer Kapoor. We created a tradition of marrying couples, who had been kicked out of their homes for wanting to marry out of caste, religion or status, on the premises.

On Mondays, the day the café was closed, we would get a magistrate to preside over the nuptials and host a small dinner for twenty people, all on the house. How many of those runaway marriages lasted? I really don't know. By this time, Genesis was doing quite well, so I did not draw a salary from Prithvi, but created a fund for my cooks who all wanted to go to the Gulf. The deal was that every time a cook borrowed money from the fund and left for the Gulf, they had to return the money in instalments until the fund was replenished; then the next cook could go. Since they all came from the same village or were related, we did not have to worry about the recoveries—the cooks left behind did all the heavy lifting to ensure the fund was replenished each time. We also voluntarily raised our rent from Rs 400 to Rs 5,000, much to the surprise and delight of Jennifer Kapoor.

Every season after the monsoon, we would open with a musical concert, a buffet dinner for the guests and well-wishers for the coming season. Mrs Pinto used to excel at it and play host with Shashi, Jennifer and Sanjana Kapoor. Shashi Kapoor would generously pay for the wine. Louis Banks often entertained us with a jazz evening. People still talk about those joyful times. Sadly, Jennifer Kapoor passed away after fighting cancer courageously for a year. And it took the heart out of the place, so we decided to hand the keys over to Kunal Kapoor, who had taken over the responsibility of running the theatre, and left heavy-hearted, but shored by some terrific memories, great friends and awesome food. All good things will come to an end, but not if you let go of them at their peak—then they remain with you forever.

Many years later, I was catching a connecting flight in Orly in France, when a little old lady came up to me and asked, 'Aren't you the gentleman in the parrot-green tracksuit who ran Prithvi Café?' When I told her I was, she beamed and said that she had eaten the best soufflé omelette in her life there! I felt so chuffed and it made my day.

27

Biting the Bullet

One day, early in the morning, just as the bachcha brigade had stared me into wakefulness at the commune, I unglued one eye open to stare in amazement at a slightly embarrassed Jean Durante picking her way delicately through the bodies in the living room. She was dressed, as always, in an immaculate, cotton organza sari—even at 7 a.m.! I leapt out of bed and shooed the bachcha party out of the room, saying, 'Gimme ten.' I sat a slightly shocked Jean on the bed, while I quickly locked myself in the bathroom to make myself presentable.

It turned out that a new client at the ad agency, Sista's, namely the Royal Enfield lot, had hit a crisis and had turned to them in a do-or-die gamble. Now, Jean knew all about the Genesis team's passion for Royal Enfield as all of us rode one. Ever the 'enthu cutlet', Jean had made her way to my abode in the children's nursery at the crack of dawn to brief me about the product and the client, and to drag me to a client meeting at 9.30 a.m. Royal Enfield had just been acquired by a young and aggressive entrepreneur, who refused to accept that he had bought a turkey on the verge of keeling over without a whimper.

You see, the 100cc invasion of the Indian two-wheeler market with the latest technology from Japan had wiped out the existing motorcycle market with the low price point and incredible fuel efficiency. All the existing brands had gone bottoms up—even Escorts, with their phenomenally successful Bobby, had switched to a 100cc Japanese collaboration with Kawasaki. Hero Honda led the pack with their brilliant campaign: 'Fill it, shut it, forget it.' Compared to all this hype, the Royal Enfield Bullet employed World War II technology, was heavy as hell and guzzled seventeen–eighteen kilometres to the litre of fuel, with oil as an extra.

But there was one thing the Bullet had that nothing could compare to: an obsolete 350cc engine that throbbed like a latent beast. Its song couldn't be compared; it was a distance marathon bike—rock solid, steady and comfortable. Most importantly, it was a man's bike, with hair on its chest. The Royal Enfield Bullet was the only Indian motorbike that a community could be built around—an exclusive club of Bullet owners, and the myths and stories surrounding it.

Enfield was also the choice of the amazing Dispatch Riders (DRs) of the Signals regiment when all else (basically communication lines) failed. It was up to the men and machines of the dispatch riders fame, who brave enemy fire, incoming artillery and impossible terrain to get the message through. The men, of course, were battle-hardened and motivated. And their choice of machine—the Bullet from Royal Enfield. Could we save the magnificent motorcycle from being relegated to the pages of history? All of us at Genesis were proud Bullet owners and were definitely not going to let the company go down without a fight. So, we all got into a huddle, including a determined Jean Durante in her crisp sari, who was an integral part of the brainstorming, though she had never ridden a bike in her life. Until I offered her the experience of riding pillion on my trusty steed, which she gamely accepted, sari and all.

We penned down a list of the most endearing parts of the Bullet. First, it had the distinctive signature sound—the dhabba dhabba dhabba heartbeat of its engine. Second, all Bullet owners were large, beefy men, who could handle its inert weight and its occasional back kick when starting. Third, the kind of instant bonding between owners at traffic lights and parking lots, to the complete exclusion of the irritating 100cc-walas, who buzz around like a cloud of flies. Fourth, the absolute pride of ownership that a Bullet owner felt, damn the fuel consumption.

'Once a Bullet, always a Bullet!' Armed with the spine of a communication idea, we set off to battle. First, we had to cast a strong policeman-type character as the main protagonist for the film, who, in his journey, would traverse long distances and terrains, meeting and greeting other Bullet owners at traffic lights, railway crossings and the like, creating a world of Royal Enfield Bullet owners. The only way into this exclusive and amazing tribe would be to own, ride and love the beast.

I recorded the unmistakable beat of the Bullet and took it to our music director, the late Nathan Sir, and briefed him about the jingle, which had to start with the throb of the bike and continue as a qawwali. The words were written by Pandit Vinod Sharmaji, who immortalized the motorbike with the words, 'Bullet meri jaan, manzilon ka nishan.' The weather had just turned from torrid and sunny to overcast when we set off for Panvel to shoot the planned sequences. Man proposes, god disposes—the skies opened up and it poured non-stop for three days.

Jean, who had insisted on attending the shoot, huddled with us in a Maruti van that had a tracking camera on its tailgate, for the better part of three days. We would leave Bombay in cloudy but relatively clear weather at 7 a.m., reach Panvel at 8.30 and the heavens would promptly open, with no let-up. So, we used to drag ourselves back to Bombay—wet, bedraggled and thwarted, but not broken—only to sally forth the next day with the same results. We took ten days to shoot a two-day film in bits and pieces.

I had long forgotten about the budget; it was imperative we create the ad the way we had dreamt of it. The final shot showed five bikes coming towards the camera with their headlights on. Once the shoot was over, we promptly collapsed in a heap without a wrap celebration. In those days, we had no rigs to mount cameras and had to innovate like crazy to get all the action—from shots of the bike from the back of the Maruti van to tying up the camera to the tail of a bike. When we edited the footage and added the music to it, the results were magical.

It captured the remarkable bonding between man and bike, and the tribe of Enfield owners. The ad film was natural, understated and relatable. Till date, I have not revisited how much the film actually cost. Today, the Enfield has a waiting line of at least six months, touchwood.

One fine day, Jean called to tell us that Sista's had also got the account for VIP's only rival brand of moulded luggage called Aristocrat. The brand was owned by an eccentric Parsi gent named Mr Engineer, who wanted to revive it and make it a contender for the throne in its category, regardless of the cost. Later, we found out that Mr Engineer wanted the campaign to get a better valuation for his company as he had received an offer from VIP to buy out Aristocrat. Smart man.

So, Jean and I started throwing around ideas that went beyond luggage advertising. Jean came up with a fabulous proposition of a tourist in Rajasthan who daydreams about the exotic past of the heritage palace, and he has a great adventure as his luggage (which has wheels!) rolls off down an ornate corridor. He follows it straight into the zenana khana, where the queens reside with their handmaidens. The queen is delighted by the vanity case and immediately starts preening, while her handmaidens open and examine the suitcase on wheels.

Our protagonist is now well entrenched in the zenana khana and is being fed grapes by the queen. Suddenly, the door flies open, and a large guard with a curly moustache and a sword enters and grabs our friend by the collar for being in a 'No Entry' zone. He is carted off kicking, biting, struggling and finds himself buried up to his neck in a walled stadium. An elephant and his mahout are about to inflict the final punishment on him and the elephant is being primed to stomp on his skull.

Our captive hero looks around frantically, sees the suitcase lying close by, covers his head with it and ducks back into the hole. *Crunch*! He wakes up in a strange place, remembers his dream and smiles in relief. He looks down and sees a clear imprint of the elephant's foot on the suitcase, dives into his pocket, pulls out a fistful of sand, and we cut to the packshot—the real hero, the luggage on wheels.

Conceptualizing the basic narrative was the easy part; the production logistics were a nightmare. To match the luggage's colour palette, we had to find a genuine palace in Rajasthan with a blue, green and red room. So, I summoned my team of trusted flunkies—the young and hungry tribe of production assistants, who had been weaned on a diet of Tennyson: 'It's not to question why, but to do and die.' They lined up and waited for the guillotine to fall. After looking at them and gauging their capacity to hang in there at any cost, I picked the young, bright-eyed Jenny Pinto. I thought she had fire in her belly as she had recently chucked up a perfectly cushy job in an ad agency and hung around my office for a whole week, waiting to meet me for a job at Genesis. Her sheer dogged determination inspired me; so I decided to test her on a real mother of a production.

My brief to Jenny was: 'Go by train to Rajasthan and find a majestic palace with a blue, green and red room. Here is some money, and don't come back till you have found it.' Off went Jenny on her Rajasthan darshan. We heard from her intermittently, from remote parts of the desert, still looking (remember, this was before Google Maps and mobile phones). One month later, when I was about to send search parties to find Jenny, she walked into the office, covered in a thin film of dust, her hair matted and her eyes bloodshot, but triumphant. She placed some photos on the table and a note that said, 'See you all in a few days. I need a bath and some sleep!' The photographs showed three rooms, bare but ornate, matching the colour palette, and the note described how to get to Bikaner and where the palace stood. Wow! Over the next few years, Jenny proved to be one of my best protégés. Tough, single-minded, intelligent and a fighter, to boot.

The palace belonged to the maharaja of Bikaner and, luckily for us, he lived most of the year in Altamount Road, Bombay. Off we went to take his permission, feeling rather nervous. He turned out to be a friendly and hospitable gentleman in his sixties, and was reputed to be one of the country's best trap and skeet shots. Though the palace was

mothballed for the summer, he said he needed only a few days for his
retainers to spruce it up for the shoot. He couldn't understand why we
wanted to shoot in Bikaner in the middle of summer and said it would
be bloody hot. But, time, tide and clients wait for no mortal man—so
summer or not, we were off to Bikaner in May.

I remember how tricky the film's casting was since we needed to
find a queen and her entourage of beauties. We got hold of a stunning
Kathak dancer from Delhi, the hugely talented and stunning Aditi
Mangaldas, who had been introduced to me by her uncle in Bombay.
She helped us cast the rest of the Kathak troupe selected from Birju
Maharaj's acolytes. Now, for the main lead, we needed a successful
Indian businessman in his thirties with a slightly bossy wife.

Inspiration struck us like lightning, and after a lot of hemming and
hawing, we broached the subject to our larger-than-life client from
Britannia, Sunil Alagh, who agreed with great alacrity. I'm sure he
thought it would be a paid holiday to Rajasthan. Ha, just you wait,
Henry Higgins, just you wait.

The entire shooting crew, with R.M. Rao at the helm, flew to Delhi
and took the one-night train to Bikaner, while the light and sound
crew travelled on land from Bombay. We had a whopping team of sixty
people from Bombay, with thirty extras from Bikaner. It was quite a
logistical feat for its time.

The shoot was a roller-coaster ride, with Sunil Alagh, Aditi and the
troupe getting along like a house on fire. We also got to see another
side of Sunil Alagh—he was funny, entertaining and thoroughly
professional. He never fussed, regardless of the logistical hardships
we were facing, and was such a sport. When we dug the pit to bury
him, he said he had only one pair of trousers that could maintain the
continuity of the film. And there was no chance of dry cleaning it for
the next shot, in which he woke up from his fantasy. So, we gently
suggested he take off his trousers and assured him that no one would
ever figure it out, and he agreed to shoot the sequence buried to his
neck in his underwear.

He thought about it for a minute, made up his mind and said,
'What the hell? Let's do it.' He stripped down to his underwear. We

dug the pit wide enough for his body to go down and wondered how we could pack it with enough sand to show that he was buried to the neck, because his hands needed to be free to grab the suitcase and cover his head. So, finally, we buried him up to his armpits, cut a piece of plywood for his head to duck into and then covered the plywood with sand right up to his body. He had enough breathing room along his lower torso that allowed him to keep himself flexible.

He could duck into his rabbit hole when the elephant (supposedly) stepped on him. We got the elephant to the hole to get him to raise a foreleg for the stomping, but he refused. Either he loved Sunil Alagh or smelled the plywood and knew it wouldn't hold his weight; so he refused to come closer than ten feet from Sunil Alagh. Shit! Murphy had struck. We wanted a composite shot of the back of Sunil Alagh's head, with the looming elephant about to step on him. But no luck.

After much coaxing by the mahout, we managed to get the elephant to the edge of the hole. Luckily, we had anticipated issues with the shot in which the foot landed on the red suitcase and we had created a dummy elephant foot for the close-up. It was hot, the elephant was about to revolt and Sunil Alagh had started complaining about streams of burning sand trickling into his fancy boxer shorts. But we managed to pull off the shot. Whew!

The films were set to the tune of Kathak bol. The girls' expressions and movements in the zenana khana were superb, and Jean soldiered through it all in her crisp kota cotton sari, slowly going limp and ragged at the edges. She was a real trooper, with her hesitant manner and nervous smile, undaunted by the enormous physical discomforts of the shoot. The film turned out to be a winner for Aristocrat luggage and it soon became the number two brand in the country. Our client, slightly pernickety and demanding, was mighty pleased with the end product and Murphy, in his cave, was happy that he had made us earn our keep!

By that time, I had moved from the commune to a barsati—a terrace room—in Trivedi Bungalow on the corner of Juhu Tara Road, which has been demolished and a high-rise has now taken its place. It was a beautiful bungalow designed by Nari Gandhi, the renowned architect. He had spent a lot of love's labour on the terrace barsati and it was truly spectacular. It also had a separate staircase of its own.

On one of my rounds of 'kissing all the pretty girls on the premises' at Prithvi Café, I came across a very attractive young woman, who actually started flirting with me. I was very enthusiastic and chatted her up, remaining on my best behaviour. One thing led to another and I invited her to my place after dinner to see my etchings. She agreed readily and I couldn't believe my luck, so I called it an early evening and took my leave from an amused Mrs Pinto. I got on to my Bullet and invited the young lady aboard. I escorted her upstairs and, while she was admiring the place, I made her a nice, sweet but stiff cocktail because as Ogden Nash said, 'Candy is dandy, but liquor is quicker!'

As we made ourselves comfortable on the terrace, she brightly asked me, 'I didn't know you painted. Where are your etchings?' You could have knocked me down with a feather; she actually thought that I had brought her up to the pad to show her some of my sketches! I gently removed the drink from her hand and told her in an upright manner, 'It's getting late, I should drop you home.' Trust her to live all the way in town on Peddar Road.

28

The Return of the Chhattisgarhis

After breaking up with Suman, it took me about a year to recover from the trauma. Every time a young lady showed any sign of possessiveness, I would instantly clam up and run for my life. That is, until I met a young lady in an advertising agency who defied the stereotypical definition of a professional in the industry. Mala was reserved, very perceptive, intelligent (not just clever) and took her time to form an opinion. She was delicately put together, belying the steel underneath. And she loved horses to boot. When I spent some time with her, it was always gentle and therapeutic. She used to look at me with great amusement and ask the most inane questions, like, 'Who are you really? Are you brash by nature or is it a mask to protect yourself?' Or she would make statements like, 'You are so different with horses as compared to humans.'

I was drawn to her wistful way of observing life and the people around her. She was very keen on chucking advertising and working with children with mental illnesses. She wanted to go to the Tavistock Institute, London, which trains psychologists to work as counsellors with disturbed kids and adults. So, I read up all about Tavistock and realized that it was very difficult to get into. I moved heaven and earth to get her an interview with them, and she came through with flying colours.

She was selected and, despite her family's reservations about her being able to hack it on her own for the first time in her life, she decided to go. I saw her off at the airport with her parents and a very disapproving young sister. For the next year, I ran up huge telephone bills trying to maintain a long-distance relationship. I thought I was doing very well—telephone bills notwithstanding—when, during one of the calls, she sounded a bit stilted and asked me to come to England for a few days. Thinking that she must be having a hard time at work and she needed me, I started shifting my schedule around and organized a cheap ticket to London.

I knew the city pretty well by now; I had spent a month with Ramesh Sippy's unit in and around the Lancaster Gate area and Pinewood Studios where the post-production on the film *Shaan* was done. I had helped them design and execute the trailer and the credits titles of the movie. Thus, I landed in England, travelling cattle class with very little money on me—in those days, we Indians were allowed only five pounds on us. I had made arrangements with an acquaintance, who had a representative in England, to transfer four hundred pounds in my name when I reached London. I had transferred the equivalent in Indian rupees to him. I arrived at Heathrow at the crack of dawn and Mala was there to receive me, much to my surprise.

She had borrowed a flat from a friend for a few days and had taken leave from Tavistock for me. I changed and freshened up, and she softly told me to sit as she had something important to tell me. Sensing something amiss, I insisted on standing and listening. She looked straight into my eyes and said, 'I can't afford to have this long-distance relationship with you; it's killing me.' I was stunned and promptly sat down. The room spun around me, but her intense gaze steadied me. A voice somehow not quite belonging to me answered her calmly, 'Oh, okay, then I will just move to London.'

'No,' she said firmly. 'I knew you would say that, but you are doing so well back home, and I don't want you to relocate and start from scratch.' I asked her what the problem was with that; I said I could hack it just to be with her. But I knew in my heart of hearts that she was right. We spent the whole night trying to come to terms with what she had said. The kind of stress that she was undergoing in the halfway home, working with mentally ill and violently inclined adults, meant that she needed a support system right there and until she had closure from our relationship, she couldn't even start looking for it. After a sleepless night of us arguing and her explaining her decision with calm finality, as dawn was breaking, I asked her, 'Why did you call me all the way to London if all you wanted was to break off the relationship?'

To this, she replied that she owed it to me and to herself to do it face to face, and be around to keep me intact and on an even keel. She hadn't wanted to give me such bad news over a telephone call. Of course, I didn't understand her good intentions then and didn't even want to. She spent the next three days just looking after me and after that, she had to rejoin the institute, leaving me a bit of a wreck. To cap it all off, the guy who was supposed to deliver the money refused to take my calls and had absconded. I used the last of my meagre funds to call India to contact the person who was supposed to have arranged the money for me in England. All to no avail. There I was, broke and heartbroken in a relatively strange city, with a return ticket that could not be rescheduled as it was a special cheap ticket that was valid for a minimum of ten days. Bloody hell!

I suddenly recalled Portobello Road and its flea market from my previous trip. Some wonderful sunny Saturdays were spent wandering down its serpentine length to the cinema at the end showing offbeat art films. I realized that I had carried five pairs of special Chhattisgarhi sandals with me to give as gifts to friends and other such deserving people in London town. Hope flared anew as I decided to find a likely corner and sell those precious Chhattisgahris to what I thought would be jostling crowds of admirers for such a unique type of footwear, fitted on location, with the look of Greek tie-up sandals—leftovers from Alexander's army.

I sat at Portobello Market, and the weather was bright and balmy, bordering on hot, and the white brigade of sun worshippers were out

Pater and Mater with Mrs Indira Gandhi.

A family portrait with mum and dad, and
my sister, Mandakini.

Me and my reluctant gurus, Shyam Benegal (L)
and K.B.K. Ghanekar affectionately known as
Kamath mama (R).

Sainik School, Kunjpura, class of '65.

A four-decade-long association between me and my director of photography, Vikas Sivaraman, which continues till today.

Me and my Tiara girl.

With god and legend Alyque Padamsee and his then wife Sharon Prabhakar.

Dumbell babysitting Arnav.

With Mohammed Khan of Enterprise Advertising fame and Shah Rukh Khan.

Shaadi? Aur tumse?'

With young Anjori Alagh.

Setting the foundation for Lacadives at the Lakshadweep Sports Institute, Kadmat Island. 1992.

The aptly named Jetty at the Edge of the Universe: our boys Varun (4), Arnav (9), Anhjin (2). This photo taken by Sheena Sippy says it all.

Our boys avidly watching a green sea turtle lay eggs over three hours, in Kadmat.

Post dive (R-L): Me, Parinita, Peter Herbst, Homi Adajania, a Bangaram guest, Mitali, Anees, Anuj, Michael, Sumer and little Arnav in the back row.

The director's POV.

With the boys and Mitali underwater.
Marsa Alam, Egypt.

Lobster whiskers!

A family that dives together stays together: (L-R) Me, Mitali, Arnav, Varun and Anhjin. Shooting for Lakshadweep Tourism on the Kadmat Island in 2021.

The new Kawasaki Bajaj RTZ 100.
The waiting is over!

Somewhere in Rajasthan for the Kawasaki Bajaj RTZ 100 film.

With the indomitable Vibha Rishi.

The Indian tigers in the savannah for a Pepsi ad film.

A candid moment with Warney.

Shooting at a Heathrow airport set with Sourav Ganguly.

'Ek lambi si train on a hot summer day … Yeh hi hai right choice, baby. Aha!

With the talented Anuja Chauhan at a Pepsi shoot.

'Yeh dil maange more!' Shah Rukh Khan, Shahid Kapoor with Mitali et moi.

Kissing SRK? Tara Sharma and Shah Rukh Khan.

In Hyderabad with Govinda, who arrived twenty-four hours late for a Wheel film shoot!

Players only! Phoot le.

Bo Kata: The Pepsi kite with two legends, Mr Amitabh Bachchan and Sachin Tendulkar.

Zor ka jhatka with Mr Bachchan … Mirindaaaah.

Post the bypass scare, taking yoga seriously.

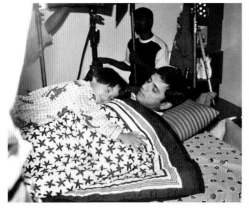

Anhjin napping on his favourite star, Rahul Dravid, during lunch break.

Ting, ting, ta ting! Anhjin with Rahul Dravid.

Rahul Dravid and Sourav Ganguly for Britannia with our youngest Anhjin. 1998.

'Main kaun hoon? Main kahan hoon?' Yours truly as the pilot with Sachin and Shane Warne.

Sharing a laugh: With Sehwag for Mayur Suitings.

The unstoppable
Cyrus Broacha with
the Genesis crew post
pack up.

'Hi! I'm Sanju!'... Pepsi 10G.

Your Guru finds you.
With Sadhguru. 2006.

The Genesis/Lacadives gang. From back left: Saif, Cedric, Naeem, Kenny, Keku, Ferzana, Pari, Mits, Shameen, Ferhana, Mama Kutty, Mridula, Stuti, Veda, Anees, Nikki, Ravi, Pranita, Sumer and the Beard!

Shooting with Varun Dhawan. Amita Sehgal taking a final setup brief from me.

L-R: Mum-in-law Ava, guest, Satoko Mitsui, direct descendent of my sensei, Miyamoto Musashi, one of the greatest swordsman of sixteenth-century Japan.

Khopchee King to Packshot King: Joel Fonseca aka Fonky aka Joel Da.

Kenny Dawson, editor, director and the Pied Piper of Saigon.

Chaddi buddies: Mitali and Shernaz, classmates from Loreto, Darjeeling.

At Pawna lake with Rakeysh
Omprakash Mehra. 2020.

Iron lady Sunitha Ram with Farah Khan
and Gemma Fonseca.

From the Flying Wing
gang, here's Stuti,
guest-starring in a
'Mera number kab
aayega' film with Cyrus
Broacha for Pepsi.

A candid moment:
Mr Bachchan in a JK
Lakshmi Cement film.

Listening intently: Master Blaster Sachin and me.

Sony Set Max with Kapil Dev.

Saif's sense of timing as an actor is impeccable.

With Jaaved Jaaferi and Aamir Khan at the launch of *Laal Singh Chaddha*.

With the Clan. 2023.

to get some colour on their half-naked and pale top halves. Hyde Park was full of these sunbathers, their bodies glistening with oil. I took the crowd as a good sign as I hopped off the tube at the nearest station to Portobello Road and, lugging my prized sandals in a drawstring bag, found my way to the flea market.

All the regular shops were closed and the pavement on both sides of the winding road was bustling with makeshift stalls of artisanal goods from stained-glass windowpanes and felt hats to ornate mirrors and clothes. I even spotted a gentleman with an ancient bioscope and an eyepatch, looking like Long John Silver with a parrot on his shoulder. The pubs scattered all the way down the road were doing roaring business and the place was crawling with tourists from all over. I couldn't find a place to even squeeze myself in, and I set up shop on top of a low culvert which didn't seem to suit anyone else, and spread out my wares—namely five pairs of soles with four slit ears, two on each side for the laces to go through and be wound, knotted and fitted on to the foot of the prospective client.

There were also five pairs of leather strips, eight feet long, with a special knot on one end to hold the sandal together. The whole exercise would take about fifteen minutes on each foot, half an hour to custom fit a pair of desi Alexander sandals. I never calculated that the biggest deterrent would be the time taken to fit the bloody sandals on. Quite a few people did stop by to enquire, mainly because I was wearing a churidar-kurta with my favourite Naga Angami shawl in a dramatic red-and-black pattern. But when they heard that they would have to hang about for half an hour while I fitted the sandals, they would beg off and swiftly head towards the closest pub.

I hung around for almost two hours with no money and no joy, until suddenly a cherry-red, low-slung two-seater car pulled up with a screech, driven by a rusty-haired, pimply young man, who had very obviously come into a large amount of new money—he was brash and loud, and had driven on to a street where it was understood that on Saturdays no four-wheelers were welcome. Yet, here he was, in his Morgan, without a care in the world. He was being very obnoxious to his girlfriend, who then opened her side of the door and flounced out, hands akimbo, looking at him really angrily. She was gorgeous. Her blonde hair was catching the late afternoon sun and sparkled like a halo around her. Her grey–blue eyes were bright with angry tears and her really generous mouth was now turned down in disapproval.

She was wearing a white summer dress that showed off her tanned calves and slim legs with open-toed, low-heeled sandals on her feet. Even as she got out of the car because the man was behaving in a distasteful manner, she was quite surprised when the lad just slammed the car into gear and zoomed off, leaving her completely crestfallen on the side of the road. She crossed over and came and sat down on the culvert to compose herself. I was so mesmerized by her that I watched her from the corner of my eye and gathered enough courage to mumble something encouraging to her as she looked quite sad.

'I beg your pardon?' she asked, noticing me in all my ethnic finery for the first time. I smiled brightly and said, 'If he has half as much a brain as he has money, he will come back for you.' She looked at me quizzically as she realized I had witnessed the sorry episode, smiled warmly and said, 'He's not a bad guy, just impatient and short-tempered.' To which I replied, 'I suppose so.' But I still thought of him as a prize idiot, and what the hell was she doing with him. She then looked at my clothes, and asked where I was from and what I was selling.

I told her all about my very special Chhattisgarhis and how long it takes to fit them on the first time. She was very intrigued and asked whether I would fit a pair on her as she had all the time in the world and, like me, nowhere to go in a hurry. I held her dainty feet and did a bang-up job on fitting them on her. She was delighted and fished out the five pounds I had mentioned as the cost of the footwear. And then, to my utter surprise, went dancing down the street advertising her new footwear to all and sundry. If they showed any interest, she would drag them along to introduce them to me as the architect of the sandals.

Within the next two hours, I had sold the remaining four pairs and collected a tidy twenty-five pounds. She was pleased with her successful intervention in my slightly hopeless state of affairs and made me feel really good, despite my circumstances. Just as I was about to ask her out for coffee, I saw a commotion at the bend in the road and the holidaymakers parted to reveal a cherry-red sports car nosing its way slowly while the pimpled driver looked furtively around for his abandoned girlfriend. I touched her shoulder and pointed to the car inching its way towards us. I nodded my head and said a tad bit regretfully, 'Told you he would be back.' She looked at me with her grey–blue eyes crinkling in the corners in delight, and I mumbled, 'Wish he hadn't.'

'Thank you for a wonderful afternoon. If it weren't for you, I don't know what would I have done,' she said as she leaned across and kissed me goodbye on the cheek before disappearing into the car like the last rays of the setting sun.

29

A Bird in Hand Is Worth Two
in the Bush

In the meantime, Rediffusion and Kamlesh Pandey, busy as beavers, had produced another campaign for their long-term client—Bush Audio Systems. After seeing the scripts, everyone was salivating over them. These were a series of films featuring a street-sharp hustler trying to buy a Bush Two-In-One from a Japanese tourist, who, at the end of his spiel, tells him that it is Indian and that he bought it locally.

In the second film, the hustler tries to pass the Bush Two-In-One as Japanese to a European tourist only to get caught by a beat cop, who then invites him to be a guest of the government for a while. Of course, he carries the Bush Two-In-One with him to jail. In film three, the hustler and his roomie try to break out of jail. As they reach the boundary wall to freedom, our hustler realizes that he has left the Bush Two-In-One behind and, much against everybody's advice, breaks back into the jail to get it. But of course, the wily jailor is waiting patiently for him to come back, playing his favourite movie song on the machine. In film four, many years later, the hustler is released from jail on parole to see his family waiting for him. Arms outstretched, they run joyously towards each other; he has left his meagre belongings at the prison gate. The family gallops past his outstretched arms to the Bush Two-In-One, as the wife plays 'Ghar aaya mera pardesi' and tells him, 'Aap to teen saal ke liye andar ho gaye aur saath-saath hamara Bush Two-In-One bhi saath le gaye!'

With great glee, we started the process of casting and getting ready to shoot these awesome scripts. We all decided that yesteryear comedian Paintal would be perfect as the hustler. Finding the rest of the cast was a cakewalk. We had started experimenting with casting actors instead of models and it was a favourable experience. Not only did they deliver great performances in half the time, but they also gave us variations for safety takes, which cut the shooting and prepping time by half. Moreover, I didn't have to pull my hair out trying to get a laddoo-faced model to give me something more than a wooden expression. The problem was always the agency and the client. They usually wanted chocolate boys and fair girls who could rarely perform like actors did. So casting was always a battle—the challenge was getting an approval for real people instead of mannequins. It was such a pleasure and relief to have an agency batting on our side for a change.

The Bush Two-In-One campaign was a tremendous success, and we were drooling as we dreamed of continuing the misadventures of the hustler for the next season! Kamlesh Pandey produced yet another amazing script. Paintal, the hustler, at the age of eighty-five, lying on his deathbed, doling out his ill-gotten gains to his daughter, who is Paintal (in drag), to his young son, who is also Paintal, and to his wife, who is also Paintal in drag but an older version! To Ranu Kaka, who is also Paintal, but all of them only have eyes for the Bush Two-In-One, cradled in the aged Paintal's arms. When he finishes his prize distribution, there is a deadly silence as old Paintal closes his eyes for his long, final journey. The family desperately looks at each other and shakes him back from neverland. To their relief, he opens his eyes and asks, 'What?' In unison, they say, 'Aur woh Bush Two-In-One?' He pauses for a few heartbeats and whispers, 'Woh to mein saath le jaa raha hoon,' and closes his eyes. We loved the script and got busy planning how to shoot each version of Paintal, by marking camera frames and rewinding the negative on a Mitchell studio camera, as it was calibrated for camera effects and Kamath mama, our resident expert cameraman.

The presentation to the Bush family was scheduled for the next morning and we worked all night to tie up the loose ends. The next morning, the Rediffusion team, led by Arun Nanda, traipsed off for the client presentation, while we loitered around their office waiting for the good news. After about two hours, the team came back, looking slightly the worse for wear, with an air of defeat surrounding them. Mr Nanda, briskly walked past us into his den and that was that: no champagne, no celebrations, nothing, just gloom!

I went up to a morose Kamlesh Pandey and tried to cajole him into revealing all. It took all my persuasive skills to get him to finally open up. The meeting started on a sombre note; the agency had been straining at the leash, the client family—they were called the Bush family—was subdued. After exchanging pleasantries, Arun Nanda got down to the business of presenting what he thought was a brilliant, but complicated script. He did a bang-up job of presenting and everyone guffawed at the punchline, except the family: Bush brothers, cousins and nephews. Everyone stifled their mirth quickly and looked everywhere else to avoid the soul-searing gaze of the family. Finally, the eldest brother got up and, with great gravitas, asked Arun Nanda to step outside for a tête-à-tête as they were good friends.

What they spoke about nobody knows, but after piecing it together this is what we think transpired: the eldest brother asked Arun Nanda if he had bothered to read the newspaper that morning to which Arun Nanda replied, 'No, no time!' After a dramatic pause, the eldest brother told him matter-of-factly that the 'old boy', the doyen of the family, had passed away the previous night without leaving a will. The whole Bush empire was up for grabs, with the family in the fray, very much like the script. Oops! The seniormost Bush son fixed Arun Nanda with a piercing stare and said, 'So you think you guys are being funny? This is in bad taste and not amusing at all.' Senior Bush stormed out, leaving a very embarrassed Mr Nanda, who was sure they would lose the account. The agency trooped back to the office and the Bush empire, split between feuding cousins and brothers, was never the same again. RIP!

30

'Oof-o! Ek Aur Naya Toothpaste!'

As the afterglow of winning multiple awards for Jenson and Nicholson one year after we had made them wore off, we got a call from the creative director of Chaitra Advertising agency. A gentleman called Brendan Pereira was on the other end of the line. Brendan was reputed to be a no-nonsense creative director. He was as uncompromising with his producers as he was with his team. This, of course, didn't make him the most popular person in advertising, but everyone had a very healthy respect for him from afar.

So, when we met him for the first time, he looked us up and down very carefully, without saying a word, while he let us fidget uncomfortably for a long couple of moments as he sat tamping his pipe. Then, when he had quite finished, he fixed us with an intense gaze and said, 'I don't know whether you guys can handle this film, as it is meant to be sexy and subtle at the same time.' We kept very still and quiet, while Brendan seemed to have lost interest in us, focusing on lighting his pipe and puffing thoughtfully. Then, suddenly, he turned towards me and shot a question, 'Who is your cameraperson?'

I was a bit taken aback and asked him to repeat the question, and he did. Now, we had spent the whole week trying to convince the reputed cameraman R.M. Rao to work with us. He was, at that time, the go-to cameraman for Kailash Surendranath and Zafar Hai, arguably the two best ad filmmakers of that time. So, Mr Rao was a pernickety, difficult man you couldn't simply hire off the shelf. Instead, you had to present yourself to him for quizzing. He would then decide if he wanted to work with you or not, and he is still like that! Anyway, after a gruelling session with R.M. Rao, who asked us all about the business of cinema to determine whether we knew our Arriflex from our elbows, he actually agreed to work with us (whew!).

So, I perked up, looked Brendan in the eye, and said, 'Mr R.M. Rao.' Dead silence stretched for a couple of seconds, after which Brendan Pereira raised a single eyebrow and launched straight into the brief.

It was for a new cigarillo that was launching soon. Now, cigarillos have a tricky positioning. They are not cigarettes, they look like a high-end beedi, though they are twice as expensive as cigarettes. They have a plastic tip that goes into the mouth, much like a cigarette holder, so you can clamp it in your teeth without wetting or destroying the rolled tobacco. It also has the aroma of a cigar. You can smoke it similarly— without necessarily inhaling the smoke, but by rolling it in your mouth and savouring its full-bodied tobacco flavour before exhaling it. The kick is in the fact that it has a nutty-brown cigarette-like look with the taste of the tobacco leaf, but without the chemicals, and the nicotine is absorbed only by your salivary glands and not your lungs. It gives you a pleasant buzz.

Brendan now fixed us with a beady eye and said, 'If I don't get an award-winning commercial from you and your motley lot, then you must never darken my door again.' God, the kind of pressure people put you under to do a stupid cigarillo film! Anyway, we got down to casting and designing the ambience for the film, and had many meetings with R.M. Rao. Since it was his first film with us, he was extra fussy. We finally shot on location in somebody's house as we needed a wood-panelled study with black leather furniture. We filmed the man lounging around topless in his swivel chair, lighting and puffing at his cigarillo, when a woman in a white clingy kaftan walks into the room out of nowhere like magic. She materializes from out to in focus in one step and looks stunning in the backlight (we had cast Sharon Prabhakar's sister, Pia Prabhakar).

Mr Rao pulled off that camera trick with a new split-focus lens, where half the frame is in focus and half is blurred, so Pia walked into focus from just an out-of-focus blob, miraculously. The entire ambience of the frame changed with a half-naked man (for a change), smoking a brown cigarillo against a rich brown wooden background, and a dusky, sexy woman in a clingy kaftan, leaving little to the imagination. Brendan loved the film, so we were on a roll and became the go-to producers for Chaitra. R.M. Rao became a regular at Genesis and there was no looking back.

Mr Rao was a stickler for detail, and we all learnt a lot from him as he would suddenly stop the shot and catch on to some minor points that nobody else had noticed. He waited while the girls leading the production team scrambled desperately to correct the anomaly, while I was fretting and fuming about the time lost. But it did make a huge difference. We took the motto 'the god is in the details' to heart at Genesis and we have Mr Rao to thank for that. If you want to be not just good but great, pay attention to the minutest detail. Period.

Brendan called us again for a job which he was hush-hush about, so off we went to Kemps Corner, to the Chaitra office. We were ushered into a vast conference room dominated by a long table and a screen on one side. In walked Brendan and a tall, lanky gentleman called Julian Almeida, the group head who was handling that particular account, and we proceeded to talk in riddles about the product. They didn't mention what the product was, but we realized it was a toothpaste. I finally got a bit pissed off and asked them, 'Just tell me the brand name and the bloody proposition!'

I imagined that the lord almighty was looking down at us and having a quiet giggle. 'What's the script?' I asked, and Julian said now in a normal voice, 'Simple! Now a new Promise with clove oil.'

I groaned and looked skywards and said, 'Oh no! Not another new toothpaste.' They looked stricken, and Julian exclaimed, 'You don't like it.'

'Like what?' I asked.

'The script,' he said, looking a bit crestfallen. Brendan, in the meantime, was busy, pretending to tamp his pipe. So, I told them how predictable and boring the script was, especially for a launch film. 'But what about the clove oil story?' he exclaimed. I replied, explaining that the audience would have switched off by the time they came to it.

Silence! Except for Brendan puffing noisily at his pipe, giving an 'I told you so' look. Julian then looked a bit down in the mouth and said, 'So, what do you suggest?'

That caught me a bit off guard, and I mumbled something to the effect of 'Let me think about it.' Then, I remembered my reaction to the opening lines of the script, and blurted out, 'Why don't you let the protagonist say what I said?'

'What did you say?' asked Julian.

'Oh no! Not another toothpaste!' I repeated.

They glowered at me, flabbergasted. Not only was I not helping, but I was having fun at their expense. Brendan stopped puffing at his now-extinguished pipe and asked, 'How will that help, pray?'

I patiently explained that it was the 'nailor'. It would surprise and hold the audience's attention just for that instant before they switched off, so we could quickly ram in the clove oil story. 'Hah!' said Brendan. 'What do you mean "hah"?' asked Julian. Brendan guffawed loudly and said, 'The "nailor" as in *Modesty Blaise*—where she walks in topless into a room with four guards, knowing that she can take out three of them, but the fourth one will get her. So, she needs something to freeze him for that nanosecond to nullify him as a threat! That's the "nailor"!' Julian thought both of us had collectively lost the plot. I was pleasantly surprised that Brendan had read *Modesty Blaise*! So it came to pass that we would use the 'nailor' for the lack of a better option.

The consensus was that everybody wanted to cast Maya Alagh, the wife of the revered Sunil Alagh, as the main protagonist. But who would bell the cat? After all, she was a doctor and the wife of one of our biggest clients. Everybody refused to ask him, of course, so I was left holding the bag as usual. With my heart in my mouth, I made an appointment to see Mr Alagh and went to the Britannia office, hat in hand, nervous as a girl going on her first date. He greeted me quite enthusiastically. I stuttered and stammered my way through my unusual request, and, much to my surprise, he laughed and said, 'Why don't you ask her?' He gave me their home landline number.

I fled the Britannia office and reached mine, all flustered. My partners gathered around to find out how the meeting went. I dialled the Alagh home number and their domestic help picked up the phone. I knew he was Nepali as I had spent a lot of time in Dehradun in the 3/9 Gorkha regimental lines as the commanding officer's sons, Tich and Ravi Thapa, were good friends of mine. So, I recognized the accent immediately. I asked for the memsahib, was put on hold and, a moment later, a sparkling voice said, 'Yes!' I tried to beat around the bush, to which Maya Alagh said, 'Tell me, what is it you want?'

I cut to the chase and told her I wanted to cast her as the brand ambassador for Promise toothpaste. There was a long pause, then she asked in a gentler tone, 'Are you sure you have the right number?' I gulped and asked if she was Dr Maya Alagh, Mr Sunil Alagh's wife, and she said, 'Yes.' I told her she was it then! After seeing her photographs at some group bash, we knew she was perfect for the role. Good-looking and very confident. She said she would think about it, and I should get back to her the following day.

Time flew and the next thing I knew, I was summoned for tea to the Alagh residence in Cuffe Parade to explain everything in detail. I arrived in my Sunday best and began discussing the script with them, and when I said, 'Oh no! Not another toothpaste!' Maya Alagh immediately translated it to 'Oof-o! Ek aur naya toothpaste!' Everything just clicked. She agreed and we shot the film in a studio. I realized at that moment that someone up there must like me. The film was received with incredulous enthusiasm, and people picked up on the line and started using, 'Oof-o, ek aur naya toothpaste!' as part of their lexicon. And it became folklore.

Maya Alagh forever became the 'Oof-o Promise' lady and, much to her frustration, the tag follows her around till today. The brand took off and grabbed 4 per cent of the market share, a massive achievement at that time as they were up against the Colgates and Unilevers of the world, who were caught unawares by this bold new campaign. They bitterly cribbed in hindsight that they also used clove oil. Too little too late, Promise forever became the toothpaste with clove oil!

31

Panther, Python and Helicopter Crashes

While we were basking in our little successes at Genesis, the big boys of ad films were busy scoring all the big-ticket projects. Zafar Hai was the go-to person with a highly evolved aesthetic reflected in his upmarket films—like the ones he had made for Taj Hotels, Bombay Dyeing and Nescafé. Then there was Kailash Surendranath, who had made the first Liril soap film, with Karen Lunel—the girl in a skimpy green bikini under a waterfall with Fa soap's international jingle, going 'la-la-la', conveniently borrowed. It was a huge hit and became the gold standard of its time.

Shama Habibullah had also entered the scene with Fanta Orange films, which she directed for Durga Khote Productions. It had broken the mould of montage films by actually telling a story with a jingle! So, there we were, the Johnny-come-latelies, still waiting for our big break. In the meantime, Shyam babu had moved his office to Everest Building in Tardeo from Jyoti Studios, Nana Chowk. Mandeep, my partner, managed to scrape together enough money for us to turn bullish and buy an office on the sixth floor of the same building. That's how we came to roost at E-20, Everest Building, for twenty-five years!

After shifting into our new headquarters, one fine day, we got a call from Maureen Wadia's office in Bombay Dyeing and then immediately after that from its agency, Ulka, headed by its charismatic founder, Bal Mundkur. We were summoned to the agency to hear a brief on the Bombay Dyeing films, both menswear and womenswear, and to make a pitch. Finally, we were in the big league! The menswear film was based on a James Bond–type character. We had to develop a script with the works: babes, guns, suiting, casual wear, chases, fights, panthers and pythons. The panthers and pythons were added later to soothe our overcharged imagination.

We worked on a creative that looked like a James Bond film trailer and was strung out as a basic story of a day (and night) in the life of Mr Bond. Full of good-looking women, sharp clothes, fabulous digs and lots of bad guys, who were trying to bump him off. We embellished the film with all our fantasies of what an Indian Bond should do. There were samurai swords, guns, pet panthers and women wrapped in live pythons instead of jewellery, with helicopter chases and bad guys taking shots at our speeding Bond in a jeep—all with him clad in impeccable suiting, shirting and trousers by Bombay Dyeing. 'Never, never say die' was our motto for this very ambitious film. Maureen Wadia heard what we were attempting to do in what was arguably the most expensive ad film of its time, looked at us sceptically, and wished us luck and happy hunting.

Putting together the whole ninety-second film was an exercise in logistics and chutzpah. We had to design the entire ad film and explain to the crew how it would come together seamlessly. There were some eight locations, of which two were elaborate sets. The first set was a 100-foot tunnel for the jeep to make a getaway in the chase sequence, and the other set was of a man cave with an exquisite sword collection and a pistol shooting range. The first hurdle was to find authentic samurai swords in Bombay. We finally stumbled across the name of a collector, the amazing Roosi Modi, not the Tata Steel Russi Mody, but Roosi Modi, the proprietor of New Empire, which was one of Bombay's oldest cinema theatres.

He was a collector, adventurer, playboy and had a black belt in karate, to boot. Roosi had the reputation of doing everything larger than life and had even survived a helicopter crash off Bombay High. He swam some ten kilometres back to the shore. He was known to avoid fools and film people like the plague, and now we had to bell this not-so-domesticated cat. Locating Roosi Modi wasn't a problem as he was well known, but getting an appointment with him was quite challenging. When he heard it was an ad film shoot, he retorted that he did not want anything to do with a film crew, for love or money. Screwed! As luck would have it, we realized that Maureen Wadia knew him, so we coaxed her into putting in a good word. The next time I called, he reluctantly agreed to meet. Somehow, I had to convince him to part with one of his precious sixteenth-century original Japanese blades for a shoot which needed some fancy footwork reminiscent of the nursery rhyme: Jack be nimble, Jack be quick!

First, I did some rapid reading about the best swords ever made in the history of the world. The Japanese katana heated in a charcoal forge topped the list. The steel was bent and beaten approximately 1,000 times to form 2,000 layers to make the heart of the sword. The blade was then shaped and the cutting edge tempered in boiling oil. It was polished to an almost mirror-like finish and consecrated in a spiritual process very much like our temple idols! Only when the swordmaker was satisfied with the energizing of the blade did he put his chop, or signature, in gold on the tang of the sword, which was sheathed in wood and held in place by two bamboo spikes. The haft of the blade was then covered in sharkskin and bound tightly. The sharkskin had a rough, abrasive surface and prevented the warrior's hands from slipping during combat, especially when its hilt was covered in blood.

Armed with this knowledge about the katana and the tanto (short sword), I presented myself to Roosi, and engaged in the history of each blade and his passion for his collection of swords. He explained the great lengths he had undergone to find each one in the jungles of Imphal and Kohima (key battlefields in World War II) where the Japanese juggernaut was stopped and defeated. The Officer Corps of the Japanese Imperial Army had surrendered their swords to the British. However, very few British army men knew the value of most blades, which were family deities, having been passed down from generation to generation ever since the sixteenth century.

It took a swordmaker a year to make each sword. The value, if calculated, is staggering. Roosi was very impressed with my meticulous homework and took me through his collection of nine impeccable blades. He then agreed to let us use one of the lesser swords for the film where Mr Bond had to test the blade's edge by slicing an orange in half as it sits on a cushion. You only know it's been slashed into two neat halves when he lifts the top half off! The film starts with that stunning shot.

Roosi proved to be a treasure trove of collectibles and knowledge, from sawed-off shotguns to Beretta Match pistols, collected between him and his brother-in-law. They personally escorted their various weapons to the set to see to it that they were not misused or manhandled, as often happens in film shoots. We had the man cave constructed in Jyoti Studios, next to Kennedy Bridge in Girgaon. For the love interest, we cast a young lady of Indian origin from the US of A, who had come for a visit to Bombay. Her name was Rose and she turned out to be a bit thorny.

Satish Shah was our in-house ordnance expert, having been a national-level marksman. He created dumdums (or hollow points) for the .22 Beretta in our attempts at getting a watermelon to explode on impact. Initially, we failed miserably as the .22 round was too small a calibre and the watermelon too soft for the dumdum to explode it, because we only managed to create a small entry hole and a large messy exit hole on the other side of the watermelon. So, we had to use a small explosive charge.

The sequence that we envisioned was a powerful series of shots starting with a katana slicing the orange and a drawer opening to reveal a dull matte-black Beretta. The magazine was locked in the gun, which was cocked, fired and the smoking empty brass cartridge case was ejected from the breach in slow motion. We concluded the sequence with a close-up of Rose's red-lipped mouth opening in anticipation and a green watermelon exploding to reveal the red pulp inside after being pulverized at 150 frames per second (which is to say, slow motion).

Cut to a scene with Mr Bond putting on his impeccably tailored jacket with a beautiful woman looking over his shoulder and running her manicured fingers over his lapel. The whole idea of this opening sequence was to establish style, lethal weaponry, a bit of sex appeal and subliminal violence in a sophisticated, male environment. The first hint of the ad working well was when we got a call from a babu on behalf of the Censor Board. He tried to tell me to change the film's opening sequence as he felt there was too much masala.

I patiently went through the sequence with him and asked him to pinpoint the exact objectionable shot. He couldn't, since no individual image was controversial in itself. So, the poor babu got confused and scratched his head while he tried to find something worth censoring. He could not put his finger on what was disturbing him. I could have told him that the individual shots weren't a problem, but all of them, in this particular sequence, underlined sex, style and violence. We got away with it because he could not recognize subliminal autosuggestion. If they had psychologists on the Censor Board, they would have caught on immediately!

———

The film featured a helicopter chase where a baddie with a repeating shotgun, courtesy Satish Shah, was shooting at Mr Bond and Rose travelling in a jeep. Their windshield explodes with a near miss and the chase is on. Their jeep weaves through a mountain road as Bond and Rose avoided getting shot, with the chopper and baddie hot in their pursuit. Finally, they screech around the corner and up looms a tunnel. Even as they make it through the tunnel, the chopper, intent on its prey, fails to pull away in time and crashes into the mountainside, drops to the road in front of the tunnel and explodes spectacularly.

Shooting this scene alone took a whole lot of planning. We needed to figure out how to position the chopper in the frame and keep communication with the pilot as there were no cell phones or walkie-talkies in those days. We needed to decide where to mount the camera on the bonnet of the jeep. The camera position was critical as the chopper was behind the jeep and the windshield would explode towards the camera. It had to be placed at an angle through which we could see the couple in the jeep and the chopper in the background, with the windshield blowing outwards, towards the camera, without touching the lens. We got everything right, except how to simulate the bullet cracking the windshield.

If we used a small explosive charge, not only would it create smoke, but there was no guarantee that the windshield would shatter outwards; and if we used an actual bullet, it would endanger the camera crew. Finally, it came to pass that I was belted in a harness, hiking out from the side of the jeep, so as to not be in the frame. I was armed with a catapult loaded with a steel ball bearing. On hearing the blank fired by Satish from the chopper, I would let fly at the windshield even as I was precariously balanced on the edge of the jeep, held up by a Carabiner and a belt. Bang went the shotgun, I released the steel ball bearing, and a spider's web of interconnected cracks spread across the windshield immediately and it fell in a cascade of small pieces ... straight on the talents' faces and chests!

We had forgotten to calculate the wind pressure on the windshield in a travelling vehicle! So instead of shattering outwards, all of the glass fell straight on the protagonists. There was a shriek from Rose and a screech from the jeep abruptly braking. Alarmed, I shouted, 'Don't move, or you will be lacerated!' Everybody in the jeep froze and Vidyadhar, the make-up artist, leapt into the fray with Irene, the hairstylist, who held soft brushes and tweezers. Mr Bond, fully dressed in a safari suit, coolly shook off the glass shards, but lady Rose was wearing a low-necked top and, unfortunately, had glass trickling all the way down to her navel. 'I can't be scarred for life,' she repeated hysterically.

It took a few hours to remove the glass from Rose's dress and her body carefully and we lost light; so filming the helicopter crash at the tunnel was rescheduled for the next day. Meanwhile, I tried to renegotiate Vidyadhar's fees because I thought he had been more than amply compensated—no joy! Just then, Rose dropped an even bigger bombshell. She refused to come back for our shoot the next day. After much cajoling and pleading, she let slip that she had accepted a role in another ad film scheduled for the next morning.

We still had many close-ups left to shoot, including the chopper crash. Now what? There was no chance of cheating on this one, so I got into a huddle with Satish Shah and asked him to dress up as a cabbie the following day to pick up the truculent Rose from her residence at 5.30 a.m., as her call time for the other shoot was 6.30 a.m. He was briefed specifically to keep nodding and saying, 'Yes!' We were going to try and kidnap her out of sheer desperation, since we had a colossal tunnel set standing with a dummy helicopter and explosives, a stuntperson, the whole works and the metre was fast running.

Satish Shah obliged and dressed up as a cabbie in khaki with a cabbies' badge. Luckily for us, Rose had not met Satish as he was in the chopper. So he went off to pick her up and rang the doorbell. A groggy Rose came to the door and exclaimed in surprise, 'You are early!' Satish mumbled, 'Yes!' So, she dressed up and leapt into the cab, and off they went! To be doubly sure, Rose asked, 'You are from X Productions, right?' Satish nodded sagely, 'Yes!' He drove through town to the burbs and beyond, and she leaned forward and said, 'I did not think it was so far!' He said, 'Yes!' He drove into Film City via Aarey Colony, and she asked, 'Where are we going?' He nodded and responded, 'Yes!' He pulled up outside the set. When she opened the door, the truth of the situation dawned on her. All hell broke loose, and she threw a massive tantrum and said she was leaving. She yelled at the top of her voice, 'You kidnapped me!' We reminded her that she came of her own free will.

She followed me and complained, 'What about my other shoot?' I explained that this would only take a couple of hours, and I'd get her there by lunchtime. I then ignored her and instructed the crew to put a mannequin in the passenger seat of the jeep for the long shot. The mannequin looked really ugly and so, she finally caved and finished the shot! Thank god for vanity. Little did she know that I had already talked to her producer, a friend of mine, to explain the situation. He knew that I'd be dropping her off once we wrapped up her scenes. He was cool about it, so all was well!

———

Mrs Wadia found a leggy blonde from the beaches of Baga in Goa. She foisted her on us as the femme fatale. I told her that she would be dressed in a towel with a python wrapped around her neck for the sequence. Our femme fatale was a bit taken aback, but was game. Meanwhile, back at the ranch, the production crew was running helter-skelter trying to find a friendly python.

We almost gave up on the python until one day before the shoot, I saw a sadhu at Colaba Causeway with a twelve-foot baby python around his neck, looking for a handout. I went up to him and he tried to intimidate me by thrusting the snake into my face. I kept my cool and asked him how much he wanted for the python. He mulled over it for a few minutes and then said Rs 500. I took the princely sum of money from a production assistant. He uncoiled the python from his neck and put it on mine, and we checked each other out—the python and me. Before we left, the sadhu said he was a baby and needed to be force-fed cubes of chicken meat by shoving it down his gullet with a pencil or stick for pythons don't eat dead meat. We named our newest crew member Snoopy.

We prepared for our upcoming shoot showing Mr Bond in his study, his pet panther beside him, accompanied by the femme fatale he had rescued from the baddies in a shipyard. Right before this sequence, we had filmed a fierce hand-to-hand fight karate style in a shipbreaking yard called Daru Khana. Our Bombay Dyeing Bond had now retired to his den after he had kicked ass, sending the villain hurtling into the water in a choreographed fight in the upper deck of the ship, supervised by another Roosi contact—the one and only Sensei Parvez Mistry.

We were shooting in our client Mr Bal Mundkur's house in Darbhanga Mansion, on Altamount Road because, though we had looked far and wide, we hadn't found a location that could emulate the character, texture and style of his home. But we had hit upon a hitch in our plan. Mr Mundkur was adamant that he would not let a film crew anywhere near his house, especially on the day that we needed it. We used every possible explanation to convince him as it was the prized account of his company, Ulka. But he wouldn't budge an inch, so we finally got Mrs Wadia to talk to him. He couldn't say no to her!

He gave in with a firmly worded non-negotiable condition. We had to clear out by 6 p.m.—no ifs or buts. We readily agreed and started setting up the shoot. Later, we discovered he was being bullheaded about the whole thing as he was getting married for the second time in his life on the day of our shoot. He would be coming straight home from a simple civil ceremony to enjoy a night of blissful nuptial delights and wanted everyone to clear out well ahead of time.

Man proposes, Murphy disposes. The first thing to go horribly wrong was that the panther, sourced from Madras, reached our set only at 5 p.m. Our local Bond hero, played by Ardhendho Bose, who was very relaxed about the lady with the python, took one look at the panther and threw a major fit. He suddenly realized he was scared of the big cat and wanted the panther's mouth stitched up, which I refused because it was cruel. I wanted the big cat to snarl in the shot! The actor professed that he needed a stiff drink to summon up some courage and disappeared. We assumed he'd be back by 6 p.m., so we could finish taking the shots and pack up. It was already 8 p.m. now and there was no sign of our Mr Bond. We organized search parties and they finally found him, slightly slurring, at his favourite watering hole in Juhu. We hauled him back to the location intent on finishing the day's shoot.

Mr Mundkur and his new blushing bride arrived by 8.30 p.m. to find his house full of crew, lighting cables and lights, and a large panther sitting regally on his drawing-room couch. He was a bit upset, to put it mildly. We immediately tried to pacify him and told him that we had vacated his master bedroom, and decorated it with jasmine flowers and rose petals. We promised him that we would be absolutely silent, so as not to disturb him and his new bride. He refused to buy into our promises and wanted to turf us out immediately. His blood pressure was climbing dangerously high and we could almost see smoke coming out of his ears in tiny tendrils. The agency executive on the job, Mira Nair, was flapping around in great anxiety.

Thanks to Murphy, we had committed large amounts of money to the shoot with no tangible results yet. Luckily for us, the new bride quickly realized that the situation was getting out of hand. Her enraged new husband bristled with anger and was ready to go to battle to retrieve their night of marital bliss and whatever was left of their shattered evening. She just about managed to soothe the old boy after which she led him off to the boudoir and soundly shut the door on us with a slight conspiratorial smile.

The shoot proceeded with everybody tiptoeing around the set and talking in exaggerated stage whispers to ensure we did not disturb the newlyweds. At around 1.30 a.m., when we were ready to take the shot of the femme fatale with the python wrapped around her, we could not find the bloody snake. After turning the house upside down, we decided to take the shot without Snoopy. Much to our dismay, we realized that we might have left him in Bal Mundkur's bedroom. Now what? Who would wake up an irate lord and master and explain to him that we had left behind a pet python, about twelve-feet long, in his bridal bedroom and could we please disturb his nuptial delights while we retrieved it?

Nobody volunteered, so we decided to pick straws. Poor Mira Nair got the shortest straw and was left with the horrendous task of waking up her boss on his wedding night. Boy, I didn't envy her at all! We waited, holding our breaths, while she knocked on the massive carved bedroom door with trepidation. No response. 'Louder,' we egged her on, standing safe out of the line of sight. Still, no response; so she knocked even harder. No luck. I plucked some courage laced with desperation and went to help her. I pounded on the door, loudly calling out his name, 'Mr Mundkur. Hello, Mr Mundkur, we need some help!' The door was flung open and a furious Bal Mundkur emerged from the doorway. His hair was dishevelled and he was draped in a bedsheet like a toga, with his longish grey locks in total disarray. He looked like an elderly Caesar, who had been disturbed during a romp with Cleopatra.

'What do you want?' he boomed.

'Sir,' a terrified Mira Nair bleated, 'we have forgotten a very vital prop in your bedroom by mistake. Could we please, please look for it?'

Silence. Mr Mundkur couldn't believe his ears. 'What prop?' he yelled irritably. I quickly stepped forward before Mira gave the game away and said, 'Sir, just a prop, but one of us will have to identify it because it's a bit unusual.'

'What rubbish!' said Mr Mundkur. 'You can't come into the room. Period!'

Inside the bedroom, we could see the blushing bride on the four-poster bed with the remainder of the bedsheet pulled up to her neck, looking like a startled doe. So now we were at an impasse. Mr Mundkur was blocking the door like a dishevelled colossus faced by a desperate film crew, trying their best to wrap up a lousy shoot and go home! Finally, he looked over his shoulder to a now relatively well-covered bride and stepped aside, saying, 'What the *fuck*?' and let the three of us in. We searched all over—under the bed, behind the curtains, on the dresser, but Snoopy was nowhere to be found. Where the hell had he gone? Suddenly, a trainee's voice piped up from the loo, 'I found him!'

'Him?' shouted Mr Mundkur. 'Who is *him* hiding in my toilet?' He bounded into the bathroom, still wrapped in his bedsheet, and came to a screeching halt on seeing a twelve-foot baby python wrapped around the base of his pristine English commode, Armitage Shanks.

His eyes bulged out of their sockets, his face crumpled in incredulity and he said in a low, hoarse whisper, 'You bastards! You left a live fucking snake in my bedroom and called it a prop! And suppose I came for a pee in the night and this monster was hungry ...' He trailed off and left the rest to our not-so-fertile imaginations.

And, on that note, at 3 a.m., ended the most ambitious ad film shoot of the time. The ninety-second film was a huge success and Bombay Dyeing owned the Indian James Bond! Snoopy, the python, was taken in style and enthroned in the spanking new Genesis office in Tardeo, and had many more adventures—or rather, misadventures. I have to say that shooting the womenswear ads was a picnic compared to the menswear films!

~~

The womenswear ad had a funny and edgy script. The main protagonist was Dalip Tahil, playing a man who ogles women. To him, the world is full of beautiful women clad in Bombay Dyeing saris and churidars made with its dress materials. So we decided to show a day in the life of this man and how the universe conspires to give him his just deserts.

It starts with him riding a bike. He overtakes a lovely young lady on a horse buggy full of flowers, aka my fair lady in a gorgeous floral dress. He blows her a kiss and she throws him a bouquet. He goes past a staircase on the road where two young ladies in Bombay Dyeing saris are traversing the stairs and ogles them. Then he spots two girls in shorts and Bombay Dyeing tops cycling past him on a tandem bike (you couldn't find a tandem bike in Bombay back then, so we had it custom-made for the ad). He follows them with his banana eyes still on his motorcycle. He fails to see a cop halt traffic at a crossroads and the car in front brakes. Eeeyagh! Our champion ogler ends up at the rear end of the 1968 model Fiat, which has a round sloping back. He climbs up the vehicle's back and lands up on the roof, relatively unscathed. The huge Iranian occupant of the car gets out slowly, rolls up his sleeves and corrects that promptly.

In the following sequence, with his nose bandaged, the man now continues his ogling in a high-end office. He ogles a young executive in a skirt and crossing her legs. Then he is at it again with a secretary in front of a filing cabinet wearing a Bombay Dyeing salwar kameez. He then turns around to stare at a lovely young executive in a sari, doesn't see a door and goes straight into it. Oops! Not having learnt his lesson, he follows a young lady past the lift, still ogling, and falls down into the out-of-order lift shaft, with a scream and a thud. The whole frame jitters with the impact as if the building shook. To get the shot (there were no post-production facilities then), we had to do it in-camera and scratched our heads on how to get an authentic shudder in the frame.

After much discussion, we finally created a base for the chhota stand of the camera. It was two pieces of two feet by two feet ply, sandwiching a set of sofa springs between them, that did the trick as Dalip Tahil goes past the camera, teeters on edge and goes down the shaft. We waited for a count of three, a nice sharp blow and, lo and behold! We got a perfect shudder in the frame, which looked like the building was shaking. Our hero now appears all trussed up with bandages in a wheelchair, still faithful to his never-say-die attitude of checking out the ladies. Now, of course, he is in a hospital corridor, checking out the hot interns wearing stethoscopes and Bombay Dyeing fabrics. He goes past one safely and then sees a lissome young doctor, and loses it, goes down a steep ramp which we had designed especially on Sophia College's main staircase, not realizing how steep it was!

During the rehearsal, we tied a rope to the axel of the wheelchair. A whole lot of production assistants had to stop the wheelchair on a mark close to the wide-angle lens on the camera, with an uneasy DOP, R.M. Rao, behind it. Incidentally, he also owned the camera. One wrong move and Dalip Tahil and the wheelchair could write off the equipment and the camera crew. We had tied knots on the rope to warn the production assistants when to stop the careering wheelchair at the right spot. Just three feet before the lens, they couldn't see the camera because they were ducking out of the frame to avoid ruining the shot with their terrified mugs.

We held our collective breaths as a screaming, bandaged Dalip Tahil careened down the ramp and the knots flew through the hands of the pullers. Screech went the wheelchair and stopped a hair's breadth away from the camera. A frantic Dalip went flying off the chair, flailing in terror mid-air, went just over the camera crew and crashed behind on some mattresses which providence had provided. We carted a shaken, but not stirred, Dalip back to the now empty and forlorn wheelchair, and tied him on to it for good measure. The next take was perfect and, to date, I believe that the terrified look on Dalip Tahil's face was not acting. Knock-out fabrics by Bombay Dyeing, indeed!

32

Snoopy

There was a brief moment of respite after the Bombay Dyeing shoots—a moment of calm. In hindsight, I have realized that work doesn't end when we finish a shoot and tick all the boxes. Instead, once all the boxes have been ticked, you sit and ponder about where Murphy is going to strike next, because strike he will! Remember, the trick is never to hope for the best, but always prepare for the worst, and you might just get away with it.

Here we were, hanging around the office kitchen, cooking up a storm. That's one of the things we did to unwind after stressful shoots. In walked Satish Shah, very keen on making an acquaintance with the now infamous Snoopy. The python had made himself comfortable in the office and had a corner to himself. He seemed very happy being force-fed cubes of chicken meat by Uttam Sirur, who also bathed him occasionally and acted as his minder. It was Satish Shah—a great outdoorsman, crack shot and animal lover, who figured out why Snoopy had to be force-fed chicken instead of pouncing on the meat of his own accord—pythons don't feed on carrion and eat hunted live bait. By the end of the afternoon, Satish had endeared himself to

Snoopy and wanted to take him home for a few days. He promised to take good care of him, so we reluctantly agreed.

The following day, at around 10 a.m., we got a slightly incoherent phone call in the office about Satish's snake and something, something. We realized that things had gone horribly wrong with Snoopy. We leapt onto our motorcycles and rushed to the rescue. We arrived at Satish Shah's parents' home in a three-storeyed building, just off Bhatia Hospital in Tardeo, and bounded up the stairs, two at a time, to the second floor only to find a large crowd funnelling in and out of the flat armed with jhadoos, sticks and suchlike, and jostling to get a peek in a slightly skittish way.

We pushed through the crowd and came upon a fantastic sight. Satish's mother was lying frozen on the bed with her eyes bulging in terror. His father was prancing around the bed with half his face covered in shaving cream and the other half clean-shaven. He was brandishing a slightly ineffectual-looking razor. Lying curled on Satish's mother's stomach was a somewhat nervous Snoopy, looking around at a frightened, hostile crowd of neighbours milling around the doorway, armed with whatever they could get their hands on, including chappals. The neighbours looked as terrified as Satish's mother. I took in the volatile scene in one glance, leapt to the side of the bed, scooped up a perplexed Snoopy, shoved him into a jute gunny bag, which was his temporary home and, before anybody could react, we raced down the staircase, jumped on to our bikes and went back to the office!

Later, we learnt what had happened. Satish had spent the evening with Snoopy and made sure he had locked the door, so that nobody in the house was aware of his house guest. He put Snoopy to bed on a soft cushion and passed out as he had an early morning shift. At dawn, he had dressed quickly, since he was late, and left in a rush, leaving the door ajar. Snoopy, who was feeling a bit cold in the early winter morning, decided to explore and find a warmer place. He slithered out into the hallway, where he found the door of Satish's parents' room open. He slid inside the room, up into the bed and under the razai.

He found that the warmest place was Satish's mother's stomach and happily curled up on it.

Sometime afterwards, Satish's dad got out of bed, brushed his teeth and was busily trying to shave using a mirror hung from the bedroom window latch, totally unaware of the python curled up on the missus's stomach. He was halfway through his shave when the wife woke up. She groggily registered a weight on her stomach and, thinking that the old boy was feeling affectionate, she paid him no heed except to turn her head and smile encouragingly at him, only to realize that he wasn't next to her.

She looked around and found her husband standing at the window, happily shaving. So, what the hell was the weight on her stomach? She gingerly lifted the razai and found Snoopy's beady eyes staring at her with his tongue flicking in and out. He looked entirely unhappy at being disturbed from his snake dreams. She froze in abject terror with the razai halfway off. In her attempt to avoid antagonizing an equally frightened Snoopy, she desperately tried to attract her husband's attention with her wildly swivelling eyeballs. No luck!

After some more swivelling and gentle grunting sounds, he finally looked casually in her direction, halfway through his shave, and couldn't understand why his wife seemed to be in a kind of rigor mortis, except for her eyeballs, which were going slightly crazy! So he walked towards the bed and flipped the razai to find young Snoopy looking back at him with an expression that said, 'Hey, what's the problem? It's cold, leave me alone!'

All these subtle niceties completely escaped Mr Shah, who, by now, was prancing around in great agitation with half his face covered with shaving lather, trying to summon some help. While the stricken wife signalled with her eyes that he needed to cool it and not get the bloody snake all het up. Of course, the entire building poured in, glanced helplessly around and grabbed anything that looked remotely like a weapon. Still, keeping their distance, they postured dramatically, trying to shoo the offending snake off the lady's stomach. Not a chance; Snoopy held his ground. The crowd grew larger and lots of generous advice was passed on from the back to the frontbenchers, like catching the snake from behind the head like they do on Nat Geo!

This circus would have continued if an intelligent domestic help hadn't added two and two and made twenty-two. He promptly rang up the Genesis number hoping somebody would pick up the phone. That's what brought Ravi and me to the rescue—flags flying, trumpets blaring. Truth be told, our only concern was to rescue our harmless Snoopy and protect him from a nervous, unpredictable mob of wannabe heroes.

———

A week later, a sheepish Satish Shah arrived in the office to make amends to a traumatized Snoopy and his local guardians. He came with a peace offering—namely a live chicken to hone Snoopy's wild instincts from scratch and see how he would react to live bait. All of us gathered around to watch. We hauled Snoopy out of his sack home and placed him in front of the chicken. The chicken looked at the python and the python looked at the chicken. Finally, they both lost interest and took on an attitude of 'C'mon, dude, let us be!'

Not one to admit defeat so easily, Satish prodded the chicken into movement with Snoopy watching disinterestedly. Then, suddenly, it dawned on Snoopy that this gawky feathered object was food and it was alive, at that. Before our eyes, the slightly apologetic, dopey snake transformed into a lethal predator—his head hardened into a diamond shape, his eyes sharpened into intense focus and his body coiled tightly into a compact figure of eight, which now was following every move the chicken made.

In the blink of an eye, our docile Snoopy launched himself at the chicken, like a coiled spring. With his mouth gaping wide open, he clamped down on the hapless bird, holding it in a vice-like grip in his mouth, whipping the rest of his body around the bird, and started squeezing it until its bones cracked. He slowly swallowed the bird whole into his unhinged maw.

We watched in fascinated horror as the dance of life and death played out. After that, we could never be the same around Snoopy again, and were now very careful and wary around him. Eventually, better sense prevailed, and we gave Snoopy to the warden at the Sanjay Gandhi National Park and he lived out the rest of his days in the freedom of the wild.

33

The Tiara Girl

We had a new client, a lady from the Singhania family. The agency was handling the entire line of J.K. Helene Curtis products. The film was for Tiara Shampoo and the casting brief was very specific. The script demanded a slim young model dressed in apsara-like apparel, representing everything natural. The client wanted her to be some kind of wood nymph, talking to animals and wading through gushing streams. I envisioned the film being shot in the Karnala Bird Sanctuary as it was densely wooded with the occasional expanse of grassland, which suited the film perfectly.

Next, we had to find the right girl. The casting was really tricky; not only did we need a great-looking girl—fit and athletic—but she also had to have long, waist-length hair. To find all these qualities in one single person seemed impossible, but for the slaves it was not to reason why. So, the hunt went on for a whole month without joy. Just when we were beginning to think that a girl like that didn't exist, in walked a young lady who did fit the bill, but was actually there to escort a probable candidate who did not suit the role at all.

As it turned out, she was not interested in modelling; she was a media student at Sophia College and was training to be behind the camera, not in front of one. Her name was Mitali Dutt. She had her hair up in a bun, so we couldn't quite make out how long it was, but otherwise, she was near perfect. We beat around the bush, hemmed and hawed, and tried to broach the fact that we wanted her to be the Tiara girl. She, of course, would have none of it and was very clear that she didn't want to be a model.

Over a chat, we figured out that Mitali grew up on the tea plantations in the foothills of Darjeeling, where she was born and brought up. Her father was a tea planter and, after retiring, he had settled down in Siliguri. I also discovered that she had come to Bombay, much against her father's wishes, to study microbiology at Sophia College, but due to an admission form mix-up, she ended up studying psychology and finally pursued the media course at the Sophia Polytechnic, which had an excellent reputation. She had since made up her mind about being behind a camera, not in front of it.

I gently coerced her, telling her that she would earn enough from the assignment to pay off a year's worth of tuition and hostel fees, and would not have to ask anyone for money. I knew I had scored a major point when she immediately said she would think about it. Sure enough she decided to do it if she was selected for it, and selected she was. For the shoot, we showed her a reference for a kind of wood nymph—pure and natural, reacting to the birds and animals in the forest. She runs through the dappled forest with her mane of hair streaming behind her, taking on a life of its own, and bathes in a sparkling stream. The secret to her fabulous hair—Tiara Shampoo.

Once Mitali agreed to do the film, we went into overdrive to find an appropriate location, and coopt all the birds and animals through an animal trainer. The only problem was that it was the middle of the monsoon season, and the torrential downpour was a major spoilsport. It would rain for days on end, and then suddenly the sun would break through briefly, teasingly, only to deceive us all. The silver lining was that we had found the perfect location in the bird sanctuary; it even had accommodation for almost twenty people. Of course, it was full of creepy crawlies due to the monsoon, from helicopter-sized mosquitoes to foot-long centipedes, leeches and frogs. Surprisingly, Mitali wasn't squeamish about the jungle and its denizens at all, unlike most city-bred young ladies. Production and costume details were being handled by the very efficient Valerie Agha, Jalal Agha's newly estranged wife.

She had temporarily found shelter in Genesis and was very useful, being a first-class production person with an awesome aesthetic sensibility, to boot. I found her hugely attractive and a great asset, so I had no problem offering her shelter in the office. I recall word getting around that Prahlad Kakar had offered the oh-so-lovely Valerie Agha a shoulder to cry on, and rumours were flying thick and fast. I once inadvertently met Jalal outside the Holiday Inn Health Club and he'd cornered me, saying, 'Stay away from my wife, or I will bash you up,' or something to that effect. In all innocence, I had replied, 'You can't do that, Jalal!' He swiftly and threateningly asked, 'Why? You think you are stronger than me?' In all humility, I had replied, 'No! But I can run faster than you can.' End of argument.

Valerie, Barun da, the DOP, Mitali and the rest of the motley crew waited for a break in the rain to head off to the Karnala Bird Sanctuary as all necessary permissions had been obtained in advance. We reached there after a picturesque two-hour drive and the heavens promptly opened up, and it poured for forty-eight hours non-stop. After waiting for twenty-four hours, I sent the rest of the crew back to Bombay and just kept a skeleton crew—basically the camera crew, the cast, i.e., Mitali, my production team, make-up and hair artists, the costume department and my assistant directors (ADs)—as we waited for a break in the rain to start filming. We were extremely unlucky—we were basically marooned in a beautiful, wet and green forest with two stunning women for company, and all of us were just fretting, constantly looking skywards and muttering to our various gods to give us a break.

Mitali had to get back to college and Valerie had to get back to looking after her house, two kids and their schoolwork. Barun da, make-up artist Vidyadhar and I had no other work. But, for some obscure reason, we felt responsible for everything and everybody. The shoot stretched on for a whole week, with us grabbing shots the moment it stopped raining. Mitali was a real trooper—she was supposed to run barefoot through the forest for one scene and, except for a few twinges, did so with great aplomb. I later realized what it had actually cost her—one evening, as we were packing up to go back to the jungle lodge, I noticed that her feet were bleeding. She had been running up a grassy slope that had sharp stones under the green carpet of grass and carried on running until we got the shot. There was not a peep or whimper from her, just a slight favouring of the other foot. I was really impressed and slightly distraught—any of our more fancied actresses would have thrown a fit until they were blue in the face.

I immediately got out the first-aid kit and washed her feet with Dettol, and bandaged them myself, much to Mitali's great embarrassment and everybody else's knowing looks. She had very pretty feet—bony but with a lot of character. What with my foot fetish and all, that was when I really started noticing her as a person. I observed her closely over the next seven days of shooting, waiting for the rain to stop, walking up and down the hill daily, and dressing her feet every evening. The poor thing never had a choice and I'm sure was excruciatingly embarrassed, dying for the shoot to end so she could escape. But that never happened. I got over Valerie and wooed Mitali until she made the cardinal error of deciding to work with us on advertising film production after graduation. She walked into Genesis one day with a colleague, Sophie Joseph, a dyed-in-the-wool Mallu Catholic from Kottayam, with a curly, oily mop of hair and an unbelievable innocence and naivety. I couldn't believe that someone like Sophie actually existed.

The first thing I did was to wash the coconut oil out of Sophie's hair and give her a haircut. I rechristened her 'Sophie Amma', and that is how she has been known forever now. Mitali and Sophie immediately started owning their responsibilities in the office, by which time I had actually started dating the former. And so that nobody could blame me for nepotism, I was really hard on both of them. Mitali, half understanding her trial by fire, held her peace to a large extent, put her head down and worked her heart out. Only when I became unbearably obnoxious did she find a corner and weep quietly. When I noticed that, I would be very contrite and ease off a little bit.

She survived the agni pariksha, and became stronger and super efficient. One day, we had a minor exodus of senior people from the office, who wanted to start their own production house. So, Mitali and Sophie, long before they were ready, suddenly found themselves running the show and were scared out of their wits! We were really busy at the time, shooting films from morning to evening, back to back, with no let-up. It was one hell of a baptism by fire. They came through the whole ordeal remarkably intact and full of beans. They not only survived, they excelled.

My respect for Mitali rose hugely in tandem with her belief in herself and, somewhere at the back of my head, I had a niggling thought: I had caught a Bengali tigress by the tail, but could I hang on? (By the way, did I mention she was Bengali?) In those months and years of inexorable pressure and stress, having to deal with a tireless PK and Murphy had tempered Mitali and Sophie Amma into people made of steel. Later in life, others who encountered them often described Mitali as the lady with an iron fist wrapped in a velvet glove. Of course, it took me a while to understand this, but, by the time I did, it was too late to escape.

Anyway, slowly Mitali and Sophie took over the production side of Genesis, and we really started rocking with the topmost brands approaching us. Meanwhile, my remaining partner, Ravi Uppoor, wanted to start a shipping company with a friend of his, an ex-naval officer called Khokar. Our earlier partner, Mandeep Kakkar, had left a few years ago and had decided to produce feature films. He passed away in an extremely tragic and untimely manner in an air crash, leaving behind his wife and daughter.

Meanwhile, Mitali and I had been dating for at least a year and a half—and she obviously wanted to figure out where it was going. I, on the other hand, was so busy between the office and the few restaurants we were running (for fun) that it didn't occur to me that Mitali wanted a change of status. I was clueless and very happy as we were. I was thirty-five by then and she was twenty-one—though, in our relationship, she was always the more mature partner! One day, she decided she needed a break. We had been working 24x7 for almost ten months, and she hadn't seen her parents for a whole year. I saw her off and she told me categorically that she wasn't in any hurry to get back. If I felt that I needed a change in our personal equation, I could get in touch; otherwise, we could review the situation in a couple of months. In the beginning, I was quite pleased at being free again, but soon it began to weigh on me. I started getting restless and increasingly ill-tempered, until I realized I was missing her at home and at work. I had a lot of friends, but no soulmate.

I became difficult and crotchety as I didn't hear from her at all, and it took a few months to realize that the ball was now in my court. I had to do something drastic. I decided to go to Siliguri to visit Mitali at her parents' place. Now, throughout my professional life, I had always wanted to look distinguished; the way I went about it was by having a touch of grey at the temples. On the day I was supposed to fly to Bagdogra, I thought I would get a makeover of sorts done, not realizing that her parents were already under the impression I was a cradle-snatcher because of our age difference. Anyway, I went to my trusty hair people, Nalini and Yasmin, and asked them to dye my temple white, with a streak from my forehead to the back reminiscent of Indira Gandhi—she looked so cool with it.

Nalini fussed over me for a bit, wrapping clumps of hair in silver foil with foul-smelling bleach. It was a tedious and lengthy process. Then I had to sit still for an additional two hours for the hair to bleach to an ash-blonde colour. Amidst all the excitement of the makeover, I'd quite forgotten about the plane to Siliguri. I suddenly remembered I needed to catch a flight and, with a start, looked at my watch and leapt out of the chair, telling Nalini to wash off the goo as I needed to get to the airport in a rush. Nalini was totally dismayed. The bleach needed another hour to set properly, she said.

I forced her to wash off the gunk and darted into the car after casually glancing into the rear-view mirror. I nearly jumped out of my skin in shock! My hair, instead of being silvery white at the temples and down the middle, was a dirty orange—somehow both stiff and rough at the same time. I looked like a futuristic lafanga and, in that state of deep shock, I landed at Bagdogra airport to meet my future in-laws. They were all there, eagerly awaiting me. Mitali took one look at me and blanched.

'*Eeek!* What have you done?' she gasped aloud. Her parents, being old school, were much more polite, but I could see that their eyes had the look of a bad dream. They grinned and took it on the chin. It was a long drive from Bagdogra airport to Siliguri, with me ensconced in the front seat of the family Ambassador, her father driving and the two ladies in the back exchanging doomsday looks. I got along famously with the old boy; he was into all the things I loved—the great outdoors, good food, shikaar, the life of the tea gardens and a free country life; the only things missing were horses and polo!

What Mitali had forgotten to tell them was that I can't stay awake for more than five minutes in a moving vehicle and, while they were still getting over the shock of my appearance, I passed out on the old man's shoulder, mid-sentence, snoring intermittently. There was stunned silence for a while, as Mitali's parents tried to figure out whether this was my idea of a practical joke. Mitali, of course, was relatively unconcerned—she was used to it—until she suddenly realized with a start that her parents had no clue about this trait of mine.

So, it came to be that I spent the next four wonderful days at her parents' house, gorging on fabulous Bengali cuisine cooked by Aunty Ava, Mitali's elegant mother, trying to evade the vital questions—were we or were we not? If we were, then when? Finally, over dinner, Mitali broached the subject. 'Why have you come to Siliguri?' she asked innocently. I coughed and choked on the food, and said, 'To see you and meet your parents.'

'For what purpose?' she then asked sweetly. I stuttered and stammered while the three of them watched me squirm with single-minded focus, never letting me off the hook, until I blurted out that I wanted to marry their daughter. There! It was out and everybody visibly relaxed.

At the end of the evening, over a Scotch, her father asked, 'So, when do you guys want to actually get married?' I choked on the drink; things were spiralling out of my control and the walls were rapidly closing in around my imaginary freedom. I took what I thought was the longest outside bet and said, 'Next year.' It was January of 1984 when I said this.

'Done,' said her father, the venerable Anil Dutt. And so January next year it was. My proverbial goose was cooked! The only saving grace was that Mitali's mother, Aunty Ava, was not only a phenomenal cook, but had aged with such grace and charm that I knew that Mitali had the right genes and would look like her mother forty years hence. Phew!

34

Finding Dumbell

During one of my trips to Goa for a reconnaissance, I had the opportunity to invest in a small house by the Mandovi river. I often visited Goa to check on its progress while staying at Jennifer and Shashi Kapoor's beach shack on Baga beach. One fine morning, I went to help the local fishermen, called Ramponkars, pull a fishing net to land. This is a team activity as the men from the fishing village collectively pull in the net—it is almost like a tug of war, chanting bolis all along.

I looked up from the net into the rising sun and, lo and behold! I saw a vision straight from Valhalla! A beautiful Nordic Valkyrie, in the nude, was slanting in on a surfboard, riding a wave with extreme ease and grace. She was blonde and tanned. And on the prow of the shiny surfboard was a wooden carving of a fully grown Doberman Pinscher. I was mesmerized and gaped with my mouth open at this amazing sight, the rampon fishing net totally forgotten. She came gliding into the shallows on her board and, miraculously, the dog came alive, jumped off the board and swam ashore. They were both stunning to look at. I walked like a zombie across to her, in an absolute daze, and engaged her in a very stilted conversation, hypnotized by her perfect, tanned breasts.

I said, 'Wow, what a beautiful dog and it surfs!'

She replied, in a heavy German accent, 'Ja, ja, she is beautiful, no?' She saw my hypnotized gaze was neither on her face nor the dog, so she put out a perfectly manicured index finger under my chin and raised my eyes to hers without any hint of anger or malice, and smiled an incredibly vivacious smile. At that moment, she looked brighter than the sun. I was rendered speechless—a rare phenomenon.

I stuttered on about the beautiful dog. The dog's name was Kalia and the Valkyrie's name was Anne Britt, and she lived in Baga with her English boyfriend and ran a beachside boutique. I also learnt that Anne Britt was expecting and so was Kalia. I eagerly booked a pup of Kalia's litter from her and gave her Prithvi Theatre's address since I didn't have a permanent one. She smiled and walked off with Kalia, a vestige from a dream. I thought that was the last I would hear from her or Kalia.

Not even four months later, I got a frantic call from my staff at Prithvi saying a very pregnant German lady called Anne Britt had left a basket for me on her way to the airport, and the basket was alive and making noises! I rushed to Prithvi, opened the basket and saw a gangly pawed wet-nosed Doberman puppy looking up at me, all of two months old. It was love at first sight! I named him Dumbell, partly because he was so smart and clever.

Dumbell as a pup was all legs and paws, and I knew he was going to grow into a big dog, and he did; he was huge. His mother, Kalia, came from the Mary Magdalene line of Dobes and their main characteristic was a long, sensitive snout. You have watchdogs and lapdogs, but Dumbell was singularly a crotch dog! His extremely sensitive nose was used very effectively to identify people by burying it deep into their crotches. The men would be petrified and hold their breaths hoping that he wasn't hungry. The ladies were a bit shocked by his curiosity, but took it much better.

Being a bachelor and living in a one-bedroom flat was definitely not conducive to raising a Dobe, especially since I treated him like my firstborn. He used to come with me to all my film shoots and was excellent with children. The attention span of an average child is about two to three hours (these days it's far less), after which they get bored at the repetitive nature of a shoot and often zone out. We tried using a TV set with cartoons to keep them upbeat and entertained, but could only extend their interest by an hour or so. But if Dumbell was around, they would be all over him. Though they were initially scared of his size, they soon realized he was their large friend.

He displayed an enormous amount of patience with them, almost as if he knew that his job was to keep them happy and upbeat. With him around, I never faced any problems with the kids—they were always fresh, focused and happy to finish the shot and head back to Dumbell for his company. I remember, during a shoot, a kid had to climb up a ladder made up of an inclined slope of planks. He baulked at the task and refused. I took Dumbell up to the ladder, explained very simply to him to climb it and that I would give him a biscuit as a reward. He went up the ladder as though he did it every day, came back and demanded his biscuit. I then looked at the kid and told him, 'See, if Dumbell can do it, so can you.' The kid took heart and went up the sloping ladder like a squirrel.

I used to teach Dumbell how to be deft and careful during a shoot by placing a biscuit in the middle of a chess set, with the pieces around the biscuit. His task was to pick up the biscuit without knocking down any of the chess pieces. He would go around the chess board looking for a likely opening, then put his forelegs on the table to get a bird's-eye view and, very slowly, with his tongue and nose, nudge the biscuit to an opening and gently lift it out. He might have even moved the pieces around, but knocked none over.

Soon, he became an integral part of the office and was treated more like a crew member than a very clever dog. People began talking to him in full sentences. They would go up to him and gently explain, 'Dumbell, I am wearing white and the shot is in continuity, so please don't jump on me with your grubby paws.' And, believe me, he understood!

Once, I entered him in a dog show; I brushed his coat to a gleaming black and tan, clipped his nails and cleaned his impressive teeth, especially the canines. Off we trotted to the show and found that all the dogs on display had been trained to obey certain rules like 'heel' or 'sit', when the master stops walking, and 'stay', while the master walks about twenty yards off and then calls the dog. Good god, we had done nothing of the sort with Dumbell. We had about half an hour to prep him to perform. Luckily, in the office, I had taught him hand signals for commands like stop, sit, lie down and roll over, but he did not know how to stay or walk next to the master. I frantically tried explaining to him what to do—the reputation of the Kakar khandaan in the office was at stake!

He seemed totally distracted by the female dogs on display, and I was sure we would crash and burn in embarrassment. Finally, our name was announced: 'Dumbell Kakar and Prahlad Kakar'. A titter ran through the crowd of dog owners and audience members. I took off his leash and hoped to hell that he wouldn't go hurrying off after some tarted-up poodle. We walked on, with me frantically instructing Dumbell to heel. Of course, he was not in the mood to follow instructions, and he kept in line with me as an equal and not behind me as a subordinate. Fair enough! Now, we came to the second hurdle—to stop and sit, when the handler stopped and asked the dog to sit.

Stop he did and I had to frantically raise my index finger a few times for him to reluctantly sit. Phew! Late, but there. Now came a game of catch. All the dogs had to sit and stay while the handler walked twenty yards away and called out, 'Come!' Dumbell had never done anything like that before; panic-stricken, I quickly invented a hand signal by raising my open palm facing Dumbell, hoping like hell that he understands.

I made him sit, turned around and walked away with my palm facing him from behind my back, and tried to telepathically order him to keep sitting. We do strange things when put to the sword. He stayed, his eyes focused on my palm, rising on his haunches every now and then, but subsiding to the sit position each time. I turned on the mark and saw, to my relief, that Dumbell was still sitting with his tongue lolling out, ready to spring into action. I showed him the palm; he subsided, still very focused. The moment I indicated with my hand for him to come, he bounded over and was all over me. He thought it was a game! We came second in the obedience category—not bad for a one-year-old first-timer.

Mitali, having been brought up in tea estates, loved dogs. She took to Dumbell like family, which he was. He used to come out on dates with us and nobody batted an eyelid. After a while, people started sending him personal invitations for events on printed cards with *his* name on it as they knew I would bring him anyway. He was always a gentleman, except for his preliminary handshake of sniffing your crotch. After the initial pleasantries were over, he was perfect, blending in seamlessly, unless he wanted to draw your attention with a wet nose or a judicially placed paw.

Dumbell was a part of many ad films and always performed to perfection—from Big Bite to ECE Bulbs to a sports cycle. Big Bite was a classic. We were sent a very interesting script by Mohammed Khan's Enterprise Agency for a snack consisting of a chicken or veg patty in pita bread; the product was called Big Bite. Off we trooped to our old friend Parle's office to sample the product. The receptionist objected to the presence of our dog, so we sat at the reception until somebody allowed us all in, including Dumbell, who had a definite role to play in the proceedings.

The product was presented for tasting with great fanfare and we all looked at it with a bit of disappointment—it was a small, dry patty, with a salad filling in half a pita bread. It all looked a tad measly. I had my own ideas on how to make it substantial without compromising costs, but nobody was listening. I took a chicken patty and offered it to Dumbell. To everybody's horror, he gently but firmly refused the offering.

This really threw a cat among pigeons and there was a sanctimonious uproar at the sacrilege. I gently reminded them that they were all vegetarians and had no clue about how to make a juicy chicken patty. The pita and the salad tasted good, because they had been able to taste and tweak them, but the patty was no Big Bite. I told them I would do the film only if I could make my own patties for the shoot and left. In the car, Mitali, who was with me at the meeting, said we would never be awarded the film for trying to feed the product to Dumbell!

They did come back to us and two weeks later, we recorded the jingle with the maestro Louis Banks: 'Doncha feel like a Big Bite now!' We had the works in the film—from dancers like Rachel Ruben and actor Jaaved Jaaferi, to models including Mitali, and the one and only Dumbell, who first catches a ball in mid-air, during a cricket match, declaring the batsman out and then runs away with the ball being chased by both teams. The film was a hit and, initially, the products flew out of the kiosks. However, it ultimately failed—even the veg offering didn't work. They should have heeded Dumbell and taken him a little more seriously.

The funniest thing happened during a site visit. I was hanging around a Big Bite stall, beautifully painted and illustrated. A car pulled up, blaring loud music, and four young Gujju studs stepped out and ordered four veggie 'doncha'. I almost fell off my bike when I realized that they believed the product was called 'doncha' and not Big Bite.

We all live and learn. Big Bite was one of the biggest flops after 'New Delhi Times', where both had brilliant advertising campaigns, but the products never lived up to its promise. We learnt to never overpromise and underdeliver. Always underpromise and overdeliver. In my career as an advertising professional, I have come across many fabulously thought-out and well-executed campaigns, which were far better than the product they were meant for. This is a cardinal error made by agencies, in the hope of bagging a Cannes Lion.

Dumbell also featured in an incident that went viral at the time; its telling has got so exaggerated that even I can't recognize which one is the correct version any more. Here is how I remember it: JWT, one of India's largest agencies, had commissioned us to do a generic fast moving consumer goods (FMCG) film for Hindustan Lever. After the job was completed and delivered, there was an additional dubbing in six vernacular languages for which we had raised a bill of Rs 1.6 lakh. In those days, it was not a huge amount, but it was nothing to be scoffed at either. This was overlooked and not paid. We did not do much work with JWT Bombay—most of our work was with their Delhi and Bangalore offices. There was no regular follow-up, except for polite and gentle reminders, which were presumably ignored by the film department.

This was around the time of our annual office bash in Goa during the first rains. Every offseason, for our annual event, we managed to negotiate an excellent package of three nights and four days at the Taj Holiday Village in Candolim, Goa, for fourteen people plus a dog. Despite numerous attempts at writing and calling the film department at JWT, regarding the outstanding payment, duly earmarked for the office holiday, there was no response. Finally, we received an official letter from the department about paying us at a certain date. We planned the Goa trip post that date. However, closer to the day, they stopped taking our calls and this really pissed me off. The date arrived, but we still hadn't received our cheque in the mail.

With no holiday in sight, the office was a sad sight to behold— and the slate-grey sky outside, heralding the monsoon, didn't help. At lunch time, I had an idea. Since there was no work or calls—everybody connected to us thought that we were living it up in Goa—I told the staff to collect all the beach balls and frisbees from the production props, and go and spend the next three days at the swish JWT office. For one, they had a bigger office compared to our little 400 square feet office—they had 12,000 square feet to themselves—and they had a VCR in their conference room, probably among the first in Bombay.

With great glee, the whole office—peons, Dumbell and all—left for Laxmi Building in Fort, which was where their office was, on the sixth floor with a terrace. The lift man refused to let Dumbell in, so he was dispatched by the staircase accompanied by a peon. The rest of the office took the lift to the JWT reception, armed with copies of the letters of promise and the outstanding bill, which we proceeded to plaster all over the walls, much to the dismay of a highly flappable receptionist, who was desperately trying to call management to inform them of our righteous invasion.

We challenged the art department to a basketball match on the terrace during their break. Sophie Amma took Dumbell's ball and hid it in the art department, and told Dumbell to find and fetch it. He took it as open season for examining crotches at will and started running around. With the men against the wall, trying to protect their goolies like the sumo wrestlers do, and the ladies standing on their desks and typewriters, hoping to avoid the scrutiny, a ruckus ensued. Those who didn't look at our activities as shocking and unacceptable actually joined in the general mayhem and decided to holiday with us on that memorable day.

We finally retired to their conference room, and managed to get our hands on some movies and watched them with great excitement, having ordered tea and pakoras from the canteen. Finally, it was time to go home and as we were making our way to the lift, an officious-looking suit, sweating profusely—as he had run up the stairs rather than waiting for the lift—came up to us and blustered, 'Who is in charge of you horrible lot?' Without batting an eyelid and with no preparation, everybody unanimously pointed to Dumbell. His face was a sight to behold. We trooped off, promising to return the next day for our annual holiday. I must say, JWT was a lot more fun than Goa!

The next morning, as we were gathering in the office to go back to Laxmi Building, a smartly dressed peon landed up and offered us the much-awaited cheque. We all cheered and took off to Goa for the next three days. Then came the best part: I started getting calls from lots of smaller production houses, who had huge outstanding payments and no clout to collect their dues, all wanting to borrow Dumbell to help them collect it.

The news of our visit to JWT spread around the advertising fraternity like wildfire and, just like the film industry, various agencies exult in the misfortunes of others—whether it's a lost account or an incident like ours. And so, various agencies used to come up to the honchos of JWT and commiserate with them about what unethical bastards the Genesis team were and how they sympathized with JWT, all the while, behind their backs, gleefully celebrating with us.

As the demands to borrow Dumbell grew, we decided to train him to actually perform. We taught him to carry an envelope in his mouth and someone would let him in to the chief financial officer's (CFO) cabin. The CFO—inevitably a vegetarian TamBrahm or Gujju—would suddenly see a huge Doberman with his front paws on his desk, dropping a soggy envelope which read, 'Please pay to the bearer of this note the sum of xxx outstanding. PS: He does not understand the cheque is in the mail. PPS: He does not understand "come back tomorrow".'

By the time they finished reading the note, Dumbell would be expecting a biscuit or a ball as his reward and would start barking and looking hopeful. The CFO, unable to differentiate between playful barking and serious violence, would immediately wet his trousers and summon security, who would then chase a disappointed Dumbell around the office. Dumbell would come back to the guy who had escorted him to the office and they would rapidly exit. The cheque would arrive a little later and sometimes even before they reached the office.

The only other home that Dumbell was comfortable in was Maya and Sunil Alagh's house, at Baharistan, next to the Parsee General Hospital. Anjori, their little daughter who only came up to Dumbell's shoulder in height, had been adopted by him as his ward and special friend. She would tie a rakhi on his paw every year and he took his responsibilities very seriously. To the extent that during Holi he would guard her against all and sundry, including her friends, and I would get a call saying, 'Please tell Dumbell to let me play Holi with my friends; he is growling at them.'

Once, I got a frantic call from Maya. 'Please bring Dumbell as Anjori is refusing to go to school!' she implored.

'What's Dumbell got to do with her school?' I asked.

'Just come please!' she exclaimed.

What had transpired was that during class, the teacher had asked the kids to describe their pets, if they had one. Anjori, not to be outdone, bragged about Dumbell, her pet and friend who was bigger than her. The class laughed and didn't believe her, and when she insisted that Dumbell was her pet, the teacher told her to bring him to school the next day.

As Dumbell was not there, she feigned a stomach ache and did not go to school. Maya, being the good doctor, immediately figured out what was bothering her daughter. Out came the story. I dispatched Dumbell to the Alagh home and she triumphantly entered a startled school with this huge Dobe in tow. She managed to convince her classmates that he wouldn't do anything to anybody, as long as they didn't fight with her. Both of them had a blast that day and Anjori became the most popular girl in class.

Dumbell was hugely popular with everybody he came in contact with. On one Diwali, he was outside our house on Mount Mary, when someone lit a string of crackers. Dobes are very sensitive to sounds, and Dumbell panicked and ran down the hill. He then lurked around Hill Road, trying to find our house near the Mount Mary steps. An old Parsi gentleman saw him, panicked and stressed, and realized he was a domesticated dog and took him home—away from the noise. We waited for three days, looking high and low for him, with no luck.

I finally put an ad in the papers describing him and his name. Over the next three days, I was bombarded with letters and telephone calls from people across the country and spectrum enquiring about Dumbell and telling me how irresponsible I was to let him out on Diwali night. I understood then how many friends he had across the country. Finally, I got a call from Mahatma Gandhi Veterinary Hospital in Lower Parel that someone had left behind a lost Dobe and could we come have a look.

We leapt into the car and, with our heart in our mouth, drove to the hospital. And there he was! He seemed to have made friends with everybody at the kennels—the doctor, the handlers and even the jamadars. After due procedure, we ran into another problem. They refused to let him go until I promised that once a week he would have to spend a day at the facility—and he did. Dumbell lived till he was seventeen years old, very unusual for a Dobe, as their lifespan is only about ten years. He died peacefully in his sleep at a friend's farm in Alibaug.

35

A Fanta-stic Chance!

One day, Kamal Oberoi from HTA Delhi arrived in office with
Ravi Dhariwal of PepsiCo. They had very exciting news for us:
Pepsi was all set to launch in India and had roped in Remo Fernandes
and Juhi Chawla to play the leads for the launch film 'Are you ready
for the magic?' They wanted to base it on Michael Jackson's ad film for
Pepsi made for an American audience.

I had been the go-to person for Kamal O when he needed slightly
out-of-the-box ideas, or even just an unbiased reaction. When they
bounced their idea off me, I loved the script—with certain reservations.
One was that there were no real rockstars in India whose following cut
across the country, only film stars or cricket players, so the Michael
Jackson model didn't quite make it. That's where Juhi came in, fresh
off her success in *Qayamat Se Qayamat Tak* (*QSQT*). It was going to
be a mega production to bring Pepsi to India. They were negotiating
with Vidhu Vinod Chopra, a very successful feature film director, to
work on this ad film.

Truth be told, I was hesitant about using a feature film director
instead of a good ad film director. I believe that telling a story in thirty
seconds or one minute is a sophisticated craft in itself, and a feature

film director would be hard-pressed to cram everything into the time span comfortably. At the time, I felt that long-format directors tended to look down on the ad film industry and did not respect its extremely critical parameters of high-quality content delivered with proper timing that makes for effective storytelling.

Very few people realized that the standards expected of us were based on international references given to us for adaptation, which originally would have cost millions of dollars, while our budget was only a few lakh rupees. Our equipment was outdated and barely adequate. It took a huge amount of planning, innovation and enormous financial risk to meet international standards even halfway.

Add to this, in our business, there were no open-ended budgets—if we exceeded the budget, then we paid for it from our own pockets. In fact, a lot of the times, when something went wrong, that's exactly what we did—reshoot it at our own cost. I was a little unhappy about Pepsi and HTA deciding to give the launch films to feature film directors. It was probably because I wanted to do it myself, as it seemed like such an exciting project with a really good budget. Feature film directors did not have to face the professional consequences of a badly done job as they were already stars in their own right and, unlike us, they weren't dependent on the odd ad film to make or break them.

But I bit my tongue, and told Kamal that it seemed like a fabulous project and he should go for it. I asked him to ensure that the cameraman and assistant director had a background in advertising. The campaign worked like a bomb and Pepsi was launched. Later, Vidhu Vinod Chopra told me that my advice to HTA and Pepsi on the cameraman and assistant director had helped them tremendously.

Many months later, Kamal called me to Delhi and briefed me on the Fanta Orange films, almost as a consolation prize. Fanta, which is part of the Pepsi family, didn't carry the kind of hysteria and stress that a Pepsi ad film did. So, we had a relatively easy time and managed to make a nice, classy and funny film starring Satish Shah and an in-house actor called Derek Afonso. The films were all about the lengths people go to get a free Fanta, where Satish Shah was seen frantically changing clothes, names and addresses to get his free Fanta.

Derek played the Fanta delivery boy. We even made our own version, where Derek rings the doorbell of an opulent mansion and a gorgeous lady in a dressing gown opens the door. She looks at the free Fanta, grabs the very good-looking delivery man by the collar, whisks him in and closes the door. A heartbeat later, the door opens a crack and an immaculately manicured hand snakes out and whisks the bottles of Fanta inside, closing the door firmly. Pepsi loved our version, but no cigar. C'est la vie.

Jean arrived one day with a client called Royal Touch, who sold artificial leather. So, we went into a huddle and brainstormed a very basic script of a guy who seamlessly transits from one location to another, where the transitions are not just left to right or right to left, but also from the bottom of the frame to the top, from one situation to another—and he always lands on Royal Touch. Since we had planned to shoot the whole film on a set, it had to be designed very well, as it would make the difference between a great communication or an also-ran. And, of course, we had Jean to contend with—she would badger us till we got the look and feel to her satisfaction.

We decided that the film would be shot entirely on a B&W (black-and-white) cut-out set in 2D against a white translucent plastic sheet, about thirty-forty feet long, stretched on a frame and backlit; it was called a cyclorama. This gives it a white limbo effect. The only colours in the frame would be the furniture resplendent in Royal Touch and the clothes of the cast. The product and the cast would be in 3D. The character was in constant movement and the sets had to be designed to accommodate that.

It starts by focusing on a crowd gathered around a single-seater sofa. They are touching and feeling the sofa, and ooh-ing and aah-ing. Our character walks in and sits on it, as soon as he does, he falls through the bottom of the frame, hat and all, and lands in a cut-out car, to the surprise of a good-looking girl sitting in its passenger seat. The car zooms down the street and stops near a couch. The girl gets out of the car and lies down on the couch with a shrink leering at her. The girl, the couch and the camera slide into the shrink's room with the background changing smoothly. The shrink feels the Royal Touch couch and his hand wanders to the girl's leg; she slaps his hand away smartly, gets up, and the camera follows her as she leaves through a door into an anteroom full of people and Royal Touch furniture.

Our original character walks past the camera, realizes he is in the wrong place, turns around and exits. A good-looking, well-dressed executive assistant–type lady wearing a skirt, jacket and heels with long legs walks diagonally into the room with a bunch of files; we follow her into an office where a young suited, booted boss is leaning on his desk on the phone—the office is completely furnished in Royal Touch. She drops a couple of files into his tray. He reacts in dismay, quickly picks up the files and drops them in her tray. He then sits on his Royal Touch executive chair, with his legs up on the desk, looking smug. Cut to the packshot.

To design all the moving sets so that they slid past in a seamless manner, we went to our go-to architect and part-time set designer, the brilliant Ratan Batliboi, who had cut his teeth designing amazing sets for theatre. Ratan put on his thinking cap, for this was not just any set, but one that was 2D with 3D elements in it, and constantly moving with the camera on a trolley, sometimes in the opposite direction. Ratan put all the sets on rolling stock, basically on wheels with ball bearings, which would create a moveable feast. And the camera would also be on a parallel trolley, so that we could get all our transitions seamlessly correct with the backgrounds being pushed manually. Those were the days of sheer innovation and in-camera effects—no post-production and easy shortcuts like the ones that exist today.

Since we had cut our teeth with the master and the genius, Kamath mama, as trainees, we had learnt to think on our feet and by the seat of our pants. The casting of the film was a cakewalk compared to the visual calisthenics. We had an ensemble cast of all the usual suspects, whom we knew to be huge talents without being fussy or moody. This turned the shoot into a picnic. We had Jaaved Jaaferi, Rachel Reuben, the late Col Kapoor, a young Ashish Sawhny, Amrita Naidu and the late Bunty Dhawan of *Nukkad* fame. The ad film was one of a kind and we managed to shoot it to perfection with a really catchy jingle that had been prerecorded.

Around the same time, we had been asked by Raymond to do a trouser commercial for their ready-to-wear trousers straight off the rack. We were relatively confident by then with in-camera movement and decided to shoot the entire film below the waist, so to speak. So, we got Shiamak Davar to help us cast and choreograph the film from his troupe of dancers. We wanted to shoot the film in one long trolley movement, following a long, leggy model in a red skirt and stilettos (never forget the stilettos) walking through clusters of men wearing the trousers and their reaction to the young lady in a free-swinging skirt.

There were all kinds of reactions, some obviously so taken by her that they would walk backwards, banging into people, standing and staring. We even had a young fellow turning around and following her—when she stops, turns and taps her foot enquiringly at him, he turns around as if he has forgotten something important and rapidly legs it out of the frame. It was one long, choreographed master shot with rapid close-ups of the fall, texture and impeccable tailoring of the trousers, set to a beautiful track by the maestro Louis Banks. The film was exuberant and pacey, aimed at the youthful professional executive.

We went off to the client to have the film approved and, during the screening, I found to my dismay that the client team led by a Mr Singhania were all fifty-plus. Anyway, they had approved the script and treatment, and so, with muttered prayers, we ran the film. Dead silence from the marketing team. We ran it again and then again for the third time. The dead silence persisted. Then Mr Singhania cleared his throat and said, 'Nice film, but don't you find it a bit fast?' That opened the floodgates and everybody suddenly found their bearings, and tried to echo the boss's opinion about how fast the film was.

I had a flashback to my job interview with Jog Chatterjee. I waited patiently for the cacophony to subside and cleared my throat with intent. Everybody looked at me including the people from the agency and just as they were about to cave in against such collective rejection, I looked squarely at Mr Singhania and started placatingly, by agreeing with him wholeheartedly that the film was a tad fast and edited to look that way deliberately. An enquiring silence followed.

I then told them how very relieved I was that the room full of fifty-year-olds, including Mr Singhania, had found the film too fast as they were not the target audience for it at all! The film was for the twenty to thirty age group. I explained that if the marketing team had found the film to be slow, we would have been in deep trouble (meaning deep shit) as the target audience would find it boring and predictable after the first viewing. A pregnant silence filled the room. Everybody shuffled uncomfortably and looked surreptitiously at Mr Singhania, as if he was the only senior citizen in the room. I must admit, he never blinked or hesitated, instead he smiled widely and said, 'You are absolutely right!' He got up, shook everybody's hands and left, and that was that.

36

Maggi in 2 Minutes!

By this time, we were on a relatively good wicket with HTA, Delhi, and had already done a few good films for them. So, they decided to give us a film from Nestlé, one of their hugely important and pernickety clients. I was summoned to Delhi to their office in Jhandewalan Extension, which was considered a slightly seedy part of Delhi. But then, they also possessed 30,000 square feet of office space spread over three floors in that part of the city. In a very hush-hush manner, I was briefed about the launch of Maggi Noodles in India.

It was an instant noodle—a product originally invented by Nissin's founder, Momofuku Ando. One boils the crispy pre-fried noodles in water with a sachet of tastemaker to give some colour and taste to the bland noodles. Variants of this product produced by different companies had taken the world by storm for the sheer number of flavours available, and the ease in cooking and serving the noodles.

India was among the last of the blocks. Partly because of its inability to buy expensive packaged foods and partly because we, as a country, were too hung up on our ethnic tastes and flavours—we loved our dal chawal, sambar rice, rajma chawal or fish curry rice too much to want to experience some bland, alien noodle curry. So, the launch of the product by Nestlé was a huge, but calculated, risk and they were willing to funnel a lot of money into it. The target audience was very carefully chosen: harrowed housewives and hungry children between the ages of five and ten, just back from school or play or wherever— too early for dinner and not quite teatime either, but the kids were hungry, clamorous and whiny nonetheless.

Thus entered the 2 minute Maggi Noodles, with its 'quick to make, good to eat' tagline. A senior suit from HTA briefed me personally, saying the ad would show a bunch of kids between the ages three and five playing together and having a good time in the garden. I suggested that they could perform as an impromptu band, banging out a basic tune, and enjoying themselves thoroughly. By giving them this idea, I shot myself in the foot because this was much more difficult to shoot than any of the ideas that had been proposed.

In the middle of the noisy soirée, the mother comes out to check on them, and one of the kids goes up to her and bleats, 'Mummy, I am hungry!' She says, 'Two minutes.' And the jingle kicks in as we get into the prep, showing the packet, the product plopping into the boiling water, the adding of the tastemaker and then cut straight to the kids enjoying the treat, watched on by a proud mom. End with the packshot. It looked simple—cute and direct. But only a production house knows that the simpler it sounds, the more difficult it is to execute, especially if it involves three- and four-year-olds. They are a law unto themselves.

I sloped back to Bombay with the sinking feeling of a looming Murphy-driven disaster, and got down to casting and finding locations for the film. The location was easy enough to find, but the task of finding cute and obedient four-year-olds was herculean. After going to tens of playschools and meeting with friends of friends, we narrowed it down to Valerie Agha's daughter and Zinia, a slightly older Parsi girl, who was a child artiste and followed the brief (thank god). As I had a personal dislike for pudgy, spoilt kids, I picked a three-and-half-year-old lean and athletic kid—he looked angelic, but was the devil incarnate, as it turned out—and another cute child, who was a bit older. What a shoot we had!

One of the kids had a small furry dog and refused to let go of it, so we included the pet in the film. We built a stand in the garden for the band to play and gave them musical instruments like a trumpet, a drum set, a guitar and a bongo. They went at it in their own way, and I tried to keep it as natural and organic as possible, instructing Mr Rao, the DOP, to shoot as many candid shots as possible of them having a blast. Luckily, the kids became friends pretty quickly and started having a good time, banging on the drums and causing general mayhem. To get them together for one establishing long shot was a huge task. Somehow, we managed to do that, despite the production assistant going ape—R.M. Rao showed us a side to him that day which I hadn't seen before; he showed the patience of Job, the biblical character.

Nishant, the athletic little boy, blew the trumpet in Valerie's daughter's face and laughed uproariously—luckily, we caught the moment on camera. The shoot was carrying along, totally out of control, but in a nice, happy way, with the kids doing their own thing and having fun. Intuitively, I knew that we should keep shooting and try to make sense of it on the editing table. Now came the tricky part. One of the kids had to run up to the mom watching fondly from the veranda and say, 'Mummy, I am hungry!' It was the shot that the entire film hung on—the money shot.

We got both the smallest kids to say it. One was Valerie's daughter, who was shy and had big eyes and a slight lisp. The other was Nishant, who was a bit aggressive, and said, 'I want my food and I want it now!' This shot alone took us the better part of an hour. Meanwhile, we packed off the kids and moved into the kitchen to start on all the prep shots, which went on well into the night. Food shots, that's one area in which you can actually play god. The food will only look as good as the effort put into making it look good. The experimentation, seeing the way food reacts to heat and to cold, how to make it steam and still have kids eat it without burning their mouths ... It's all part of the process.

No post-production special effects, no cleaning up the shot later, everything in-camera and what you saw was what you lived with. When we threw Maggi into a glass beaker of boiling water to film a point-of-view shot from inside the cooking pot, we found that the flour separated, and instantly the liquid became milky and opaque. It took us many days of prep to figure out how to stop that from happening so that we could clearly see the tastemaker spreading its goodness and mingling with the noodles. It doesn't just happen—it was engineered with a lot of time and energy put into it, so that we could avoid unpleasant surprises on the day of the shoot.

Luckily, we had a state-of-the-art kitchen in our tiny office and everybody learnt how to cook, including Joel, the peon, who was in charge of the production peti. He went on to become a master packshot artist and is probably the highest paid professional in the business today. Genesis actually introduced the business of food shoots in India, as there were no food stylists and speciality camerapersons—even for shooting tabletops. Especially with food, one requires a tremendous amount of patience and a certain kind of temperament.

Almost everyone who subsequently became a food stylist actually learnt on the job with us. So, preparing for the shooting of Maggi Noodles was a huge learning experience for the entire crew. It was because of this shoot that we started insisting on setting aside a whole day to shoot packshots and food shots in the future, and also plan and cost for them separately instead of just clubbing them willy-nilly with the shoot concerning the talent. The value addition, by focusing on the food and packs, was huge. Seeing the changes taking place in advertising in the 1980s and 1990s, an extra day to shoot food soon became the norm.

Anyway, back to the Maggi launch film. After a tedious preparation segment the night before, we began shooting the consumption segment the next morning, where the kids were supposed to eat their noodles, neatly and politely, with their napkins tucked under their chins. They were also supposed to nod vigorously with big smiles of appreciation and a few 'wows' had to be thrown in. It was all nauseatingly predictable and oh cho chweet! We shot as per the board and I almost threw up as I saw all the suits nodding vigorously as we shot the kids eating. Jesus H. Christ! This was definitely not turning out to be a Genesis film.

So, we quickly ran through the required set of consumption shots and sent all the suits off the set, saying we needed to shoot the packshot again as the cellophane was reflecting light, which meant we couldn't read the brand name clearly in the shot and, therefore, had to do it again. The suits, of course, had never heard of dulling spray. They left rapidly having done their due diligence. Clearly, they also wanted to escape an enthusiastic Dumbell. The kids, on the other hand, were promised that whoever found a new way to eat the noodles, no holds barred, while having a lot of fun, would get to take Dumbell home for a day.

The only rule was that they couldn't sling the noodles on any of the other participants in the ad. The kids, having been released from all constraints, leapt on the bowls of noodles placed in front of them with gusto—some used forks and tried to twist the noodles around it, some used their hands and lifted the noodles high and slowly lowered them into their wide-open mouths, some put their mouths directly into the bowl and slurped noisily and messily. Most importantly, they had a blast and it showed—yelling and screaming and egging each other on. It was a riot and we loved it, and caught most of it on film. And that was the portion we used for the consumption segment. We got Louis Banks to do a really lovely tune for the film, keeping in sync the blowing of the trumpet and the dialogue, 'Mummy, I am hungry!' We now had two segments in the film that were spontaneous and slightly out of control, but I loved that natural quality of it. So what if it wasn't on the storyboard?

Off I went, carrying the doubleheader for an agency–client screening. On reaching the HTA office, I assumed that we would toodle off to a preview theatre, which could screen doubleheaders. There was one at the Taj Palace, on Sardar Patel Road. No such luck, I learnt to my dismay. HTA had a makeshift screening room on the second floor of its office and in that theatre of the absurd was an old Russian mobile projector running on a light bulb—no arc lamp either. They had a separate sound system rigged to it to run a separate soundtrack, roughly in sync. When I say roughly, I mean quite roughly. It was not meant to run lip-synced dialogue, only background music. Ambar

Brahmachari, the senior suit, and the rest of the cohorts settled in to watch the film.

The lights dimmed and, with a massive clatter, the ancient projector sprung to life with its feeble projection lamp, throwing the images on a makeshift yellowish screen. The film looked terrible and the sound was even worse. To be fair, this was the first time I was seeing the film projected, having edited it on a machine with a 6×6 inch screen. I actually thought the film looked awful and incoherent, with bad sound and very bad camera work. I went numb with shock.

They ran it three times and each time it looked worse and worse until, in acute embarrassment, I wanted to run, hide or just disappear. It took sheer willpower for me to remain in the room. Then began a trickle of comments that slowly became a torrent: 'This is hopeless!' 'I can't understand anything!' 'It's too fast.' 'The sound is out of sync.' 'The main kid looks like a malnourished refugee.' 'The consumption is messy and all over the place.'

On and on it went.

In my paralysed mind, it was all white noise and I nodded dumbly at all the comments ripping the film apart as I did not believe that it was defendable either. So, in this darkest gloom, the team sat down to suggest changes to improve the film. There were twenty-four shots in the film and there were thirty-two changes suggested. In any other circumstance, I would have found this funny. The decision not to show it to the client was immediately taken. The client was a tough, no-nonsense gent named Pradeep Pant, called 'Punter' by his friends. The call to an eagerly awaiting Punter was made and a mumbled excuse was given. He would have none of it and said, 'What's the problem? Share it with me.'

Mr Brahmachari told him that it was a disaster, and they would have to reshoot most of it, so he would rather not show it. Pradeep 'Punter' Pant insisted on seeing it in all its rottenness. After great hemming and hawing, they agreed to show it to him. When Punter wanted something, he usually got it. We went to the preview theatre at Taj Palace, and I sheepishly handed over the doubleheader to the projectionist and told him to set the volume on medium. Everybody settled in the plush seats with kadak air conditioning. I was studiously ignored, while Mr Brahmachari furiously tried to prepare Punter for the disaster that was about to unfold.

I crept into the last row and gave the signal to start. The film sprang to life in the colours of Kodak and the jingle came through in all its fidelity: catchy and in sync. There was a stunned silence after it ran its course, finally broken by Punter. 'Hey, Brahm, that's not so bad! What are you talking about?' Mr Brahmachari, equally shocked and embarrassed, mumbled, 'Yeah, it's looking okay here; must have been the projection.' Punter was actually quite relieved by then and was really enthusiastic about the film, and so was an embarrassed but relieved Ambar Brahmachari.

At this point, I took my chance to save the agency's face and my ass. I interrupted all the backslapping and celebration by loudly clearing my throat, and, in the pause, interjected, 'I do agree that the film is a tad fast, but don't worry, I will re-edit it and bring it back for approval next week.' Ambar Brahmachari quickly jumped into the fray and said, 'We thought so too. Please make the necessary corrections.' Punter, not to be left out, said, 'Don't change anything from the consumption sequence; it's perfect.'

Everybody agreed happily and the rest is history. Maggi Noodles still uses the same tune and Nishant, 'the malnourished refugee', went on to become the national face of Sundrop Oil from ITC as the kid doing a perfect cartwheel and running away from an oversized, toppling poori.

37

The Jhinghh Thing

Rediffusion had just bagged the Gold Spot account and, in their due diligence, had figured out that the positioning of the product was only aimed at kids. However, the product was not necessarily consumed only by children. The group that consumed soft drinks the most, and mainly colas, was the fifteen- to twenty-five-year-old lot—so why not make Gold Spot attractive to this segment? If they positioned the brand for young college kids instead, it would not alienate their present kiddy group, causing the consumption to increase and the group to grow.

Gold Spot had started strong with their infamous line, penned by Kersy Katrak, 'Live a little hot, sip a Gold Spot!' The ad featured a young and sultry Rekha sipping on a Gold Spot. After this, the brand had lost its way and had been aimed at children. So the team sat together with the amazingly talented Kamlesh Pandey to create a line even better than the original. The tagline Kamlesh Pandey came up with was: 'Gold Spot. The zing thing!' It translated fabulously into the vernacular as the 'jhinghh thing'.

The agency had designed the TV campaign around a peppy jingle and about four to six scenes where great-looking young ladies in different locations would profess their desire for the product and a young Lothario would disappear in a flash and appear mid-action, carrying two bottles of Gold Spot. For instance, a guy is driving a motorcycle in the middle of traffic and the lady pillion rider sings of her desire for a Gold Spot. He disappears, leaving the girl holding herself in thin air and the motorcycle still running driverless down the road, much to her consternation. Cut to a close-up of the bottles popping open as an introduction to the brand and then the young man lands back in the frame from the top, facing her, and hands her the bottle—all the while the bike is still running.

In those days, there were very few post-production facilities and the ones that were available were of very low quality. So, we had to plan the shoot in-camera as usual, with all the logistical nightmares attached. We had to fix the motorcycle on a flatbed truck along with the camera, so that it was locked on to the frame. Then we had to move the flatbed through traffic, with the couple lip-syncing the jingle, pop the guy out and drop him back on the motorcycle from just out of the frame, holding the bottles of Gold Spot.

We had to be very careful as, on the first take, the poor male model landed with a thud, groaning in agony. He had landed smack on his goolies. Ouch! Luckily, the bike was on a flatbed or he would have fallen on the road and probably been run over. He recovered after a while with lots of fanning and ice packs. We had about four or five scenarios for the series of ads: a pair on roller skates, a café with lots of college kids and so on. The campaign was one of the most successful product relaunches of its time and the toast was 'Gold Spot. The jhinghh thing'.

Mohammed Khan's agency, which was handling the Charminar cigarettes account under the banner of Vazir Sultan Tobacco Company (VST) was told that the company needed help revamping its image as sales had stagnated. Charminar was a cult brand among students and blue-collar types, as it was a very basic smoke, unfiltered and raw. But it was losing market share since it was far from premium. I remember, when I was in college, at the beginning of the month, when everybody was flush with cash, the choice of the new generation was Wills or Gold Flake. But, by the end of the month, everybody was broke and the choice—out of desperation—would shift to Charminar.

It was nicknamed 'Khopadi Chaap', skull and crossbones, as it was strong and unfiltered. VST tried to launch a milder version called Charminar Virginia, which bombed, just as Mohammed Khan had predicted. That's when they looked to him to pull their chestnuts out of the fire. Mohammed Khan had left Contract Advertising and had started his own dukaan, called Enterprise.

He worked on the look and feel to build a premium value for the product with young and aspirational consumers, who sought an upwardly mobile lifestyle. Mohammed Khan and his team came up with a cigarette that had a filter, but the greatest innovation was in creating a soft pack, fashioned with the look and feel of denim. They called it Charms, to create a pedigree for the brand.

Charms was launched in Bangalore as a test market. It just took off like a rocket. It soon went national and it was truly the choice of the new generation. Mohammed Khan called us in to design a film worthy of the brand's youthful image—keeping up with the exuberance and aspirations of the young. We batted ideas around and finally narrowed the film down to a day in the life of a fashion photographer. It was a new, bold career option for talented young people who didn't want to be doctors or engineers.

We designed the film around a spectacular fashion shoot with international-looking models moving in a choreographed sequence to music from a really well-designed studio with a lighting stage and backdrops, to a lounge area full of stacked soft cushions in rich reds, scarlets and pinks. We didn't want to show anybody actually smoking, so we planned to place the pack very strategically in most of the frames and have the protagonist wear denims.

His assistant was a no-nonsense young lady, dressed in tracks, and as good-looking as the models on the studio floor. We decided to show the protagonist and his assistant preparing for the shoot in a swift montage sequence. Those were the days of celluloid still cameras. The choice of film was Kodak Chrome, resulting in slides, and the choice of cameras were Nikon and Hasselblad for large-format stills.

The film then opens on to the shoot with six exotic Indian and international models moving to the music in a choreographed sequence, with our photographer shooting them from different angles. The sequence was in slow motion, at sixty to eighty frames per second, and, with the 'khachak-click' of the shutter, the image would freeze into a photograph. The brand was always subliminally present as an extension of the photographer (in denim).

A sexy, husky voice crooned the jingle and a strong driving beat pushed it along: 'Charms is the spirit of freedom. Charms is the way we are.' As the shoot ends and the photographer calls it a wrap, we see him in a sports car with his assistant navigating a narrow road going into the sea, like a sea wall. A Charms cigarette is lit and we reveal the car parked on a finger of a road in the middle of the sea. The assistant sits on the bonnet of the car strumming a guitar and the photographer stands with one leg up on the fender, seemingly relaxed as he smokes. 'Charms is the way we are!'

It was quite difficult to find six women who looked international and kickass, to boot. We also needed someone who didn't look like a typical chocolate boy to play the photographer. He had to have character and charisma, and we had to find his sexy no-nonsense assistant, as well. It took us a month to cast the film. We found a Tibetan girl and an Anglo-Indian girl in Bombay, and a Somalian girl from Delhi to play the models. The assistant was from my office—none other than Mitali, who was playing herself!

Charms was an unprecedented success as far as cigarette launches were concerned, and it took a Mohammed Khan to throw the book out of the window and reinvent cigarette advertising for the next generation.

⌢

Now, on to the story of how I cast a girl from Somalia in the ad film. Around that time, I had to make a trip to Delhi for a client meeting and had a few hours to kill. I found myself in the Defence Colony market. Defence Colony used to be my hangout during my college days, because my mother used to live at A-339. That day, I was wandering around, checking out all the fancy new places like Moets and such when I noticed a statuesque, attractive African girl, in a strappy top and really short denim shorts, walking along with a bag of groceries. She had legs that stretched on forever and an hourglass figure. Obviously, she had also caught the attention of some local louts, who were double-seated on a bicycle and following her, passing lewd comments.

She ignored them and kept walking. They followed, and seeing how she was not retaliating, they pedalled up to her boldly. The passenger sitting on the connecting bar reached out and put his arm between her legs, lifted her bodily (quite a feat), carried her for about ten to fifteen yards, in the crook of his arms and dumped her unceremoniously on the road in a heap. Joined by a third friend, they stood around laughing like jackasses. Nobody said a word (that's Delhi for you). She quietly picked herself up, gathered her groceries, put a hand into her handbag and, with her head bowed, tried walking past them.

This time, they blocked her way. So out came her hand from her handbag, holding an olive-green can of military-issue mace. She gleefully sprayed it all over their faces, and almost instantly the three tormenters collapsed into a heap of boneless bodies, making choked, gurgling sounds, with fluids running out from every orifice in copious amounts. She smartly flipped on the safety catch of the can, casually put it back in her bag and walked away!

I was shell-shocked by the whole episode and rather thrilled to see this young lady destroying three huge louts in a matter of seconds. I walked up to her with great trepidation and congratulated her on her amazing feat. She smiled a dazzling smile with perfect teeth and I asked her if she had ever modelled. 'A little,' she responded. Later, I learnt she had modelled for Gucci, Versace and the likes. Emboldened, I enquired whether she would come and do an assignment for me in Bombay. She actually agreed and said that a visit to the city was on her bucket list. And that's how I met Hodan from Somalia and cast her in the Charms film.

Hodan arrived in Bombay by flight, and was received and escorted to my old Dariya Mahal flat, which was being used by three of our office girls—Mitali, Sophie Amma and Dinaz. Of course, with due permission from Suman, who was now settled in Munger at the Bihar School of Yoga. Hodan and Sophie Amma hit it off immediately—both of them Mad Hatters, dark-skinned beauties, with gleaming teeth and bright, wicked eyes. Thus, the legend of Hodan started from Om Dariya Mahal on Nepean Sea Road, a building full of Kutchhi and Gujarati diamond merchants from Zaveri Bazaar.

One evening, Hodan and Sophie were coming back from a fitting in Colaba when the latter realized that she had forgotten the house keys inside the flat. Both Mitali and Dinaz were scouting elsewhere. Screwed! They hung around outside the flat for a bit (remember, cell phones didn't exist yet). Finally, they decided to try and talk a neighbour into letting them into their flat so that they could leap from that neighbour's balcony into their own—about a four-foot jump—hoping like hell that the door to the drawing room was open. Now, it seems relatively simple in planning, but Murphy always manages to put a spanner in the works. All Gujarati houses have two doors: one main door and then a grille door on the outside.

On ringing the bell, the neighbour's door opened halfway to reveal an eighty-year-old lady who didn't know a word of English or Hindi, trying to understand two dark-side-of-the-moon girls—one who knew English and Malayalam and the other that spoke Somali, a bit of Swahili and a kind of English, but neither knew Gujarati or Hindi. They tried to request an alarmed eighty-year-old to open the door and let them in, so that they could jump from her balcony into their own flat as they had forgotten their keys inside it (all this was done in an elaborate mime and with rolling eyes).

The more they talked, the louder they got, but there was no way the old lady was going to let them into her flat—especially these two: one five feet, four inches and the other six feet and one inch in her socks. Not a chance! After half an hour of a pantomime in English, Malayalam, Swahili and Somali, they had reached a stalemate.

Surprisingly, the old lady hadn't closed the inner door and was feeling quite safe behind the outer steel grille door.

Suddenly, Hodan decided enough was enough. Her powerful hands shot through the grille, grabbed the old lady by the collar, pulled her against the grille and, by sheer strength, lifted her off the floor and said, 'Open.' Sophie's limited Hindi came into play and she remembered 'kholo'. The terrified lady immediately unlocked the door. Sophie scurried through, went to the balcony, climbed on to the ledge and leapt. She landed smack in her own balcony. Phew! And luckily, the door to their drawing room was open.

She quickly opened their main door and called out to Hodan, who released the terrified old lady, did a quick, apologetic namaste and quickly vanished into the flat. The next day, I got a long letter from the society, complaining that two African guests of mine had molested a senior citizen and broken into her house. Luckily, nothing was stolen, they said.

When leaving Bombay, Hodan presented Sophie with her prized can of mace. Sophie used to carry it around like a weapon in her handbag and had no idea of the potency or deadliness of this weapon-grade mace.

One day, Sophie was in a car full of wannabes from Hyderabad, some of her downmarket vernacular friends—relationships she had cultivated from somewhere. They thought they were really cool and reeked of expensive aftershave and wore shiny synthetic shirts. They cruised around Marine Drive in a borrowed car, blaring loud music in Telugu, sure that they were going to score Bombay chicks, with Sophie egging them on for her own amusement.

Just as a conversation piece, she pulled out her green can of mace and asked them what they thought of it. Before you could say 'Jack Robinson', one of them grabbed the can. As Sophie desperately tried to tell them to be careful, he flipped open the safety catch and liberally sprayed himself under his armpits in a closed, air-conditioned car thinking it was a can of deo. Sophie, in anticipation, opened her window and stuck her head out into the fresh air. The car started weaving around erratically and came to a grinding halt next to the sidewalk. For a while, nothing happened, except Sophie breathing deeply with her head sticking out of the car.

Then, dramatically, three doors opened simultaneously—first the driver's door flew open, followed by two side doors at the back—and three bodies crawled out on to the road coughing, puking and weeping. They collapsed on the kerb. An embarrassed Sophie hovered over them with a handkerchief pressed to her nose, shocked and worried. She had, in the meantime, quickly retrieved her precious mace and hidden it deep in her handbag. It must have been the most powerful deo that the three Hyderabadi Lotharios had ever used. Hodan had struck even in her absence!

38

Billy the Kapoor

Mr Anil Kapoor of Boots (popularly called Billy Kapoor) had just moved to Ulka Advertising—a rare piece of reverse engineering where a client takes over an agency. It was quite the opposite of the norm, where the agency suits were dying to join the client and kick ass, instead of being ridden roughshod over. Mr Kapoor had always been a rough client to his agencies, bouncing everything brought to him—all of them, without exception. After meetings with him, it was not uncommon to see agency creatives wandering around shell-shocked and desperately trying to hold on to the tattered remnants of their teams, who wanted to, at some stage, migrate to some unknown country far, far away. For some strange reason, he took a shine to me—probably because I had learnt a different way to skin the cat.

We heard that he had been trying to get a TV commercial out of his agency for Strepsils in three different flavours. Its tagline was 'Gale mein kharaash? Strepsils!' And whatever they pitched to him came boomeranging back, slightly worse for wear. In despair, they finally gave up and were about to resign the account, when he decided to brief us—Genesis—on a whim.

We came up with the idea of doing a take on the MGM lion, where, with the fanfare of the introduction, the animal takes a deep breath to blow the house down, but instead we had him wheeze out a meow in falsetto, and cringe in embarrassment and shock. A VO asks, 'Gale mein kharaash?' The lion nods sheepishly as a strip of Strepsils appears with the VO legend, 'Agar gale mein kharaash, Strepsils!' The lion then pops a Strepsils, perks up and lets fly an earth-shattering roar. A packshot of Strepsils follows in the three flavours—orange, lemon and ginger lemon—all within the searchlights of the famed MGM logo.

We all felt very chuffed with the idea and I could see it so clearly in my head. The agency, in their bruised and battered state, refused to present it and the onerous task of belling the cat fell to our lot. I knew he would not play ball with us if we didn't impress him with our belief and commitment. We decided to go for the 'shock and awe' treatment. We presented the entire creative as a pantomime—with sound, smoke and fanfare.

We arrived early at the Boots office in Ballard Estate and requested Mr Kapoor's assistant to clear his room for half an hour, as we had to prepare the presentation. He was petrified to ask his boss to vacate his room. He hemmed and hawed, and offered us the conference room instead. That was not at all suitable; so I barged into Mr Kapoor's office and asked him very pleasantly to let us have the use of his office for half an hour, after which we would present our idea. He was most unhappy, and grumbled and threatened that it had better be worth it before he slouched off. The team immediately took control and we quickly got into the groove.

Uttam Sirur crouched under the desk with four cigarettes in his mouth to create smoke. He also had two torches in his hands to simulate the searchlights that crisscrossed over the MGM logo and lion. The smoke was for the torchlight to be seen clearly. One of the girls held a cardboard cut-out of the logo on the desk and another was in charge of the fanfare. I was playing the sheepish lion and also doing the VO. Finally, we invited Mr Kapoor and his team into the now smoky office.

Uttam was frantically puffing and intermittently coughing. The Boots team couldn't believe their eyes—they didn't know whether to run for their lives, in anticipation of what Anil Kapoor would do to them after the circus was done, or to stay and brazen it out. They finally chose the latter and settled down. Mr Kapoor was startled enough to not be his usual abrasive self and just sat down to see it through. On cue, the smoke billowed, searchlights cut through the gloom and the fanfare kicked in. *Tan ta rah!* The lion looked around ferociously and started to belligerently emulate Mr Kapoor himself (this fact did not escape his flunkies, who had a hard time keeping a straight face). The lion opened its mouth wide ... And out came a feeble meow. The lion looked embarrassed as hell its paws covering its mouth in shock.

VO: Gale mein kharaash?

The lion nods sheepishly.

Now came the product window, as the lion ducked out of the logo and a hand appeared holding a strip of Strepsils. The lion reappeared, popped one tab, looked slightly relieved and roared magnificently. Smoke billowed from under the table, with Uttam desperately trying to muffle his coughing. Fanfare. *Tan ta rah!*

VO: Strepsils in three delicious flavours: orange, lemon, ginger lemon.

The hand now held three strips. The end.

What followed was dead silence, except for Uttam's desperate coughing, of course. I got up and took a bow, waiting for thunderous applause. No such luck. One flunkey quickly started opening the windows to let the smoke out (thank god, this was before the ban on smoking in offices). Everybody slunk sheepishly out of the room, leaving us with the original 'loin'. He looked at us with his heavy-lidded eyes and rumbled, 'So you think that's funny?' I nodded vigorously. He finally cracked a smile and said, 'You guys are totally and completely mad! But I love it.' That was the best compliment he ever paid to anybody in his life, I believe, including his wife!

So, the Strepsils MGM lion film was made exactly as I had imagined it in animation by none other than *the* Ram Mohan. It was a huge hit. Even MGM loved it! Nine years later, after trying desperately to top it, everybody gave up and killed the ad. Genesis, the mad production house, became Mr Kapoor's favourite go-to, boys and girls. We were then contacted in desperation by a very battered Trikaya, who had been struggling to do something unique with a small brand called Sweetex, a sugar substitute, which was way ahead of its time. Trikaya was at the time reputed to be a highly creative agency and had done some amazing campaigns, including the launch for Thums Up and they had taken on a piddly small account like Boots' Sweetex purely as a prestige thing, that is ... until they came up against 'Billy' the Kapoor.

Six months later, Trikaya had a bruised and shattered creative team on the verge of jumping ship, with one creative director already an illegal immigrant in Singapore—who had left without even informing his girlfriend and secretary or collecting his dues. So, we were summoned and briefed to 'Please, please, do something. Anything!' I met Mr Billy Kapoor in the same office and he was at his belligerent best. With great foreboding, I went to the agency, which by this time was looking like a war zone—WWSCP, or Walking Wounded Stations and Collecting Posts.

I found, to my surprise, our very own Uttam Sirur, as a part of the Trikaya creative, and he looked pretty unscathed. I quizzed him about his bulletproofness. He grinned in his typical toothy way and said if he could survive Genesis for a couple of years, he was surely certified bulletproof. So, I sat with him on all the work that had been done on Sweetex. When I checked Uttam's wastepaper basket, I stumbled on to a gem of an idea, which of course had been bounced by Mr Kapoor. It was amazing, a line scribbled on a crumpled piece of paper. So typical of Uttam, who in my opinion always was an eccentric genius. The line said, 'No squeeze, no wheeze, no sugar in my coffee, please. Sweetex!'

It was awesome, it was visual, it had rhythm and most importantly, it had 'goonj' like a tuning fork. I just loved it. Now, how were we going to get past Billy the Kapoor with it, considering that he had already rejected it. So, we decided to just go for broke and make the film without his approval and take our chances later. I met with Mr Kapoor and told him that we had a great idea for the brand but that we were not going to sit and bust our chops trying to convince him. I told him we were going ahead and shooting the commercial, and he could then accept it or bounce it as was his prerogative. We did not have the stamina or the patience to play Russian roulette with him.

He was almighty pissed. I explained to him that we were not asking for an advance and since we were funding it ourselves, we did not need his approval at this stage. When the film was complete, he could view it and buy it or reject it. It would be his decision then. He was still pissed; I think he felt deprived of his entertainment: playing god with his creatives. So off we went and recorded a jingle with Louis Banks and cast and shot the film to the song. It was a lark and worked like a bomb. We edited the film and invited a still sulking Mr Kapoor to view our efforts. He came, glowering at everybody.

I wasn't perturbed as I knew we had a winner on our hands. He saw it without comment three times, got up and left. He loved the film, but he didn't want us to gloat. Since it was such a small brand in India, there was very little money to put behind it for exposure, so we were all wondering when we would see it on TV. The funny thing that happened was that Mr Billy Kapoor went to a conference in London with the parent body of Boots and carried a reel of the work they had done in India. On showing it, they dismissed most of it as relatively pedestrian but Sweetex caught their attention. I believe they made him an offer to buy its copyright. Mr Kapoor, being a hard-headed businessman, latkaoed them, kept them dangling for a while and finally made a tidy profit on the film over and above the credit and the kudos.

———

Now, as mentioned earlier, Billy Kapoor of Boots infamy had bought a managing share in Ulka Advertising from its founder Bal Mundkur and had become an agency man. He had to cater and pander to his own clients. One of whom was the tobacco giant ITC. They were diversifying into agricultural products and one of their offerings was a cooking oil called Sundrop, made from sunflower seeds—a healthy alternative to groundnut oil.

It was critical for ITC to break into a very competitive and cluttered market, and they could only do so with an original, visually exciting campaign. And it was also Ulka's test to see if they could hack it with the big boys. The pressure was palpable and a lot was riding on it. So, Billy the Kapoor sent for his favourite punching bag: his A-team, Genesis. Ever since Sweetex, where we successfully converted an idea he had initially rejected, he had wanted to extract his pound of flesh. So, he would always single us out for his most difficult projects, hoping that we would crash and burn.

We sat with the Ulka creative team and started batting ideas around; the production design was a given. Brand colours—basically, yellow— would be liberally sprinkled across the film. What we finally zeroed in on was a day in the life of an energetic seven-year-old, starting with him getting up, leaping off a bunk bed and cartwheeling his way into the kitchen, wearing yellow trackpants. He is hugged by his attractive, slim mother in a yellow sari and he sees a healthy spread of delicious food laid out for him to sample.

The boy interacts with the food and sits down for the meal. Basic but doable; the trick was to make the film edgy and different from all the other cooking oil films. We started looking for a six-to-seven year-old who could execute a perfect cartwheel. I had come from a school that had very high standards of fitness and calisthenics, and knew precisely what we required—no ifs and buts. The cartwheel had to be perfect for it to be aesthetically appealing. No sloppy bent knees, no bent back, no getting an 'almost fit' kid to attempt one. He had to be confident, supple and fearless. And the only one who fit the bill was none other than Nishant from the Maggi ad, now a six-year-old, who was as fit as a whip. Ambar Brahmachari's disparaging comment about how he looked like a malnourished refugee still rankled.

There were many Ambar Brahmacharis in Ulka, who looked at the slim, whip-like Nishant, and promptly said he was too thin and not 'ha-althy' in the very North Indian concept of 'khaate peete bachche', who are basically podgy and unathletic. The battle lines were clearly drawn. None of the overfed kids could do a simple cartwheel, forget about a perfect one.

The creative team at the agency argued that Sundrop was a healthy cooking oil, so our young protagonist had to conform to the North Indian concept of the khaata-peeta type whom you could lift by his blubbery cheeks, and to hell with him actually being fit enough to jump off a double bunk bed and do a perfect cartwheel. The dispute went all the way to Billy the Kapoor, who, for once, erred on the side of logic and good sense. He had the balls to defend my casting all the way to the client; this included the slim, hot, yummy mummy.

Buoyed by this small but significant victory, we decided to really push the ticket. We suggested that since the oil delivered a big taste, let's dwarf the kid with the food, so that he cartwheels straight on to the dining table into a city of giant food. We even thought of him going up a mountain of piled pooris, and as he approaches, the top of the poori pyramid starts to topple and the kid runs for his life, all in good humour, as the poori lands and bounces around him.

Eventually, that was the money shot—and it is remembered by that generation of consumers even to this day. But having stood our ground and pushed the casting and the script through, how the hell were we going to execute it? With no post-production gimmicks, no special effects, no digital labs, only low-band pneumatic recorders and the whisper of a rumour of in-camera blue-screen chroma keying, we set out to make the ad.

We followed the rumour trail to find the elusive chroma keying technique and found ourselves in Wankhede Stadium's outer boundary, where, under the bleachers and stands, was a photography studio run by a very successful advertising photographer, Suresh Seth. He had invested in a basic video setup of two cameras, editing suites, etc., on low-band recorders. And there, fiddling around in a forest of wires and screens was a brilliant young man named Shyam Ramanna, the non-conformist son of atomic scientist Raja Ramanna.

We asked about chroma keying and he explained a part of the intricacies of digital in-camera blue-screen techniques. Basically, he told us that if we shot and edited the poori and food sequence on to a film and transferred it on to low-band tape, he could play it back for the six-year-old Nishant on the video monitor. Nishant could then run, duck and dodge on cue in a small studio with a blue background. Shyam Ramanna, sitting in the control room, could miraculously marry the two images together into one magical sequence of the giant poori tumbling, and a little kid running and dodging around it in great glee. We were elated at the seamlessness of the effect.

Shyam Ramanna later confessed to us that even he hadn't done a chroma key shoot before, but based on our brief, had gone back and read up on the possibility of doing it and the theory of how it could be achieved. Those were exciting, impossible days, where we ventured into areas that only we could imagine were possible. Shyam Ramanna went on to become the go-to person for computer graphics and special effects, and started his own company called Z-Axis Communications. He now lives in Bangkok with his own post-production studio and a bevy of attractive girls who help him run the show.

In those days, there were no readymade platforms for computer graphics, so programmes were written in code for specific jobs and the rendering process was painfully slow. Doing post-production computer graphics was like watching grass grow! Shyam's most recognized work was making a Kawasaki motorcycle turn into a leaping panther against the backdrop of a moving city street.

39

'Shaadi? Aur Tumse?'

In the thick of work, I had completely lost track of my impending marriage until, one fine day, Mitali announced that she had to help her parents set up the ceremony. I looked at her blankly and asked, 'What ceremony?' She stared daggers at me and very slowly but clearly elucidated, '*Our* marriage, which you committed to one year ago, which my parents are getting their act together for. I suggest you get your act together yourself, unless you want to bail!'

I gave her a sheepish look and mumbled something to the tune of 'will be there' and quickly became patla to turn up in Siliguri well in time for the nuptial delights. Now, I felt very stressed because it suddenly felt like everything was happening too quickly, leaving me wholly unprepared. But then again, when it comes to marriage, who is ever fully ready? Luckily for me, with great foresight and clarity, I had convinced Mitali's father to hold the ceremony in Siliguri: not only would it be convenient and affordable (since he was footing the bill), but it was also halfway across the world, close to the Chinese border, with very little connectivity.

That meant no jhund of Punjabi freeloading relatives and friends would arrive and demand after-parties. It worked like a dream. My mom, sister, an uncle and his wife and two diehard friends were able to make it; the rest were told to read about it in the news. From Mitali's family, her mom and dad, her sister and her husband and kids were the ones who arrived. Some of my father-in-law's tea garden friends joined in too. That was it. Period. Of course, there were also one pandit and Mitali's two trusty roomies from Sophia College, Dinaz and Vandana.

I arrived in Siliguri via Calcutta into Bagdogra through a long drive, but I had already done that once earlier with orange sidelocks! That time, I had blotted my copybook by passing out on Mitali's dad's shoulder and dribbling gently while he was driving. This time, somebody else was at the airport to receive me and I was made to sit in the back seat just in case. I looked around, wondering what happened to the 'band, baaja, baraat'. I arrived and found Mitali busy with her mother, sister and friends, getting lathered in haldi, as is the tradition.

Since my lot hadn't arrived yet, I drifted around the house aimlessly and spotted a pile of magazines called *Gentleman*. Published in Bombay and of a very recent vintage, there were sixteen of them in the pile, all the same issue. Leafing through one of them, I nearly jumped out of my seat in fright. Staring at me from the centrefold was none other than yours truly! 'The Eternal Bachelor' proclaimed the headline. I couldn't believe it. I read and reread the article, and tried to remember when I had been interviewed by them and recalled that it was a year and a half ago before we decided to get married. I had been celebrating Mitali's departure to Siliguri, and now, one and a half years later, right in the middle of my nuptials, this article had cropped up in a national magazine.

I looked around furtively to see if anybody had noticed me. All was calm, all was quiet (before the storm, I was thinking). But why were there sixteen copies here? Suddenly, there was a commotion and my father-in-law, Anil Dutt, came striding into the room, holding aloft a seventeenth copy of *Gentleman*. 'Got the last one!' he said triumphantly and slammed the offending magazine on the existing pile.

He grinned at my shock and told me that a friend of his had rung him up about the article, and knowing that not too many people read that publication in Siliguri, he had decided to collect the lot from the various outlets. After a hectic morning chasing down all the copies, he had finally come home with the seventeenth and the last copy in triumph. Saved from acute embarrassment by an astute and understanding father-in-law.

After this hiccup, we were immersed in the rituals and ceremonies of a regular Indian wedding (specifically, a Bengali wedding), from being rubbed down in haldi paste to the actual pandit-driven havan and saat pheras. Everything was going well until I quizzed the pandit on how long the ritual would take, to which he immediately replied, 'Three hours.' I quailed at the thought of sitting cross-legged, chanting 'swahaa' and pouring ghee on a fire to purify me for three hours. Even twelve hours of purification would not have washed my sins away, so what to do? I promptly decided to bribe the portly Jabba the Hutt of a pandit.

First, I tried sympathy, 'Sirji, I can't sit for so long cross-legged; I have haemorrhoids.' No luck. I then slipped him a five-hundred-rupee note and he promptly brought down the time to two hours. I flashed another five-hundred-rupee note at him, it became one hour of excruciating torture. Since my exchequer was fast emptying, I offered him a bottle of rum. His eyes lit up and the ritual was reduced to an acceptable forty-five minutes.

No more compromises, he told me. Of course, I got an army friend, Bill the Sapper, to purloin another bottle of rum from the army canteen and we were down to fifteen minutes now. So, it was half an hour of fast forwarding the chanting with telescoped rituals. I was even allowed to sit on a low stool to stop me from squirming. Finally, it was over with one last, enthusiastic 'swahaa!' Everybody hit the bar and the pandit loped off, a thousand bucks richer and cradling two bottles of Old Monk.

And so it came to pass that at the age of thirty-six, I was finally married to Mitali, all of twenty-two, but significantly more mature than me. My mother took to Mitali with great relief as she had practically given up on me. My uncle, Dr Prakash Nath Sehgal, got along famously with my in-laws thanks to his extremely dry sense of humour. The rest of us just hit the delicious Bengali food and drinks, and made merry on the terrace. Except poor Kripal Singh, a diehard North Indian who couldn't handle the rice and shorshey maachh, and was dying for decent roti-shoti and maa di dal.

On to Calcutta for take two, where my father-in-law had managed to book the Fort William Army Club through a friend and had planned a grand reception. Half of Calcutta's who's who was there, as everybody wanted to know who the delectable Mitali was getting hitched to—she was quite the catch. They found this slightly grizzled thirty-six-year-old, nothing much to look at, who had a reputation for calling a spade a spade, especially on national TV. Maybe they were even a tad disappointed in her choice of a life partner.

After a night of drunken revelry, Mitali and I staggered off to the New Kenilworth Hotel for our first night as a married couple. I don't recall much of the night as I was happily inebriated and probably passed out on an exhausted Mitali. Such is the tale of most weddings—where the groom is happy and blotto, and the wife is long suffering and relieved it's finally done!

———

Getting back to Bombay was not something I was particularly looking forward to. By now, everybody had figured out that the Kakar had finally managed to cook his own goose and get married. They all laughed their heads off at my expense, and, after meeting Mitali, nodded their heads in sympathy and started taking bets on how long the poor thing would last.

Little did they know what I had learnt in our year and a half of courtship: looks can be deceptive. Mitali embodied an iron fist in a velvet glove. The first thing that she did after our wedding was to take over the finances of Genesis, leaving me free to dream and create. She even put me on a stipend so that I wouldn't run the company into the ground.

Arriving in Bombay was a minefield—everybody wanted to know when the reception was and when they could formally meet Mitali.

Not so much to congratulate her, as to commiserate with her. I had not the foggiest clue about the reception as I left in a flurry for the Chinese border having totally forgotten that my friends and colleagues in Bombay would expect a reception. Now that I was back in the city, I had to start from scratch to make a guest list, book a venue, procure booze and food, create invitations and whatnot.

So here was take three and I was in a tizzy, ensuring we left no one out of the guest list, especially vital people. And how were we going to print the invitations on time? How were we going to arrange for caterers? To boot, we had no money! Mitali had not yet taken over and put our finances in order. Riding to the rescue, with trumpets blaring, was the one and only Mohammed Khan. Being a Hyderabadi of nawabi lineage, he was, and remains, a food connoisseur par excellence. He offered to send a coterie of khandaani cooks from Hyderabad at his expense to cook us a meal for royalty. We will always be eternally grateful for his timely intervention.

Next, we had to find a venue that was good enough for an intimate gathering and large enough for a big party, as we had no idea how many people would come. After much scoping around, we chose the scenic United Services Club annexe at Colaba Land's End. Next, I got hold of twenty army and navy officers who agreed to contribute their monthly booze quota for a good cause; they surprisingly agreed (remember, the booze quota for a service officer is as precious as his wife). I ended up with sixty-five bottles of booze at Rs 20 a bottle, so all I spent was 1,300 bucks to get my regiment hammered.

Then came the bloody invitation—a logistical nightmare. I decided to just fuck it and put up a hoarding that read: 'Prahlad weds Mitali, Reception at the US Club Annexe, 7 p.m. sharp (Dress code: A decent shirt, pants and *shoes* please. No flip-flops will be entertained). Friends, relatives and dependent animals are welcome (basically Dumbell).' We crossed our fingers and let word of mouth take over. Our duty was done. The last on the list was to get the royal khansamas organized.

Three days before D-Day, I got up at the crack of dawn to meet the Minar Express coming from Hyderabad to greet the head chef,

Khan Sahib, and his bunch. I saw them at the far end of the platform; they had minimal luggage and two enormous sacks. I enquired about the sacks and was told that one of them contained carrots from Hyderabad. I scratched my head as carrots were also available in Bombay. Anyway, the second heavier sack intrigued me, but I only received stoic silence when I asked about it. I persisted and was told they were granite stone chips from Hyderabad. I was a bit taken aback. After digesting the information, I asked Khan Sahib why he had hauled half a tonne of broken stones from Hyderabad by train when there were plenty available in Bombay. He stopped walking, drew himself up to his 6 feet, 2 inches and looked down at my 5 feet, 6 inches disdainfully and said in chaste Urdu, 'Aap ke pattharon aur hamare pattharon mein zameen aasmaan ka farq hai.' I swallowed the next question, and nodded sagely as if I truly understood what he was saying.

We had put them up in a reasonable lodge on Marine Drive. Once we dropped off their luggage, Khan Sahib immediately wanted to go select the goats for the dum ka bakra and the biryani, and nothing would deter him. So off he went to the slaughterhouse, where he spent the next two hours talking to goat vendors, examining and weighing different goats. And after much to-do, he selected six young animals, all of them six kilos of weight. He then insisted on giving specific instructions to the supplier as to how precisely he wanted the whole carcass dressed and cut as they were meant for stuffing.

Next, he ordered 'pasandas'—which is a bunch of muscles from the thigh, or raan, of the goat—which needed to be cut precisely at the ligament and kept separately. He then explained how he wanted the different cuts for the biryani, extremely specific instructions from a master craftsman. I spent the next two days with Khan Sahib as he personally selected everything from the cooking vessels (deghs) to the spices to the dry fruits to garnish the dishes. Even the quality of the malai in the desserts mattered. He refused to cook on gas and wanted a wood fire in a traditional choolha and a charcoal sigri for his cooking.

I had to get special permission from the US Club to erect this temporary kitchen in the annexe. Col Lobo, the then secretary of the club, thought about it and was intrigued; so, he let us go ahead. I, of course, invited him for the feast. I sat with the cooks as they marinated the meat and watched the process of stuffing a whole lamb carcass with chicken, in turn stuffed with boiled eggs, cooked in dum in a sealed degh.

I observed the traditional way of cooking mutton biryani in dum and then watched them cook a vegetarian version of the same (incidentally, the vegetarian version was far more complicated than the mutton). The highlight was the treating of the pasandas to make patthar ke kebab. The whole business of lugging a sack full of granite chips from Hyderabad made sense; that particular stone, quarried from the rocks of Banjara Hills, imparts a special flavour to the kebabs. The menu was to die for—from assorted nawabi starters to dum ka bakra, patthar ke kebab, shorba, kacche gosht ki dum biryani, baghare baingan, hung yogurt ka raita, mirchi ka saalan, gaajar ka halwa and khubaani ka meetha.

It was finally 27 January, and the sun set as the hordes started arriving and made straight for the bar. Drinks were flowing, and a noisy advertising and production crowd intermingled with a few suits who were glued to the bar area like Fevicol. Khan Sahib was busy building an igloo of chipped stones around a round charcoal choolha. He had slit the pasandas down the centre and peeled them back, exposing their delicate core. He lightly marinated the insides with dahi, masalas and khus seeds.

When the stones had been heated to a white-hot intensity, using a leather bellow to pump air into the core of the choolha, he placed a pasanda on its open side on the stone, which stuck there and sizzled deliciously. The unbelievable aroma wafted into the night sky. All my exhortations to pry my friends away from the bar to the feast had been to avail and I was afraid that they would be in no state to appreciate the food for kings prepared specially for the occasion! I need not have worried though.

When the smell of the sizzling kebabs drifted to their booze-addled nostrils, they tore themselves away from the bar and, in a dreamlike manner, walked towards the kebab zone, licking their chops in anticipation. The kebabs, with their unique flavour of poppy and the granite stones, simply melted in the mouth. My guests just couldn't get enough of them. The taste was so unique that people still come up to me today and recall the patthar ke kebab.

Once we had managed to crowbar the boozers off the bar, there was no looking back. The food was just awesome with Khan Sahib personally supervising the carving of the dum ka bakra, ensuring every guest was served a generous portion. With each helping, he managed a healthy slice of mutton, chicken and egg. Altogether, it was a masterclass in fabulous cooking. Watching him go through five succulent melt-in-mouth bakras, everybody ate and drank till they needed to walk around the Golf Course Promenade, only to come back for another helping.

The desserts were unbelievably exotic: the gaajar ka halwa, very different from its Punjabi cousin, was decadent and delicious. But what took the cake was the khubaani ka meetha: gently stewed dried apricots in a rich sauce under a layer of fresh malai. It was not at all artificially sweetened, but full of natural flavours. I have not had anything like it since then.

The evening was a huge success, a feast for the gods, with Dumbell playing host to all. And the bill to the exchequer was a royal sum of Rs 25,000 with tips and all thrown in.

40

Lacadives and the Kon-Tiki Expedition

During a slight break at work, Pradeep Uppoor, a dear friend and fellow producer, decided to go to Mauritius to check out locations and the food scene there and meet people to scope out new business prospects. He asked if I would be interested in coming along. Our instigator-in-chief was Parag Jamsandekar, who had some connections in the island country. Of course, we flew Air Mauritius, cattle class and proceeded to chat up all the exotic air hostesses on board—an incredible mix of Indian, African and French women, with cute, slightly Frenchified English accents.

It was a six-hour flight and they plied us with fabulous South African wines, including a Pinot Noir to die for. We arrived at the airport at Port Louis gently inebriated, maudlin and in love with all the air hostesses on board. We sobered up instantly when we saw a huge poster proclaiming, 'Life imprisonment/death' for carrying any form of drugs into the country. We cleared customs quite easily, though we were sweating profusely throughout, and headed for our digs at Trou aux Biches, about thirty kilometres from the airport, in a cab. It is a beautiful island country, so the drive was easy and relaxing.

We arrived at our B&B and were introduced to our landlady, Mrs Merday. Mr and Mrs Merday were a Mauritian couple whose origins were somewhere in South India and who spoke English, French and Bhojpuri, in a sing-song kind of way. We were amazed that 60 per cent of the island had origins in India—carted from Bihar to Mauritius by the British as agricultural labour to tend to their main cash crop, sugarcane. They had stayed on and prospered. We spent two wonderful days checking out all the Indian eateries, relishing dishes like curry poulet, and examining the possibilities of going to one more restaurant before the night ended. The population of Mauritius at the time was about 1.5 million. During the summer tourist season, it could go up to 3 million people. They also had about five world-class luxury beach hotels and hundreds of other resorts all around the island.

On the third day, we decided to just relax. A really nice bunch of guests from France invited me to go scuba diving with them down the road. I didn't know the first thing about diving, but decided to tag along just for the outing, it being a lovely Sunday morning and all. We arrived at the dive centre, run by a short, bald, authoritarian diving instructor, Hugues Vitry (pronounced 'Oogh'), who kitted out all the divers, and ignored me since I was only tagging along and taking up space on the boat. The sea was a bit choppy for my taste, but what the hell? A boat ride is a boat ride. We went out to the reef and Hugh briefed all the divers about the location, how deep it was, what the duration of the dive would be. He rehearsed all the underwater signals and then buddied them up in pairs. Off they all went, backwards off the boat, into the water all together and, within a second, they disappeared leaving a trail of bubbles on the surface.

There I was, all alone in a boat, somewhere on a reef in Mauritius, with a windy, roughish sea and a disinterested boat boy listening to music on a small transistor. I was beginning to feel seasick and queasy. In the excitement of the outing, I had forgotten that I could get seasick in a bathtub. The generous portions of breakfast I ate now sat heavily in my stomach and I felt the taste of bile in my mouth. I looked desperately at the horizon to stabilize the fluid in my inner ear. But eventually, I couldn't handle the rocking, heaving boat at anchor and told the boat fellow to take me back to shore before I chucked up my breakfast in his boat.

He looked at me a bit alarmed—not so much at my condition but at the fact that he would have to clean the boat. However, he could not abandon his post or the divers, so thinking out of the box, he handed me a diving mask and told me to immediately get into the water. I was most reluctant as it was October and the water was bloody cold. I remembered the song 'She was afraid to get into the water in her itsy-bitsy, teeny-weenie yellow polka dot bikini (sic)' like an idiotic ditty in between the lurches in my stomach. After one particularly large lurch, I took the bit in my mouth and slid over the side, into the water. The cold hit me like a sledgehammer and I immediately forgot about the seasickness.

After thrashing around a bit, I steadied myself and pulled on the mask, which was airtight and helped my vision to stay focused in the water. I ducked my head into the cold, briny and clear water, and lo and behold, my wariness of the sea changed forever. I could see as easily as I could have if I were above water. I saw the divers on the reef, beautiful coral formations and multicoloured fish. I forgot my queasy stomach and held my breath. I came up with a whoosh. I looked around and saw the boat still rocking in the water, with an anxious boat boy looking down at me. Taking a deep breath, I dunked my head back into paradise. I was hooked.

I spent the whole journey back shivering in the cold and begging the instructor to take me for an introductory dive. He ignored me, saying he was busy and didn't want to waste time on a non-serious Indian. I thought, 'Shit! Racism in Mauritius, an almost 60 per cent Indian island.' Then I realized that they don't think of themselves as Indian, but as Mauritian. Us tourists were Indian. He had probably had a bad experience with Indian tourists. I persisted and the more he said no, the more I pursued him. I stuck to him like a leech.

Out of sheer exasperation, he finally agreed to take me for a dive the next morning at the crack of dawn. We had a flight back at 7 p.m., but I dared not tell him that as it required a twelve-hour gap between that last dive and the flight. I knew he would say no, so I kept my mouth shut. I went home and told an indifferent Pradeep Uppoor that we were going diving the next morning—the both of us. He wasn't interested, so of course I stayed up half the night, trying to convince him. He finally agreed. The next morning was cold, overcast and choppy. We rode double-seat on Mr Merday's bicycle to the diving centre and arrived at 6.45 a.m. sharp. Not a sausage in sight and a big lock on the door. We asked around and somebody told us where Hugues lived in Grand Bay.

So off we went to track down the elusive and reluctant Hugues Vitry. We found him having breakfast with his wife and his ten-year-old daughter, Claire. He had completely forgotten about me, thinking I had just been fooling around. He reluctantly came back with us to the school and kitted us out with scuba masks, wetsuits, booties, regulators and tanks, and then briefed us on the way to a shallow dive site. As we stopped at the site, he looked at the two slightly stressed and now frightened individuals in front of him, shaking his head ruefully. At least, Pradeep had a genuine reason for feeling scared—he couldn't swim. In my single-minded determination to convince him to come diving, I had ignored that very vital piece of information and forced him to come.

Now, in Hindi, he nudged me to tell Hugues the sorry truth; I hadn't done so till now as I was afraid that he would abort the exercise. Reluctantly, I informed an exasperated Hugues about this. He looked at Pradeep and said, 'No problem, I will take you first and I will handhold you; so don't worry!' They soon disappeared in a flurry of bubbles and left me shivering on the boat with my vivid and now scary imagination.

Surprisingly, fear knocks the shit out of seasickness. Twenty minutes later, they both surfaced with a whoosh, and I was relieved to see a smiling and buoyant Pradeep Uppoor. I asked him how it was, and he replied, 'Fantastic!' Now, whatever excuse I had to abort the exercise was void—a non-swimmer had done it and survived! It was my turn. I went into the water, which was surprisingly warm, and awkwardly swam across to Hugues, struggling with the cumbersome equipment. He deflated my jacket, gave me the okay sign and we sank below the surface, with me hyperventilating, despite him holding my hand.

Suddenly, I was weightless and could see forever in the ocean. Since I was so scared, I saw nothing. I could only hear my own breathing, like an out-of-context steam engine in the water, my eyes, wide open in fright, registered nothing. Hugues calmed me down by pressing on my solar plexus to slow down my breathing and started a handheld guided tour of the shallow reef. My mask wasn't powered to accommodate my short-sightedness, so the view in the distance was a bit hazy, but I could see something fluttering on the reef. I pointed it out to Hugues, who then let go of my hand and nudged me to check it out.

I was totally mortified, but managed to clumsily fin to the object. Realizing that it was a book fluttering along with the waves, I grabbed it and clutched it to my chest. As I swam back to Hugues, I realized that I had used up most of the air in my tank; something that should have lasted for an hour was nearly finished in fifteen minutes. Much to my relief, we surfaced in one piece. I had just done my first dive, by god! I checked out the book on the boat and it turned out to be the Koran, which I cleaned up and dropped off at the Islamic Department in the local university en route to the airport. Serendipitously, five years later, I founded the first scuba diving school in India in an almost 100 per cent Muslim island in the Lakshadweep group of islands: Lacadives.

The journey between that first traumatic dive and the subsequent trips that I made back to Mauritius and blue water diving with some hardcore adventurous friends were exhilarating. Hugues Vitry was so surprised to see me back with a whole gaggle of Indians, including two very attractive young ladies—Mitali (my wife) and Sophie (my minder). He thought he had gotten rid of me forever, considering the blue funk I was in during the first dive. I had managed to buy some second-hand diving equipment from Bombay and was happily conducting classes in the erstwhile Sea Rock Hotel swimming pool on Sundays. We attracted a lot of attention as quite a few good-looking women also attended these classes. A large contingent of Lotharios would hang about, checking them out. It was the incompetent teaching of the newly converted as the two unqualified instructors were Nikhil Rawley and yours truly.

Subsequently, we went back to Mauritius and Hugues, to get certified—we assumed we already knew how to dive. He led us to a shallow reef that he called the classroom and all hell promptly broke loose, as it was our first experience of a real ocean and real coral and real fish. Being relatively comfortable with the equipment and with no discipline, we were like excited children—we were all over the place, pulling at each other when we spotted some small colourful fish, gesticulating wildly, trampling on the coral and generally ignoring the real instructor, Hugues. It was crazy.

Finally, he banged on his tank to attract our hyperactive attention and wrote on his underwater slate: 'You are destroying my reef! Get to the surface *now*!' The moment we surfaced, we were hauled to the shore by a furious Hugues. On the shore, he proceeded to give us a right royal bollocking. His little moustache literally bristled! He was only gentler on Mitali and Sophie as they professed to be terrified of the ocean and wanted to call it quits.

He decided to take them by their hand and took it as a challenge upon himself to get them certified. As far as the rest of us were concerned, we were relegated to three metres of water in the lagoon until we got the hang of being neutrally buoyant and less destructive on the reef. He also taught us the fact that diving is a buddy sport, and the safety of one's buddy and oneself is of paramount importance, not macho posturing. It took us the better part of a week to unlearn and start from scratch.

We were, of course, staying with the Merdays and had rented cycles to travel the three kilometres to school every morning at the crack of dawn. Evening was party time. We had a kitchen and we stocked it with provisions. Everybody pitched in to turn out some amazing dinners. Vikas Sivaraman, our cameraman-turned-diver, and I were in charge of the BBQ, and we managed to turn out some amazing meats and fish. Our favourite barbecuing fish was the dorado, white, succulent flesh marinated and barbecued to perfection. The girls went at the rest with great enthusiasm and, all in all, we did ourselves proud. We could even afford to entertain all the friends we picked up on the way, as long as they brought the wine.

What really got to us was the fact that, to certify, we had to pass a written exam that included physics. I hated physics and hadn't looked at it since school because I used to be quite stressed out during theory class. But now, at the age of forty, I found that I could cope as it was all about my body responding to pressure and volume, and not some stupid laboratory shit. We all passed our diving exams, including theory. The girls, of course, excelled at theory. Sophie had an issue clearing a flooded mask at depth and, try as she might, she couldn't get the hang of breathing out from her nose underwater to push the water out of the mask. Her results were held back.

She was given one last chance and she took it with all the strength of her faculties while we held our collective breath. Sophie being Sophie could never follow the straight path. Since she couldn't clear the water out of the mask, she actually sucked it through her nose and drank it up. Bloody hell! Hugues had never seen anything like that in his entire diving career, but he had to pass her, despite her not following procedure. We celebrated our certification with a rocking party for all our friends and instructors, and left the next afternoon for the airport, desperately hung over but enormously triumphant.

The core group of divers—Mitali, Nikhil, Vik, Brian, Captain, Anuj Kapoor and I—kept going back every year in October to improve our certifications from One Star CMAS to advanced-level divers. As our skills improved, the certifications became tougher and took longer, but, by this time, we were really hooked. I even wanted to start a school somewhere in India. The search was on to find a likely spot somewhere on the vast Indian coastline.

We zeroed in on a little unknown coral atoll 400 nautical miles of Cochin, called Lakshadweep. We had heard of this island from some of our naval friends, about its clear blue water and white sands. We got hold of some maritime charts of the area and tried to figure out how to get there. I spent a lot of time in Delhi, in the home ministry, as the islands were Union territories and, thus, were restricted. After much to-ing and fro-ing, I managed to get a letter from the Ministry of Tourism to allow us to recce four islands in the region for the possibility of scuba diving.

We mounted the expedition by rounding up the right, qualified people and the equipment. The crew consisted of Nikhil Rawley, Dipika Dayal, who insisted on coming along, a senior naval diver called Mukhs—short for Mukherjee—a journalist named Ashok Motwani and Karl Brietkoff, the son of a German frogman diver who got stuck in Goa during World War II and ended up marrying a local beauty, resulting in Karl, Jr, who owned a portable compressor and some equipment. He was a self-taught diver and keen underwater photographer.

This bunch of mismatched individuals left Bombay by train for Cochin, lugging all the equipment and compressor, and our precious permit, to then board the *Tipu Sultan* (a huge passenger ship) for a voyage to the islands. We set off from the muddy water of the Mattancherry docks for an overnight voyage to Kavaratti island, the capital of Lakshadweep. Here, we were set to meet Shaukat, our host and guide, and a national wind-sailing champion whom I had met during a conference in Goa. We arrived early in the morning during the holy month of Ramzan. The sea, as we got closer to the islands, was incredibly blue and amazingly clear. We could see twenty metres into the depth, as clear as day from the side of the *Tipu*. We went ashore in a small fishing boat, bobbing on the ocean alongside the large cargo hold of the ship. We all had to take a leap of faith to land on the small craft.

The equipment was another thing altogether. They passed our priceless diving gear—including the chhotu compressor and our precious diving cylinders—from the ship to a fishing craft, as we watched with our hearts in our mouths. We finally landed on the jetty inside a pristine lagoon and were greeted by Shaukat and a one-eyed Liakat Ali, nicknamed Arjun, master sailor and fisherman. Kavaratti island was somnolent, as everybody was resting during the fasting times and nobody was stirring. After a bit of cajoling, Liakat agreed to take us out of the lagoon on to the main reef purely out of curiosity.

We quickly got our gear together and started filling the tanks as the compressor took thirty-five minutes to fill one tank to 200 bars (one bar is one atmospheric pressure). Our excitement was palpable. We were probably going to be the first people to ever dive off the Kavaratti wall. With butterflies in our stomachs, we went backwards off the boat and descended to eight metres on the lip of the wall. It was spectacular—the visibility was at least a 120 feet. We were surrounded by hundreds of colourful, curious reef fish and resplendent tabletop coral for miles. I was overwhelmed by the sheer beauty and life surrounding us. We finned towards the lip of the wall and our stomachs lurched as the bottom fell out from under us into an inky abyss at least 300 metres deep.

The wall was resplendent in soft coral of all hues and colour—a cascade of beauty—and, in the depths, we saw a few patrolling white-tip sharks; all of us were wide-eyed and enchanted. We levelled off at twenty metres as planned, gave the okay sign and started cruising along the wall with a mild current. Suddenly, out of the crevices and little perches, huge turtles started shooting out of the wall to circle us (the only sound a diver makes underwater is his expulsion of breath in loud bubbles).

They were huge hundred-year-old green sea turtles and some Hawksbill turtles, graceful, curious and stunning. We forgot about time (a cardinal sin) until Nikhil tapped his pressure gauge and signalled all of us about our air—we were all on reserve. Fifty minutes had flown by in seconds. We surfaced with our mandatory three-minute safety stop at five metres and came up with a whoosh, all talking at the same time. We named the Kavaratti wall the 'Wall of Wonders' and it holds that name even now. The expedition was to visit four islands—Kadmat, Amini, Agatti and Bangaram—and dive off them, and then compute a report. Since it was Ramzan, nobody was willing to come with us or hire out a boat and crew for us to travel. Shaukat was trying his best to convince a boat master to go with us for eight days.

And then arrived P.K. Kasali, a tall, suave English-speaking gentleman of authority in a sparkling white shirt, a mundu and with a swagger. He pitched in to help after hearing our predicament. Both

Shaukat and Mr K (as we took to calling him) would go on to play a huge part in setting up our operations and running a diving school in the islands. We managed to wrangle a just about seaworthy fishing craft with its surly master and crew, only to realize it had no compass, safety gear or communication set for an emergency, and no shade. So, we had to get two boats, just in case. On a full moon night, during high tide, we loaded up the boats—one with equipment and two of our people, and the other with Nikhil, Mukhs, Dipika, Karl and me.

We headed out of the lagoon on to the ocean, which was as flat as a billiards table with the moon at eight o'clock, rising on the gentle swell. We set off. It was truly magical. Words are woefully inadequate to describe the feeling. Off we headed on our Kontiki expedition, first to Kadmat island, forty nautical miles away, in two noisy fishing crafts with unsilenced Kirloskar marine engines. Our boat was overrun by resentful roaches. One hour out of Kavaratti, our engine wheezed, spluttered and conked out. Holy shit! In the middle of nowhere.

The other boat luckily stopped and came alongside. The two masters talked furiously in Malayalam and after tinkering around for half an hour, gave up and gave us a tow line to pull us towards Kadmat island. Our speed dropped to three knots from six and, as beautiful as the night was, we were just waiting for the second boat engine to conk out as well and leave us marooned. We had to sleep on the gunwale of the boat, with one leg down for balance and boy, did it take some getting used to. And so, it was for the next eight days, travelling by night and diving by day, two days on every island and two dives a day. It was by far one of the most memorable journeys of my life.

———

Each island was unique in its layout, coral growth and the terrain below the water. Kadmat was just thirteen kilometres long at one end and only five hundred metres wide where the Water Sports Institute was located—on the southern tip of the island. You could watch the sun rise over the eastern shoreline, where the small lagoon would empty out during low tide, leaving beautiful wave formations on the spectacular white sand. Without having to move from your spot, you could watch the sun set on the western lagoon, which had a wide reef with a long, narrow sparkling white beach.

The diving was amazing, especially off the wall on the western side and coral-infested drop-offs; there were sandy flats resplendent with stingrays on the east, which Mitali later christened Stingray City, there was Barracuda Point and a fabulous Shaukat Alley (Sharkat Alley) named after Shaukat Ali, who discovered it. Two days were not enough for Kadmat, but we quickly did our recce dives by hanging a masked Nikhil Rawley upside down off the side of the boat. As and when he found an interesting dive site, he would bang on the side of the boat, and we would stop and dive in.

On the eastern side, we found some spectacular tabletop slopes that went on for kilometres, which later Mitali aptly named Eden, East of Eden and Return to Eden. The island was surrounded by thousands of fusilier fishes, turtles, nurse sharks, lobsters and moray eels. We made a day trip to Amini Island and accidentally descended on a coral reef about a mile wide, which stretched forever into the clear distance. It was full of tabletop coral like flat filigree fans, staghorn coral, huge brain coral and fronds of soft coral teeming with reef fish of all kinds. We just hung in the water at twenty metres and were comfortably gobsmacked by the life we saw all around us. I realized that nothing on the reef was perfect individually, but the whole reef was perfect in its imperfection. We called it the Forever Reef because it stretched into infinity with its aching beauty—a work of nature and god. We had never experienced anything this resplendent manmade; it truly humbled me.

On to Agatti island, which sports a quaint, tiny airport sticking out into the lagoon like a finger. When you land on the island, you feel as though you are landing on water because that's all you see from the windows of a fourteen-seater Dornier aircraft. The lagoon on Agatti was full of turtles feeding on the seaweed that grew there. We must have counted at least a hundred of them swimming about. After a short boat ride, we finally arrived at Bangaram island, which, at the time, had the only resort in Lakshadweep—we could finally have a hot bath and a cold beer!

Initially, the staff at Bangaram tried to shoo us away. Burnt black by the sun, with blondish streaks in our hair from the salt, dressed in native attire, a bamboo-and-straw fisherman's hat, lungis and tees, we certainly looked a sight. We finally convinced them that we were Bombay types and had friends staying at the resort, which was run by the Casino Group of Hotels (now called CGH Earth). We dived in Bangaram with Andreas, the resort's German diving instructor, and exchanged notes on the trials and tribulations of running a diving school in the Lakshadweep islands.

Soon, our Kon-Tiki expedition of four islands of Lakshadweep ended; we were elated at how pristine the ocean was, and the fact that it was teeming with coral life, fishes and creatures of all sorts. We wrote our extensive report and waited and waited and waited for some response from the tourism ministry and the home ministry on the possibility of starting a diving school in the Lakshadweep islands. And we waited another six months before I began to personally land up at the two ministries for permission. Whenever we did some paperwork on the lesser brands, I would get paid-for tickets to Delhi for my meetings. Once the meetings concluded, I would head to the home ministry and be passed around like a ping-pong ball, only to gird my loins and go at it from the beginning, again and again and again—for three years! I was not willing to give up.

One day, I was sitting in the corridors of the home ministry, waiting for Godot—that is, the deputy secretary incharge of the Lakshadweep islands—when a neat-looking South Indian gentleman wearing a blue shirt and a pair of trousers walked past. I knew he wasn't an Indian Administrative Service (IAS) babu as they all wore a kind of uniform: trousers, safari short-sleeved jacket in various shades of grey or khaki, and Kabuli sandals without socks. The gentleman in the blue shirt hesitated and stopped, then walked back towards me. I looked up from my Louis L'Amour novel and arched an eyebrow at him. He cleared his throat and, in a melodious South Indian accent, said, 'I have been noticing you for the last two years, waiting for somebody. What is it you want?' By this time, I was pretty fed up and needed an audience. So I vomited my frustration and ire on him in one tirade. 'Whoa,' he said, backing off a few steps. 'Slowly; one thing at a time.'

I gulped my bile and followed him to a canteen, where, over a cup of good filter coffee, I narrated to him my tale of woe. He looked at me quizzically and asked whether I would make any money if the project were approved. 'Of course not,' I replied before I could think better of it. I proceeded to tell him why it was a passion project— that it was in the middle of nowhere with very bad connectivity and how Indians didn't scuba dive much, so we would have to start from scratch and pioneer the sport in this country. He put his cup of coffee down and asked to see my project report, which I reluctantly showed him. He looked at it and said, 'But you will make no money for *ten* years!'

I nodded dumbly, but dug my heels in. He then took out a pen and started changing all the projections, and, after he had finished, looked me straight in the eye and explained that the babudom does not understand love, passion or charity, unless they are the direct recipients of it. So, he told me, they will always be suspicious of my motives to start something like scuba diving in the boonies for love or passion. It had to be a moneymaking venture, not searching for treasure or sunken wrecks or some windfall. Besides, it was a life-threatening sport, so no babu in their right mind would put their signature on it.

He unscrambled the figures to show that there was a healthy profit in it from the start and, since he knew there was no precedent, nobody could cross-reference his workings. I now docilely followed him to his desk and realized he was the TamBrahm personal assistant (PA) to some big shot in the system. He started making phone calls to a whole bunch of TamBrahm PAs until he got the PA to the Union Minister of State, Home Affairs, P.M. Sayeed, who, I was informed, hailed from the islands. If he couldn't do it, nobody could.

I ended up at the desk of the PA to Mr Sayeed to seek an appointment with my now revised project report. The PA told me that the minister was very busy and that I should return after two days. I pleaded with him, told him that I lived in Bombay, I had a flight at 6 p.m. and it would not be feasible to come back after two days. He hemmed and hawed a bit, spoke to my saviour in Tamil and then called P.M. Sayeed to tell him that someone from the islands was there to see him.

I was told to report to P.M. Sayeed's residence at 1.30 in the afternoon, so he could see me for twenty minutes before leaving for a parliamentary meeting at 2 p.m. I was at his residence at 1.15 p.m. sharp and was ushered in by his PA to an anteroom, where I awaited Mr Sayeed's summons. He called me into his office and saw immediately that I was not an islander—yet. So, he said, 'You have come from Lakshadweep?' I mumbled that I had spent some time on the islands to assess the possibility of starting a scuba diving school there. He didn't bat an eyelid and I am sure he didn't know what the hell scuba diving was. But he shot a question at me: 'What will my islanders get from it?'

I was prepared for this, thanks to my new-found TamBrahm friend. 'Direct employment for the island people and a huge impact on the island economy with high-end tourism landing up there and spending money,' I responded quickly. He thought about it for a bit and nodded absently. He then asked his PA to connect him to the administrator, which he did. He spoke to him and then handed me the phone; I was suddenly talking to a Mr Cheema (IAS) in Kavaratti island in Lakshadweep.

I explained to the forward-thinking Mr Cheema that I wanted to start a tourism-based scuba-diving during school on the islands and would love to get started on it immediately.

It was done in two months—after three years of pounding the corridors of the tourism and home ministries in vain. I then realized that the most powerful organization in the capital was the TamBrahm PA Network. It actually makes things happen if it chooses to. Try it sometime.

That's how Lacadives, the first scuba diving school in India, was set up in Kadmat, in 1993, as Mitali and I pioneered and promoted the sport for the next twenty challenging, yet unforgettable, years. The administrator, Mr Cheema, very kindly built us a jetty to get on and off the water for our scuba diving trips. The jetty became the centre of our universe and we named it the Jetty at the Edge of the Universe.

While Mitali and I were setting up and running the diving school in Kadmat, our kids were having the time of their lives on the island, swimming in the lagoon, climbing coconut trees, catching crabs, and learning to respect the ocean. The ocean taught them more than any educational institute could possibly have taught them about the rules of nature and therefore life. It taught them never to take the ocean for granted and it taught them humility. It centred their energies, how to keep still and listen and follow their instincts.

It taught them the way of the adventurer, the curiosity to see, learn and go that extra mile, to feel the embrace of the ocean, to follow their intuitions and be patient. They are who they are because of the ocean, despite our efforts to teach them otherwise. While Arnav and Varun started diving long before Anhjin (pronounced Anzain), who was the youngest and the most enthusiastic, he had to wait years before he was allowed to dive. In the meantime, he had been introduced to the ocean at six months of age, and by the time he was three, he believed he could do everything that his elder siblings could do, including swim, without water wings.

One day, after two spectacular morning dives, we were chilling on the front porch of my small prefab hut, watching the kids, happily playing at the edge of the jetty (yes, the Jetty at the Edge of the Universe) when Anhjin, suddenly, lost his footing because of the dip in the sand, and disappeared. He came up spluttering and gasping for air and was thrashing about looking for some high ground. Mitali, like a true mother hen, was about to charge down the jetty to rescue her flailing youngest. He was very close to the steps on the jetty so I stopped her to see if he had learned his lessons from the ocean and would keep his head and his bearings right. He did! Gasping and thrashing he made it to the steps and clambered on while we cheered. He finally caught his breath and came running to us across the wooden jetty. He reached Mitali, who was still a bit shaken, and blurted to her, 'Mommy, Mommy, I drownded!' We all collapsed laughing.

The other memorable incident in Anhjin's life was when he was all of ten, a tiny figure who stood at the edge of the jetty to see off the diving boat from it, and was still there two hours later, waiting for the boat to return, dying to hear first-hand all the excitement and the creatures sighted and the state of the sea and its visibility. He would just love the shark encounters and play them back in his imagination again and again, always embellishing them with his own take, as if he was there. One day, as we were coming towards the jetty from a dive, we could see a small figure waiting patiently to hear all about our adventures.

Mitali, who was the senior instructor, couldn't bear to see him waiting every day to grow up to get his turn. She finally called Seemant, the diving instructor, and mentioned to him that he could take Anhjin down to five metres and not more than that. So just imagine the scene, two figures at the end of the jetty, where the equipment was being washed, one a tall instructor and the other, a small ten-year-old.

Seemant: 'Anhjin, kit up! Your time has come!'

Anhjin, looking up with great gravitas, replied: 'Do you know I have been waiting for this moment all my life!'

End of scene.

Arnav (Nobby) had a very special relationship with the ocean and could uncannily predict the myriad moods of this enormous body of water. Once we had gone to Alibaug by boat and the car brought Dumbell, because it was a long and arduous journey. On the way back, he took one look at the placid sea and said, 'I am going with Dumbell by car.' We couldn't fathom the reason until he told us that there was going to be a storm. And as we were getting on the boat to head back, there was a sudden wind that brought in a whole lot of thunderheads. There was lightning and thunder and we were in the midst of a storm. We just about scrambled back to land for our safety and had to wait it out. Meanwhile, Arnav and Dumbell reached way before we did.

Another time, when he was old enough to dive, I remember he was sitting at the prow of the boat and looked down at the water and said, 'I am not diving today.' Mitali asked him, 'Why?' The conditions were so idyllic. He looked at her gravely and said, 'There's jellyfish down there.' Mitali looked, couldn't see a thing and told him so. He stuck to his guns and said they were there because he knew. Sure enough, as we were submerged, we were surrounded by thousands of jellyfish, which you couldn't see from the surface because they are transparent! We all got right royally stung in all the exposed parts of our bodies.

Nobby grew up to become a marine biologist and diving instructor, underwater filmmaker and surfer. Varun studied law in London and is an avid diver and Anhjin has become a cameraman and crack underwater camera operator. Thank you, ocean, for looking after our children and teaching them things they would never have learned in a classroom.

Here is what Seemant, one of our diving instructors, who was in-charge of Kadmat island at that time, has to say:

> It has always been a pleasure to have Prahlad, whom we call PK, over when he would come to Kadmat and chill. For me, as a young instructor taking care of the Lacadives Diving Centre, it was always exciting when the baap came visiting. There would be a palpable buzz of mixed emotions between all of us at Team Kadmat, including those who had occasionally screwed up enough in the diving season to get the famous PK mouthful. And the rest of us looked forward to all the fun and frolic that arrived with him.
>
> Fact: Almost everyone who got the mouthful also secretly looked forward to it. It was a badge of honour to be told off by none other than the baap! It was nice to also see a version of PK I would never see in the brief 'off-seasons' at the mainland and office [Genesis], when monsoons would shut down the diving season in the islands.
>
> At Kadmat, PK would take off his shoes (literally) and settle into his usual mundu, chappals and a comfy T-shirt. He would unpack his Louis L'Amour novels, something that he would religiously carry on his trips there, and a good—contraband— bottle of Gentleman Jack or something equally welcome in those dry lands.
>
> He would immediately start diving the day after arrival and there was no changing that two-dive, sometimes three, a day

routine of his. PK would doze off in the transit boat rides and snap back as soon as we reached the dive site.

Diving with him was always fun; I could see his childlike wonder at being underwater all the time. All local chaps in the dive team would suddenly display professional behaviour, which was a struggle to maintain during the rest of the season as S would have his PMS days or U would decide it was time to become politically active in the team. When PK was around, everyone reached before time, smiled through the full days and even managed to show up for the evening barbeque. There would be special made-at-home lobster or tuna deliveries from the dive-team boys and the choicest snapper would end up in the BBQ. Jolly times for all, basically.

Most nights, as was his ritual, I was happy to arrange his mattress, bed sheet, blanket and pillows on the jetty. The Kadmat jetty is still a magical place. It truly exists in its own universe. Anyone who has been there knows. PK named it the Jetty at the Edge of the Universe. He christened the part at the end, where he slept, the Starlight Suite.

After I first saw him sleep there most nights, I gave it a shot too after his visit was over. It is surreal beyond belief to lie down with the tide lapping under you as you look up at a crazy night sky glittering with stars. You can see the Milky Way and shooting stars most nights too. PK never changed this ritual on Kadmat—unless there was no breeze; then the mosquito hordes could carry one off to the neighbouring island, Amini. And it was always great to see him enjoy some of the simplest pleasures of life at Kadmat and her jetty.

Thanks to him and his love for that jetty, generations of us laddoos (all novices were laddoos first and divers later) became scuba instructors and lost our souls to the ocean in Kadmat and Lakshadweep—a place where one still steps back in time. Where the jetty still stands with its Starlight Suite overlooking the lagoon.

41

Limca and All That Jazz

From the beginning of my career, I have somehow been involved in the making of most soft drink campaigns. I started with having an observer status on Gold Spot, starring Rekha. This left a subliminal impact on my young and fevered mind. Later, when Shyam Benegal went off to do the Hindustan Steel films (Pulsating Giant) and left the ASP film department in my inept hands, loosely supervised by Shama Habibullah, I grabbed the opportunity to do a whole lot of Limca films for our client Parle, who wanted a cheap and cheerful stopgap reminder film for Limca. The proposition was: 'When you are feeling hot and thirsty, and you want some fun and frolic, take one chilled bottle of Limca, open it . . . Aaahh, Limca, it's very, very lime and lemony.'

Being free and unsupervised, I decided to have some fun and frolic—literally. I had enough of a budget to build one college canteen set and cast a whole bunch of college kids with one main protagonist. For once, I didn't cast our go-to actor, Dalip Tahil, but I found a youngish theatre actor, Jayant Kripalani, as our main lead and irreverent protagonist. I remembered Rekha sipping a Gold Spot straight from the bottle and made a spur-of-the-moment decision to talk about what to do with a straw, and instead drink Limca straight from the bottle. We thought of half-a-dozen ways on how to use a straw creatively without drinking from it: 'Take a chilled bottle of Limca, open it, now take a straw, pinch the straw alternately and chant, 'She loves me, she loves me not, she loves me not, she loves me, she loves me not! Shit!' Throw the straw over your left shoulder and drink Limca straight from the bottle. Ahh, Limca, it's so lime and lemony.'

We shot seven of these ads, furiously brainstorming and improvising on set between shots; everybody got into the act and either contributed or applauded the ones they found funny. In one day, we shot seven one-take commercials and could have gone on if we hadn't run out of shift time. We came up with 'Take a straw, blow gently into your partner's ear.' 'Take four straws, crisscross them on the table and play knots and crosses with her. When she makes her move, drink *her* Limca straight from the bottle!' 'Take two straws, bend them in the centre and then use them to make loud, snapping sounds.' 'Take a straw and with some moong dal, use it as a pea shooter, *ouch*, quickly hide the straw after shooting someone with it!' And so on and so forth.

We loved the films, but the marketing manager hated them and, at the presentation, objected vociferously on behalf of the straw manufacturers and said it would upset them. I told him that if we were successful, we would not need straws any more; and anyway, they were unhygienic and not eco-friendly. He grumbled on and on about these issues until I realized that he was past fifty years of age, and had completely missed the point and the inane humour. I asked him to test it on his teenage children as they might find the ads irreverent and fun. He sulked and reluctantly approved them, only because he had seven commercials for the price of one. The campaign was launched, garnering great reviews from teenage consumers and a lukewarm reception from the adults. C'est la vie! We were a little ahead of our time. A decade later, we were to follow the same style and pattern for the Maggi sauces films.

One day, I got a call from Clarinda (Clarrie), a senior copywriter from JWT Delhi. She proceeded to sing a jingle into my ear for Maggi Hot and Sweet Tomato Sauce. In a husky, breathless voice, she sang, 'Hot sweet! Hot sweet! Hooottttt and sweet! VO: Maggie, Hot and Sweet

Chilli Sauce!' Clarrie wanted jazz maestro Louis Banks to record the jingle; she was going to fly to Bombay to supervise it. I quailed at the thought of dealing with Clarinda. She was completely off the charts. I knew this because I had indirectly dealt with her in Bombay for a suitcase advertisement. I barely escaped with my hair intact. I called Louis Banks (Unca Looey to my flunkies) and, after hearing the brief and her name, all he said was, 'By jove!' That was Mr Banks for you.

The critical day arrived and Clarrie was landing at the crack of dawn. I dragged myself out of bed, having pulled a graveyard shift the night before, and surprised her at the airport by personally picking her up and driving her to the film centre in Tardeo, where the recording was taking place. She sang the jingle all the way to the studio. I settled Clarrie and Mr Banks as quickly as possible, and while they sorted out their preferences, I told them that I would take a quick shower and be back in a jiffy.

I went straight back to the airport, bought myself a ticket on the first flight to Goa and skedaddled! The finished jingle was ready by the evening, but not without Clarrie making incessant calls to my office. Everyone at Genesis was too terrified of telling her the news that I had flown the coop out of sheer self-preservation. They then coopted Mitali (still my girlfriend then) to finally tell her. It was all done and peti packed by midnight. I promised the battered Louis Banks a bottle of feni for stepping into the breach for me like a true trooper.

The film was beautifully shot by Vikas Sivaraman, with lots of fabulous food and product shots, and no story. Not surprisingly, it bombed at the box office, and back we went to the drawing board. We heard nothing from the client or the agency for a year. And then I got a call from Dennis Joseph, creative director of JWT Delhi, to get my arse to Delhi for an important brainstorming session on Maggi Hot and Sweet Chilli Sauce (I groaned).

I landed up and found an extremely worried creative team headed by Dennis, who had come up with a great line after watching *Kramer vs Kramer*: an extended dialogue between Satish Shah and Naseeruddin Shah, in a series titled 'Shah vs Shah', where Satish loves the sauce and Naseer hates it. That is where it came to a grinding halt as whatever we thought up wasn't funny, but pedantic. I had a brainwave and told Dennis that I would have to go back to Bombay and brief my friend and talent Jaaved Jaaferi, because he wouldn't anticipate the kind of restrictions that brand managers put on agencies—he wasn't conditioned, unlike us battle-hardened advertising types—and would give us a fresh perspective on the subject.

I met Jaaved, who was full of filmi anecdotes and references. He came up with lines like 'Sau din sauce ke'; 'One day in the "loin's" den', the 'loin' being Ajit, the villain; 'One day at a tennis match'; 'Hero to zero'; 'One day at night'. He not only got the gist of what the agency wanted, but took off, writing it the way he spoke. It wasn't Hindi and it definitely wasn't English. Instead, it was a sort of Hinglish—the typical language of the Bandra boys. Even though the entire country, especially the youth, talked the talk, it had never been accepted by the oh-so-propah advertising copy crowd. This style of Hinglish was funny and real, especially if you had the guts to be a first-mover.

We wrote about six scenarios for the launch and I instinctively knew that if we presented them on paper, even as a narration, they would be bounced around like a basketball. We decided to test the scripts out on videotape; VHS had just made a huge dent in the way people were going to consume content in the entertainment world. I had decided very early in my career that relevant entertainment was the only way advertising would be effective and engaging. Storytelling was the only way for us because we were damn good at it. We went into a huddle with the agency's creative team and decided to budget a small one-day video shoot on a VHS handycam, for which we would share the cost with the agency. Dennis Joseph was thrilled with the idea and agreed to our proposal.

We set up a space in a photography studio and, since we did not have a budget for sets or costumes, decided to innovate. We got our set designer and poster illustrator, Promod Guruji, to paint us flats of the necessary backgrounds, such as a park for 'One day at the park'; a movie theatre for 'Sau din sauce ke'; bleachers for the spectators of 'One day at a tennis match'; and the 'loin's' den for 'One day in the loin's den'. Since the flats looked pathetically two-dimensional and our characters were three-dimensional, there was a huge jump between the two. To avoid that, we decided to add a layer of reality between the characters and the flats by putting in real objects and people. It was magical how seamless it started looking when we added a bench in the park, a row of real people in the movie hall, and a row of real people on the bleachers to watch the tennis match and so on (today all this can be done with the click of a button).

We were a bit stumped for the casting, as both Satish and Naseer were too busy to write off a day, and we couldn't afford their sitting fees anyway. Jaaved volunteered to take Naseer's place and we browbeat a rather plump boy from the office, the curly-haired Sailesh Chandrakant, to play Satish for the scratch films. It was an excellent choice! Jaaved, who is a brilliant actor, had also written the dialogue. So he took on the role of the detractor and Sailesh played a credible Satish Shah, who loved the sauce. Jaaved was inspirational and egged Sailesh on to perform outside of himself. We laughed the whole day away. Since we did not have the time to break the commercials into shot breakdowns, we planned them in one shot with zooms and pans and sometimes, just one close-up. The dialogues were so well written and the performances so stellar that the scratches already looked excellent in thirty seconds.

I took the scratch films to JWT Delhi and shared them with Dennis; he was thrilled. We went over to the Nestlé office in Connaught Place to show it to the marketing team. We were as buoyant as the Nestlé team was stoic. We set up the system in the conference room and ran the commercials. Dead silence! We ran them again and a small trickle of whys streamed in, which quickly turned into a bedlam of wheres: 'Where's the consumption? Where's the sauce's moment? Where were the mouth-watering close-ups?' Poor Dennis's explanations were wholly ignored and he had to shut up.

Dennis is about six feet in height, and when he wants to disappear from an unpleasant scene, he tends to lean back and slowly slide under the table. He was doing precisely that as the tirade of inconsequential comments on inconsequential issues went on. Nobody told us that the films were not working, nobody said anything about how well they had been put together and how many times the brand descriptions were embedded in the dialogue. It was quite a mouthful too! 'Maggi Hot and Sweet Chilli Sauce.'

By this time, Dennis had practically stretched his entire length under the table and only his eyes were visible. Just then, the door of the conference room flew open dramatically. A mild-looking Parsi gentleman peered benignly at this frozen tableau. He was D.E. Ardeshir, chairman of Nestlé India, the whole room shat bricks! He was, by reputation, not someone to take lightly. He did not tolerate fools and he was an unpredictable Bawa to boot. In a deceptively gentle voice, he said, 'I can see you guys are having fun! Give me a moment while I take a leak.' Like Schwarzenegger, he said, 'I'll be back.' He turned around and left.

The room ran a gamut of emotions, from blue funk to furious. 'Now what? How do we get rid of him?' Dennis slowly emerged from under the table and blinked owlishly. People like me never got to meet D.E. Ardeshir; I had only heard of his reputation of cutting to the bone and not fiddling around. There was a pregnant silence while everybody looked for a place to hide in the tiny room equipped with only a large table and some chairs. Dennis, by first-mover advantage, had already got cowering rights under the table. (It transpired later that D.E. Ardeshir's private loo was under repairs, which was why he was heading past the conference room to the general loo, when he heard the clamour and popped in.)

Door opened less dramatically this time, and in walked Mr Ardeshir, now looking visibly relieved. He refused a chair, tekoed (rested) one bum cheek on the table and, sitting hip shot, said dramatically, 'What's happening? Please include me in your fun.' The brand manager cleared her throat and said, 'We were just reviewing some preliminary, possible creatives for Hot and Sweet.' D.E. Ardeshir looked pleased and said, 'Great, show me!' We reluctantly ran the scratches for him, and halfway through, he started giggling, then guffawing. Shit, we thought, he's going to sack the agency! He saw the lot again, laughed some more, turned to us and said, 'Very good, just lose the last commercial (where Sailesh forces Jaaved to finally taste the sauce).'

He then stood up and said, 'It's different!' He was echoing the tagline we had used in the ad films.

He looked around and asked the brand manager how much money they had put towards this variant. She mumbled something like Rs 30 lakh, but also mentioned that they had asked for only one TV commercial (TVC). He raised an eyebrow and asked, 'How much for the mother brand, Maggi Tomato Ketchup?' To which, she said about a crore and a half. D.E. Ardeshir hesitated a split second and said, 'Use it all for these ads and run them.' She knew when to keep her powder dry and nodded. One of the assistants blurted out, 'But ... but, sir, what will happen to the mother brand if we put all our money on Hot and Sweet?' D.E. Ardeshir gave the offending naysayer a hard look and said, 'Don't worry, you nitwit, the takeaway for people will be Maggi sauces and we will sell shitloads of both variants!' He then turned to me and asked, 'When can we release them?'

I stammered that these were scratches, and we had to shoot them on film with proper sets and with Satish Shah and Naseeruddin Shah, which would take time considering their dates. He looked at me and stressed, 'Don't change anything, not even the cast. Keep the style the same; I love it. If you change the tagline, "It's different", I will personally kill you.'

Off he went, out of the room. We did change one thing. We cast Pankaj Kapoor instead of Satish Shah for we needed a star and he had become very popular as the carrot-eating detective, Karamchand. As a pair, they were brilliant: Jaaved's volatility versus Pankaj's understated matter-of-factness. 'It's different, boss.' The campaign made history and after its release, as predicted by D.E. Ardeshir, both products flew off the shelf—it became the favourite success story for all B-schools to refer to. But nobody, except the people in the room, knew that it was the universe conspiring and not human deliberation that made the campaign successful. The case history was written, in hindsight, by some senior suit who just wanted a piece of the glory. So, just for the record, I had to write it exactly the way it happened.

42

The Waiting Is Over

Life kept moving at a frantic pace and Mitali was expecting our second child. However, she was restricted to the house as she was having a difficult pregnancy, and we were really missing her cool, efficient handling of agencies and difficult talent. One day, I got a call from the Lintas film department to come and hear a storyboard for Kawasaki Bajaj's relaunch. They had had a disastrous start to their previous campaign as it had overpromised and underdelivered. They had gone back to the drawing board and, a year later, were ready to relaunch the RTZ 100.

I thought I had heard them wrong when they asked us to 'listen' to the storyboard. Very curious, I landed up at the meeting and was promptly introduced to a bright young copywriter, Adi Pocha, who greeted me very seriously and led me into a small recording studio–like room. He sat me down and switched off the lights. I thought that perhaps Lintas was going through one of their economy drives, and had asked their staff to switch off all appliances and lights when leaving the room. But no, Adi was still in the room; well, at least his voice was, and he instructed me to close my eyes and listen. It was pitch black, so it didn't matter if I closed my eyes or not. But, from hidden speakers in the room, I suddenly heard the sound of the wind.

Adi described a desert and a pair of shiny railway tracks stretching into infinity. Squinting into the horizon, he said, is a young man, rugged and good-looking; he is nature's child, an outdoorsman, he is waiting ... How long is anybody's guess. But his footprints in the sand are already half-covered by the gusty wind. Suddenly, he stiffens and looks searchingly down the rail tracks. The distant tooting of a train engine is almost lost in the roar of the wind. But yes, a gleaming engine grows out of the shimmering distance like a mirage. The young man smiles in anticipation, and his body language changes from patience to alert anticipation as the train comes thundering down the track, gleaming black and gold.

It stops in front of the waiting man. It is a goods train full of cattle bogies. A ramp drops down from one of the bogies. Our young man spins around in excitement, his eyes wide with hope, a smile lighting up his face. He starts sprinting towards the ramp. A pair of men in grey–blue overalls, with the legend 'Bajaj Motorcycles' on their chests, lead a gleaming machine out of the compartment. The men park it and jump back on to the train. Our hero sprints up to the bike, runs a worshipping hand over its shining tank and leaps in the air in triumph. The VO goes: 'The new Kawasaki Bajaj RTZ 100. The waiting is over!' There was no specific mention of a steam engine, which we added later as our contribution to the narrative.

The lights came on with a crescendo of music, leaving me blinking owlishly in the sudden brightness. I had been transported magically to a desert with a train, a bike and a young man in the middle of nowhere, waiting for the new Kawasaki Bajaj RTZ 100. It was one of the most powerful and vivid narrations of a TVC script I had ever heard. I looked at young Adi, looking shyly around, and clapped. He blushed. I could see the film etched permanently in my mind's eye with an antique steam engine. Awesome! But proverbially, there is many a slip between the cup and the lip, and in walked a slightly portly, obnoxious suit, who claimed to be the group head in charge of Bajaj. I promptly nicknamed him 'Walrus, the pugnacious'. All he was interested in was the *when* and *how much*. He wanted it now! I blandly told him to take a flying fuck at a rolling doughnut.

I tried explaining to him that it was a major film to be shot somewhere in the desert with an existing railway track. Then there was the matter of finding an antique steam engine; god alone knew if that existed and in what state it was to be carted to the location. There was also the logistics and costs of taking a crew to the middle of nowhere, and then setting the whole bloody shebang up from scratch. He blustered and fumed and reiterated that the bike was ready for launch, the campaign was ready, only the film needed to be done, like, yesterday. I told him he should have briefed his producers months ago if he was in such a tearing hurry. Then I thought a bit and asked him to run the narration as a radio spot for it was brilliant; he wasn't amused by my suggestion.

It was April and summer was galloping in—so the desert would be especially hot. I sent my team, divided into pairs, to look for a likely location. I briefed them that there shouldn't be a single tree around; it should be stark and barren, highlighting the loneliness of the waiting man. I also sent one lot off to Rail Bhawan in Delhi to figure out the engine and its availability, and whether it would work or not.

Also, almost in hindsight, I informed the desert searchers by telegram that the bloody steam engine would be narrow gauge and the railways were busy converting the network across the country to broad gauge. A month later, we got news from one bedraggled crew that a narrow gauge track was still available between Jaisalmer and Jodhpur and that some steam engines had been mothballed in Jodhpur's railway yard. Nobody knew whether they were working or not, but thank god for small mercies.

By the time we got one engine working by cannibalizing two others at Jodhpur, paying a hefty deposit to the Railways for its use and permissions, it was May—quite sweltering even in Bombay. Luckily, we had already cast the film and our hero was quite a find. I had met Feroze Gujral when she was a top model and had cast her in a red-and-white cigarette TVC (unique for its time, as we designed the entire film and all its activities in the red and white brand colours, including Feroze). Anyway, during that shoot, I met her younger brother, Hanut

Ewari, who was in college at the time and remembered him as a strapping, fit and exceptionally good-looking young man. He was a natural, good at games and very well put together.

I got hold of him, and Adi and the creative team loved him. Basically, we were ready to go and started planning the logistics of the shoot. By the time we were greenlit, it was the end of May and even more blisteringly hot. Mitali was due any day. Walrus, meanwhile, danced a tandav on his team's heads; he was a bit wary of me by then, but we knew we just couldn't delay it any more, summer or not. So off we went to Jaisalmer and sent most of the crew ahead by train from Delhi. Coming out of the aircraft at Jaipur, the heat hit us like a sledgehammer. It was 45 degrees Celsius in the shade and you could fry an egg on the bonnet of a car.

The wind came in swirls, little dust devils, and fine sand got into every orifice. We were miserable. The first order of business was to buy a couple of mulmul saris and cut them up into keffiyeh, like the Bedouins use in the Sahara, for the entire shooting crew. We drove down to the locations literally in the middle of nowhere. God alone knows how the kids (namely my tenacious intern, Chitra) in the office found it. It was a whistle-stop in the middle of the desert with nothing except a shed and a bench. We had carried a brass bell with us for a coolie type for the ad, whom we had dressed up in the classic Rajasthan style with a saafa and a brass billa on his chest, and he was to ring the bell when the train was to arrive. We had also given him a nice, thick curling moustache, reminiscent of Rajputs.

We realized that we would be able to shoot only early in the morning, from about 4.30 a.m. to 10 a.m., and from 4 p.m. to 6.30 p.m. The remaining hours of the day were too hot, even for the locals. The call time was set at 3 a.m. We set up whatever props we needed and, since the steam engine was expected to arrive by 6 a.m. the next morning, we decided to shoot from the next day on. Vikas Sivaraman was the DOP and, wrapped in his sari headdress, he was trying to figure out where to place the storm fans to create the wind.

We need not have bothered; during the night, there was a huge sandstorm that was still lingering the next morning. On arriving at the location in zero visibility, we quickly realized we couldn't find the station, the platform or even the railway track! Instead of our location, there was this massive sand dune. Everything was buried under it. We called the local sarpanch and hired the entire village to dig our location out. Nothing happens in isolation—especially not when Murphy strikes. When the engine was nowhere to be seen till 9 a.m., we got a bit frantic and tried asking the station that lay between us and Jodhpur where it could possibly be.

We learnt, to our dismay, that the bloody engine had derailed five kilometres from us by hitting a sand dune. All the villagers were dispatched to dig the track out from under the dune and try to get the engine back on to the rails. So that's how day two went; we actually never needed the storm fans. On day three, Adi arrived from Bombay, fresh for the slaughter, and we were finally ready to roll. This is Adi Pocha's version of what transpired next:

It was 1988, I think, if my memory hasn't totally deserted me. I had just written the script of my lifetime, or so I thought. I called it 'The Train in the Desert'. It was a simple, yet dramatic script, but I knew it wouldn't be a simple film to make. Eventually, after many rounds of hard-nosed negotiation, which I, as the creative person, was not really privy to, the bottle spun to the original Mad Man of Indian advertising: Prahlad Kakar.

Now Prahlad, during a shoot, was a creative director's worst nightmare. He was capable of haring off down some new creative rabbit hole that caught his fancy, abandoning months of carefully crafted strategy, on a whim. He had eternal trust in that very important advertising tool: his gut. However, Prahlad, once the TVC was actually aired and proven successful, was more often than not every creative director's dream. The trick, I thought, was to give him his head up to a point, like a thoroughbred thundering down the final straight.

The production crew got down to it. They had to find a desert, or more specifically, a truly empty stretch of desert, with a railway track running through it. Finally, news filtered in via STD, fax and telegraph. The team had found the ideal location—a small place in Rajasthan that probably didn't exist on any map. It was called Lathi. It looked like we were all set, except we still needed a locomotive that would stop exactly where we wanted it to and allow us to shoot the bike being wheeled out. Once all the permissions were in place, we were ready to go. I landed in the blistering desert in the middle of nowhere and was greeted by a director who looked like a cross between an Arab and Captain Haddock.

'Baashturd! So ... ?' It was his customary greeting with a questioning look and an upturned palm. It was meant to indicate great affection and an undying curiosity for the darkest secrets of my life.

'Come, baashturd! Let's go.' There was no point asking 'where'; I just followed him. The camera was set up; the DOP was a young, lean, languid, bearded fellow who went by the moniker Vikas Sivaraman.

'Here's our model ...'

I turned. It was Hanut Ewari, and he looked good—tall and tan. There was something that niggled at the back of my mind, but I pushed it away. He was wearing a cowboy hat; I guessed it was because of the sun. He would take it off, I was certain.

I was wrong.

'Okay, okay, c'mon ... Get your finger out of your nose before I nail your foreskin to the wall ... Let's go!'

I jumped. Was he talking to me? I didn't know, but I certainly didn't want any bit of me nailed to any non-existent wall.

'Yes, Prahlad,' I said dutifully.

'Not you,' he muttered brusquely. 'You're the agency. You don't have to work. Those other baashturds!'

The shot was all lined up, the camera was poised to roll and, in slow motion, I saw two things simultaneously: Prahlad's mouth beginning to open to call action and the hat.

'Stop!' I yelled. Now, it is sacrilege for anyone, especially agency anyones, to yell anything before, during or after a take. But I didn't have a choice. Prahlad turned to me; I could see the smoke coming out of his ears, but maybe that was just Rajasthan, I thought hopefully.

'P-P-P-Prahlad ...'

'*Whattt*, baashturd?'

'The hat.'

'What about it? It's made of genuine camel foreskin. If you stroke it—'

'Prahlad ... he can't wear the hat.'

'Balls! Of course, he can wear it.'

'But it wasn't discussed at the PPM [pre-production meeting].'

'So?' he asked, jutting his bearded chin belligerently at me.

It was bloody hot in the desert. 'You could fry an egg on your goolies if you stood outside,' he would later lovingly remind me. But we went at it for quite a while.

'He can't wear a hat. He looks like a cowboy.'

'So what? It's a fucking film!'

'But ... Please ...'

'Fuck off!'

We went on and on until, finally, we reached a compromise.

'Okay, baashturd! I will shoot it both ways. One with the hat and one without the hat.'

True to his word, he did. When I finally saw the finished film, I knew which version we would go with. I knew what made Prahlad such a great filmmaker. When that train pulled in, it did not stop conveniently beside Hanut, as I had naïvely scripted. It overshot him by a bit, which made Hanut whirl and run to the compartment. As he ran, his hat—*the* hat— flew off his head. In that one shot, I saw all the anticipation, the excitement, the sheer joy that a man feels for his new bike.

With that one shot, I knew what it meant to be a filmmaker. My wait was over. Thank you, Prahlad.

After two days of shooting in extreme conditions, we actually finished the shoot with sand in every possible orifice in our bodies, and I got a telegram informing me that I had become a father.

43

'Hi! I'm Sanju!'

My long and amazing run with Pepsi actually started quite slowly and with trepidation: both parties were still feeling our way around, looking for a comfort zone. We did some of their non-cola brands first and even launched the potato wafer brand, Lays, for PepsiCo. Back then, they were very enamoured by big names in the film industry, especially the stars that Pepsi has traditionally signed up with. Their launch film for Lehar Pepsi with Remo Fernandes and Juhi Chawla, 'Feel the magic', was done by Vidhu Vinod Chopra, as mentioned previously.

At that time, Pepsi was looking for national-level rockstars and it took a bit of learning for them to realize that the only national-level stars that we have in India are not musicians, but cricketers and film stars. On top of that, the South has its superstars and the North has its own—from the Hindi film industry. After the launch, they signed up with a few cricketers, starting with a young and promising Sachin Tendulkar, who proved to be a bonanza for them as he grew into a phenomenal global icon.

Pepsi also went through a small but significant change as Vibha Rishi replaced a recently promoted and internationally bound Ravi

Dhariwal as marketing manager. Vibha's style of functioning was very different from the typical marketing managers, sitting in their ivory towers. She was a hardwired, result-oriented professional, who had no qualms about her own (very few) shortcomings. She always included and trusted her agencies for all major strategic and creative decisions. She also realized very quickly—by attending most of their shoots—that nothing is cast in stone except the end result, and a creative director and film director can only realize on the set whether the script needs tweaking.

As a result, a lot of latitude was allowed during execution as she was working with the best professionals of her time. It was a slow but sure way to build trust, since she had to make sure both her agency and the producer–director of the TVCs were firmly locked into the brand values and target audience, along with the strategic importance of the yearly campaign and its objectives. This is why all the strategic meetings included suits, creatives and the production house—everybody became part owners of the brand and its future. This inclusivity was at the heart of great Pepsi advertising during her tenure.

I first met her during the shoot for the Mirinda special offer TVC, where Pepsi was testing our overall capacity to cope with high-value, high-pressure international brands. I was pleasantly surprised by her willingness for us to innovate during the shoot. We even managed to squeeze in an extra where the Mirinda deliveryman, a smartly dressed Derek Afonso (an assistant from the office), rings the doorbell in a stately mansion for their free four-pack sample. The door opens a crack as he straightens up and a beautifully manicured hand shoots out, grabs him by the collar and whisks him in.

A startled Derek disappears and the door slams shut, while the camera remains on the sweating four-pack of Mirinda. But the door opens a crack once more and the same hand now whisks the product inside before slamming it shut again. We all loved the film and Vibha promised to keep it in the archives as it was a bit too 'non-vegetarian' for the brand at that time. I think she approved of our slightly irreverent approach to brands, regardless of their stature, and decided to really test our mettle with a biggie.

JWT Delhi (née Hindustan Thompson) called to give us the good news: Pepsi's biggest film of the year was coming our way. I was called to Delhi for the briefing. It turned out that after much hemming and hawing, the agency and Pepsi had decided to remake an all-time successful film from the PepsiCo library called 'Apartment 10G'— Michael J. Fox's flat number in the ad.

The story goes Michael J. Fox hears a knock on his door and he opens it to find this very pretty girl who tells him she is his new neighbour and asks him if he has a Pepsi. 'Sure, come in,' says Mr Fox, and turns around and jumps for joy at his luck. He goes to the fridge and nada, no Pepsi. He calls out and asks if he can offer her something else. She refuses and is about to leave, so he tells her, 'No, no, I got it!'

It is pouring outside, but a faint heart never won a fair maiden. He slides through the window and goes down on to the landing. The window slams shut behind him as he drops to the street. Now, he tries to cross the busy road to a 7-Eleven, and a guard dog in a car sticks his head out of the window and barks furiously at Mr Fox, scaring the daylights out of him. He tries to cross the road by jumping from one car roof to the next, slipping and sliding. Just then, he is surrounded by a motorcycle gang of hoodlums, but he escapes and runs into the 7-Eleven. We see him running up the fire escape to the landing, only to find the window closed with no handle on the outside. We see an impatient girl about to leave when there is a crash and the tinkling sound of shards of glass falling. Mr Fox appears at the kitchen door— wet, bedraggled, but triumphant, holding, a can of Pepsi to the fair maiden who is most concerned about him.

There is a knock on the door and she mentions a flatmate, Danny. He looks visibly crestfallen, but looks around to see a bombshell of a girl in the doorway, who smiles invitingly and asks, 'Got another Pepsi?' Mr Fox is caught in a dilemma—to do or not to do. He rises to the occasion and says, 'Sure.' The film ends on his 'never-say-die' expression and the rest is left to your imagination. It was a beautiful film and hugely successful as Michael J. Fox was a trending youth icon of that time.

The original Michael J. Fox film was ninety seconds long; Pepsi wanted an Indian copy of forty-five seconds for TV and sixty seconds for cinemas. We were the ones chosen to cast and shoot the film, preferably with Shah Rukh Khan—an up-and-coming actor at the time. I was faced with a huge dilemma—to do or not to do! Here was a plum assignment, ripe for the picking, and we were caught dithering. If the quality slipped compared to the original (there was always a budget constraint), we would forever be branded as the arseholes who couldn't even copy an ad properly. If we did a fabulous job, the naysayers would say, 'Big deal, it was copied, there's nothing original about it.'

The challenge was to try, cast it and make it better and more relevant to India than the original. We got into a huddle, and we figured that the popular choice for a Michael J. Fox equivalent or more was, at that time, Aamir Khan—though Shah Rukh was a very close contender. *Qayamat Se Qayamat Tak* had catapulted Aamir to teen heartthrob status in 1988, and Mitali absolutely insisted that she would be the one to present the idea to him and convince him to do his first TVC. We were still desperately looking for the cute neighbour and the bombshell friend.

Pepsi was not overjoyed by our choice of Aamir over Shah Rukh as they had already negotiated with Shah Rukh, and Aamir was asking for the sky and not budging—partly because it was his first TVC and he wasn't very keen on doing it anyway as doing an ad film was looked down on by the film industry then (it was seen as only meant for film stars who were out of a job at the time).

Pepsi put a lot of pressure on us to accept Shah Rukh, but, calculating the stakes involved, I dug my heels in as I knew that Aamir was a better fit for the story. It went to and fro and, finally, we showed Aamir the original film, which got him excited enough to at least sound enthusiastic. He still wouldn't budge on the price. Finally, Pepsi also saw the sense in it as well and upped their budget to sign on Aamir Khan. Phew, first hurdle crossed; now for the girls.

JWT came up with a really pretty girl from the tea gardens; her name was Ritu Chaudhry. She was selected to be the girl who rings the bell at Apartment 10G—one down, one to go. We were looking for somebody who not only looked good, but someone whom the camera loved as well. Often, clients recommend talent for various reasons— based partly on the fact that they are easy on the eyes—and, when put in front of a camera, they turn out to be disasters and no one is willing to bell the cat. We had no such compunctions; so, we put Ritu through the grind and she came across as really cute on the camera— and the camera doesn't lie. Now for the bombshell. We looked high and low, but just couldn't find someone with the magical quality of an instant connection. We looked and looked and just weren't happy with whomever we found. She was to be the clincher in the film, the secret weapon, the bombshell that exploded on the screen for three seconds and left everybody screaming for more.

In the hustle and bustle of a normal day at Genesis, two young college students with huge architecture portfolio folders strolled into the office to meet Mitali and show her their work—one was Zhya Jacobs, a friend's son, and the other was his tall, green-eyed friend. My trusty assistant, Monia Sehgal, barged into my room and announced, 'I've found her!' *What?* I thought and leapt up to see this goddess. Monia led me to the editing room to see the attractive college girl with her hair tied back and no make-up on. She was wearing a kurti, a pair of distressed jeans (as was the trend) and work chappals, and carried a jhola—nothing earth-shattering. The thing that arrested my disappointment were her mesmerizing eyes—slate grey and green, depending on her mood. I asked her to loosen her slightly oily hair and out tumbled a mane of wavy, auburn tousled hair. Not bad, but not the jackpot. Not yet.

Monia saw my disappointment through my bland and polite expression, and followed me to my cabin, saying, 'Just let me test her; she is really quite unique and fabulous.' I looked at her in grim exasperation, but she said with great conviction, 'We will give her a makeover. Watch how the camera will love her. I stake my life on it!'

She was one of my better assistants and loyal to the core; so, against my better judgement, I decided to go with Monia and see where it led us. Maybe back to square one. But at least she wouldn't argue so vociferously if she was proved wrong.

I told Monia that I wanted the wet look for one of the tests, with only light make-up on, just her eyes and her mouth, with her hair plastered close to her skull—and bingo! She looked quite stunning because of her bone structure; the camera loved her. We had our showstopper, with a mane of auburn hair and a wet look—both shots were fantastic. It was Aishwarya Rai.

To completely foolproof the plan, we also cast Aishwarya in a short film for Prudent mouthwash. Vidyadhar, the make-up man, was briefed: 'Inko bhagwan ne bahut fursat se banaya hai! So don't even think of improving on it. Just enhance her eyes and mouth, and try and give her a zero-make-up look!' He grumbled a bit, but got to work. Her entry on the top of a staircase was mind-blowing. We all stopped and gaped, before getting on with the shoot. Jalal Agha was playing the dentist, and even he lost his irreverent and nearly constant deluge of 'non-vegetarian' jokes.

Off I went to the Pepsi office in Gurgaon to show them our coup. With Vibha out of town, Neal Chatterjee and an assistant took care of the approvals. Neal was an old buddy from our McCann and Nestlé days, so we got along well. In a darkened projection room, I showed them two stills of Aishwarya (Ash)—one with her hair open and one with a wet look. Neal sat up and asked, 'Same girl?' We nodded, turned off the projector and waited. They all looked at me expectantly for more and Neal, a bit chagrined, said, 'That's only one.' I looked at them with great solemnity and said, 'I am sorry, guys, but they don't make them like her in twos! You are looking at a future star; enjoy it!'

So it came to pass that Ash was the chosen one and we prepped furiously to make the film a truly Indian experience. Now that we had the cast of our choice, there was no excuse to flub it. The first change we made in the narration was that the 7-Eleven became a kirane ki dukaan about to close for the night, with a rolling shutter, which our hero spots the moment he gets on the landing. The girl next door is shy and uncertain when she rings the doorbell and asks for a Pepsi. He, though surprised, is pleased to make her acquaintance, but can't overdo his delight in front of her as he would come across as lecherous. It was very important for him to look very appreciative and clean (in an Indian context, she would never come in if she suspected him to have any ulterior motive).

She checks out his chess set while waiting and tentatively makes a move, a subtle suggestion that she is not a bimbo. Aamir is known to like playing chess. All the cars, of course, were Indian with Indian number plates. The final touch was the kirana shop. The most important part of the identity of the film, in my opinion, was the casting. The combination of Ritu, Aamir and Ash was a minor coup and they were fabulous together. We branded the film even in Aamir's jump from the balcony into a puddle of water, which reflected the brand name Lehar Pepsi. Aamir sliding under a closing shutter to get the Pepsi is the crowning moment and, now that we know the shop is closed, where the hell is he going to get the next Pepsi?

The shoot was full of adventure as we finished the indoor segment, including the classic scene with Ash playing Sanju/Sanjana, where I had to get a really inviting posture from her when she appears in the doorway. I don't know who was more stressed—her or me. We tried different postures and finally settled for one hand on the doorjamb, with her hair wet and slicked back as if coming straight from the shower. Her body was poised slightly provocatively, wearing a pair of beautifully tailored slacks, a silk shirt knotted at the stomach with just a hint of grey–black make-up around her eyes to enhance their unique colour and a touch of deep red on her lips. The visual result was stunning. Now came the performance and body language. Since it was Ash's first really big campaign, the pressure and stress really got to her—and to me—as we realized that this was the money shot for the entire film and everybody was watching her.

In the beginning, there were many suggestions flying at her from me, the agency, even the client. We did take after take, confusing and stressing her out, until she just threw up her hands and said she couldn't do it. She was close to tears. There was dead silence in the studio; everybody was shocked. I stepped up, told everybody to shut the fuck up, took her aside and calmed her down. I told her she was doing fine, but that she just had to imagine a roomful of attractive young men, and to stand and deliver her line, 'Hi, I am Sanjana, got another Pepsi?' as a challenge to them, so that they would leap to it and compete with each other to get her that elusive bottle of Pepsi, even when everything was shut and it was pouring outside.

Listening to me, she burst out laughing. Taken aback, I asked her what was so funny. She sobered up and told me that she had been so protected thus far at home that she had neither a boyfriend nor the inclination to have one as she had been focused on her studies. What I was telling her was as remote as the moon, but she would give it a try. Boy, did she get into the groove. Not only did she deliver, she also knocked us all out with her performance. It took only a few more takes for us to wrap up the scene, and Aishwarya Rai became a part of legend with her four-second debut—to the point that thousands of parents named their daughters Sanjana after the character in the TVC! (A little-known fact was that it was Vibha Rishi's idea to name her Sanju/Sanjana, after her own daughter.)

While we were shooting in the studio at Raj Kamal, Parel, late into the night, Murphy was busy throwing a monkey wrench into the smooth functioning of the shoot. As we packed up the indoor shoot with Ash's segment and emerged outside into the real world, we ran smack into one of the biggest communal riots in the history of Bombay, and Parel was at the heart of it all. It was unsafe for anybody to venture out, Hindus or Muslims, and we had a crew of eighty people with both Hindus, Muslims and a Parsi assistant cameraman, who looked like a Muslim. One-third of the crew was women.

We were wondering what to do when Vibha Rishi took over, and ordered all of us suburban types to get into a convoy and head for the President Hotel in Cuffe Parade (a safer route) until the riots subsided. She also took full responsibility for the bill. We were stuck for three days at the President before we could get home. We left Ritu at the hotel thinking she would be able to fly out to Delhi, her base, directly, but the airport was totally cut off. So, a few days later, I chanced a run to the President Hotel to pick her up and bring her home. She was stuck in my house in Bombay for nearly ten days.

We had kept the street set standing, thinking we would be able to complete the film in a few days. No such luck; it took us a month of fretting before the crew could risk going back to Parel. After sprucing up the street and the kirana shop, we informed Aamir about his revised schedule. He was game, but his nervous family was putting a lot of pressure on him to abstain as things had just about settled down. I sent a very pregnant Mitali to escort him to the studio, reassuring him that we had security for him.

He was so embarrassed about Mitali landing up—a picture of pregnant serenity amidst the carnage—that he meekly followed her to the studio, looking for his security detail, which he was promised. The truth was that Amita Sehgal, our cracker of a producer, had requested the harrowed local police station to provide us some security and they had refused point-blank. After much cajoling, they gave her a scrawny-looking constable with a lathi to fend off the imagined marauding hordes.

Amita Sehgal came back to the set and dressed up some of our male staff in police uniforms with lathis, and told them to act big and tough between shots. In the meantime, we got a friend, Ashok Motwani, to engage Aamir in a game of chess in his downtime, to get his mind off what might happen if the riots broke out anew. We finished the shoot without incident and even got Aamir to slide under a rapidly closing shutter of the kirana shop without a raised eyebrow. Thank you, Murphy, for not screwing us yet again.

The film was edited into its required lengths, and the music was recorded by the enormously talented drummer and musician, Ranjit Barot, over three days—through which he kept ordering food from the Taj Hotel, until I was convinced that the food bill would cost us more than the film. When I mumbled my fears to him, he was a bit peeved, but finished the job in double quick time as I threatened to order vada pavs for everybody next. The film looked like a million dollars and everyone—the agency and Vibha included—were thrilled. We were dying to release it as quickly as possible.

In our self-congratulatory mood, we forgot to thank Murphy, who, true to form, struck again. During the shoot, in the segment where

Aamir opens the door to a shy neighbour, Ritu, his expressions were surprise, hope and pleasure, but there was definitely no flicker of lechery. We tried many takes and would have repeated ad nauseam—Aamir, as always, wanted it to be perfect—so I told him we got it. We had only been trying for a safety, but it was in the bag, I said. He looked at me sceptically and said, 'Show me the take you have chosen in the rough cut.' But in our hurry to make the schedule for Pepsi, I selected a perfectly fabulous take and sent it to Pepsi, while sharing it with Aamir slipped my mind completely.

Later, on being congratulated by Vibha for a job well done, he threw a petulant fit and told her that he had been promised a viewing before its release. He wanted to see it and approve the offending take himself. Vibha called me in a flap and I called Aamir to assure him that the take looked fab—but he was not happy. I told him that I appreciated his professionalism, but was not going to compromise *my* film for his convenience.

He sulked, I sulked—we reached an impasse. It took a pregnant Mitali lugging the rough cut to Aamir's editing room in Juhu to get him talking again. She showed him the film on a Steinbeck, a film editing machine, about thirty times. Finally, a friend of Aamir's, who was also there, told him it was fantastic and to stop hyperventilating. He gave us the okay and Mitali immediately called a very relieved Vibha.

The film did amazing things for Pepsi—it made movie stars out of Ritu (who changed her name to Mahima), and Ash became Miss World the next year and went on to do blockbuster movies. Aamir remained Aamir, but realized the power of good advertising and the money in it, and hasn't disengaged till today. Genesis became the Genesis Film Production house, the most difficult but also the most creative production house of its time.

I want to conclude the story of this amazing project by leaving you with a thought: loose bowels, death and Murphy can strike any time, so do not react, but anticipate. Be prepared for any and all eventualities. It sounds better in Hindi: Maut, tatti aur Murphy kabhi bhi aa sakte hai!

44

'Nothing Official About It'

There was massive excitement in the Indian advertising fraternity as the fifty-overs Cricket World Cup was being played in the subcontinent and would be the single largest event in recent history. The advertising fraternity was salivating as they would finally get to push their clients to loosen their purse strings and participate in this mega event! Pepsi had bid to be the official sponsor of the World Cup.

Pepsi, having had a couple of years of a head start over Coca-Cola in the region, had gauged the mood of the youth of India and had invested heavily in cricketers, movie stars and rockstars. They had also signed up 80 per cent of the Indian cricket team, plus some prominent players from England and the West Indies. But there was some apprehension as a newly resurgent Coke had come back to the Indian market, with deep pockets, and had also entered the fray to sponsor the World Cup at any cost.

In between the planning and ideating to create advertising around the greatest sporting spectacle in five years for the cricket-crazy citizens of India, Pakistan, Sri Lanka and Bangladesh, we were waiting with bated breath for the sponsorship bid results. Surely, there was no way Pepsi would lose the bid—it was practically a given! The day arrived and the announcement was made—Coke had won the bid to be the official sponsor of the World Cup. We were bereft. 'Ab hamara kya hoga, Kalia?' HTA was summoned to the Pepsi office in Gurgaon and a more sorry lot was difficult to find or even imagine.

There was gloom all around when the HTA team was asked to come up with something—anything—to counter this disaster. Now was the time to actually prove their pedigree. HTA briefed all the senior creative types and they all set about to find a solution. After two days of frantic confabulations, Shankar Rajan—senior suit, strategist and stakeholder in the future of the brand—reviewed all the ideas that were churned out. Nada. None of them were worth pursuing.

In desperation, everybody with a creative bone in the agency was roped in for this last-ditch rescue effort, including the trainees. Among them was this dewy-eyed young lady called Anuja Chauhan, recently married and very pregnant, about to take off on maternity leave. Shankar briefed everyone to come up with something by the next day. The next day, Anuja returned with three ideas, not just one (such is the enthusiasm of trainees). The first idea hit the jackpot and Shankar was quite gobsmacked. They bandied the idea about for a bit, but Shankar stood by the idea and they decided to take it to Pepsi. Anuja was left plaintively complaining, 'But there are two more ideas.' By this time, jaan mein jaan aa gayi thi, so nobody even read them.

They all trooped into the conference room with a flicker of hope. Vibha walked in briskly to call the meeting to order, as the topic of discussion for the day was: How is Pepsi going to respond? Hers was the only cheery face in the room as Shankar Rajan got the ball rolling. He presented the one idea that had caught his imagination.

In the sombre Pepsi office, with the whole team present (Vibha Rishi, Neal Chatterjee, Nilanjan Shome and a few other motleys), the arguments centred mainly on whether it was too clever. Would people understand it? Would it work? So on and so forth. In the middle of all this carnage, a small voice piped up, 'But why do we have to be the *official* sponsor? It's not like it's the end of the world.'

Everyone, except Shankar Rajan, turned towards this offending voice trying to make light of this enormous dilemma. It turned out to be the new copywriter trainee, who had been given specific instructions that, for her, this meeting was a privilege to attend and she was not meant to be heard. But now she had gone ahead anyway, and dared to open her cute mouth and make a comment! Sacrilege! She was quickly shushed and the meeting moved on. Until Vibha suddenly said, 'Hold on.' Turning to the offending newbie, she asked, 'What exactly did you mean by that?'

Anuja went on to explain that if Coke was the 'official' sponsor inside the stadium, then why couldn't Pepsi be the 'unofficial' sponsor outside the stadium (where there are 60 lakh people who couldn't get in)? In other words: Why be official when it was in Pepsi's DNA to be unofficial? The brand positioning was all about being antiestablishment, young and irreverent. Vibha Rishi made a split-second decision, then and there, to go ahead with the idea and put an end to all discussions.

'Pepsi: Nothing official about it.'

Now it was left to Anuja to extend the idea into workable scripts before she went on maternity leave, which she did fabulously. Genesis was given the privilege of bringing this great idea to life and we took it on with utmost glee. We made some really wacky, antiestablishment commercials for the campaign, starting with 'Cricket is a gentleman's game, played in white.' The fifty-overs game was definitely not played in whites, and most players played to win and not score brownie points trying to be a gentleman. They would sledge, browbeat, occasionally throw bouncers to intimidate and appeal decisions vociferously, and even try and hector the umpire.

We made a series of films on all the larger-than-life characters in the sport. Dicky Bird, the legendary umpire, was dressed up like a Supreme Court judge, wig and all, sitting behind his desk in the middle of the pitch, passing judgment. When he puts his hand up, it's always holding a Pepsi. 'Pepsi! Nothing official about it!' Dicky Bird loved the commercial and, as he was about to retire, he didn't give a shit about what the powers that be thought of him. 'Meet Dickie Bird, you can't ruffle his feathers or get a bad decision out of him. So when he raises his hand, you can be sure he's made the right choice.'

VO: Pepsi: Nothing official about it!

We did one on Sachin trying to snitch a Pepsi from a delivery truck and being chased by an irate sardar driver, who, on catching him, realizes it is Sachin and offers him the whole truck and says in Punjabi, 'Oye, Sachin-e, haavve a Pepsi!' 'Meet Sachin Tendulkar, just plain greedy. When it's runs, wants a tonne. When it's Pepsi, wants a truck. Oye, Sachin-e, have a Pepsi!

VO: Pepsi: Nothing official about it!

We shot scenes with a whole lot of cricketers—Indian and other teams. Mohammad Azharuddin was hilarious, cracking Hyderabadi jokes all the way through, leaving us in splits. 'Meet Mohammad Azharuddin, no getting past the guy, grabs every ball that comes his way, or doesn't. So, when he asks for your Pepsi, just hand it over; it won't get past him anyway.'

VO: Pepsi: Nothing official about it.

We shot with fast bowler Dominic Cork in the ruins of Mukesh Mills with the sea as a background. We had him running up and down on his bowling run in the sun. He turned out to be a real sport. 'Meet Dominic Cork. Dead-eye Dominic, they call him. Bang on target every time he shoots, so watch him go for his Pepsi like a bullet out of a gun.'

VO: Pepsi: Nothing official about it.

The best was going all the way to the West Indies to shoot Courtney Walsh and Ian Bishop. Accompanying us on a shoestring unit was Mahesh Aney (Anee for short, for his long silky hair). Anees Adenwala was sent in advance to test his mettle as a resourceful production manager. There was Neelanjan Shome from Pepsi, who became a great friend and we did a whole lot of work together for Pepsi Vietnam, and Pooja Malik, the pint-sized dynamo from HTA Delhi. Anuja Chauhan couldn't make the long and arduous trip as she was on maternity leave already by then.

West Indies was a blast. It's one of the most laid-back countries of the world, where there is a boom box at every street corner playing reggae and I noticed that nobody walked normally; they all walked to the music—men, women, children, everybody had an internal rhythm and they bogeyed to the beat. There were plenty of Rastas, with their long, matted hair—no surprise as Bob Marley was considered a god there. The cricketers, led by Brian Lara and Viv Richards, came a distant second. A few roads and a couple of city centres were named after them.

Shooting in the West Indies, we discovered, was a nightmare and everybody moved in slow motion (except their fast bowlers). As far as shoots were concerned, there was very little equipment and few options available, but permission to shoot on the streets was a cakewalk as we had some very good-looking lady cops helping us with the traffic. We had hired a local coordinator—a very attractive lady called Maria. As Anees had gone ahead to check out locations and a road roller, he had spent two days with her and was a bit smitten. After dropping her home one night, he spent an evening in the back seat of an abandoned car opposite her house, because he forgot the name of the hotel that he was staying in!

A shattered Anees and a buoyant Maria greeted us at the airport with the news that the stadium had been booked for the Ian Bishop shoot. But the road roller for Courtney Walsh's film did not exist on the island and the hiring of a West Indian steel band was in progress. I was furious, as the road roller was a very important part of the Courtney Walsh film as his vehicle of choice. We first shot with Ian Bishop—a sweet, gentle soul and a terrific bowler, feared by all. 'Meet Ian Bishop, batsmen shake when he plays. How does he make them move like that? Must be all that Pepsi dancing inside him.'

VO: Pepsi: Nothing official about it.

The shoot went well, but now we were left with Courtney and no road roller or a steel band. At this stage, I tore into Anees and Maria, and they promised they would find the two props, come hell or high water. We finally had to make do with a bulldozer, which they found. Anees turned up with a slightly lightweight band that I promptly named the tinpot band as opposed to a steel band. Courtney Walsh, driving in the bulldozer, sees a crate of Pepsi on the sidewalk and makes a beeline for it, going through everything from hedges, parked cars and traffic—anything that comes in the way of getting his Pepsi, basically.

'Meet Courtney Walsh, the gentle giant flattens wickets and anything that comes in his way, but boy, when he sees a Pepsi, you can't put the brakes on him! Got a Pepsi? Sure.'

VO: Pepsi: Nothing official about it.

Anees, I realized, was never going to make a crack production manager, but he did find his true calling with Lacadives, our diving company, and became one of the finest diving instructors in this country, or, arguably, any other. He is a god underwater and now successfully runs his own dive company.

The 'Pepsi nothing official' campaign was launched before the World Cup and fired everybody's imagination to the point of eclipsing the Coke campaign completely—not that Coke had taken anything for granted. They had got a huge talent from USA to direct and produce their film, namely the brilliant director, Tarsem, who made a beautiful film for them called 'Red Is the Colour of Passion' (the Pepsi colour is blue.) Despite that, the Coke ad never made it into public imagination and Pepsi ruled the cup. The campaign went ballistically viral for its time.

The sheer audacity and irreverence of its tone, going against established norms and the status quo caught not only Gen X's attention, but even the silvers grudgingly acknowledged and quite enjoyed its unfettered glee. The advertising fraternity were also pretty amazed by the route Pepsi and HTA took to take on Coke—the number one cola in the world by far, with its reach, influence and very deep pockets. By the time the cricketing extravaganza was over and the dust had settled, Pepsi was the drink of a new generation and a winner of the World Cup stakes by far.

There was a literal buzz among the Pepsi drinkers and they walked cock-a-hoop, full of confidence, swagger and attitude. The campaign reverberated long after the World Cup and in a lot of B-schools became the go-to example for what was then being described as a disrupter—for not only did it set the focus for the Pepsi campaigns of the future, but also clearly defined the value proposition for the brand: young, sassy, irreverent, bold, with a great attitude to bend rules rather than break them and to be funny to boot. It was one of the most one-sided advertising duels that kicked off the cola wars in India. Aha!

———

After our World Cup success, Pepsi was on a roll and Vibha placed all the faith in her agency, HTA, and her favourite production house, Genesis. Not only was she willing to take risks with edgy scripts, but we could also dream to be flexible on set. As long as we remained within the brief and the core values of the brand, we had the liberty to chop, change and innovate. This was such a morale booster for the HTA creative team and Genesis that we were very careful about not only the end product but also the DNA of the brand. All in all, we had a lot of fun in the process and that was the magic the consumers felt too. It built solid brand loyalty.

The next great script—this time we cast Shah Rukh—was one where a guy driving in an SUV, with his date, spots a petrol pump with a Pepsi vending machine. The guy stops and drives into the place, craving a cold can of Pepsi. Nobody seems to be around and when he calls out, a big golden retriever comes charging out, barking furiously, chasing the thirsty couple back into the car. They escape by the skin of their teeth. The girl looks disappointed and asks, 'Now what?' Shah Rukh, never one to give up, says, 'Pepsi toh main pi ke hi rahunga.'

He wriggles out of the window and goes on to the roof of the car, and opens the door on his side to let the dog in and, as the dog gets in, the girl quickly gets out and closes her side. They lock him in and go up to the vending machine, and retrieve their Pepsi cans. Now that they are out and the dog is in the car, the girl asks, 'Now what?' Shah Rukh shrugs nonchalantly, jumps back on to roof and opens his side of the car. The dog charges out, and the girl quickly gets in and Shah Rukh gets back in through the window. Now both are in the car with their Pepsis and the dog is out. Shah Rukh triumphantly asks for the car keys, the girl looks confused, saying, 'You have it!' The dog growls and they both look out—and he has the keys between his teeth! Touché.

We built the entire petrol pump station with a vending machine inside a studio, as it was a late evening scene, which we could control inside and shoot through both day and night. Shah Rukh was a dream to work with; he was professional, on time, created no fuss, didn't put out those 'star vibes' or have any nakhras. The girl was a find (young Sandali Sinha, who went on to do a movie called *Tum Bin* after the TVC). The dog, whom we thought might be a problem as he had an extended, difficult role to play, was surprisingly excellent, and did everything asked of him to perfection, including his expressions. The film, as predicted, carried the Pepsi campaign through a good six months of non-stop cricket.

One day, Sachin was gliding his way to a century and Mumbai came to a grinding halt as everybody was trying to attach themselves to a convenient TV set. Nothing could bring the city to a halt—not even the monsoons—in its mad frenetic pursuit of business, except for Sachin on song, on his way to a century. I pulled up at the Opera House in front of an electronic shop; they had turned their TV in the shop window to face the road so the public could watch the match. There was a huge crowd outside watching with bated breath.

Heart-stoppingly, Sachin was dropped off a top edge and instead of an action replay, the Pepsi commercial came on for the nth time. Everybody standing there got very pissed off. It was such a critical moment in the match. When Shah Rukh said, 'Pepsi toh main pi ke hi rahunga,' a smartass in the crowd quipped, 'Behen de take! Tu Pepsi pi, par humein action replay toh dekhne de!' That's when I rang up Vibha and told her we needed a new commercial for Pepsi. This one, successful as it was, had now run its course. We desperately needed a TVC every four to six months, considering the amount of exposure Pepsi gave its commercials.

45

'Yeh Dil Maange More!'

As we were using up creatives for Pepsi and discarding them as quickly as underwear, the team was constantly under pressure to come up with better and newer ideas, and the go-to person was Anuja Chauhan. She came up with a really neat script about a young scriptwriter writing a hero's story. Since we were always using top film stars or cricketing icons in the ads, we had to be very careful to ensure that Pepsi remained the hero of the story.

So it was with the train script—the writer introduces the scene with a lambi train on a hot summer day. A beautiful girl sitting in the compartment, melting in the heat, looks for water and calls out plaintively, 'Pani.' 'Nah,' says the writer as he looks at the bottle of Pepsi in his hand and switches the water to Pepsi. The pyau (water vendor) instantly turns into a Pepsi vendor. The girl is delighted. Ab hero entry maarta hai: A sleeping Shah Rukh throws off the blanket around him, enters the scene with a dramatic front roll, looks at the beautiful damsel in distress and volunteers, 'I'll get it.' He then jumps off the train and gets two Pepsis—one for her and one for himself. Meanwhile, the train moves off without him and his lady love woefully only rues the loss of the Pepsi.

Not to be outdone, our hero spots some horses tied to a dhaba wall. He 'borrows' one, leaps on to it and chases after the train, with the owners of the horse in hot pursuit, one lot even riding double seat. Our hero gallops alongside the train and clumsily switches vehicles mid-stride, stumbling into the train with two chilled Pepsi bottles. The lovely damsel's eyes light up and we pause for a romantic music change. We now come back to the writer, who also pauses as the film and soundtrack come to a grinding halt. He is unhappy with the way the story is unfolding. He suddenly gets an idea and thinks, 'Shit, this is my story,' and quickly switches roles with Shah Rukh.

The dewy-eyed damsel looks up to the top berth and asks, 'Darling, would you like a Pepsi?' A blanket is thrown off and our writer emerges, much to Shah Rukh's surprise and dismay, as the lady snatches his Pepsi and gives it to her real lover who is the writer and has written himself into the script! Before Shah Rukh can react, the horse's owners arrive, grab him and jump off the train, leaving the two lovebirds drinking their Pepsis and looking into each other's eyes. 'Yeh hi hai right choice, baby. Aha!' says the VO.

The moment we got the script, we started layering it with detail to make it visually exciting and memorable. We put in an old steam engine for better visual effect, the pyau was a small Rajasthani boy in a turban, whose water stall magically becomes a Pepsi station. We decided that the owners of the horses should be daakus and we cast the actors who played Kalia and Samba in *Sholay*. Shah Rukh dramatically opens the Pepsi with his thumb. 'Pop pop' they go, as he hands one to the thirsty damsel. We added a small scuffle on the train when the daakus arrive; Shah Rukh takes an ineffectual swing at Kalia, who ducks and lifts him on to his shoulder and exits the train. We all decided that the film needed a dramatic ending other than the romantic one, so we had Shah Rukh spreadeagled and tied to the tracks with the train receding into the background and he adds a plaintive 'Aha' at the end of the jingle.

I must say, Shah Rukh was a real sport for not wanting to change the script. Only an actor with great confidence in himself could have accepted being the fall guy. I can't imagine anybody else agreeing to the end.

———

Meanwhile Pepsi International developed a new campaign and Pepsi India was expected to follow suit, albeit with an Indian flavour. The new slogan was a straightforward consumer statement: 'Ask for more!' It obviously meant ask for more Pepsi. There was nothing clever or cool about it, and the creative team at HTA was flummoxed as it didn't sound inspirational or aspirational at all. After knocking it around, they came up with the amazing 'Yeh dil maange more'. Indians are a very emotional kind of consumer and this tagline hit the nail on the head as it talked of the heart. Pepsi simply became the vehicle to deliver what the heart desired.

We were all very excited about our version of the international line. Pepsi and HTA were planning a huge launch for the new campaign. They managed to rope in the entire cast of *Kuch Kuch Hota Hai*—a huge hit at that time and Karan Johar's claim to fame. What was needed was a new Pepsi kid, who was to be destiny's child. It had to be someone who could be plucked out of obscurity, except for a growing hunger for more—more entertainment, more taste, more Pepsi, more life—and to suddenly be catapulted amidst his dream team of stars from the biggest hit of the year.

Pepsi and HTA decided that the scale of the film would be unprecedented, and we decided to shoot it all over Bombay—from a baroque movie theatre to the steps of the Asiatic Library to Ballard Estate in the middle of the night. We'd have a cast of thousands of screaming fans as our Pepsi kid gets introduced to each of his dream stars, from Rani to Shah Rukh to Kajol. Yeh dil maange more, and how! The logistics of the film was humongous, and the shoot was outdoors and night-for-night, which meant the graveyard shift of 7 p.m. to 5 a.m. It was not the most ideal situation, especially when shooting with top stars of the time and crowds without total control— not at all what we were used to in a studio.

A new jingle had to be recorded to deliver the larger-than-life promise of 'Yeh dil maange more'. We needed a raw, high-voltage voice to shake the market out of its complacency. We found it in Krishnakumar Kunnath, or K.K., whose voice was pitch-perfect. Well-known composer Juku's style suited the mood of the jingle and so we went to him. The rest is history.

We recorded the jingle first, so that we could illustrate the song with the visuals and get the length bang on. I needed to visualize the film in my head so that I would get the timing of the music track just right. The other major task was to find the perfect young dreamer for the ad. We decided to leave that to Amita Sehgal, the executive producer, who had a damn good nose for casting. As K.K. and Juku got started on recording the jingle, I sat down to visualize the film in my head.

It opens inside a movie theatre as the lights come on and people trail out, leaving a young man refusing to get out and wanting more. The usher rudely tells him to leave. Cue jingle: 'Par yeh dil na maane, yeh dil maange more.'

He steps outside on the road and kicks an empty Pepsi tin can. Almost like magic, the can skids across the street and a delicate, high-heeled foot stops the can. We tilt the camera up and see Rani Mukerji, who looks at him and asks, 'More?' She slides open the shutter of a garage to reveal a group of dancers grooving to the beat. Rani collars the young man and dances with him, and he cannot believe his good fortune. Then, with a change in music, a huge Pepsi truck drives up in front of the Asiatic Library; it's got Shah Rukh on top, holding a bottle of Pepsi. The kid and Rani join Shah Rukh on the truck as hundreds of fans run down the steps to surround the truck, the camera cranes down and, suddenly, police sirens go off as a motorcycle cop clears his way through the crowd.

Shah Rukh immediately puts his hands up, still holding the bottle of Pepsi. The cop takes off her helmet, revealing a stunning-looking Kajol, who flicks her hair and holds up a pair of handcuffs pointed at the young lad, who grabs Shah Rukh's Pepsi and leaps off the truck, sliding on his knees to offer Kajol a Pepsi. She grabs his collar, hauls him on to the bike and disappears through the crowd with the siren blaring. Rani and Shah Rukh are still on the truck as the latter does a spectacular twirl, leaps into the air and lands on his knees (ouch!). The scene fades like a dream, leaving an empty Pepsi can rocking gently in the breeze. Was it real or a dream?

VO: Pepsi! Yeh dil maange more.

I have always loved the motif of a tin can and steam engine and have used it often in my films.

Meanwhile, Amita finally hit pay dirt and hauled a very clean-looking young dancer from Shiamak Davar's troupe, namely Shahid Kapoor, to the office. He was a bit scrawny for my taste, but very nice looking in a boy-next-door kind of way. More importantly, the camera loved him. We pitched him to Pepsi. They seemed to have a lot of reservations about Shahid initially—he was a bit too pretty, too thin, not macho enough, they said. Amita, ferocious as hell about her find, dug her heels in, and I just stood back and watched. She cut through all of their reservations and came back triumphant. So, Shahid Kapoor made a dream debut with a star-studded Pepsi TVC and a cast of hundreds. He never looked back from that launch, and became a teen heartthrob and very big star.

Working with Shah Rukh, Rani *and* Kajol was a high for me. They were all consummate professionals and superb to work with. Shah Rukh, in particular, would go out of his way to put the unit at ease and go that extra mile to get the shot right. Kajol's call time was at 3 a.m. and she arrived driving her own car, completely unescorted, with no fuss. She reported to her make-up van and only asked me two questions—how long for her shot and how long would it take. I, in my enthusiasm, said two hours, and when my two hours were up, she looked at me and pointed to her watch very sternly.

We hadn't finished and I had two more critical shots with her, so extremely embarrassed, I went up to her and apologizing profusely, told her we needed her for another hour and waited, hat in hand, for her to fly off the handle. Kajol had the reputation for not tolerating inaccuracy or incompetency, both of which I was guilty of. She thought about it and relented, much to my relief. Amita, Mitali and the rest of our hard-working production team did an amazing job of handling the logistics and permissions for the shoot, and the 800 extras who constantly wanted to sneak off the set and become soomdi mein komdi.

It was a fabulously smooth shoot considering the massive arrangements. Everything was larger than life, and Vikas Sivaraman, DOP extraordinaire, and his merry camera crew did a superlative job on the visuals. The film was really well received and 'Yeh dil maange more' became a part of folklore. It was used even during the Kargil War in 1999, when Captain Vikram Batra, PVC, who, while being congratulated for a particularly hard-fought victory, was asked, 'Aren't you scared?' He quipped, 'Yeh dil maange more!'

46

Kissing Shah Rukh Khan

When all things are on a roll and you feel invincible, beware of the ides of March, for overconfidence invariably leads to an unforeseen disaster. Pepsi and Genesis were on a roll and whatever we created turned to gold. So Pepsi decided to sign on a young superstar, whose first film had broken all kinds of box-office records and who had become a teen sensation overnight. His name was Hrithik Roshan, and the film was *Kaho Naa ... Pyaar Hai*. Pepsi was in advanced negotiations with Hrithik's father, Rakesh Roshan, who handled all his commercial affairs. To our great surprise, we heard Coke announcing that Hrithik Roshan was going to be their brand ambassador. It seemed that Coke had caught wind of Pepsi's negotiations with the Roshans, and preempted and outbid them, leaving Pepsi with egg on its face and hopping mad.

So, we all went into a huddle to figure out what to do next. Out of a desire to get back at the Roshans, we decided to spoof a film where Hrithik Roshan is a loser and loses a spin-the-bottle game to Shah Rukh, the prize being a kiss from a young lady named Tara Sharma. It was all done in a studio—very hush-hush as Coke had a knack for finding out what Pepsi was up to and was playing spoiler. So, in a highly secretive manner, we erected a set in Raj Kamal Studios, and quickly and quietly started casting it. We had already signed on Tara Sharma and Shah Rukh, and, luckily, we found a near-perfect double for Hrithik. He turned out to be a terrible actor, though, and I had to spend a lot of time coaxing a performance out of him.

Anuja had added a nice touch to the proceedings by casting a kid as the main instigator; it immediately made the film light-hearted and fun. Tara, of course, was a find. She looked fresh and wholesome—not a femme fatale as most people wanted their leading lady to be. We decided to put steel braces on the Hrithik lookalike as somebody had researched his early years, and he was believed to have worn braces. Also, they are very awkward when kissing. The film was set up in a bowling alley with a few guys, girls and a perky little kid, who, when Shah Rukh wins, says, 'Winner gets a kiss!'

Everybody looks at Tara, who immediately picks up a bottle of Pepsi and says, 'Pepsi hi batayega.' Tara spins the bottle as everyone gathers around. The Hrithik Roshan double looks hot and gets an appreciative look from Tara. Shah Rukh intervenes and asks him to smile, which he does, revealing his steel braces—a flash. *Ting!* He looks like Jaws from a Bond film. A bit taken aback, Tara says, 'Yuck,' and spins the bottle again.

Shah Rukh stops the bottle when it points to him to jeers of 'Cheating! Cheating!' Tara ignores the jibes as the kid pipes up, 'Kiss! Kiss!' Shah Rukh ruffles his hair, gently pushes him down and tells him his turn will come when he grows up. Tara goes up to Shah Rukh, and tells him to close his eyes and pucker up, which he does. She backs off and starts laughing with her pals. Shah Rukh is hurt and disappointed, and walks away. Tara looks chagrined and runs after him, turns him around and smooches him. 'Aha!'

The fact was that Tara had never kissed anybody but her parents, and looked dismayed at having to kiss Shah Rukh. She said she would only kiss someone on the lips if she loved him and dug her heels in. We all got really tough with her and insisted that she follow the script, while Shah Rukh just looked at her disapprovingly. I yelled a bit and did a very Rumpelstiltskin act. It was the most spontaneous

jugalbandi between Shah Rukh and me. When poor Tara was close to
tears, but still adamant, we couldn't help but burst into laughter and
she realized, with great relief, that we were both pulling her leg and we
fudged the kiss. But by god, it looked real.

This is Tara's version of what happened that day:

> Shah Rukh and Prahlad convinced me I had to kiss the former
> on the lips in the commercial and the prude in me was adamant
> I would only kiss someone I was in love with. So I got more
> and more nervous as Mr P yelled good-humouredly that it was
> crazy to refuse to smooch King Khan, insisting I oblige. Both
> of them burst out laughing saying it was a joke, immediately
> putting me at ease. A megastar playing a joke on a newbie with
> such humbleness and fun was endearing, and sure enough
> the kiss was a peck on the cheek or a cheat kiss. This story
> continues to be one I love to recount.

The film turned out to be cute and funny, but not particularly earth-
shattering. On release, the reaction we got was nothing like what we
expected. The teen world exploded with resentment and hated the film
because it ridiculed their hero, Hrithik Roshan, and they couldn't and
wouldn't tolerate it. The backlash was so intense that we had to remove
the film after a while. We had not calculated for the almost fanatic
following that young Hrithik had garnered amongst the youth. It was
one of the few faux pas that Team Pepsi made during my time and it
was huge! Pepsi even lost market points temporarily. It was a lesson
well learnt as we had not followed our instincts and got carried away.

47

Zinta and the Ape

When Pepsi approved a script starring Preity Zinta and a chimpanzee, à la Tarzan in Johnny Weissmuller's 1932 film *Tarzan the Ape Man*, we were all quite excited for we would have to shoot in South Africa as no chimpanzees were available in India, especially for shooting. Chimps were only in zoos and were quite wild. We sent an advance team to SA to source a trained and tame chimp, and to get a place to build two sets—preferably on the beach. One would be a shack run by Preity Zinta, and, next to it would be a glitzy, new-age shack with disco lights and Russian dancers wearing skimpy outfits, to turn people away from Preity's very modest but homely shack.

The die was cast and the recce was on. The one thing that nobody had anticipated was that a full-grown chimp was as big as an average man and weighed as much. We confidently figured that since the six-foot-two Johnny Weissmuller could happily lug a five-foot chimp around, a five-foot-two Preity Zinta would be able to do the same! Not a chance of a snowball in hell. The advance team now had to search for a malleable baby chimp, who would listen to directions!

The amazing part of the whole sorry episode was that Kalpu (Kalpana Kutty, the executive producer at Genesis at the time) and her team actually located a baby chimp somewhere in Congo, whose mother had been killed by poachers. She was now in the care of two trained human parents, who were extraordinarily protective of her; they treated her like their own child. She had a strict feeding and resting schedule.

Regardless of the shoot timings, she had to be fed every two hours and be put to sleep. Besides, she was only partly trained and knew only basic instructions. As she was the right size for Preity to lug around, she was the only option we actually had. I decided to go for it and hope for the best, despite a slight sinking feeling in the pit of my stomach. For Plan B, we located a gorilla costume in Kenya and bought it, just in case it all went down the tube. The gorilla outfit was all wrong as it was meant for a full-grown man and the face was awfully scary, to boot.

Now it was all up to Preity and the baby chimp (with lots of disapproving noises from the foster parents-cum-trainers). Preity rose to the task like a trooper and went way beyond the normal professional commitment that she has a stellar reputation for. She hung out with the chimp for two whole days, getting familiar with her so that she would allow Preity to carry her around the shack, greeting the regular customers with whom the chimp was also supposed to interact while looking cute. It was simple on paper, but was a *mother* in actual execution—what with a wild baby chimp and overly protective human parents who had only agreed to the shoot because we had offered them large amounts of money. Even the simplest close-up of the two became a game of patience and chance. Did we get it? Didn't we get it? Was the chimp's expression happy or scared? And so on and so forth.

We weren't worried about Preity because she was always on point. We shot humongous amounts of footage as we were not sure about the bloody monkey at all and it was all on Kodak negative stock. Our ratios jumped from 1:20 to 1:80—i.e., one foot of usable footage to eighty feet of hope and a sinking feeling as film stock is bloody expensive. After a while, we just stopped counting and hoped we had a usable film at the end of it all. And if we didn't sink the boat in the process, we would be lucky. Of course, Murphy wasn't far behind.

After the first day of balmy weather and a relatively slow, but relaxed shoot, we were caught in an unseasonal storm, which huffed and puffed and blew our sets down. The second day dawned on a complete disaster as we surveyed the shambles of the outdoor location. The temperature dropped to two or three degrees, and the Indian crew plus agency, who had only prepared for summer, froze their goolies off. Everybody returned to the hotel, leaving the primary crew to repair the damage, and immediately purloined the hotel blankets. We were roaming around looking like a Jat village in winter—all huddled in our various pink and powder-blue hotel blankets. Thank god we had decided to shoot the interiors in a real nightclub.

Preity, poor girl, was stuck in continuity in a bright, summery cotton dress. She had to keep hauling off the blanket, pose in front of the camera *and* deal with a frozen baby chimp, who clung to her for dear life, looking for any bodily warmth that she could get. In the middle of this total disaster appeared Joel Fonseca, the ingenious production manager, dressed in the gorilla suit minus the scary gorilla head! Joel had realized that the warmest thing in the production peti was the gorilla suit and immediately got into it, as it did not impede his efficiency in the shoot. It was a sight to behold!

The shoot was extended by two whole days, which doesn't sound like much—if it was in India, everybody could have just gone home until law and order prevailed, but sitting in SA with an Indian crew, hotel bills, logistics, renegotiating with the set people to put up the set again in double time ... Well, it cost a lot of money and we were fresh out of it, stuck in a foreign country with archaic Indian currency laws. To the rescue came our client, Pepsi, flags flying and trumpets sounding, as they managed to transfer the extra funds from Pepsi SA.

The real heroes of the shoot were Preity Zinta, a real trooper, Nikhil Rawley, who was playing the bad guy, and Joel Fonseca, in the gorilla suit with his never-say-die attitude. Eventually, even the chimp delivered in the crucial nightclub sequence when she is up in the rafters wearing her tuxedo. Her handlers finally decided that we were not going to give up and go away, come hell or high water, and managed to get the chimp to actually open a can of Pepsi and drink into an amplified mic, saving the day. We thanked our stars for having finally shot a coherent film—not a great film but a good one regardless of the cost incurred and no thanks to Murphy.

48

Bheel! Bheel! Burma!

During a lull in our hectic schedule in Mumbai, I got an unusual offer from Lintas, who handled a large part of the Unilever account. They asked us whether I would be interested in going to Myanmar, and checking out if we could shoot a TVC for CloseUp toothpaste and Wheel detergent soap for Unilever, UK—with local talent in local locations. There was a total blackout on conditions in the country, so I would also have to figure out everything on the lam— from whether there were budget hotels for us to stay in, to what kind of equipment and post-production facilities were available. There was also the possibility of having to brave a draconian regime of military dictatorship that had locked up Aung San Suu Kyi, who had recently won a national election, and was immediately deposed and put under house arrest. The country had exploded into riots, which the military quelled with an iron fist. To boot, there was very little money to be made on the productions, but how little, insignificant things swing huge decisions.

My parents had grown up in Burma, as it was known then, and I was immediately intrigued. Besides, the trip seemed full of the unknown, and smacked of risk and high adventure. Nothing like a bit of danger to tickle one's adrenaline diet to do something different. But the real motivator was that a lot of us had just been converted to a new religion—scuba diving—and we were to travel via Thailand. Of course, I decided to take a slight detour on the way back via Phuket in Thailand to go diving—all on the house, courtesy of Unilever, UK.

We put together a crew of four key divers, other than Ashish Bhasin (whom we called Oily), who was representing Lintas, and Chien Wien Lee, our go-to photographer, and my man Friday, Joel Fonseca. The rest of the crew were all divers including Vik (Vikas Sivaraman), Nikhil Rawley, Johnny Pinto, who was a director in his own right, as post-production and yours truly, as director and dogsbody. I was fed on stories of Burma from my mother's youth: my grandfather was a colonel in the Unified Medical Corps. He was in charge of the Rangoon Military Hospital just a few years before the Japanese invaded and drove General Slim's British Army all the way to Imphal and Kohima—in what is known as Northeast India now—before they could get their act together and take a stand.

Armed with these tales, our motley expeditionary force then made its way to Yangon (Rangoon) via a six-hour transit through Bangkok. We arrived a bit bleary-eyed at a raucous fish market–like airport, where nobody seemed to know what the hell was going on. The military personnel manning the airport were in rumpled uniforms; everybody else was in sarongs and sandals and milling around, being pushed by touts, who were all over the place and seemingly in charge.

Luckily, we were met inside arrivals by our official liaison bloke, who could actually speak English, and had the unlikely name Stanley. Stanley didn't look particularly Burmese, and we later realized he was Anglo-Burmese, or Eurasian. He guided us past customs and made all of us cough up a hundred dollars each for which we got six kyats to the dollar officially, when the black market exchange rate was one hundred and twenty kyats to the dollar just outside the airport—an official highway robbery by the government.

We all headed to an air-conditioned van en route to our destination, which was actually a government guest house. We stepped out of the airport and found ourselves smack in the middle of a street battle between the followers of an ousted and deposed Aung San Suu Kyi and the military. It took some deft driving through the back streets of a decaying Yangon to be hustled to our guest house.

It was rather plush and ornate, but all of us had to double up and share a room as there were only three suites available. Just my luck, I drew Ashish Bhasin as my roomie and found, to my horror, that our room only had one large king-sized bed. By this time, it was close to midnight—I was totally knackered and didn't give a shit. I changed and was about to dive into bed when I saw Ashish Bhasin very carefully collecting long bolsters from the settees and arranging them neatly down the centre of the bed. When I asked him what the fuck he was doing, he—very primly dressed up in a matching nightsuit—answered, 'This is my side, and that is your side of the bed. Please make sure you stay on your side.' Out of sheer cussedness and his 'oh-so-propah attitude', I wanted to sleep in the centre—preferably with one leg over his chest!

Myanmar was one hell of an experience, not only because it completely lacked any infrastructure for the making of professional commercials, but because it is also one of the most xenophobic countries in the world. The regime was a cabal of army generals who ran the country and were so suspicious of everything, including themselves, that they considered enemy number one to be the citizens of Myanmar. So they decided the only way they could perpetuate their extremely unpopular and oppressive rule was to turn it into a draconian police state where everybody was encouraged to spy on each other.

Neighbours against neighbours, family members against family members, office staff against office staff, and so on, until they had managed to divide the whole country against itself. Everyone reported any and all activity to the various monitoring police cells, while the generals laughed all the way to the bank. Corruption was rampant, and the smell of fear seeped into every nook and corner of society. By this time, we had realized that Stanley himself was planted to keep tabs on us and whom we fraternized with. After all, contact with foreign elements was strictly frowned upon. Into this hellish stew landed some of the most irreverent and rebellious bunch of creative people, whose main entertainment in life was to push the establishment.

Our trip to Myanmar was not without its own brand of humour and incident. Other than being in the middle of pitched street battles between the army and the followers of Aung San Suu Kyi, we spent our nights in a mosquito-infested, post-production studio and had an AK37 shoved in our face by an overzealous guard every time we wandered anywhere near the broadcasting studio that carried all the news—i.e., propaganda about the glorious military dictatorship that the generals allowed. As the guards themselves were very poorly trained country bumpkins handling real firearms with their safeties off, it could get really hairy sometimes. Like, 'Oops! Soo solly it venta off by mistake.'

We spent the next four days, shooting by day, editing by night, in a battle-scarred and curfew-hit Yangon, where the government-run TV centre was the only place with high-band shooting equipment. We were locked into the studio at 7 p.m. sharp—as soon as the sirens went off and announced the curfew—till 7 a.m. the next morning.

———

The most indelible memory I have of that trip was one of Johnny Pinto in the middle of the night. Having collected a group of guards and electricians, he was trying to get them to rehearse singing the Wheel jingle to the best of his memory. There Johnny was, with his wild, curly hair, blue jeans and a matching blue shirt, doing a Zubin Mehta on this completely besura bunch of Burmese who knew no English and pronounced Wheel as 'Bheel! Bheel! Bheel!' Johnny tried to correct their harmony and diction by making them sing along with him—to no avail. God, it was awful.

At the end of the tunnel, we produced a very quirky ad for Wheel (or should we say Bheel?) detergent soap, shot in Myanmar with

Burmese talent, edited in their very own studio, sung by a bunch of armed guards, canteen boys and one lady who was in a tizzy, flapping around, as she didn't know whether she would get into trouble for lending her voice to a Unilever product. The best part of the entire exercise was that Unilever had no manufacturing facility in Myanmar, but were allowed to smuggle in their soaps, shampoos, toothpaste and detergents from Thailand, where they were actually manufactured.

Once a year, for a two-month window, the government of Myanmar would open its borders with Thailand to unofficially allow the smuggling of consumer products into the country. Of course, there was also the rampant smuggling of rubies, jade, timber and other unique precious goods to be sent out of the country at the behest and convenience of the generals for their personal benefit. No wonder the prime pieces of real estate in London are owned by Arabs or Burmese generals. The government also charged Unilever in dollars for broadcasting the TVCs.

The high point of our trip was the food in Myanmar—fresh, affordable and really scrumptious. Especially their sweet water fish, prawns and crabs, which are so plentiful that restaurants only serve crab claws (the rest of the crab is sold for making crab cakes for the marginalized). Khaw suey, the dish most bandied about in five-star hotels in India as the national dish of Myanmar, is actually street food and served in haath-gadis on street corners. There is no such animal called a vegetarian khaw suey—that's a completely Indian Gujju invention, just like gobhi manchurian.

Finally, the day arrived when we were to take our flights to Bangkok and then to Phuket for our much-awaited diving trip. Vik and Rawley had an early morning flight while Johnny, me, Joel and Chien Wien Lee were to take a later flight. We spent our last evening purloining a decent stock of alcohol before the curfew kicked in and spent the evening watching a football match on TV, while Rawley and Johnny Pinto got through the better part of a bootlegged bottle of bourbon. Early the next morning, before sunrise, I was rudely awakened by a frantic Vik saying the transport had arrived, but he couldn't wake Rawley up as he might have left for the 'happy hunting grounds'—he wasn't breathing! I jumped up with a start and headed to where he was curled up on a settee in a loose-jointed foetal ball. He was indeed not breathing and was surrounded by a cloud of alcohol fumes. It was the first time in that whole trip that I really panicked. If Rawley had croaked, we were screwed, I remember thinking. I imagined spending the rest of my life in a Burmese jail.

I quickly got a small hand mirror out and held it in front of Rawley's red nose—the faintest hint of vapour coated it. By god! The fucker was alive, but blotto. We now tried desperately to wake him, while Vik sweated it out, thinking he was going to miss his flight. He was just about to dump Rawley on us and leave. Perish the thought! I procured a bucket of cold water and threw it over the inert Rawley. He came up sputtering for air and tried to go back to never-never land. There was not a chance that was going to happen; we hauled him out of the settee, draped him over a really hassled Vik, bundled them into the car and went back to sleep—or rather, we tried.

The adventure didn't stop there. Yes, we made it in one piece to Thailand, and yes, we went diving. But it was monsoon season and we had the roughest dive ever. It was very touch and go. The dive operator decided that since all of us were advanced divers, he would abandon us to our own devices in a very rough sea. We arrived back in Bangkok a bit shattered, got caught in a massive traffic jam on the way to the airport and missed our flight back home. Blimey! After shelling out some extra money, we booked ourselves flights for the next day.

Now, we had a day to kill, so I floated the idea of getting a much-famed Thai sandwich massage; we had heard all kinds of lurid stories about it. Johnny, the prudish little Catholic boy, immediately baulked and said he was not having any woman touch him below the waist, and dug his heels in. Since he was the only one with some money left on him and he was key in funding the whole activity, we had to at least pretend to humour the little shit. I couldn't believe this side of Johnny Pinto—I had only interacted with him at parties and get-togethers, where, after three drinks, he went berserk! There was no controlling him then. Seeing this pious, holier-than-thou version of Johnny left me completely gobsmacked.

Anyway, Rawley, who seemed to know his way around the seedier side of Bangkok, finally led us to an address that was recommended to him by the concierge. Here, we were confronted by a pristine building with a sign that proclaimed, 'By appointment to the Queen of Thailand'. Johnny Pinto's (now dubbed 'Sphincter') eyes lit up, and he said we were at the right place as we walked into the reception area. A very polite, well-dressed young lady took our request, including Johnny's outlandish one about not being touched below the waist by a strange woman, and told us to wait.

As I looked around the immaculate lobby, I noticed a neat line of men sitting very upright on a line of chairs. What was remarkable was that they all wore the same brand of dark glasses, almost like a uniform. My mind flashed back to a book by Graham Greene that I had been reading pre-Burma. It was about Haiti and Papa Doc Duvalier, the dictator whose secret service—the Tontons Macoutes— wore similar dark glasses. I assumed that these were the queen's secret service security detail. I leaned conspiratorially towards Rawley and Sphincter, and sotto voce, I said, 'She is here!' Johnny, of course, piped up loudly, 'Who's here?'

'The queen, you idiot,' I said.

'How do you know?' Johnny asked.

I was about to launch into an explanation but then I decided to fuck it—who cared.

We were ushered into a spartan room with a raised concrete platform in the centre. It had three straw pallets on it, roughly divided by hanging bamboo curtains for some modicum of privacy. We had just about made ourselves comfortable in the cotton dressing gowns that had been supplied to us when I heard a tapping sound down the corridor. I looked around and saw three of the guys from the reception tapping their way into our room, dark glasses and all.

I realized that these were three blind masseurs and not the queen's secret service after all! They assigned themselves one to each of us and started exploring our bodies gently at first, with Johnny bleating, 'Hey, tell them I am ticklish!' ending with an 'Uff ...' as his masseurs stuck his elbow into his ribcage with controlled violence.

It began—the three blind masseurs proceeded to pulverize us with their elbows, knees and callused palms for the next two hours, turning us into pulp. Our initial grunts and moans were reduced to whimpers and holding of breaths, waiting for the ordeal to end. It seemed to go on forever. Even the bleaty Johnny Pinto was reduced to little cries and whispered groans.

Finally, it was over just before we passed out, and the tapping receded down the corridor, leaving us splayed like beached whales after a particularly vicious storm. Somehow, we gathered ourselves—too aching and embarrassed to make any eye contact or conversation—and limped back to the hotel, holding on to each other for support.

Making it to the airport was a small miracle, but, by that time, we were feeling surprisingly good and seemed to have miraculously recovered. Now, whenever someone mentions a Thai sandwich massage, I smile a painful secret smile to myself.

49

The Vietnam Veterans

Vietnam, for all of us at Genesis, was an eight-year-long love affair, and we called ourselves the Vietnam Vets. The usual suspects included Vik, Annie (Mahesh Aney, DOP), Mistah Lee (the late Chien Wien Lee), Fonqui or Khopchee King (Joel Fonseca), Kenny Dawson (editor, director, and the Pied Piper of Saigon), who always had a gaggle of street kids following him around, Dean Affonso (assistant cameraman and chick magnet) and Raj (the master editor). We grew to love the country as we travelled in and out of it for nearly a decade doing films for Unilever and Pepsi—from toothpaste and detergents to soft drinks. We started going there in the early 1990s, after our trip to Burma, and continued into the 2000s.

The country was very poor and basic in terms of infrastructure and even consistent electricity, but what a beautiful people—they were full of zeal, very hard-working and artistic. The best part was that even fifteen years after the Americans abandoned their embassy, fled and sanctioned them, the women of Vietnam stood shoulder to shoulder with the men in running the country. As the only Indians in 'Nam, we took to the conditions without a hiccup! We went to ground immediately.

Our local hosts were two remarkable ladies, Kim Loan and Kim Phuong, sisters with a small quasi-government-aided production house called Youth Films, housed in a dilapidated movie hall-cum-office called Youth Studio. That became our headquarters in Saigon, or Ho Chi Minh City, as it was renamed after the war. From the Youth Films office we used to foray out for our location recce or food adventures, and we discovered hundreds of little war memorabilia flea markets dotted across Saigon, selling anything from uniforms, flying overalls and dog tags to bayonets and hundreds of Zippo lighters, some authentic and others fake.

Vietnam had been embargoed by the US of A and had suffered a severe economic crisis for fifteen years, which was why they were a country lost in time. They more than made up with a people who were warm, hospitable, clever and gifted, and dying to catch up with the rest of the world. Of course, they also had a cuisine to kill for—their food is fresh, healthy and full of pleasant surprises. My greatest motivation for going to Vietnam was actually a gentleman named Vo Nguyen Giap, who, in my opinion, was one of the greatest military generals of the century.

Being a student of military history, I had studied General Giap (pronounced Ziap) very closely. He had burst into the world's imagination in 1954, having successfully conducted an amazing campaign against the French in the most decisive battle of the Indochina war at Dien Bien Phu. It broke the back of the entrenched French Army, and they subsequently actually pulled out of Indochina. General Giap has been hugely underplayed in the West, considering he defeated the French, the Japanese, the Chinese, the French again and the Americans in 1973—all in the space of some forty-odd years ... So I suppose it's understandable why they didn't give him his due. I was dying to meet him and, if possible, tape an interview. He was eighty-one years old in 1993 and lived in Hanoi, the capital of Vietnam.

Having read extensively about the Vietnam War and its conduct, I was really curious about the country and the unbelievable tenacity of its people. Vietnam was, and still is, a communist country, but, by the 1990s, they had decided to open themselves to investment from the outside world and move forward. We were witnesses to this rapid change. Money flowed in from Taiwan, France and South Korea, but not America or China. Our base of operations was basically Ho Chi Minh City, but in the eight years I spent in and out of Vietnam, I got to travel quite a bit, saw a lot of the beautiful country, met a lot of local people, and learnt about their food and culture.

We learnt that, like India, it is basically an agrarian country, where most of the population lived and worked in the Mekong Delta—the rice bowl of Indochina. However, because of the war and its massive displacement, a lot of the population had moved to a few cities for safety, putting these areas under enormous pressure, leaving them with a massively crumbling infrastructure. With the reunification of North and South Vietnam came the problem of re-indoctrination of the latter, and it took almost two years for the communist government to cleanse the South of collaboration tendencies.

As the only Indians who visited Vietnam in those days, we were very well received with cries of 'Andao' (Indian); they would come up to us and shake our hands, or even touch my beard! For a long time, I couldn't fathom this behaviour. Having travelled all over the world, I have never been so enthusiastically received anywhere else. Over a period of time, I sort of realized why. For one, as a government, we had always supported the Vietnamese struggle for independence in all international forums, also, simultaneously Russia collapsed after Gorbachev and the rice harvest in the Mekong failed.

What with the American embargo and 10 million Cambodians and ethnic Vietnamese refugees fleeing a Pol Pot–ruled bloodbath by the Khmer Rouge into Vietnam, the country faced starvation and huge hardships. This was when the Indian government extended them a generous amount of 1 million dollars in credit to tide them over. They have never forgotten that gesture. Also, I realized that the ugly Indian tourist had not discovered Vietnam yet, as it was suspected to be a war zone. Unlike Bangkok, we had not blotted our copybook totally yet.

They were beautiful, shy, cultured, intelligent people with small delicate women who looked like porcelain dolls, but were tough as nails—the product of a grinding forty-year war. Into this rapidly changing landscape arrived us Indians. We quickly adapted and went to work. The first thing we realized was that to be accepted and liked, we had to also give back. So we immediately set up shop. In our spare time, we started teaching anybody who was willing to learn, and they came in droves.

We operated out of the premises of Youth Films. I held classes on brand building, film scripting and production of ad films, while Raj held classes on editing. Vik and Dean taught them the intricacies of the digital camera, Chien Wien Lee taught photography and Joel taught them how to innovate equipment that did not exist then. We would shoot the films that Unilever or Pepsi had commissioned and stay on for a few days extra to run classes. In the evenings, we would party (and how)!

Nobody believed what an amazing party town Saigon was. Even in its most dilapidated state, there were parks with live bands, restaurants, bars and dance halls that played retro music with people dancing the cha-cha-cha. The streets were alive with throngs of Vietnamese, all togged up for their evening out. It was like rush hour. We loved it!

We were all introduced to the tradition of the dance bars by Kim Phuong, who went with us on the first visit to show us around. Everybody was charged a small fee for entering the plusher dance bars. When five Indian men settled in and ordered their first round of drinks, a lady would appear and ask us through very broken English and many gestures whether we would like company for the evening. She was the Mama San, a very important part of the management of the establishment.

At first, we were all very shy and diffident, not used to the tradition. But with a little coaxing from Kim Phuong, we mumbled something like, 'If she can speak English, please.' Kim Phuong rattled off in Vietnamese and, like magic, a few lovely young ladies trotted out, wearing gowns that were a bit dated, but quite fashionable for the fact that all the girls on the street were always dressed traditionally in their áo dài (pronounced aao zai), which was very like a silk salwar kameez—full sleeved with the top fitted like a blouse. It's long and flows down to the calf with a slit down the side up to the waist, the pyjamas or bottoms are straight cut and loose. They looked stunning.

In the dance bar, the girls usually wore Western-style formal gowns, and chattering away in Vietnamese, would make themselves comfortable between us. They were all good dancers and could put away copious amounts of alcohol. The problem was that their English was nonexistent, except for solitary words like 'numbah one', 'cannow' (cannot), 'caan'. Other than dancing with them and buying them drinks, all communications were conducted in elaborate mime, which we all became damn good at, with a smattering of Vietnamese words.

All the post-production facilities existed only in the government broadcast studio and we spent a lot of time there. It was very chilled out compared to Burma. We got comfortable with miming and we met all kinds of people—ex-colonels from the ARVN (South Vietnamese Army) driving cycle rickshaws, as they were considered collaborators and couldn't get normal jobs; non-resident Vietnamese, who had escaped as boat people and were coming back to invest in a rapidly opening up Vietnam; flea-market owners, who collected war souvenirs from old battlefields and outlying villages; owners of small soup kitchens called Pho shops; little old ladies that ran food handcarts on the street corners where the food was to die for; government officials of varying capacities; and even a very successful actress, who had trained in Kyiv in a ballet academy and was a prima ballerina.

Her name was My Duyen (pronounced 'Me Zuyen'). She was an amazing person, a fine actress, a fabulous dancer and one of the best-looking women I found in Vietnam. We had cast her in a few films for Unilever and then for a 7Up film for Pepsi. She didn't know a word of English, but was proficient in Russian and Vietnamese, of which I was clueless, except for Da and Nyet! I was fascinated by My Duyen's journey—a nine-year-old suddenly transported to Kyiv to train as a ballerina, and then her return to a completely war-torn and devastated Vietnam at the age of twenty-three to become a leading actress in that country after having to refamiliarize herself in her native tongue all over again.

I spent a lot of time with her, conversing in my exaggerated mime, which was totally over the top to her extreme embarrassment, as it was done in public view while having dinner in a lovely little restaurant. When she had recovered from the shock of her 'Andao director', in full flow, she giggled furiously and we got along like a house on fire. She was a complete knockout! I remember watching her come into the Youth Film's office for her first audition; she climbed up a set of stairs and sat down in her áo dài, looking like a delicate doll. I asked her whether she was a ballet dancer. This was translated by Kim Loan, who knew a bit of English. She looked a bit startled and said, 'How did you know?' I cleared my throat and said, 'Because you walk like a duck!' She dissolved into laughter and we became as thick as thieves.

I even managed to invite Kim Phuong, Kim Loan and My Duyen to India; I still have a beautiful photograph of her that Chien Wien Lee, our star photographer, took. When she came home and found her photograph next to Mitali's in my bedroom, she went into a state of shock and embarrassment. She grabbed the photograph and vehemently declared, 'Cannow! Cannow!' She refused to let me have it back until Mitali placated her by saying, 'It is all right, don't worry, that's just how Prahlad is. He obviously values you a great deal.' She finally calmed down and gave me back the photograph, checking with Mitali all the time.

Chien Wien Lee was a huge hit in Vietnam. Initially, they thought he was a local, only to realize later he was a foreigner when he pulled out his glasses to wear. The funny thing in Vietnam was that they never needed to wear glasses; their diet and their habits were so healthy that in my eight years in Vietnam, I never saw a native wear glasses.

Many years in Vietnam left me with many beautiful experiences, especially with their people, and some very funny incidents, which I can blame on cultural incompatibility. I remember meeting a very serious gent at a bar who got talking to me and asked a whole lot of questions about what I did, where I came from, etc. I, in turn, asked him what he did and whether he told me deliberately or inadvertently, I don't know, but he admitted to being a part of the Internal Intelligence Bureau, and his job was to keep tabs on all foreigners and what their agendas were.

I was a bit taken aback and professed that I didn't know we were all under surveillance. He smiled and said, 'If you had known, then we would have failed at our job. The idea is that you don't find out.' So I asked him why he was telling me this since I wasn't supposed to know. He smiled indulgently, and told me that my Indian crew and I were a bit intriguing—if not frustrating—as we didn't follow the pattern most foreigners followed. Most expats hung out together, at familiar watering holes and entertainment centres, and were actually quite predictable as they didn't know too many local people socially.

But we were different—we knew lots of locals, who seemed to like us back, to the extent of taking us home to meet their families; the Vietnamese never did that normally. I thought about this and it was true. We didn't know or hang out with any expats, and mostly spent time with the locals talking in mime. He went on to add that after landing in Ho Chi Minh City, we just vanished and it was one hell of a job tracking us down. I thought about it and laughed. He was bang on. We were not predictable at all!

Joel used to spend all his spare time in tiny, unpronounceable villages with the local crew and some of the dancing hall girls, who had all migrated to the cities from rural areas. Dean was a natural chick magnet and attracted all kinds of girls, who wanted to take him home to meet their parents and feed him. Kenny spent a lot of time with the street children, buying them chocolates. Vik and I spent most of our time exploring the wet markets and dingy flea markets. By then, I had become fascinated by the plethora of war memorabilia on offer—from French bayonets to American dog tags and Zippo lighters. I was also trying to wrangle a meeting with General Giap.

Over the course of the eight years, I had become an expert at figuring out authentic Zippo lighters from fake ones and started a collection of war lighters—tracing the historical progression of the American involvement in the war from 1962 to 1973, as seen from the ordinary GI's point of view. All the lighters were inscribed with the owner's name, regiment, key battle location and, most importantly, his personal feelings. I had lighters from 1962 that had inscriptions saying, 'Yea, though I walk thru the Valley of Death, I fear no evil, as I am the evilest son of a bitch in the valley!' There was one that stated, 'No mission too difficult, no sacrifice too great, duty first' and another said, 'Live by chance, love by choice, kill by profession!'

As the war progressed and there was no easy end in sight, the inscriptions started changing 'Fighters by day, lovers by night, drunkards by choice.' Or, 'If you think sex is exciting try incoming.' I found one from 1967–68, which proclaimed, 'Fighters by day, lovers by night, drunkards by choice, army by mistake,' and yet another bore the inscription 'If you haven't been there, shut the fuck up.' The Americans were convinced that they were winning the war, until North Vietnam launched a series of counter attacks across the South, called the Tet Offensive, during the 1968–69 lunar year holidays. It was only then that the American public and media realized that they were being led up the garden path. Though the North was driven back with heavy casualties, the morale of the war changed and so did the American soldier:

'We are the unwilling, led by the unqualified, doing the unnecessary, for the ungrateful.' (Khe Sanh 1968–69)

'Please ask me not why? I am sad.' 'If you kill for money, you are a mercenary. If you kill for fun, you are a sadist.' (Vang Tao, 1970–71);

'When I die, I know I am going to heaven because I've spent my life in hell.' (Phu Bai, 1970–71);

'One thousand marines will shit today and wipe their ass with the green beret.' (Dong Ba Thin, 1971–72).

I even found a Black GI's lighter that said, 'They call me Coffee, not only because I look that way, but because I grind so damn good.' (Nha Tnong, 1966–67)

I carefully collected thirty-five Zippo lighters from 1962 to 1973, tracing the progress and morale of twenty years of American involvement in Vietnam until their ignominious and scrambled evacuation from the roof of the embassy in Saigon, when the world woke up to the first American defeat in their history. I have been asked many times, by various people, how a poor agrarian country could fight a sustained war for forty-five years for the independence of their country.

They fought the French colonists, the Japanese who had occupied Indochina during World War II, and the Chiang Kai-shek faction, who had been asked to run the country while the French were trying to figure out how to double-cross the Vietnamese in their promise to give them their independence in 1949–50. The French were finally and decisively defeated at Dien Bien Phu by General Giap in 1954. They handed South Vietnam, under President Ngô Đình Diệm, to the Americans, who, in turn, were finally kicked out in 1973, and the country was unified. The Vietnamese even fought off a Chinese invasion of North Vietnam in 1979 after they went into Cambodia and removed the genocidal Khmer Rouge regime under the despotic and murderous Pol Pot and Ieng Sary, supported and funded by the Chinese.

One of the best books that I read on the Vietnam War was written by a war journalist on his kaleidoscopic vision of the events, in fragmented vignettes, where he had witnessed everything from courage to stupidity, to the futility of the whole exercise, while travelling the length and breadth of the theatre of combat. The book was called *Dispatches* and was written by Michael Herr. One very telling episode in it was from an airfield called Khe Sanh, which saw some extremely heavy fighting. The North Vietnamese and Viet Cong were hell-bent on surrounding the American airbase and knocking out the landing transport planes, supplying the troops. The North Vietnamese were trying a repeat of Dien Bien Phu, but the Americans controlled a lot of the high ground, plus they had complete air superiority.

It became a cat-and-mouse game, while the North and the Viet Cong soldiers had dug themselves into a maze of tunnels. On spotting a lone Viet Cong soldier, the Americans, in their typical overkill style, called in a B-52 airstrike and pulverized the hill they saw the trooper on; the bombardment was intense and devastating. When the smoke cleared, the odd leathernecks suddenly saw the VC soldier pop up from a trench and scuttle across the smoking landscape. They called in a napalm strike by a fighter bomber squadron. The planes roared in and poured fire and brimstone on the unfortunate Viet Cong's position; it was like the fires of hell had been let loose! Nothing but nothing could survive that! As the American GIs were packing up to go to their bivouacs, the little indestructible VC pops up again and scampers to another position. Unbelievable! The Americans to a man spontaneously got up and cheered the cheeky little survivor.

For a long time, I thought the tenacity of the Vietnamese was in the fighting quality of the men and generals. It was only after being in the country for many years and travelling extensively through it, meeting and interacting with lots of people, that I realized the truth of why Vietnam will never lose a war. You see, it's relatively easy for men to arm themselves and go to war, depending on their fervour and belief; for them, the choice is simple—to kill or be killed, and pride, honour, patriotism and ego play a huge part. Equally, they can very quickly tire of the process, and feel sickened by the hype, rhetoric and bloodshed, unless they have something to come back to, which is more precious than country, patriotism, pride, or propaganda—family.

The women of Vietnam, other than actually physically running North Vietnam during the war, became the currency of the war in the South. To ensure that families survived the worst years of the war, vast numbers of people migrated from the countryside to overextended cities, which became refugee camps for the displaced, and food and money were almost non-existent. In this scenario, it would have been very easy for family units to disintegrate and be lost forever, if it hadn't been for the single-minded resolve of the women.

At great cost to themselves, they kept the families intact, so that the men would have something to come back to. This is why, in today's Vietnam, women are considered more than equal in the social fabric of the country. Anyway, despite being in and out of the country for eight years, I never got to meet and talk to General Giap as the Vietnamese government was very protective of him. He died in 2001 at the age of 101. What a man!

My weakness for Fedora-style felt hats has defined a large part of my identity and persona—I had made quite a collection thanks to my travels all over the world. My favourite was the Aussie Akubra made from genuine rabbit fur. It is water resistant, keeps its shape, lasts forever if looked after, and protects the head from heat and cold. I swear by them! Many of my friends are intrigued by my fascination for hats, so I tell them my favourite Vietnam story. Our trips to Saigon were always an arduous roundabout journey, via a six-hour stopover at Bangkok and then a late afternoon connector to Saigon, where we would arrive a bit worse for wear by 6.30 or 7 p.m.

We would check into our budget hotel in Downtown District 3, change and head to District 1, where all the bars and dance halls were. We were determined not to waste time and hit the party scene immediately. I was always in my Akubra hat. On one of our trips, I was a bit knackered, so I left the crew to carry on partying and called it a night by midnight (Cinderella time), making my way back to the hotel. Vietnam, as mentioned, was undergoing a massive economic embargo by the Americans and their good-weather friends in retaliation for kicking their asses in the war.

They were dirt poor and struggling to keep their infrastructure from collapsing. They were also a very proud and dignified nation, and very concerned that the easiest victims would be their very beautiful, but vulnerable, women, who could be exploited by the thousands of tourists and foreigners heading into the country as it was opening up after years of war and economic isolation.

The government at the time had put in some very basic but drastic rules of engagement, especially for all the small-budget hotels dotting Saigon. The rules were very simple and direct—if a man was caught entertaining a local girl or lady in his hotel room, he would immediately be deported, the girl and the manager of the hotel would be arrested and would spend some quality time in a jail.

To implement this rule, the local police would periodically raid random hotels in the middle of the night just to keep tabs on the hotels. When I staggered back to my hotel room at midnight, I was so exhausted that I just removed all my clothes, put my hat on the TV set and passed out on the queen-size bed, which took up 90 per cent of my room. I didn't even have the energy to climb over the bed to go to the loo. Suddenly, at some godforsaken hour, I woke up to pounding on my door. Highly disoriented about where I was and what was happening, I groggily got up, intuitively put on my hat and opened the door.

I saw a man in a police uniform holding an AK-47 with the safety off at a nine o'clock position. Behind him was a horrified lady, who I presume was the manager of the hotel, with her eyeballs popping out. Fuzzily, in the distance, across the hall, I recognized Mahesh Aney and Chien Wien Lee. They also seemed to be in a state of great agitation; I couldn't see them too clearly as I had forgotten to put on my glasses in the confusion. I didn't realize that I was standing there with my hat on and nothing else; completely starkers! I could imagine the reaction of the good lady as I am sure she had never seen such a hirsute human in the altogether in her life (the Vietnamese, by and large, are pretty hairless).

My adrenaline shot up immediately after seeing the AK-47 with the safety off. This removed the cobwebs from my mind and I could focus. I realized that Mahesh and Chien were jumping up and down, pointing to my nether regions. I looked down and, to my horror, realized that I had nothing on. I quickly whipped off the hat and covered the essentials, relieving a lot of tension for the policeman and the poor manager. She was simultaneously trying to translate for the policeman and my colleagues, who thought it was going to be curtains for me.

I was pushed aside rudely by this time, as the cop was sure I was hiding a nubile in my postage stamp–sized room with a wall-to-wall bed. He looked everywhere, including on top of a very narrow wardrobe and, of course, in the toilet and under the bed, but no cigar. They finally left to check out some boisterous and drunk Koreans next door. The motto of the story is, 'Never leave home without the hat; you never know what you might need to cover.'

50

'Tod de Talle, Khol de Bandhan!'

Before the Cricket World Cup, there is always frenzied activity in the advertising world, especially when the Indian team is on a song. During the run-up to the 1999 World Cup, Pepsi decided to create a smaller build-up campaign. It was on individual players and the team at Genesis loved the one on Sachin, where a bunch of kids wearing Sachin masks would play gully cricket. They take a Pepsi break and when they lift their masks to drink, they realize that Sachin is behind one of the masks right there with them, drinking his Pepsi!

Everything was based on the reaction of the children seeing the real Sachin amongst them. The Genesis kids loved the possibilities of the script and immediately started working on it, on their own. However, things got delayed and the World Cup loomed large, and therefore, this interim campaign got canned—much to the dismay of the team, who moaned and groaned and begged me to try and get Pepsi to allow them to at least do the Sachin film alone.

I reluctantly took it to Vibha Rishi and tried to cajole her into letting us do a one-off TVC. She was very non-committal and told me to concentrate on the World Cup theme film, which was a biggie. But the team refused to get off my back, so I rang her back and told her we would do it at any cost—whatever she could scrape up. She hemmed and hawed, and, seeing our enthusiasm, finally gave in and said what the hell: 'Do it, but I only have twelve lakh.' I accepted the challenge and the team went at it, all guns blazing. Somehow, in my mind's eye, I always saw the film revolving around a stunted tree in the middle of nowhere and, of course, all the kids would wear Sachin masks.

The team scurried off to find such a tree. They looked all over Maharashtra—from Panvel, Pune, to Nashik—and no luck ... Finally, when we were all about to give up, a trainee found the exact tree we needed behind Aarey Colony next to a basti. It was perfect! Kenny Dawson then found a bunch of kids from the basti actually playing cricket with the tree trunk acting as the stumps and a wooden clothes phatta for a bat.

He loved the visual so much that he wanted to cast them as the kids in the masks. This would change the whole perception of the film and give it a lot of depth, but the kids were scruffy, wearing mismatched torn clothes and sometimes only in chappals—very real, but 'downmarket' in advertising parlance. I knew it was going to be a task to sell the basti kids to Pepsi and Vibha; they would definitely baulk at the idea as the script was written with upper middle-class kids in mind, who could afford a crate of Pepsi during a break.

With great trepidation, I presented the idea to Vibha during the pre-production meeting, where the agency, client and production house discuss the details of the script and its vision until everybody is on the same page so there are no unpleasant surprises later. As expected, Vibha was alarmed by the suggestion and immediately rejected it. So I asked her a crucial question, 'When our line is "Yeh dil maange more" and it's all about dreaming big, what could be a bigger dream than this? A kid who has everything and also wants to be a Sachin ... Or a kid from a basti who has nothing but his talent and wants to grow up to be a Sachin?'

'That's not a fair question!' she said.

I replied, 'Life is not fair, Vibha!'

She finally gave in and allowed us to shoot with the basti kids, but with certain caveats—such as new school uniforms, socks and shoes for the kids, and all of them would have to get proper haircuts.

Kenny, who was directing the film, was ecstatic and got down to work with a vengeance. Then came a bombshell—Pepsi informed us that WorldTel, the agency handling Sachin, had bounced the script. One of the terms of the contract was that all creatives meant for Sachin had to be vetted by them. I was hopping mad. How could a talent agency decide on a creative script without even discussing it with the talent and creative people? I decided to bypass them all. One of the clauses in their contract was that nobody could meet the talent without their permission and without them being present during the meeting. What they hadn't realized was that Sachin and I lived in the same building. He was on the tenth floor—ten for Tendulkar. I was on the second floor.

One sunny Sunday, I decided to play the liftman in our apartment, and spent the better part of the day going up and down in the lift, waiting for Sachin to go down to the car park. It took a few hours, but finally, bingo! He arrived at the lift to go down. I got exactly five minutes with him and sold him the script, also telling him that we would need him for precisely one hour and no more. He loved the script, and on being told that WorldTel was making an unnecessary fuss, told me not to worry and that he would handle it. I immediately told the team that it was a go and informed Vibha accordingly.

She was a bit peeved initially, as she didn't want to rub Sachin's agency the wrong way. But when I told her about my morning in the lift, she was tickled pink. The film was on, and my only real contribution was the tree and the idea that when Sachin came out of the van, all masked up, the basti kids wouldn't have a clue as to who he was. This way their reaction when he removed the mask was going to be a killer. We could only do it once, so I told our DOP, Deohans, that he had better get the kids' reaction to Sachin in the first take or I would murder him. He got it and the rest is history. But the saga doesn't end here.

The edited product was fabulous, but I felt like something was missing, something to lift the film to its true potential—maybe a jingle or a song to mould it into shape. The song had never been planned and we only had accounts for a background score. Zap, the writer of the script, then penned one line for the jingle to follow 'Tod de talle, khol de bandhan, yeh dil maange more.'

I looked at Kenny and Zap, and asked who they would like to use for the song. They both said Raghubir Yadav, the actor. I was a bit taken aback as he was a theatre actor and lived in a village in Madhya Pradesh. I immediately vetoed the idea and told them that we had neither the time or the money to find Raghubir—surely we could find someone who sounded similar. A week later, the song had been recorded, and I was to have a look and approve it. It was brilliant! 'See, you didn't need Raghubir Yadav,' I reminded them.

They all looked sheepish as hell and muttered, 'It *is* Raghubir Yadav.' They had searched for him all over MP, found him, and convinced him to come to Bombay to compose the music and record the song. The song was so original and fresh that it just lifted the film, even though it had a very raw, folksy cowbelt sound. I thought about how these little shits had disobeyed a direct order and needed reprimanding; but, on the other hand, they had done what they thought was best for the film, proving ownership! I promoted a lot of independent directors who took the initiative, and stood by their ideas and owned the campaigns.

When we presented this little gem to Vibha, she saw it just once, and said, 'What can I say, guys? Well done! I only hope I don't get sacked for this.'

In my opinion, it is one of the best films we have made for Pepsi and will live long beyond all of us.

51

'Players Only, Phoot Le!'

Immediately after the Sachin mask film, we plunged into the production of the Pepsi World Cup film—featuring practically the whole Indian cricket team, minus Sourav Ganguly, who had been snapped up by Coke. Since Shah Rukh, who was the most important part of the film, was shooting in Hyderabad for *Main Hoon Na* and couldn't budge from there, we had to cart everybody to Ramoji Film City.

Sachin could arrive later as his part was a while away and he had some prior commitments. We built a changing room set for the players and copied the main gate for the Marylebone Cricket Club (MCC) in London, because the UK was where the World Cup was being played. The logistical nightmare of coordinating with twelve players of the Indian cricket team, plus Shah Rukh and Ramoji Film City, was humongous. It was entirely handled by Amita Sehgal and Mitali, both tough and battle-hardened by this time. And pull it off they did!

We arrived at Ramoji Film City in Hyderabad, only to be told by Shah Rukh's minders that he could not shoot before 9 p.m. and after 6 a.m.—he was required on Farah Khan's set (Farah was also, incidentally, a semi-Genesis product). We sent everybody to bed while

Anuja (from HTA), Vik, Amita and yours truly hung around the set, breaking the ad film down into its various shots so that the lighting department and the camera lot could get on with it. It was going to be a night-for-day shoot (we had to light it in a way that it looked like day), and the production, props and camera departments actually got no sleep at all.

The script was very simple, written by Anuja: Shah Rukh is loitering near the gate of the MCC grounds and sees a stack of Pepsis being wheeled into the player's dressing room through the gate. He is promptly stopped from entering by a proper English gatekeeper, with the warning, 'Players only, phoot le!' Shah Rukh dresses up like Sachin and crashes the party, looking for his free Pepsi. After walking in on many players in various stages of undress, he mistakes Rahul Dravid for Sourav Ganguly and sees him glugging Pepsi. He quips, 'Acchha, Sourav, pi le, pi le!' We added this during the shoot to get a dig at Coke (to imply that even though Sourav is the brand ambassador of Coke, he secretly drinks Pepsi). Shah Rukh would then finally find the cooler and grab a can when Mohammad Azharuddin taps him on the shoulder and tells him, 'Pad up, Sachin, you are on.' The film stops here with a 'to be continued' caption.

During the World Cup, with the whole country watching, the film comes to an abrupt halt. This was the first ad film in Indian history to be shown in two parts. I must have received a thousand phone calls asking, 'What happens now?' A week later, we released the next half of the film. It opens with a distraught Shah Rukh with a Sachin wig and all, fully padded up and clutching a can of chilled Pepsi, stumbling into the corridor leading to the grounds with a bat. He suddenly spots an amused Sachin leaning nonchalantly against a parapet, looking at him. Sachin feels sorry for Shah Rukh and taking the bat from his hand, says, 'Don't worry, I'll take it from here.'

Much to Shah Rukh's relief, of course. I think Sachin was on song that day and decided on his own to grab the Pepsi can instead and went back to the dressing room, leaving a completely flabbergasted Shah Rukh to look into the camera in a desperate appeal and croak, 'Ahaa!' The film ends. The last part was entirely Sachin's idea and I realized he had come a long way from the reticent, reluctant sixteen-year-old whom I had worked with not too many years ago.

I was amazed at Shah Rukh's stamina and dedication. He had shot the whole day on his own film set, shot the whole night with us and shot at sunrise outside our mock-up gate for the opening of the film. No nakhras, no 'star vibes'; he was just an amazing professional and was going back on his set to shoot for the rest of the day. What energy!

52

Bo Kata!

Meanwhile, back at the ranch, Pepsi had scored yet another casting coup and had managed to rope in Amitabh Bachchan and Sachin Tendulkar—two of the biggest stars in the country—for a TVC. Anuja had come up with a script where both would compete in a kite duel (pench). It was a biggie and even the media was hyper-excited about it.

We went about it furiously, trying to find a suitable location for the duel. We finally zeroed in on Jodhpur, not only because we would get the spectacular fort as a backdrop, but also because the town below had been recently painted blue (Pepsi's colours). The unit consisted of forty-odd people from the crew—including make-up, hair, lighting and rain machine guys—to the Genesis gang of super enthusiastic flunkies and ADs.

It was winter and we had to factor in not only the travel time, but also the fact that the 'kite duel' could be disrupted by rain, and that meant we would have to keep people from freezing their goolies off. Logistically, it was a bit complex, but we had been there and had survived. This time, it was a bit different. We were also dealing with two superstars and a cohort of the national press that was following us around, knowing that the coming together of Mr Bachchan and Sachin was a scoop. And of course, Murphy, lurking in the dark corners of the fort, struck one night before the shoot.

Both Sachin and Mr Bachchan fell ill with high temperatures, colds and coughs. We got the local doctor involved and waited with bated breath for the next morning. The cold and cough persisted, but the fever vanished. And both of them, being the incredible professionals that they are, reported to set at 9 a.m. sharp. Wow! The shoot went wonderfully until the time the rain disrupted the duel in the ad film and they all got wet! We kept hot towels and some brandy for the stars, but neither of them touched the booze—so we drank it ourselves with great glee.

In the script, the rain plays spoilsport. Everybody is sitting gloomily under a stone stairway, teeth chattering, when a kid comes up to Mr Bachchan and Sachin, and, in a woebegone manner, asks, 'Khatam?' The music picks up as an idea flashes across their faces and the next thing you know, they have made paper boats out of the kites, and, in the pouring rain, are racing them in a flowing nallah, with the rest of the cast cheering them on. It was fabulous. For the cutaways, we had a lot of chokras racing down the narrow gullies of the town with long sticks to try and snare the floating kites as they wafted gently down to earth with cries of 'Dheel pe dheel, bo kata!'

Kenny, my trusty AD and editor, really good at managing street kids and chokras, was given the task of shooting these exuberant kids racing down narrow streets gleefully. He did a great job as always; those shots actually lifted the film, and made it watchable over and over again. I realized that despite the cold weather and hardships, the professionalism of both Mr Bachchan and Sachin, shooting through the day and prancing about in the rain, without a care despite being sick, was a lesson to remember.

53

The Beard and the Bypass

Thanks to Pepsi and my other clients in Delhi, my trips to the city were quite frequent, and I made some great friends. I normally used to spend the night at either Feroze and Mohit Gujral's place or at Radhika and Ajay Bahl's place (Feroze being our favourite model for all seasons. She was always ethereal and the camera loved her). Radhika used to be a lawyer, and then became a homemaker and interior designer par excellence; Ajay is one of the top corporate lawyers in Delhi. I used to call them Chachi and Chacha even though they were much younger than me. There is a story behind this, like everything else.

In those heady early days, I was coopted by Nirja Shah to help run RG's in the erstwhile Natraj Hotel on Marine Drive on Saturday nights. My bar name was 'PK Tun', and Tony Singh of Pritam da Dhaba, with his loose hair and beret, was 'Che-gon-rong'. We did away with their membership scheme and invited all the professionals who make this city what it is to come party with us. We rocked the place—it was the go-to place on Saturday nights. It had a capacity of 200 people and we usually ended up with 400 eager-beaver party animals—all friends and friends of friends. Sure, it was strictly by invitation and a list of invitees was left at the counter, but it became a big deal to be invited as a regular.

I used to get a lot of requests from my Delhi friends and their friends to be invited to RG's on a Saturday night. One such Saturday night, Aparna (Appoo), an up-and-coming choreographer and impresario, and her sister Nisha, wanted to tag along. I was to pick them up from Marine Drive, where they were staying with a friend. I landed up at 7 p.m. sharp and found these two Delhi girls still trying to tart up to the hilt (Delhi style). I got a bit miffed and told them to hurry up, or I would have to leave them behind.

They quickly did whatever they had to and sat down on a sofa very primly, waiting. I got up and said, 'Let's go; I am getting late.' To this, they replied, 'We have to wait for Chachi. She is also coming with us.'

'Chachi!' I exploded, imagining a stout, Karol Bagh–type behenji of middle age, landing up at the wild nightclub in Bombay, escorted by yours truly, sitting in a corner going haw at everything. All this with her hand covering her mouth and her eyes popping out. There was no way I was taking any Chachi to my club; not a chance of a snowball in hell. They sulked; I sulked. I paced up and down in agitation when the door flew open, and in walked this bombshell in her mid-thirties in a little black dress. I gawked at her as the girls jumped up and, in unison, all three of us said, 'Chachi!' They said it in relief and me in pure surprise! That's how Chachi came to be called Chachi by me forever.

On one of my trips to Delhi, I landed up at Chachi's to have dinner; I had an early morning flight to Bombay scheduled for the next day. At night, the lights conked out. It was a hot, sweltering Delhi summer, and I tossed and turned, bathed in sweat, waiting for the morning. I caught my flight, reached home and tried to get a few hours of shut-eye before heading for the office in Tardeo. I just couldn't sleep and felt quite uneasy. I showered, changed and was heading to the office when we passed Lilavati Hospital.

On a whim, I told my trusty driver, RC (Ramchander), to pull into Lilavati and wait for me. I hopped out, went into the outpatient department (OPD) and told them I wanted a complete heart check-up. The lady at the counter asked if there was anything wrong. 'Not yet, but it will be,' I replied. She looked startled and sent me off for an electrocardiogram (ECG). On seeing the results of the ECG, the attendant called the doctor, who looked very worried and wheeled me out to do a hurried angiography.

What amazes me about hospitals is that when nurses and doctors find an anomaly, they huddle around the report and talk to each other in hushed voices, putting on doomsday expressions on their faces, while the patient is right there! Yet, nobody looks at or addresses the patient at all. There I was, lying on a trolley with a bunch of technicians and doctors talking across me in medical gibberish as if I didn't exist. I raised myself on my elbow and loudly intervened, 'Excuse me! Would somebody mind telling me what's going on?'

Dead silence.

One young doctor finally came up to me and said, 'Is there a family member or a family doctor we can talk to?' I told him nobody was in town as Mitali had gone to Marve and I had never had a family doctor. The closest I had to one was Maya Alagh, a trained doctor, and my dentist Aparna Pinto. I decided to ring up Aparna, since she worked out of her Bandra clinic, which was closer to the hospital, and told her to come to Lilavati pronto. Aparna, of course, panicked and turned up looking really hassled.

The doctor at Lilavati took one look at her and asked me who she was. I told him she was my dentist and the only doctor I went to regularly. He almost fainted. By this time, Mitali called me, and told me that Maya Alagh was coming straight from the airport and to just hang in there. The huddle of doctors still ignored me, but told Aparna that I had a huge blockage which might need surgery. By this time, Maya Alagh also arrived in a flurry and got hold of Dr Nitu Mandke, senior surgeon extraordinaire, who checked the reports and told me to go home as they had stabilized my condition. He told me that I needed a heart bypass surgery and to schedule one. Maya also said that we could take a second opinion and come back.

By this time, I was a bit pissed off and decided to just get it over with instead of procrastinating, as the blockage was going nowhere, regardless of the many opinions. And that changing my lifestyle overnight to maybe avoid the procedure was not a possibility. I asked Dr Mandke a straight question, 'Will I be able to dive after the procedure?' He looked at me a bit surprised, thought about it, and said, 'Yes!' That was it. I told him that since I was already in the hospital, there was no point in dithering. We could just get on with it, and how soon could that be? Everybody went into a tizzy when he said, 'Tomorrow morning, first thing.' So, there we were, at the moment of truth.

Aparna was most concerned and was trying to get me to defer the timing with no luck. Mitali, who would be directly affected by the responsibility, was solid as a rock and cool as a cucumber—at least for my benefit. She sent the boys to see me before the visitors' hours ran out, and they looked at me solemnly and nodded sagely at all my instructions of how I expected them to grow up overnight and support their mum. Finally, everybody left.

With a loud knock on the door, a barber entered and set up shop in my room. He hauled out a gleaming old-fashioned razor and started stropping it on a leather belt to give it a sharper edge. I looked at him nervously and asked what he was going to shave. 'Everything above the belt,' he said. He proceeded to cover me in talcum powder and started to dry shave my upper torso. I must say, he was an ustad—not a nick or cut, smooth as silk. He then arrived at my beard, which I had cultivated for the last thirty years.

I stopped him dead in his tracks. 'You are not touching the beard!' I said.

'I have to,' bleated the poor fellow. It was standard procedure for a bypass.

'Not on your life!' I said adamantly.

Finally, to break the impasse, he had to summon Dr Mandke, who, luckily, was still doing his rounds. The doc arrived in a flurry, surrounded by young interns, and said in his booming voice, 'Well, what's the problem, young man?' I explained to him that the barber wanted to shave my precious beard. 'So? It's necessary. Even if a single follicle goes into the incision, it will screw up the whole procedure,' he said. I then asked him whether he would give me a guarantee that I would walk out of the operation theatre alive.

He looked at me seriously and said, 'Nobody can guarantee that!' I gulped, nervous for the first time that day, and I explained to him that since he couldn't give me a guarantee, and god forbid something did go wrong, then I would end up on a slab of ice, clean-shaven, surrounded by grieving young ladies. My friends and family would look at me and say, 'Who the fuck is this? There is a mistake, we've got the wrong body!' I would have to get a blow-up of a colour photograph and keep it behind my head, for me to recognize myself. QED! Meanwhile, by the time Mitali and the office organized a photograph, I would be smelling a bit high. 'Don't you think, doc?' He threw up his hands in exasperation and told the barber to go to the chemist and get a tube of Fixo, which sardars use to stick their beards with, and a beard hair net. I probably am the only patient ever who went into open-heart surgery with his beard intact and lived to tell the tale.

I came out of the anaesthesia with a sore throat, and a beard as hard as a rock, thanks to a generous slather of Fixo, and tubes sticking out of my chest cavity, which also sported a neat set of stitches running down my breastbone. And, of course, a congested chest, which comes with the territory. It took me one day to figure out how to collect the phlegm in my chest before coughing it up in one spasmodic heave, and to get used to the pain and lack of manoeuvrability.

What I couldn't get used to was the bedpan to perform the ablutions in and, of course, I was constipated as hell. On day three, with the tubes still sticking out of my abdomen and chest, I browbeat the on-duty nurse to help me sit up, stagger to the loo, and sit on the pot. God, you cannot imagine how good that felt! What a sense of achievement.

I was tentatively released from the bed that had held me captive. And, since I slept all day, I was a nightbird. The new-found freedom allowed me to prowl the corridors of Lilavati's seventh floor in the middle of the night, full of recovering patients—to meet with them and exchange small talk. Some of them hadn't gotten out of bed for a month and so, of course, I used to prod them into taking a midnight walk with me. On day four, my tubes came off, and that was a relief and made me totally free to visit the other patients nocturnally.

On day five, a delegation of doctors, nurses and admin types gathered around me. Basically, they were pissed off that my nightly activities were disturbing and upsetting many patients who were recovering slowly. I was asked, in no uncertain terms, to go home. I have a strong feeling that they wanted the patients to take their own sweet time to recover and run up huge bills, and that I was a bad influence on their billing system. I was on the set shooting a commercial exactly one month after my open-heart surgery. Such is the power of the mind!

After my bypass surgery, I used to take long walks on Bandstand, and watch Mitali go through the stretching and contorting of yoga asanas with her amazing yoga teacher, Jaya. Mitali grew slim and fit, while I slowly expanded my middle. So she insisted that I do yoga with Jaya just to become fit again. I resisted as much as I possibly could, but knowing Mitali, I should have realized it was a losing battle. I reluctantly agreed. Because of my post-operative condition and the fact that I was dying to get back to work, Jaya worked out a tailor-made regimen for me, which started like a cakewalk until she began tightening the screws and stepping on the accelerator.

By this time, I was hooked, and it actually made me feel much better. Slowly, I got into the rhythm and realized why Mitali was so fanatical about her yoga practice. If anything, twenty years down the line, if I can cram in so much into a day and not keel over, I think a lot of the credit goes to yoga and to Jaya's perseverance, despite my initial lackadaisical attitude, which can be very tiresome.

54

Ting, Ting, Ta Ting!

Having worked with Britannia and Sunil Alagh from the beginning of my career—especially as 'Britannia Marie' was Genesis's first national-level film, catapulting us to very high visibility—we witnessed quite a few changes in the company, such as when it moved its headquarters from Bombay to Bangalore (now Bengaluru) and Sunil Alagh rising from product manager to chairman of the company. We were very involved with a lot of their campaigns that are now being handled by the Bangalore office of Lintas.

Their go-to copywriter was Ashit Desai, and we got along extremely well. Sunil, having known me practically forever, was very comfortable with both of us and used to brief us directly, to the exclusion of the suits, who were really pissed off that they couldn't put their contributions and names in the case histories of campaigns. The suits used to corner poor Ashit Desai in the office and give him a hard time, to the extent of reporting him to his boss, Balki, national creative director of Lintas in Bombay. Desai, of course, told them that Mr Alagh called him directly along with Prahlad Kakar for a brief, and if they had a problem, they could take it up with Mr Alagh directly. All of them took the patli gali and disappeared.

One reason for Sunil Alagh being so comfortable with us was that a lot of the strategic ideating came from him as a brief, and the moment we locked on it and embellished it cinematically, we would be off and running. We would also knock them off at a relatively affordable and competitive cost, with very little to-ing and fro-ing. This was exactly how things went for the amazing campaign we did for Britannia during the 1999 Cricket World Cup, during which Mr Alagh had coined the line 'Britannia khao, World Cup jao'. The winner of the competition would get to go to England for one India match, all costs paid. But the twist was there would be not just one winner, but 300! A whole section of the stands would be taken over by these fans wearing Britannia T-shirts. Awesome! That was when we made eight films for the World Cup on the fly.

The campaign was a huge success. And Britannia ruled! Mr Alagh once made a statement that resonated with me tremendously. He said, 'I have some thirty brands to sell and only about Rs 1.5 crore for each of them, which, as advertising professionals, you know is peanuts. So I just don't have the luxury to be mediocre in my advertising. It has to be bold, risky and totally out of the box for it to work for me.' And so it was, starting with his first campaign as a product manager for Britannia glucose biscuits, called 'Gabbar ki asli pehchan', produced and directed by Kailash Surendranath. The campaign was a take on a scene from *Sholay* and was an all-time classic. It ran just before *Sholay* in theatres. Even ushers in theatres would stop to watch the commercial for the nth time. They couldn't get enough of it.

One day, Mr Alagh summoned Ashit and me to the Bangalore head office for a brief on a new corporate film to follow the line 'Swast khao, tan man jagao', meant for young kids and mothers. He sat us down and started the brief by stating he wanted my youngest son, Anhjin, for the film and that he wanted three sports as the themes—football, cricket and tennis. He proceeded to show us an international film as reference featuring a five-year-old scoring a goal and celebrating in typical football fashion. I sat there a bit stunned, as Anhjin was a completely out-of-control three-year-old brat. And the idea of trying to direct him in three films of a specific discipline was something straight out of my nightmares. Moreover, how was I going to break the news to Mitali!

I told Mr Alagh as much, and suggested a slightly older child who could be directed. But he was adamant about only using Master Anhjin. Obviously, he saw some merit in the little monster that had escaped us all. After a long and exhausting session, he browbeat all of my reluctance and perfectly rational reasons to not use Anhjin for the films, and said as a clincher, 'I am going to give you all a budget for a three-day shoot with the kid—just follow him around with a long lens and shoot whatever he does. Shoot him eating, sleeping, playing, throwing tantrums, doing whatever the hell he chooses to do, with a little hint or directions from us. At the end of this harrowing exercise, we will all review the footage and see if it makes any sense whatsoever.' He was willing to take a gamble on a cute, but devilish three-year-old who was a law unto himself.

On returning to the office, I immediately excused myself from the shoot, as Anhjin was too familiar with me, and the whole exercise would go off into a tangent if I couldn't control myself and started losing it. It would compromise the whole shoot and end in an unmitigated disaster. I appointed two of my most trusted to the job—Sunita Ram, on the entire production, and Kenneth Dawson to deal with Anhjin. Kenny had had a few encounters with the brat and actually liked him.

Kenny was ably supported by Vikas Sivaraman, our go-to DOP, to keep the little bugger in focus. So off they went into the valley of the unknown to do battle. It was not to reason why; it was to do or die. I was there a safe distance away. After the first-day shoot of the football sequence, everybody trooped back into the office, looking exhausted and drooping, except Anhjin, who was still full of beans as he had had a blast. On my asking how it went, Sunita shrugged and crossed her fingers—not a reassuring sign at all.

Day two was the cricket segment. The group came back at the end of the day looking worse for wear. I was hoping they would outlast the schedule—one day to go. The third day was a bit different as, by now, Anhjin had realized that his new besties were duty-bound to accept whatever he did and wanted, and came out bouncing happily to cause some more serious damage. The unit followed, slightly chastened by the experience of the previous couple of days. The third day actually went off better than the first two. Anhjin and Kenny had become friends of a kind.

When I saw them at the end of day three, they were all a little more buoyant; maybe it was also because the ordeal had finally ended. The jubilation lasted until I reminded them that if part or most of the footage was unusable, then it wouldn't surprise me in the least if Mr Alagh asked us to do it all over again. Practice makes perfect, after all. On that sombre note, Kenny was given the footage, and he left to see if he could make some sense of it (Kenny was also our brilliant in-house post-production pro). He called me after a week of disappearing into the editing suite and seemed quite pleased with the results.

It was still a rough cut without music or VO, and Kenny had put in a rough scratch track on the films. I saw the films for the first time and thought they were like no advertising films I had ever seen before. There was no logic, there was no continuity, there was no resemblance of a storyline or even an attempt at one. It was all hearts and mind. I watched them five times, with my mind trying desperately to fit them into some category, but not a chance! They defied all logic, but, at a very visceral level, they worked! Kenny recorded the track and Mr Alagh saw them only once and loved them.

I now feel that he knew all along why they would work, specifically, as Anhjin wasn't at all aware of the camera, but was only trying to raise hell on the shoot in a spontaneous, organic manner. The films are a classic example of when a client puts his money where his mouth is, he gets magic. For Britannia, the films were magic and, in my heart of hearts, I know they will be almost impossible to replicate. Ting, ting, ta ting!

55

'Main Kaun Hoon? Main Kahan Hoon?'

Before the run-up to the Cricket World Cup, we were all wracking our brains for a suitable hatt ke idea for the brand. Pepsi had on its roster a lot of international players like Shane Warne and Carl Hooper, besides Sachin, our favourite star. The HTA creative team, headed by Anuja Chauhan, came up with an amazing idea of Warne (who had a running feud with Sachin on the field) and Hooper following Sachin around a mall, hoping to kidnap him and send him to Timbuktu, thus ruining the Indian cricket team's chances at winning the World Cup. Hooper accidentally knocks over a huge pyramid of Pepsi cans, which buries Sachin. Warne and Hooper pull him out of the mountain of Pepsi cans, and realize he was knocked on the head and lost his memory.

'Main kaun hoon? Main kahan hoon?' asks a dazed Sachin. Warne and Hooper exchange gleeful looks, and tell him that he is a famous cook. They put a chef's hat on him as they load him into a shopping cart and start wheeling him out, saying, 'You are famous in Honolulu.' They then wheel him to a private plane and load him on. Unfortunately, a Pepsi can slips out of Sachin's hand and he runs after it as it rolls down the stairs. Sachin then quickly shuts the ramp door on the plane and tells the captain, a sardar, 'Praji, go to Honolulu.' The two unfortunates, Warne and Hooper, are left stuck to the windows like glue, gesticulating wildly as the plane takes off.

We had to build a huge set of the shopping mall and dress it up to look authentic as we needed it for a full day. We also needed total control of the environment. This was quite a mammoth task, as I insisted that we needed an establishing shot of the location, so no cheating was allowed. Amita and Mitali worked all night with the set crew to have the place ready for the 9 a.m. shift. Everybody arrived bang on time, except Warne. We tried calling him, then his hotel and his agent in Australia, but no luck. We tried everybody, but it seemed as though he had disappeared off the face of the earth. The hotel booked for him said he hadn't even checked in.

When there was still no sign of Shane Warne at 11 a.m., we panicked. Suddenly, I got a call from an unknown number and a strange, but authoritative voice informed me that they were holding Shane Warne at the airport as he had arrived without a visa. They were in the process of deporting him. The only reason for the call was that Warne claimed that he had come to Bombay at the behest of Genesis Film Productions and Pepsi to shoot an advertisement. So, if this were true, the call had been made to inform us that they were sending him back. Clearly, they weren't cricket lovers and had not recognized the famous player.

We leapt into action and rang everybody we knew—from the police commissioner to the local politicians (not that they took our calls). But we were very persistent and hared off to the airport. We begged and pleaded with the officials to let him into the country for just the day, and promised that we would return him before 12 a.m.—Cinderella time. No luck. Then we got serious and started calling Delhi; Pepsi called the Directorate General of Civil Aviation and I called the home ministry to talk to our Lakshadweep MP, P.M. Sayeed, who was also the minister of state for home. Finally, something worked, or someone finally recognized good old Warney, and I was made to sign an indemnity bond to make sure that he reported back to the airport by midnight, only to be flown back to Australia.

On seeing a sheepish Warne at the immigration office, as he was being escorted out, I asked him, 'How the fuck did you get on the aircraft without a visa?' He shrugged and said, 'Nobody asked me for one; they were too busy taking photographs or autographs.' That was Shane Warne for you—not a care in the world; always joking and laughing. On the set, he was always amazing and on point; he was just a natural. There was no way we could even be angry with him. We scrambled to reach the domestic airport by late afternoon to shoot the second half of the film and found, much to our dismay, that the plane we hired came without a pilot!

We had given a crew and talent list to the security people days ahead, presuming that if we hired the plane, a bloody pilot should accompany it. It was too late to add a new person to our crew list as the airport security was justifiably anal about it. Finally, I had to dress up as a sardar in uniform and act as the pilot myself. And so, as it is with most shoots, somehow, Murphy always lurks in the darkest corners of sets, and it takes great resourcefulness and adaptability to actually stick to the schedule without running into another shift. I did manage to get Shane Warne back to the airport in time and saw him off for the last time. He had a cheeky smile and a jaunty wave as he was hustled off at immigration. We miss you, Warney. They don't make people like him in twos.

56

'Mera Number Kab Ayega?'

One fine day in JWT Delhi, Anuja Chauhan came up with a quirky, amazing line that is echoed by every loser in the world, 'Mera number kab ayega?' for a Pepsi promo. The line was a winner. We were excited about doing the thirty-second version and then the quickfire fifteen-second ones. The basic script of the film was the story of a prime loser for whom you feel bad. The loser, on the other hand, lived in a state of perpetual hope all his life, never giving up in the hope that ek din uska number zaroor ayega.

We immediately cast Cyrus Broacha—not only was he a very good actor, but he also didn't look like a typical hero-type model. He grew on you gradually. Now, where were we going to get a five-year-old, ten year-old and sixteen-year-old Cyrus lookalike? Namumkin (not even in Dadar Parsi Colony)! We hit upon this fantastic idea of putting a curly haired wig on Cyrus. And because his hair was so dominant in the frame, we could cast any five-year-old, ten-year-old and sixteen-year-old, put them in similar wigs and get away with it. And get away we did!

Cyrus was brilliant! With his plaintive look and appeal of 'Mera number kab ayega?' until, in one commercial, even god feels bad for him and reassures him. The voice of god tells him, 'Tera number ayega, beta, ayega.' The campaign took off to such high visibility that the line and Cyrus became instant stars. We even got actual people reassuring him: 'Cyrus, don't worry, tera number ayega, zaroor ayega.' Eventually, the campaign captured so many hearts and minds that it started vampiring the main campaign for Pepsi, which at that time was 'Yeh hi hai right choice, baby. Aha!'

So, with a heavy heart, Vibha and the team actually had to can it! Ahaa!

In the thick of the ongoing shoot for 'chhota' Pepsi with Cyrus, his *MTV Bakra* team sidled up to me and asked if I would help do a reverse 'Bakra' on Cyrus himself. They had rigged his vanity van with hidden cameras and sound mics. I was tickled pink by the idea, as Cyrus had pranked a series of Bombay's best and worst on camera for MTV. I coopted my stunt director, Alan Amin, and figured out a plan of action.

I was all wired up and went to Cyrus's vanity during our lunch break, where he was chilling. We were in deep conversation when the door flew open, and a slightly 'drunk' and irate stunt assistant, Geeru, staggered in and started berating me about some payment he hadn't got. I tried to placate him, but to no avail. By this time, Cyrus got involved, and told Geeru to stop cursing and get out of his van. Geeru got even louder and more vituperative, so I slapped him. Phataak!

At this point, Geeru pulled out a gun. On seeing the gun, Cyrus naturally ducked for cover under the table. And then, Geeru fired a shot at me. I grabbed my chest and doubled over, frantically searching for the button to explode the condom full of false blood strapped to my chest. The damn thing was in my pocket and I was fumbling for it. Finally, I found it and the blood exploded out, drenching my jacket (ten seconds after the shot).

Geeru, in the meantime, hurling vitriol and waving the pistol, leapt out of the van in the middle of a crowd of the crew and agency having a leisurely meal. Disturbed by the gunshot and a wild-eyed Geeru running amok, firing blanks in the air, there was pandemonium all around. People were scattering in all directions, some falling over in their haste. One brave model type was actually trying to catch Geeru. Meanwhile, I was writhing on the floor and beseeching Cyrus for help, but he was frozen with fear under the table. He scrambled out, relieved that he hadn't been shot too, looked around wildly, and said, 'He's gone!' He jumped out of the van and took the patli gali, while I called after the bugger, 'Cyrus, you bakra, I have been shot! Do you mind helping me?'

This entire mayhem was captured with the hidden cameras placed all around. And when the crew finally emerged, laughing their hearts out, Cyrus realized he had been set up. Boy, he was not amused! The show went on air and Cyrus sulked for a whole week. I must admit, though, Geeru deserved an Oscar for his sterling performance that afternoon.

This is what happened from Cyrus's point of view as the Bakraa!

This ridiculously stupid show caught on very quickly, but the crew had even more fun making it than the viewing audience. However, there was a slight twist, on every shooting day, we'd end with a 'Bakra' on one of our own. We used to call this the 'reverse' Bakra. Now this felt like being in the Government of Maharashtra, as in you have to constantly watch your back. I have to give this background, before we plunge into the gag Prahlad pulled off on me, which I'd like to term by its short name, 'Chota Pepsi Reverse Bakra, Lunch Time Gag Cyrus Ke Upar'.

We were shooting for Chota Pepsi, early morning in the suburbs. I mean like 'early' morning, I was on set at 7 a.m. This is important because my malicious crew led by two of my favorites, Sajeeth and P.M. Satish, had come to rig up the trailer at 4 a.m. and were out by 6.30 a.m., so that I wouldn't suspect a thing. These guys, who were rarely on time for 9 a.m. shifts, had no problem coming in at 4 a.m., such was their love for me.

If I remember, I was dressed up as Elvis, a common practice in ad films in those days, and during the lunch break, Prahlad invited me to eat with him in his trailer. So far so good.

All was just going fine, when 'Geeru', the stunt assistant, knocked on the trailer door. I opened it and immediately smelled alcohol, which was odd. Prahlad wouldn't pay for a Chota Pepsi, forget a chota peg on the set. Then it was all Geeru. He put on a part Devdas, part Tony Montana show. At first I couldn't believe it, to be frank. After asking Prahlad for money owed to him, (extremely believable), he then spoke about his sick son and raised his voice, and in the final act was spewing gaalis. Listen, on Prahlad's set, only Prahlad raised his voice or used gaalis. I tried to reason with Geeru by saying 'Tameez se baat karo', I didn't want him to get blacklisted.

At that time the 5 families ruled ad films. The Kakars were one of them. So, for Geeru's sake, I tried to tone it all down. Prahlad played his part magnificently. He was dismissive, rude and demeaning to Geeru. At this point, Geeru pulled out a gun. P.K. on one side Geeru on the other, like Djokovic vs Alcaraz with me as the 'net' in the middle. When Geeru pointed the gun wildly, I decided not to take a bullet for Prahlad.

I mean, I was fond of him, but a bullet? Then Geeru shoots, Prahlad goes down like the Titanic. I see my world coming to an end. Keep in mind, I'm still dressed as Elvis. Geeru then points the gun at me, and I beg him for my life. Again, I loved Pepsi, they paid well, but a bullet? Geeru then exits like a Third World Al Paccino, spewing threats and abuses. I think Prahlad is dead, should I take off his Rolex? No, now was not the time.

The funny thing is back at MTV, they laughed at me for running from Geeru when he pointed the gun. But, tell me, if someone points a gun at you after shooting at somebody else, what is the correct reaction?

Anyway, I had to take it on the chin, and still have to whenever it's replayed. And for 5 mins, 20 years ago, Geeru was the most popular man on MTV.

57

Auld Lang Syne

We all knew it would happen some day, but when it did, we were left feeling very distraught and unhappy. Vibha Rishi had been promoted to the Pepsi New York office and we bid her bon voyage with a heavy heart. She had been a huge support, and stood behind HTA's creative team and our production house like a rock. She had so much faith in us that she even pushed me to represent Pepsi at national-level debates and address controversies on news channels. An era had passed. Then, Anuja left HTA to pursue writing—she made a very successful second career of writing quirky bestsellers.

That left the suits totally exposed to the new team at Pepsi and they were in a tizzy—running around like bats straight out of hell, covering their arses with multiple folds of cheap toilet paper in case of a breakthrough when the shit hit the fan! The new honcho at Pepsi was a proper corporate type, who followed the book to the letter and took the pants off the servicing team, who had had it very easy so far, as the creative team had their backs.

Now, with a brand-new creative team of newbies and a brand-new client who wanted everything in writing and by the book—no casual behaviour was tolerated—Pepsi swiftly lost its mojo and spontaneity.

The suits took charge and started following briefs to the T. There were no sudden flights of fancy and imagination, no adding or subtracting from a thoroughly researched script, but they wanted the humour to be there. After all, irreverent humour was Pepsi's DNA.

The problem was that the jokes soon became forced and the humour fell flat, because they were trying too hard to be funny simply for the sake of it. In life, there are people who can laugh at themselves and do, and then there are people who take themselves very, very seriously and can't bear the idea of being laughed at—they always have to laugh at someone else. That's exactly what happened to a hapless Pepsi India, who started taking themselves very seriously, especially the fact that for the first time in their history, they were the number-one cola brand in any country.

Pepsi's whole attitude to Coke has always been that of an underdog, and, therefore, they could cock a snook at the monolithic Coke and get away with it internationally. Coke, of course, chose to studiously ignore the pipsqueak Pepsi, but in India, Pepsi had become number one. For the new team, this was a big deal, and, unfortunately, they decided to behave like number one and lost the plot. We realized this when HTA summoned me to Delhi to brief me for a small 7UP promo featuring Mallika Sherawat, who had become infamous overnight for her kissing scenes in movies. Incidentally, she was a good friend, as we had helped her at the beginning of her career. No, I didn't give her kissing lessons or vice versa!

On arriving at HTA, Delhi, I was surprised to see a rather sombre team, which was unusual because they were usually an ebullient lot. I thought maybe they were having a bad hair day. I was led into the conference room full of suits and I started looking for a familiar creative face. Nada! All the suits were very serious as they briefed me on a promo script for 7UP where Mallika is lying on a bed, being fussed over by her handmaidens, when she declares she is bored. In pops Fido Dido, the animated mascot of 7UP, and asks her what she wants. To this, Mallika replies, 'I wanna be cool! I wanna be curvy and I wanna be close to all my fans.' Fido says, 'No problem.' He points at her and zap! She becomes a curvy 7UP bottle. End of the commercial.

I agreed to do it, as it seemed quirky and simple enough to be shot from one angle. We just needed to embellish her boudoir. I suggested that she should be on a kind of love couch, à la Cleopatra, and they went into a tizzy, referring to a kind of corporate checklist and not a script or storyboard. After a serious huddle, they came up for air and said no Cleopatra, stick to the boudoir. I asked what her posture was supposed to be—lying, sitting or in the lotus position? Another flurry and they came up with a blank. Now, they finally dropped the egg in my lap and said, 'Pepsi wants to storyboard it and test it. Whatever you want to do, put it in the storyboard!'

Thunderous silence.

'Have you guys gone mad?' I asked politely. 'We have not done a storyboard in my fifteen years of working for Pepsi. Why now and why do we have to make one for such a simple execution? One shot at one angle, with a close-up.' All I wanted to do was discuss the details with the client and get on with it. When I said as much, all hell broke loose. 'Meet the client? Without a storyboard? No chance,' I was told. I was totally taken aback by the fear generated by the suits and their reluctance to let me discuss the script with the client, which we did all the time with Anuja and Vibha.

I realized they were all in a blue funk and there was no sign of the creative team. I refused to do a storyboard. A doomsday pall hung over the room. Some of the suits I knew begged and pleaded with me to just once, just once, do a simple storyboard, and then all would be okay. As far as I was concerned, all was okay, god was in heaven and it was cool. I just couldn't figure out why everybody was shitting bricks and refusing to let me meet the client.

Obviously, the boss had opened a chhattri up in the agency's wazoo! Everybody was running around with their knickers in a twist. To me, the question was, why? We had done a great job for Pepsi so far; if nothing else, we were all equal stakeholders in the future of the brand. The new team at Pepsi thought otherwise and had put the fear of god into the suits. The good old times were over! No more fun and games; we had to be deadly serious about the work and the brand. Everything had to be checked and double-checked before it was presented to the new Pepsi team, and all the creatives had to be tested and researched before execution.

There was now a protocol in place: no casual behaviour or deviating from the pecking order. Only the suits would meet with the clients, et cetera, et cetera. I was flabbergasted that the whole style of functioning had changed overnight. Pepsi had become a protocol-driven corporate like any other, and everything had become uptight and formal. Good grief! No wonder Anuja had quit the leaky and slowly sinking boat! In the middle of this circus, I had a brainwave and told them with a very straight face that I would do the storyboard.

There was palpable relief and joy at the announcement. I flew back to Bombay with a sense of great foreboding. I called the team and briefed them about the storyboard; we would not do it in drawings, but actually shoot the whole thing on a low-end handycam. I would be playing Mallika Sherawat and needed to be kitted out in a grass skirt and a humongous bra, size 44D. We were to shoot it in my drawing room, on my sofa. And my four-year-old son Anhjin would play Fido Dido.

We would have to pick the ugliest guys in the office to play the handmaidens and they would need one of those big, feathered fans on a pole to fan me like I was some holy book. I thought, what the hell? If we had to do the storyboard, we should at least have some fun in the process and teach our uptight client a small lesson on how to laugh at yourself. We shot and edited the storyboard, replacing my voice with a sexy female version.

The opening of the film had me talking to myself in a hand mirror that covered my face and only the voice could be heard. Later, I whipped away the mirror, revealing my hairy mug in all its glory. It was one of the most obscene pieces of film I have ever seen. Just imagine—me, slightly overweight, with my hairy torso, a large, hairy belly protruding over a grass skirt, with two hairy legs sticking out in repose, trying to be Cleopatra (more like Kilo-phattara). A bunch of equally ugly guys, also bare-bodied, just wearing grass skirts, waving a feathered fan above a corpulent Kilo-phattara, eating grapes. And a devilishly cute four-year-old Fido Dido with a lisp completed the entire tableau. It was gross and hilarious, if you took it in the right spirit.

I arrived in Delhi with the DVD tucked firmly in my coat pocket and refused to show it to the agency suits. I said that since the client wanted a storyboard, everybody could watch it together. This dismayed them no end, as they wouldn't know what they were getting and, therefore, there was no way to cover their collective arses. I also told them that the storyboard was a complete scratch film on videotape, and that they would need to make arrangements for a screen and video player to show the exercise to the client. All this was done with reluctant haste for they knew my reputation for springing completely unexpected surprises, both pleasant and unpleasant.

We trooped off to Pepsi in a small cavalcade, and set up the projector and DVD player in their conference room. I insisted on no rehearsals as it was only one thirty-second promo repeated three times. Everybody fiddled around nervously for Her Ladyship to arrive. She swept in, making no eye contact with anybody, raising the tension in the room palpably. 'Is she in a good mood, or is she in a bad mood? She loves me, she loves me not.' And so it went, until she looked at me and said, 'Alright, what have we got?'

I explained that we had done a storyboard for her, on video, more or less following the narrative and dialogue of the film. And we ran the DVD. As the first viewing, with all three repeats, came to an end, there was dead silence, except for a choking sound from one senior suit and a delighted giggle from a newbie trainee at the back of the room, which was instantly cut off as many horrified eyes swivelled in his direction and nailed him to his cross. I had eyes only for the client and watched in glee as her jaw dropped open, and remained so, for the duration of the entire screening. I was dying to close it with a gentle finger under her jaw, just in case a fly crawled in. In the horrified silence in the room, the client recovered first and spoke in a pseudo-jovial voice, 'Haha, that was a Prahlad joke, I presume.'

She then turned to me and said, 'Go ahead and make the film.' And then she looked towards the bunch of distressed suits and said, 'Follow me.' She then flounced out. I believe she took their pants, chaddis and the works off. But she let me make the film the way I wanted to, pretty much like the storyboard—with the real Mallika, of course! The film was a huge success and the launch of the curvy bottle was awesome.

But we never worked with Pepsi again. That was the last film we made for them.

Just goes to show that very few people in advertising and marketing learn that if you want the world to laugh with you, then you have to first learn to laugh at yourself. And so, over the next few years, followed the partial demise of a brand that had become 'iconic' because of its advertising in the following years, with campaigns like 'Oye Bubbly' and 'Yeh hai youngistan meri jaan' and so on. I can't even recall the rest. The brand slipped to number three behind Coke and the home-grown Thums Up.

Que sera sera.

58

Your Guru Finds You

And so it was with me! In the early 2000s, one bright Sunday morning, I was happily sitting on my favourite sofa, reading the *Sunday Times* with my cuppa chai, when the doorbell rang. One of my sons opened the door to reveal a stocky gent with a shaved head in orange robes. He introduced himself as Swami 'Udyavar' from Isha and asked for me by name. Now, I am used to irate neighbours, occasional clients and sometimes cops with warrants showing up unexpectedly, but definitely not a sadhu type. I arched an enquiring eyebrow and settled him in with a glass of water.

Then, I waited with bated breath for him to state the purpose of his visit. He looked around and in a matter-of-fact way said that Sadhguru had invited me to the Isha ashram for a five-day 'Inner Engineering' yoga workshop. I politely asked him, 'Who is Sadhguru? And why would he want me?' I was the last person that any ashram would want anywhere near them! He patiently repeated that Sadhguru had followed my work on TV and my sporadic 'writings', and thought I needed to go to the ashram. I was totally foxed. I felt that my life was near perfect—why would I need to go to a yoga ashram?

Okay, so I was diabetic, had had a bypass surgery, my blood pressure was erratic, my diet was out of control, but I didn't drink alcohol or smoke cigarettes. I didn't see a problem; whereas, obviously, Sadhguru did. Mitali then piped up and said, 'Maybe he is the same über-cool guru I was talking to you about? He has a great sense of humour and doesn't talk mumbo-jumbo about ancient texts and practices, but makes everything a relevant science in our day-to-day lives.' She was quite keen that I meet him. 'He is your kind of guru,' she added. I was still very reluctant as I couldn't imagine myself sitting cross-legged and chanting 'Aum' for five days straight, looking for an out-of-body experience. In any case, I couldn't sit cross-legged because of an old knee injury that prevented me from doing so.

With glee, I told the swami that I couldn't sit cross-legged and, therefore, was unfit for the ashram. He countered by saying I could do the practice sitting on a chair. Checkmate. Finally, I threw him a curveball and totally innocently asked, 'Are there lots of pretty sanyasins at the ashram?' He looked at me completely nonplussed, then nodded his head sagely and said, 'Yes, there are.' Very sceptically, I decided to go to the Isha Foundation for their 'Inner Engineering' yoga course, which was to be conducted by Sadhguru himself. Since we were all hand-picked media invitees, the course was made really 'special'. Not the practices themselves, which were distilled and proven in their efficacy, but the resplendent evenings, the music performances of the 'Sounds of Isha' and the delicious satvik food, among other things.

My first experience of the ashram was actually what determined my lasting relationship with Isha and Sadhguru. As I entered the gate and passed the Shiva temple, Dhyanalinga, I could feel a palpable energy that seemed to envelop the entire space. It was subtle, intangible, but permeated the space and the people who were thronging the temple for meditation. We were taken to our accommodation, which was clean, comfortable and spartan. I noticed that it had a very nice, large toilet (that's important!) and a rain shower. We had an hour to get our act together before meeting all the other chosen ones over a quick snack. Most were writers and creative people.

Our first session was all about simple yoga asanas, breathing and the awareness of it. The five days soon passed by in a blur. All throughout, I was a backbencher. Our first encounter with Sadhguru was quite impactful; he looked and behaved like a spiritual guru, which he is, but spoke like a modern visionary with a wicked sense of humour—irreverent as hell. He resonated with me immediately and I decided that I was free to be my own person in the ashram, because Sadhguru was. I had a blast, I laughed, I played pranks on other participants, was borderline inappropriate, but I diligently attended every session and learned my yoga practices.

We got up at 5 a.m. to the beating of drums and the melodious strains of a flute—quite a pleasant alarm. I walked around the ashram, met many swamis and maa yoginis (some of them very good-looking, as promised), and was amazed by the attention to detail and aesthetics of everything. I had spent all my waking hours, trying to explain to my interns and assistant directors that the god is in the details, and never quite succeeded 100 per cent in instilling it in them. But here I was, in an environment where, wherever there was human intervention, it was seamless, highly detailed to match its surroundings and as close to nature as humanly possible.

I started noticing little details in the most unlikely places. For instance, in the place where we stayed, there was a rainwater drain at the gate, which ran into a round water collection spot. The drain was covered by a stone slab, but the round culvert was exposed at one end. It was uneven—in an oval shape, with lots of irregular borders. Someone had thought to put a grille on it, in case somebody might inadvertently step on it and hurt themselves. The grille had been made to fit every contour of the drain perfectly, without it wobbling. Someone had taken the trouble to customize the grille with great effort, so it wouldn't stick out and spoil the symmetry of the surroundings. It was a one-off, as one size doesn't fit all. I was speechless when I spotted it.

We were soon all highly invigorated and energized, almost as if we had absorbed the energy of the Dhyanalinga, despite the crack-of-dawn drumming and flute alarm. I even got used to the vegetarian food (me being a total meat eater). I used to joke with the volunteers and sanyasi maas that every time I ate a pure vegetarian meal, I would have to take a snan, and they would look at me and ask, 'Why?' I would tell them that it was dharam-bhrasht (ungodly) for me to eat pure vegetarian food, and I would have to purify myself by bathing as I was a pure non-vegetarian. It takes two to tango.

As a conclusion to the five amazing days spent with Sadhguru, in our last gathering, he asked each of us what thoughts and memories we would carry back with us, and whether we would continue our practices. Of course, everybody very enthusiastically swore to continue the practices we had learned. When it was my turn to speak, I mentioned the attention to detail and the fact that nobody in the ashram was paid to be there; they were all volunteers. I also told him how I had struggled all my professional life in trying to impart the fact that the god is in the details—with partial success—whereas, at Isha, it was like a symphony, and it had truly blown me away. He laughed at my frustration and said, 'Remember, your interns work for you for money, whereas my volunteers work for me out of love.'

I will never forget that.

Yoga Marga

Six months after returning from Isha, I realized that I had been burning the candle at both ends. Despite my bypass surgery, after which people tend to slow down, I had, on the contrary, picked up speed. I was working and travelling at breakneck speed for multiple projects, which included restaurants, my diving school in Lakshadweep, making ad films and writing feature film scripts. I was also giving talks at various B-schools and colleges.

I realized I needed to go somewhere to detox and I thought what better place than the ashram, since it had a full rejuvenation setup following three medical disciplines: Ayurveda, Siddha and allopathy. Every candidate, depending on their comorbidities, would submit various tests and reports. They would then be examined by a doctor from each discipline, and each person would go through the diagnosis of the traditional disciplines of Nadi Pariksha (Ayurvedic pulse reading) and the Siddha procedure. All three doctors would then sit and exchange notes to determine the treatment to be given to each individual.

The course was called 'Yoga Marga' and included the traditional Ayurvedic procedure of Pancha Karma. The whole thing lasted twenty-one days with rigorous treatments, dosha-related diets and meditation. I decided to opt for Yoga Marga and was lucky to get a place, as these courses are always chock-a-block. I decided to take a small break and return to Isha, and the yoginis, of course. Little did I know that the group of twenty-five people was divided into comorbidity groups, like diabetes, arthritis, and other ailments of the lung, skin and so forth.

Three of us were acutely diabetic and were put in one group from the second day onwards. We were each plied with a glass of bitter karela juice on an empty stomach, which gave us all loose motions till the afternoon, after which it let up a bit. As there were only two dedicated toilets in the centre, and the need to purge often and frequently was enormous, we had to guard one toilet exclusively for the 'loosey brothers', as we called ourselves—much like a rock band.

We guarded the toilet fiercely till evening, as one never knew when the urge would strike and whom it would strike. We fully believed in the ancient proverb 'When you gotta go, you gotta go'. We became quite notorious, as we had lost all our inhibitions quite early on, and announced to all and sundry when we had to go, we just had to go, come hell or high water and that one toilet was reserved only for us.

There were two treatments a day—massages and frequent bitter kashayams at regular intervals. Call time was 5 a.m. with the now familiar drums and flutes. The day would start with a guru pooja and proceed with talks, Sadhguru videos and Shunya meditation in between massages with medicated hot oils and lean, muscular masseurs, pummelling our soft city bodies into shape. And then, the yoga teacher would stretch and bend them at will.

The day's regimen would leave us drop-dead knackered, and we would stagger back to our digs and sometimes crash with all our clothes on. Only I had a little respite—Sadhguru had recommended that I spend forty-five minutes to an hour in the Dhyanalinga temple every day, to avail of its curative powers. Since that time was a part of my treatment, even though he was in Kailash, Sadhguru used to keep a tab on me every time he had network, because he knew of my penchant for goofing off on a whim. So, I was pretty heavily monitored.

My slightly irreverent behaviour, however, didn't change and many an overzealous participant complained that the loosey brothers' behaviour was very inappropriate for the ashram. When we were told to tone down our laughing and merrymaking, I was very amused. On one occasion, when we were having a group discussion, we were told what had happened when another overzealous guest had asked Sadhguru on one of his darshans what Prahlad Kakar was doing in the ashram, as he didn't look like an ashram type at all. Sadhguru called the person up to him and, sotto voce, but in a way that everybody could still hear, said, 'You see, Mr Kakar is a madman and has travelled all over looking for someone as mad or madder than him. After a long search, he found him in the ashram'—dramatic pause—'me!' Sadhguru burst out laughing and that put an end to all complaints of inappropriate behaviour.

The course was tough, the regimen even tougher and our swamis unrelenting. Maa Ujwala, who was in charge of the rejuvenation centre, was a hunterwali, and very strict about the timetable and treatments. All in all, I survived ... Barely. On the last few days of the course, the participants, according to Isha tradition, have to put up a talent show (a skit, songs and/or dances). We could even make fun of the staff and teachers. Us loosey brothers three, of course, had a song worked out about our loosey adventures. It was totally inappropriate, but hilarious. Then there would be a big feast, including some forbidden fried foods.

I also wrote a skit loosely based on the Mahabharata about the run-up to Draupadi's vastraharan (celestial stripping) and the real reason for the war. It went something like this: Arjun wanders into Draupadi's swayamvaram when he hears about her beauty and, in order to win her over, he would have to perform a great feat of archery. He does so to everybody's delight, including Draupadi's, as he is a good-looking lad. The skit starts from here, as Arjun returns to his brothers' abode with a purdah-swaddled Draupadi in tow.

Now, he hasn't had the chance to check her out as she is covered in a purdah, so he brings her home and tries to tell his mother about his prize. Kunti is busy doing her Isha Yoga practices and dismisses him by saying, 'Share whatever you have won with your brothers.' The brothers are elated and so is Draupadi. They all gather around a truculent Arjun and demand to see the prize. At this stage, Draupadi halts them and says she will only show her face and her lily-white body if they can play 'Munni badnaam hui', which they promptly do, as it is their favourite song too. And it is to this song that Draupadi, for the first time, reveals herself. All the news about her beauty is true, in reverse; she turns out to be Prahlad Kakar in the flesh.

There is a scramble amongst the Pandavas to bail and bounce, and they start a game of volleyball to see who gets stuck with her. Finally, they decide to present her to their cousins, the Kauravas, as they were also vying for her in the swayamvaram. Krishna then steps forward and advises them that it's not going to be so simple: the Kauravas had been schooled and tutored by Shakuni mama and would smell a rat. So, they would have to make it worthwhile. The Pandavas challenge their cousins to a game of dice, which they agree to. The Kauravas win, hands down, and finally, the Pandavas put up their half of the kingdom to wager, which they lose.

Now what? Draupadi, in the meantime, is hanging about coyly, casting big googly eyes at the Kauravas. This does not escape Duryodhan, who wants her at any cost. The Pandavas challenge the Kauravas to one last hand. Shakuni mama asks them what they would bet next since they had lost everything. Arjun stands up and offers Draupadi. There's dead silence. Even the Kauravas are shocked. Shakuni mama is about to refuse when Duryodhan intervenes. 'Done,' says he, and they roll the dice.

The Pandavas lose yet again, and the Kauravas celebrate. Then they notice the Pandavas also celebrating, and a pall of suspicion falls on the proceedings. Duryodhan drags Draupadi to the centre and tries to disrobe her. She stops them in their tracks. 'Thehro!' She demands 'Munni badnam hui' once again. To the beats of the song, Draupadi disrobes and reveals her mug to the Kauravas, who are shocked at the misinformation. They try and give her back to the Pandavas, but no such luck—they refuse. Stalemate. Shakuni mama loudly pronounces, 'This is cheating.'

'What do you mean by cheating?' ask the Pandavas. 'That's an insult; a bet is a bet.'

'War!' says Duryodhan.

'War!' echo the Pandavas.

And thus, the Mahabharata started over Draupadi.

We pulled off this skit against all odds, and had the swamis rolling in the aisles, laughing. It was a milestone of inappropriateness in the ashram and has not been beaten to date. To top it all, I decided to reward all the participants of Yoga Marga on the last day of looseys (by that time, we had got better control of our sphincters with hot oil, pummelling, bending, stretching, being put on a starvation diet, etc.) for having barely tolerated me. I ordered T-shirts from my Bombay office, which had arrived the previous day. On graduation day, I gave everybody, including the mentors and swamis, T-shirts with the legend, 'I Survived Yoga Marga'.

59

The Clan

Looking back at my journey, I realize that the centre of it all was Genesis, and the amazing people we trained and set loose into an unsuspecting world. Genesis came about when three of us slaves from Shyam Benegal's team decided to start an ad film production house of our own—Mandeep Kakkar, Ravi Uppoor and myself. The fourth member of the founder's group was Smita Patil, who was our great friend and supporter. As mentioned earlier, Smita gave us the name 'Genesis'.

All three of us hauled out our wallets and put up Rs 250 each to print the letterheads. We never had visiting cards since all of us also had 'real' jobs. Our address was wherever we were at any given moment—most of the time in a coffee shop. We got our first office after I was sacked from Radeus Advertising for moonlighting at Genesis. I had been summoned to K. Kurien's office and asked to choose between working for the organization and working for myself. My stomach lurched and I felt a little giddy; I desperately wanted to say 'Both', but managed to croak 'Myself'. And so, the die was cast. We cut the umbilical cord, and the adventure began. It was huge and is one of the scariest decisions I have ever made in life, including marriage.

So, what is Genesis? A production house? A correctional institute for waifs and strays? It is, among other things, a café, a borstal, a state-of-the-art kitchen, a training school for future disrupters, a scuba diving school, an experiment in life, a training ground for entrepreneurs and risk takers, a breeding ground for flights of imagination and fantasy, where the office functioned 24/7 and was the only place on the planet where the debt collector was a Doberman Pinscher called Dumbell, and the waiting room for all the smokers and faltus was the staircase outside the office. It was all this and more.

All out of a 400-square-foot office, where one-third of the space was a kitchen and the first meeting of the day was to decide what we wanted to eat for lunch. We also served the best chicken soup for the soul, a Shankar speciality (Shankar was our resident office boy, whom we had promoted to head chef at the office). Other than making some very interesting and unique ad films, Genesis will always be known for the unique people who came out of our portals—each one exceptional in their originality and personality. We are a clan.

All ex-Genesis survivors have a small tattoo on their left bum cheek that reads 'A Quality Product of Genesis', because each member of the clan has survived at least two years of extreme prejudice by Prahlad Kakar, and that's a mark of resilience, courage and sheer dogged tenacity. That's why I have always said that there is the Genesis clan and then there are the others, and I would only trust my life in the hands of the clan.

I have talked about several members of the clan in the book, but let me write about them in detail now.

'Idunknow'

Among our first full-time employees was Uttam Sirur. Uttam was, and still is, a slightly reticent man with a brilliant but deviant mind that is perfect for advertising, but needed careful handling as he was relatively antisocial and laconic in his speech. His preferred reply to most questions was 'I don't know' said as one word: 'Idunknow.' This was especially true when answering the phone. He used to doodle very detailed, complex drawings—a bit dark for my taste, but interesting nonetheless—and I knew that lurking behind that very standoffish exterior was an untapped mind. He spent about two years with us and eventually joined Trikaya as a copywriter. He wrote that amazing tagline for Sweetex: 'No squeeze, no wheeze, no sugar in my coffee, please.'

Jenny Joins Genesis

As Genesis grew, so did the number of interns. And thanks to Mandeep's herculean efforts, we bought office space on the sixth floor of the Everest building in Tardeo, above our guru and mentor Shyam Benegal's second-floor office in the same building. Kailash and Jit's office was on the ground floor. One day, as I entered the office, I fleetingly glimpsed a short, young girl sitting on the steps outside, and promptly forgot all about her as we were in the middle of multiple productions and there was no time for anything else.

The next day, she was on the staircase again, as if she hadn't moved since the previous day. On the fifth day, when there was a lull in the madness, one of the office boys came to me and said that there was a girl to see me, and she had been waiting for five days. I had her sent in and made her as comfortable as possible. In those days, only the accounts team had a cabin and everyone else sat on the long desk we had—there weren't enough chairs, but we had five landlines, all ringing at the same time. So, I got her the rare chair, sat her down and asked her what she wanted.

She was only about five feet tall, with a clear, innocent young face. I thought she must be in school. She looked straight at me and said she had come to join me and Genesis. I was about to tell her to finish school and then come back when she said that she was working as a copywriter in an agency, and had resigned to come and work with us as she wanted to make films. I was a bit shocked that someone had actually resigned from their job before getting an offer to join us. I told her to look around—we were bursting at the seams and there was no place for anybody else. She just shrugged, smiled and said, 'I will wait till there is a vacancy.' Then she went right back and sat on the stairs again.

I was a bit resentful that she was holding me to ransom, in a sweet, non-aggressive way. So, I let her sit, to see who would blink first. By day ten, I just couldn't handle it. I was upset, distracted and couldn't focus on my work. The girl just sat outside the door on the steps—not reading, not asking us of anything, just smiling and sitting. She didn't even use the office loo! Finally, I got fed up and called her in to give her a job. Her name was Jenny Pinto, and she is as stubborn and tenacious as ever—a dynamite in a small package. She changed the office, organized it, brought some order into the franticness of our work and ordered new chairs. She wrote well, learned quickly, and was really hungry, hugely independent and fearless.

After her first year, which flew by, I decided to test her mettle with a tough job. I called her and briefed her about the location for the Aristocrat luggage film to be shot in the desert of Rajasthan. I wanted a palace that had a queen's room, a blue room, and a red-and-gold room to match the colours of the luggage. I gave her a train ticket to Jaipur along with some money and sent her off alone, with the instruction, 'Don't come back without the location photographs and if you need more money, send us a telegram.' She came back after a month, with sand in her hair, looking dishevelled but triumphant. Throwing some colour photographs on my desk, she told me that the location was a palace in Bikaner and that she would be back after a bath. She left for the day and was in the thick of things the very next day—pitching in with the casting, costumes, and logistics of getting a crew and cast of fifty people to Bikaner.

That was Jenny Pinto, who spent four years doing hard labour at Genesis. She also introduced me to her amazing mother—one of the finest home cooks I have ever known and whom I persuaded to partner with me to start the Prithvi Café, with the full support of Jennifer and Shashi Kapoor. Jenny Pinto finally outgrew Genesis and left to start her own production house, and she did exceptionally well in a highly competitive advertising film business. I do believe that she will excel at whatever she chooses to do; she's the real deal.

Fonky

Then there was Joel Fonseca, also known as Joel da or Fonky. Joel came to us as a peon through an ill-fated courier service called Docu-Del (Mitali appropriately renamed it Docu-Delay for obvious reasons). It folded within four months, leaving us with a much-inebriated Joel, who refused to leave. Every morning, he would arrive at 8.30 a.m. sharp and after collecting his pauwa of local snake juice from the corner speakeasy (an auntie's joint), he would consume it on the way to the office. He would then find himself a khopcha and pass out. The rest of the office would toodle in at around 10 a.m. and find no Joel. You could smell him, but you couldn't see him. His favourite cubbyhole was behind the editing machine in the editing room, which was all of eight feet by eight feet. To be able to curl up behind the Steinbeck machine (flatbed editor) was quite a feat.

One day, Mitali and Sophie—both interns at the time—decided that they couldn't bear the smell of stale alcohol mixed with sweat any more, and decided to take Joel in hand. They realized that he actually had nothing to do and lacked self-belief, as Docu-Del had closed shop. They also found out that Joel's family business was making hooch in the marshes of Sahar, and he had made the cardinal error of becoming the main taster of his house product and got hooked. They both went and met Joel's wife, Gemma, who was also at her wits' end and became an immediate co-conspirator.

The girls then briefed a slightly groggy Joel about being in charge of the production peti—a tin trunk that had anything that might be needed on a shoot (from a safety pin to a giant canopy). They made sure that he knew everything that went into it, to keep it topped up at all times, under the threat of Prahlad Kakar's wrath if it wasn't. Slowly, over a period of time, Joel went through a significant transformation— from resentment to a sense of belonging, and then to pride and possessiveness over his work. Mitali and Sophie got regular reports from Gemma about the change, and how he would sit in front of the TV at home, with the family, and show off the commercials that we had shot with an element of pride, after successfully weaning himself off the juice.

I saw the beginnings of hunger in Joel after a few months and started involving him in our packshot shoots. Genesis was the first production house to keep a separate day aside for packshots and didn't club them with the main shoot with the talent. We realized that since the product was the hero of the film, it needed careful design and movement to end the commercial on a high note. Joel became a very keen participant in that process, and started contributing and innovating according to my brief.

Soon, he owned the space, and was very gung-ho about improving on the brief and adding enormous value to the process. He threw himself into the dynamics of shaping liquids, and creating perfect models of soaps and gels out of acrylic and other materials. It was quite amazing how he would stay up the whole night figuring out how to get something to work on camera. Remember, in the 1980s, we had no special effects.

Joel became my man Friday for all shoots, in and out of the country, and, wherever he went, he always carted the production peti along with him—it was his magic box! He came with us for shoots to Vietnam, the Philippines, Myanmar, Thailand, Russia, Romania, and South Africa, amongst other countries. Over time, he started taking more initiative, until he came to be known as the 'Packshot Man'. We allowed him to freelance for other production houses as well, since he was so proficient at his work.

By the 1990s he also bought an industrial gala and converted it into his own packshot studio. As he grew in confidence and stature, he never forgot his roots or where he came from. He became a mother hen for all our interns and shielded them from the brunt of my wrath whenever there was a foul-up on the set, by taking responsibility and taking my reaction on the chin! For that, many generations of filmmakers will be eternally grateful.

Joel and Gemma started their own company, Sparkle Productions, and never looked back. Today, they are among the most respected professionals in the ad-film space and Joel has now graduated from

Fonky to Joel da, the master. Both of his sons have inherited something from them: Silver is a crack, award-winning DOP after graduating from FTII and Goldwyn 'Goldie' has taken his father's mantle of creating gorgeous packshots to another level.

Life Comes Full Circle

Seema, who was the famous writer Ismat Chughtai's daughter and was a crack producer, initially worked at Lintas with the legendary photographer Gautam Rajadhyaksha. One fine day, she arrived at Genesis with her young son Ashish in tow and left him with us for his summer holidays. I don't know why parents—usually our friends— would dump their kids on us.

It was sometimes just for their holidays and, other times, it was forever. Ashish was a bright young boy of thirteen and immediately took over the office phones. The girls in the office loved him and he was spoilt rotten. So, he kept coming back during his breaks and practically grew up in the office. He had a hidden talent for acting and superb comic timing. Seema would also be in and out of our office a lot—so we considered her one of our own.

Seema also had a very keen eye for talent and good-looking young men. So, it came to pass that she found a struggling young photographer called Prashant Gupta, who used to hang around the Oberoi Hotel's swimming pool, trying to impress the Lufthansa air hostesses. He would claim that he could make them famous—quite an original line. He always had a Nikon camera around his neck, with no film in it. Seema found young Prashant and offered him a trial shoot for Lintas, and if he passed muster, some serious work thereafter.

Prashant was to report to her house in Churchgate at 10.30 a.m. on a Sunday morning. Now, Seema had a cat that lived under the settee and would occasionally shoot out of her hidey-hole to career around the room, ricocheting off the walls and furniture at great speed, before diving back under the settee. If one caught her blurring around the room from the corner of their eye, they believed that she existed. But most people missed the cat's trajectory completely and didn't believe that she was real at all. Nobody could have guessed that young Prashant was highly allergic to cats.

Prashant reached her house on the second floor of an old building and was let in by Habib Miya, the khansama of the house. After a while, Seema breezed in and started briefing Prashant on the job. Suddenly, the cat shot out from underneath and ricocheted around the room in a blur. Prashant grabbed his chest in a wheezing fit, his eyes suddenly rolled in his head and he started frothing at the mouth. Just as suddenly, he keeled over with a thud. Seema didn't know what hit him and tried her best to revive him, but no luck.

Habib Miya heard the thud and came rushing out of the kitchen. Seeing Prashant lying on the ground with his eyes rolled up, he felt his pulse and immediately said, 'Aapa, yeh toh mar gaya!' He sat on the floor with his head in his hands, rocking back and forth, keening. Seema snapped at him and asked what his problem was. To this, Habib Miya, still rocking backward and forward, replied that the cops would come and arrest him as he was the servant. They would take him to the thana and beat the shit out of him to get a confession. Seema told him to shut up and grab one of Prashant's legs while she grabbed the other (only a seasoned production person could think on their feet like that).

The two dragged the body out of the house, bumping his head in the process on the doorjamb, and left him outside the rickety lift. They then scuttled back into the house and watched through the keyhole to see if anybody would notice the body lying still on the landing. The lift stopped and the liftman peered out, and laconically commented, 'Piyela padela,' and carried on. Half an hour later, the dead body suddenly came to life and sat up, feeling the lump at the back of his head. Suddenly, he remembered that he had a 10.30 a.m. appointment with Seema and it was already 11.30—he was late. He got up and gathered himself, and rang the doorbell. Habib Miya, still scared shitless, went to the door, closely followed by Seema.

He opened the door and saw a dishevelled Prashant standing there, trying to figure out where the lump on the back of his head came from. On seeing the dead body standing before him, Habib Miya let forth a high-pitched shriek. This set off a chain reaction: Habib Miya shrieked, Seema shrieked, Prashant shrieked too. He then pushed his way into the house and apologized for being late. Seema went along with it in great relief, as if nothing had happened.

Prashant soon left Bombay for New York. He lived there and was last seen driving a taxi. If he ever reads this chapter, he will finally know the cause of the bump on his head and the lost hour that day. Seema went on to start her own production house with Mahesh Mathai, also a Genesis product, and eventually retired to Coonoor with Gautam Rajadhyaksha as her neighbour and both of them passed away peacefully a few years later—so life comes full circle. Ashish is now a producer–director and did a lot of films in Sri Lanka. Habib Miya went back to his village in Uttar Pradesh.

Lock, Stock and Barrel

We had gone to Delhi on a shoot for Hero Honda, at Bhatti Mines, with a young Salman Khan and his *doppelgänger*, when I took the bike for a spin. I skidded on a gravel patch and broke my arm, and was carted off to the hospital, put in a plaster and sent back to the shoot in great pain. The two young executives from the agency were Rakeysh Mehra and young Vikram Oberoi, I called them and gave them a detailed shot breakdown, and told them to go and finish the films. I added that Vikas, our cameraman, would help them. They were really startled by this responsibility, but had no choice—it was not to question why, it was but to do or die. They managed remarkably well and I was very impressed by young Rakeysh.

On the way back, he was given the responsibility to make sure that I caught my flight on time. I took a small diversion near Defence Colony to meet Feroze Gujral, who was then staying with her father-in-law, Satish Gujral. She was a favourite of mine. Time flew and I disregarded it as usual, much to the chagrin of young Rakeysh. I cut it really fine and finally, when I realized it was time to leave, I noticed Rakeysh was on a motorcycle, which was the fastest mode of transport in the traffic at that time. I leapt on to it behind him with my arm in a plaster and told him to go for it as we had exactly twenty-five minutes before the gate closed.

Rakeysh, in true fashion, stepped on the gas, and we flew through Delhi traffic with our hair standing on end and reached the airport, skidding in just in time. I looked back at him and said, 'You are wasting your time in Delhi. I want to see you in Bombay.' And one month, later, he arrived with his bistar and bori and worked for me, until Vikram Oberoi and he could start their own company called Lock, Stock and Barrel.

Surviving Genesis

Once Genesis started getting a reasonable amount of work, we became a little choosy and started picking the more difficult, slightly crazy scripts because that's how we were. And due to the workload and the schedules, we used to throw the interns into the deep end to see who would survive without having their hands held. The ones that did manage to come out on the other end were the salt of the earth.

I found that women performed better under stress than most men. One such survivor was Deepu Mudholkar. She was tough, detail-oriented and tenacious. She was always prepared with a Plan B in case Murphy made an appearance. She left us to get married to her childhood sweetheart, Shilpin, who ran a factory in Aurangabad. She moved there after four years of working with us and had her first child, Tara.

One morning, as she was getting Tara ready for playschool, she got a frantic call from their driver saying that the plane Shilpin was on had crashed. Deepu immediately went into overdrive—she packed enough food and water for her little one, bundled the maid into her car and drove to the airport. She could see a plume of smoke in a distant field beyond the airport. In the meantime, all the surviving passengers had been brought back to an ITC hotel for treatment and care.

A police contingent had rushed to the crash site first to try and rescue their officer, Additional Inspector General S.K. Ayenger, who had luckily survived. In the meantime, the passengers from the front of the plane had managed to scramble out and were carted off from the crash site. The more severely injured survivors were taken by the police to the local government hospital, which was totally unprepared for the calamity.

Deepu raced to the site in her car with the baby, maid and driver to look for Shilpin. There were bodies strewn around, with explosions and flames coming out of the fuselage, which was lying on its side in three pieces. There was no Shilpin in sight. Somebody told her that the survivors had been taken to an ITC hotel, so she reached there and met the duty manager, who was a friend, and looked for Shilpin with no luck.

As a last resort, she went to the hospital, to find the place in total disarray, with lots of people hanging around just out of curiosity, oblivious to the fact that the burned and wounded survivors needed to be isolated from infection. Deepu looked at all the rooms and beds full of the dying. The dead bodies lined the corridor with white sheets covering them and the barely living were being treated in front of a large audience.

Just as she was about to give up and start checking the corpses to find her husband, she glimpsed at what looked like Shilpin's shirt, half-burnt, on a body that had third-degree burns on the hands and face. She rushed to the bed, pushing people out of the way, and found her husband—burnt, but alive, barely. He was in great pain and was probably the only passenger to have escaped from the rear end of the plane, which was engulfed in flames. According to Shilpin, the rear wreckage was on its side, fire burning and the door above him was white-hot. He stood on the seat to reach up and push the door open with his hands—his skin sizzled on contact—while his shoes melted on his feet. He managed to pry the door open, getting third-degree burns on his hands. He stumbled out as a gust of flames fed by the oxygen of the open door burnt his face and neck. He had to roll on the ground to put out the fire on his flaming shirt.

Deepu took one look at his condition and realized that she had to get him to Bombay at any cost to save his life. She got hold of an STD landline (remember there were no cell phones then) and started making calls, first to charter a special flight the following morning and then to get the burns unit of Nanavati Hospital to organize an ambulance from the tarmac to the hospital and prepare to receive a critical patient.

She then took on the doctors of the government hospital, who were refusing to let him travel in his state. Deepu put her foot down. She single-handedly organized the entire operation of springing her badly wounded husband out of Aurangabad. At the last moment, Shilpin, who was just coming out of shock, refused to go by plane, as he had just come out of a traumatic situation involving one.

Deepu got him tranquillized and comatose, and supervised his journey to the plane by the only ambulance available—against the doctor's advice—got him to Bombay and admitted him into Nanavati Hospital. After all this, she took a long breath before she threw herself into nursing Shilpin back to health. The doctors at Nanavati told her that if she had not managed to get him to Bombay, he would have definitely lost his hands at least, if not his life.

People still ask her how she managed to coordinate and choreograph the multiple layers of overlapping situations single-handedly and still keep her cool in such a crisis. All she ever said was, 'My experience in Genesis prepared me to deal with anything that life can throw at me!' Once Shilpin was out of the woods, she called and thanked Mitali and me. Resourcefulness, tenacity and single-minded focus are qualities that you learn on the job while working in production and it holds you in good stead in any situation.

Good Morning, Bombay!

I inherited Shernaz from my wife, as she and Mitali attended Loreto in Darjeeling together. She was affectionately called Dinsh by her buddies and homies. Her prior experience of successfully running a restaurant in Darjeeling and working at a steel mill in England made her very resilient and resourceful. Her trial by fire was when she had to get me snow boots for a shoot involving an Inuit (eskimo) in the middle of the North Pole. I arrived on the set, where everything was perfect, except the shoes. It had been pouring incessantly and half of

Bombay was underwater. I threw a blue fit. I pulled a Rumpelstiltskin and sent her out to get said boots.

Wading through waist-deep sewage water outside Raj Kamal Studios, Lower Parel (where local residents had invested in small rubber dinghies to combat the floods), Dinsh was sent out to battle against the elements and the odds of finding furry white boots before lunch break. Four hours later, a slightly bedraggled and a much worse-for-wear Dinsh returned, triumphantly holding up a pair of boots in a plastic bag. Halfway through a narration of her misadventure, she was handed a mug of hot tea as the boots were impatiently snatched away and a dishevelled Dinsh was left muttering expletives under her breath. The boots were perfect. To her great dismay, they were never seen in the final edit.

She was also in charge of the outreach for the AIDS consultancy programme, which we ran out of the office and all our girls had been trained by the World Health Organization (WHO). She went on to become the voice of 'Good Morning, Bombay' and soon became the first popular radio host on FM. Dinsh now runs a successful boutique in a quaint, beachside town called Whitstable, in England.

This is Dinsh's version of what transpired on that rainy monsoon day when she was reluctantly booted out of the studio to find a pair of eskimo boots:

> It was a particularly hopeless day. Day four of unceasing rainfall. The kind that floods roads and brings a city to its knees. A relentless rain that delays flights inordinately, shuts down schools and disrupts life as one knows it. And so, we hoped against hope that the shoot planned at Raj Kamal Studios in Lower Parel, one of the lowest lying regions in the city, would perhaps be rescheduled, and we would be spared the ordeal of a shoot in such arduous weather. No such luck. The cavernous studio, with no air conditioning, had been the scene of activity for the past few days, at great cost, to erect a gigantic snow set and losing a day just like that would just not work.

The film we were to shoot had just one protagonist. An Eskimo, one solitary one. So, the brief was that he was to be in a suitable Inuit attire—sealskin and furs, of course. Prahlad was notorious for showing up at no particular or fixed time on the day of the shoot, but he always allowed us enough time to set up, iron out hitches and sometimes even drum our fingers in the air in impatient anticipation. However, his journey would be even slower than usual as the city was flooded.

Still, we were ready and the shoot could begin no sooner than he got here. We were relaxed. How misplaced that relaxation was I soon found out, to my own personal detriment. PK arrived and, in his inimitable, disarming manner, he cast his eyes around the set with a salient lack of approval—even if he did actually approve—exchanged pleasantries with the cameraman, Mahesh Aney, if I recall accurately, then greeted our actor, Mishal Varma, joyously as he cackled at him in costume. Everyone started to prepare and set up for the first shot.

At this point, all was right with the world and we were ready to roll. When 'lights, camera and action' was called, the actor was meant to emerge from the igloo. At the first sight of the Inuit, head and body, we heard a thunderous 'Cut!' None other than PK had called for all to stop and in an even louder voice, he shouted, 'Dinsh, what's with the fucking boots?'

I said, 'Prahlad, you said no long shots, so I didn't think it was a focal point as they won't be seen.'

'Like hell, Dinsh,' PK replied with a scowl. 'Of course, they will be seen! Are you stupid? Look, we will do all the mid shots and close-ups, just go and get a pair of snow boots in the meantime. Just go!'

'But, Prahlad,' I protested. 'There are no taxis running.' These were the days of the Fiat black and yellows with soggy delco points, and the shoot taxi had long since given up its ghost. 'I don't care, Dinsh. Just go and find a pair of fucking snow boots,' came the reply.

Important lesson number ninety-nine: Always prepare for the unexpected, come hell or high water! So, cussing and swearing, I made my way to Maganlal Dresswala on Grant Road, hoping against hope as the water lapped higher and higher. I tiptoed to avoid the lapping soup of toxic sewage water. This is the kind of sacrifice one makes for a man like PK. Make what you will of that!

Locating a pair of boots in the middle of Grant Road on a monsoon-madness day is easier said than done. The shop was closed, but some determined hammering woke up a sleepy assistant, who opened the door in his kachha and banian. But, of course, there were no such boots available, so I found a pair of calf-length moccasins, which were two sizes smaller than the model's feet and quickly located a pair of argyle stockings around which we wrapped faux fur found lying on another dusty shelf.

And so, armed with these DIY boots, I began my journey back, hoping they would stand up to PK's scrutiny. Thankfully, the water had abated slightly and the streets were a little livelier with more cars than before. I managed to flag down a taxi not far from the shop and was back in the studio about three hours after I had left the set.

The mood was jolly upon my return—all shots were nearly done, and laughter and good humour wrapped itself around the set like a clammy glove, except for a profusely hot and sweaty male model, who exclaimed repeatedly that no remuneration was worth this level of discomfort. Apparently, I had done him dirty by not warning him about the level of resilience and strength he would require to get through this—he said it in jest though, so all seemed well.

The boots received a cursory examination and were then attached to our model's feet. They took one long shot that wasn't even used in the final edit and, just like that, it was all over. All puff and fury, signifying nothing and everything.

Another day at Genesis done, and several lessons learnt and unlearnt, all in the space of less than a day.

Life was often like that in the company of Prahlad Kakar and expecting the unexpected just became a way of being. What it succeeded in doing was making even the ordinary and mundane rather extraordinary and sometimes, even profound.

The Eager Beaver

Monia also joined us after graduating from Sophia College's mass media course, like Mitali and Sophie. Monia was a real eager beaver, bright-eyed and bushy-tailed. Before I could complete a brief, she was off the blocks. She would sometimes come back with the goodies and sometimes not, but she learned very quickly from her mistakes. She did, however, have a huge problem keeping her opinions to herself.

As justified as she was, she would always jump the gun. Folks in advertising didn't really mind, but the film industry is a different ball game, since it is highly caste- and hierarchy-ridden. When Monia would blurt out the obvious, sometimes out of turn, the so-called stars would be highly offended that a mere assistant was correcting them, making a suggestion or daring to instruct them. Of course, they didn't know at all that this was the environment that Genesis cultivated and encouraged (though not always successfully).

Monia always took ownership of a job from very early on in her career and I loved her for it. She was instrumental in finding a young Aishwarya Rai and convincing me to test her out. After Monia had spent a couple of months at Genesis, her mom insisted on her going back to Calcutta. So, a tearful Monia came to bid adieu to her stillborn film career. I was aghast and asked her if she wanted to relocate, and she said miserably, 'No.'

So I bought two tickets for Calcutta, travelled with her, sat down with her mother over a cup of tea and convinced her that her daughter had a brilliant career ahead, and that I would take full responsibility of her. Her very distrustful mother reluctantly agreed to let her come back for a year. Monia travelled back with me, much chastened but happy as a lark. She got married to the successful, but incorrigible ad filmmaker, Johnny Pinto, after she met him at a very drunken New Year party at my house in Goa. We all went to Calcutta for the wedding. That is another story, perhaps for the next book. Monia now successfully runs her own production house.

This is her version of her journey with us:

I am guilty of living a dream job at twenty-two—one where it was explained to me that dildos were a perfect substitute for non-performing partners, where the catchphrase in the office was 'It's not on if it's not on', a great advertising line for condoms, incidentally, where murgi chaal in public was your punishment for a prop not having been delivered to the set, where a truck driver as a model meant you travelled to every hotel in the city to find the quintessential big-moustached, tall watchman who suddenly found himself in an ad, where a Dumbell was not your exercise friend, but a beaut of a dog, who was also your travelling partner to Goa, where you learnt that the god is in the details, to never shy away from being vocal, to never compromise with your work and to always follow the feeling in your gut, because that's the truth of life. All this, courtesy of one man and a small office.

The Genesis of almost half the media talent that exists in this city was this big, burly, hairy, obnoxious, loud, extremely talented, witty, incomparably creative and one of the most imaginative people that one would be lucky to meet in this lifetime. They say you have to love the person or organization you work in to survive and succeed. Over twenty-five years later, I have survived and still love, adore and totally respect this human who taught me the bare facts of life and career.

A Punjabi girl from Kolkata, whose mother looked at Prahlad as the big bad wolf when he first convinced her to let me work with him, it is all thanks to this man today for opening up my limited exposure to the world of aesthetics, creativity and madness. I love you, Prahlad, and I forgive you for making me get Aamir Khan a security guard while the riots were on in Mumbai. I forfeit all the money I spent on breakfasts for you even when you raised my salary by only one rupee. I am sorry for making a video of you on 'I am too sexy for my body' as an ode in the biggest advertising hall of fame event in Kolkata.

I never complained to my mom about you teaching me the importance of kissing many to choose the one that excites you the most. I really want to forget about cleaning props and products for the first few months of my internship with you. I hated you for sending me to every nook and cranny of the city to find one small artefact that only you thought was necessary for the shot till we all saw the doubleheader.

I also forgive you for making us write scripts on the morning of the shoot under dire pressure, only because you felt the clients' creativity was not your style. So yes, 'it's different' to work with this maverick called Prahlad. Genesis is truly and honestly 'the right choice, baby' as a start to your career, and the 'zor ka jhatka' Prahlad gives his prodigies is what stays with you forever. Enough said. 'Ting ting ta ting!'

The Army Brat

Tanushree was an army brat like a lot of us, and a little nudge from Neil Chatterjee, my friend from Clarion McCann and now a client from Pepsi, got her a quick audition, without any waiting on the steps of the staircase. Tanushree was young, petite, deceptively soft and as tough as an old drill boot. After all, she was a general's daughter. It took her very little time to figure out the method in the madness, and she took to the mayhem and bloodshed in Genesis like a battle-hardened trooper—reliable, detailed and loyal to a fault. She could take the punishing schedule on the chin and come back for more. A perfect dyed-in-the-wool Genesis product. She always had ambitions to direct a feature film and after opening the doors to her own production house, she actually made one. She is now located in Delhi, temporarily I hope and will be back for more.

No Starry Vibes

Raveena Tandon walked into our office one day during an audition, and I discovered that she had a lively attitude and a mouth to die for. She professed to be more interested in the production side of movie-making than modelling. She badgered us for a couple of days, and because of her very positive attitude and commitment, we took her on. At the time, I realized she came from a long line of film producers. She was a very quick learner and took criticism on the chin. She also followed Joel around like an eager puppy, emulating his do-or-die attitude.

One day, we were on a Cadbury Eclairs shoot, with young Aftab Shivdasani as the child model, on a pristine white set. With white furniture, white walls and white carpets, everybody was very careful not to leave grubby footprints on the set, on pain of death. Raveena was standing right next to me as Aftab went from one eclair to fifteen (fifteen takes later)—he wasn't getting the expression right. He was slowly turning a shade of green. At this stage, Raveena whispered, 'I think he is going to be sick, what do we do?' I said, 'Get a bucket and be prepared, I don't want him to bugger up my set.' But before she could go looking for a bucket, Aftab started upchucking his breakfast.

A frantic Raveena said, 'He's vomiting; what do I do?'

I said, 'Bloody catch it in your hands!'

My only concern at that point was the shot and my white set. She committed herself like a trooper and caught the warm vomit in both her cupped palms, quickly deposited it outside the shooting area and rushed back for more! After the kid had finished, we gave him a glass of water and cleaned him up, while Raveena, in a state of shock at what she had just done, looked at her mucky hands in great dismay. I gave her a pat on the back for her timely action, told her to clean up and get back to the shoot. C'est la vie.

When wrapping up, Joel scored her ten on ten (in the secret Genesis Roster of Flunkeys, Raveena had arrived as a true resourceful professional). She went on to become a top star in the Hindi film industry, and to date, whenever I need the perfect mouth for a product close-up, I always think of her.

Shankar's Bhojanalaya

Our office boy, Shankar, showed an inclination towards cooking. I gradually started training him in my spare time to cook for the office and he turned out some legendary dishes. His 'chicken soup for the soul' was to die for, and many an ex-Genesis assistant director would sometimes drive an hour to the office just to have his soup. His fish moilee was the highlight of our Saturdays and he perfected the art of cooking rice in the microwave. He learnt how to make an authentic Burmese khow suey from my mother, titbits and all.

He fed many a generation of the hungry Genesis clan. I decided to partner him with my driver and major domo, Ramchander—who, by then, had become our barbeque champion—to start a catering service for our shoots out of the 'Brothel', my bungalow in a lane opposite Elco Market, with a lazy Goa vibe. We christened it 'Shankar's Bhojanalaya'. Shankar went on to become a full-time chef at a restaurant. Ramchander, or RC as he is popularly known, continues to be my trusted charioteer.

The Tiger Ladies: Sunita Ram and Mama Kutty

Sunita Ram joined Genesis after a short stint with Mitali's company, Offspring, and had excellent credentials, but had a tough rite of passage initially. She was a very private person and extremely wary of me, so it took her some time getting used to my very in-your-face style of criticism and praise. There were no grey areas for me. Sunita, having been trained by my wife, a self-proclaimed control fiend, had passed the trait on to her. While this can be a good thing sometimes in production, mentoring young interns and delegating was a very Genesis style of management, and she needed to get used to that.

Both of us were cagey at first, until we learnt to trust one another. She grew to be one of my most trusted colleagues and never ever let me down. I always recommended her to foreign units that contacted us for help. My only issue with her has always been that she holds everything very close to her chest. It's only now that she has begun sharing some things with me and we are much better friends. She went on to become executive producer of some outstanding feature films, first with Aamir Khan's *Taare Zameen Par* and then with Zoya Akhtar in *Zindagi Na Milegi Dobara*.

Kalpana Kutty also started out with Mitali and then swiftly became Mama Kutty to the lost souls at Genesis. She was tough, compassionate, patient and protective. Her loyalty was unquestionable and to a very large extent, we shaped each other's lives. Whenever I had a completely hare-brained, out-of-the-box project to do, she was my first bouncing board. One such project was setting up the tea centre lounge—she put it together with the rest of the Genesis girls.

It quickly became an iconic destination and tea lounge, right from the menu design and the tea tasting soirée, to the décor and look, Kalpu took ownership of everything. She was not only a good production person, but also a tremendous cook, interior designer and leader. Today, she is relentlessly headhunted by some of the top media houses and production companies to head high-end projects. She, along with Aarti, ran the Lakmé Fashion Week for four years, smoothly navigating all the inflated egos of models and designers. Quite a herculean task!

The RVs Three

Despite the stress of shooting films and working on productions where the Genesis office was stretched to its limits, we still managed to have quite a bit of fun. One day, I discovered to my dismay, that we had three resident virgins in the office. I named them RV 1, RV 2 and RV 3. It became my bounden duty to find them likely partners so that they could hopefully shed their burdens. So, when we got a brief to shoot a moped film for the rural areas, I summoned the three RVs and briefed them that they had to find me a bull. I put them on a train to Pune—they were to be sent to a friend's farm. The copy of the film compared the two-wheeler's stamina and toughness to that of a bull. I reminded them as they were leaving that they were looking for a bull, not a bullock. One of them asked, 'What's the difference?'

'Look into its eyes and you will see the difference,' I replied.

A week later, I got a call saying that they had found a bull that we could shoot with, close to Pune. So, we packed up a unit of thirty people and headed off to Pune to shoot. When we arrived at the location, I asked them to trot out the bull. The owner walked out with a magnificent beast. It had a good spread of horns. On closer examination, it turned out to be a bullock. I lined up the three RVs and gave them a sound dressing down. To which they plaintively said that the owner had promised that it was a bull.

I asked them if they had looked into his eyes and they swore they had. So I bundled them into a car and drove to a nearby temple town. I took them straight to the sabzi mandi, where a few bulls were loitering around eating vegetables off the ground. They had been released by some farmers in the name of the Devi. They were big, sleek, well fed and, to put it mildly, a bit unpredictable. Nobody had ever tried to tame them, so they roamed free. I told the three RVs to very carefully hide behind vegetable carts and sneak up to one of the bulls, and look into its eyes.

Off they went. When they got close enough to an unsuspecting bull to peep out from behind their sparse cover, he noticed them. With a loud snort, he lifted his magnificent head and stared at the three offending girls. At this stage, they quickly scuttled back to the car, where I was waiting. I asked them if they had looked into the bull's eyes and they nodded, a little overwhelmed. I asked, 'What's the difference between your bullock and this bull?' They hesitantly said, 'Our bull looks very sad compared to this one.'

'So would you be, if someone cut your balls off,' I told them.

Eventually, RV 1 and RV 2 found their true loves within the clan and are happily married to this day. Last I heard, RV3 was still looking.

The Chaska Maska Girl

One day as we were casting for a film for Bazooka TV sets, with an extra loud sound system. The script was based on the *Sound of Music* kind of scenario, and we were looking for the main lead. My brief to the team was that I had not liked Julie Andrews at all and would prefer an Audrey Hepburn pixie like character. The team turned up with this petite, young lady called Vidya Malvade, and were really rooting for her. I was a bit irritated, as they were really pushing, and I found her pretty but a bit 'docile' and lacklustre.

I called her into my cabin to have a chat, in the process of trying to figure her out, I found that her spirit was totally crushed, but despite her present state, she was willing to audition for the part. On an impulse, I decided to see how hungry she was, despite her acting inexperience. When the team informed her that she was on, it was as if a huge weight had been lifted off her shoulders and an impossible hope flickered in her eyes.

Vidya's transformation from that moment till the shooting was quite remarkable. The office girls had sort of adopted her and taken her under their wing with Mama Kutty being the chief mother hen. They had all sensed her desolation and the little flicker of fire that still burnt in her tiny frame. Vidya became a part of the Genesis clan, more through adoption than a trial by fire, but then she had already been through her agni pariksha in her own personal life.

Vidya was an air hostess and had met and married a young, dashing pilot of her dreams, a few years ago, and life was so perfect and happy, until on that fateful day his plane crashed, killing him and his co-pilot and some passengers. As her world crumbled around her, she had to keep it desperately together for the sake of her elderly in-laws who were equally bereft. After all the formalities had been completed, only then did she allow her grief and desolation to overtake her.

And now, she had arrived at our doorstep to try and put her shattered life back on track. Vidya became a part of the office seamlessly, and the girls pushed her to do more work.

She was lucky as the camera loved her, and she slowly got her spirit and confidence back and secured the amazing campaign for Britannia's 'Chaska Maska'.

The hoarding featuring her as the Chaska Maska girl was splashed across Bombay, and almost overnight she was a star in red who had finally arrived. When she landed from her flight and was being taken home in the wee hours of the morning, completely knackered, she woke up with a start as she found herself staring down from the hoardings. Vidya like all our other waifs who had transformed into something spectacular, was very much a Genesis story.

Papa Pancho

A lot of interesting endeavours came out of the Genesis kitchen— one of them was a Punjabi restaurant started by young Mamta Sekri, who came to me as she was looking for a name for the restaurant. I suggested the name 'Papa Pancho'. She was taken aback and slightly horrified at my suggestion. I reminded her that among Punjabis, 'pancho' is no longer an abuse, it's a term of endearment and that we would create a home away from home for all homesick Punjabis in Bombay, looking for mummy de haath da khana. In this, we had found a niche that didn't exist in the city for our adopted Punjabi brethren.

We had no money to even print a pamphlet to distribute on the street, when we were ready to launch, so we did the next best thing. We cooked a handi full of maa di dal—it took six hours on a slow flame. We packaged them in little kulhads as a sample of what to expect and wrote a personalized note on it: 'A dhaba lives and dies by its dal! If you like our dal, you will love everything else.' We distributed it to 400 homes in the neighbourhood and that's how Papa Pancho was born.

When I exited the business 14 years ago, I suggested it be called 'Mama Pancho' as Mamta and her sister were to run it, but the PP name stuck I guess!

Toolie to Kasby

One rainy day, a tall portly gentleman walked into my office with a gangly youngster in tow. It turned out that the gentleman, Mr Kasbekar, Senior, had a problem. His gangly son, who was a state-level scholar with a gold medal in chemistry, did not want to follow in his father's footsteps and become a chemical engineer, but God forbid, wanted to study photography. His father was aghast, he did not consider photography a real profession and believed it to be a hobby only. So, he hauled his errant brat to us, as recommended by a friend, to talk some sense into his head that if he followed his passion for photography, then he would be a pauper all his life.

I patiently heard him out, took the boy aside, and asked him what he thought! Atul was very clear that he wanted to follow his passion and damn the consequences. He just needed me to pacify his father temporarily. I talked the old boy into leaving his entitled son with us for a while, and he would rapidly learn the price of eggs and atte–dal ka bhav. So young Kasbekar became part of Genesis, and paid his dues, by cleaning the ladies' toilet with a toothbrush and many a time, I could see him bolting for the fence, but the alternative would be to go back to his father and enroll in a chemical engineering degree.

Toolie, as he was nicknamed in the office, hung in there and did his diligence and the better he became at production, the more determined he was to become an ace photographer. After a year his father made him an offer, which he refused. Back they came to the office to sort it out. As it transpired, Atul's dad had bought him a factory in Panvel, and wanted him to run it forthwith or else. I sat and reasoned with the old boy, while Atul lurked around trying to hide in our tiny 400 square feet office.

I finally explained to Mr Kasbekar that his son had the talent, brains and passion to make it big by taking up fashion photography as there was also lots of money to be made. After much brow beating, his father agreed to send Atul to America to study photography professionally, and invested a kingly sum in the equipment required.

Atul spent a fun time in California and returned with a new moniker 'Kasby', and made good, shooting skimpily clad women for the Kingfisher calendar (his claim to fame and envy (what a life!) and quite a few top advertising campaigns. Thank god Atul made good, otherwise I would have to face a very irate and disgruntled father. Now, Kasby's life has come full circle, and he has started producing full-length feature films . Good for you, Atul!

The Flying Wedge: Aarti, Stuti and Nikki

Stuti arrived with two other interns from Sophia College for a really tough outdoor shoot in Banganga. It was hot as hell, and people were really exhausted and we only had daylight hours to complete the Atlas cycle film (the chief villain was a dwarf called Aaja bhaiya), as there was a cultural festival starting the next day. The location was not therefore available and there was a frantic scramble to finish the shoot with no lunch break (and no shade). And the last man standing at the end of the day was young Stuti. Everybody else had keeled over and collapsed in a heap. I immediately coopted her into the clan, and she proved to be hugely resourceful, organized, tenacious and stubborn.

She always managed to stand her ground, even with me. She was a huge asset and loved what she did. She had the face of an angel and even clients insisted I cast her in some of the ad films we did at the time. She always delivered, both off-screen and on-screen. After spending three years with Genesis, she decided to go to film school in New York City. I wrote her a completely off-the-charts, much-deserved recommendation letter. And with her Genesis experience, she topped her class. She came back to us two years later, but we lost her to holy matrimony and the UK. But nothing, nothing can keep a good man (or woman) down. Today, she is with Excel Entertainment and is the executive producer for *Gully Boy* and other successful projects.

Aarti Patkar arrived with her dad at Mitali's Bandra office, where she ran the production office and managed most of our international work for Pepsi, Nestlé and HUL. We knew Aarti's parents, and they couldn't understand why she wanted to leave a seven-figure salary job and do production flunkey work for practically no money. Within a week of her joining, Mitali realized she was unshakeable, extremely intelligent and would take great pleasure in seeing the other interns struggle with the hectic pace of work and the multitasking required to do six-to-eight films a month. These were things Aarti could do with her eyes shut, especially when it came to costume styling and accessorizing the sets. Remember, this was an era where production assistants did everything from casting and costumes to art and locations. Today, there are separate departments for every task.

We were to shoot for a massive production in the deserts of Rajasthan and Mitali suggested I give Aarti the opportunity to head the production. The first thing I said to her was that she was underperforming because she was putting in half her potential to be as good as everybody else. I told her I needed her to be the best that she could be (without comparing herself to anyone else) because I thought she had great potential. I threatened to send her back to her banking job if she didn't deliver. And boy, did she deliver, and in spades! I named her the 'chabuk' of Genesis, because not only did she do her job, she owned it.

And she got the whole team to perform to their full potential too. She may be diminutive in her build, but she was a powerhouse and a first-class leader. I could trust her with my life! When her father passed away suddenly, she had to leave Genesis and take over his incomplete villa development project in Lonavala. Today, other than doing event design and being the executive producer on feature film projects with her husband, she successfully runs the Vintage Garden Artisanal Bazaar.

Nikki was sent to us reluctantly by her Delhi-based parents, at her stubborn insistence (post a brief meeting with me at Chachi's farmhouse party). She came to us as a complete fresher from Dilli 'Twon' and was amazed at the kind of liberty, freedom and responsibility we used to give our interns. She threw herself into production work and took to it like a duck to water. She improved every day in front of my very eyes. She managed to be independent and a team player simultaneously.

Aarti, Stuti and Nikki were what I called the 'Flying Wedge' of Genesis. A flying wedge is a combat team that cuts through all opposition, however deeply entrenched it might be, so the girls were very appropriately named, trust me. They bonded so well that they are inseparable even today. When Genesis entered the all-women's team for the inter-corporate office go-kart rally, my Flying Wedge, along with Sunita Ram, formed the core team, called 'Kakar's Angels'. The only exception—as a male backup driver—was Anees Adenwala. Aarti recorded the fastest lap time of all time and we made it to the finals, only to lose by a whisker. We came in a very close second to the all-male Burmah Shell winning team. I treasure the trophy to this day.

Aarti was very camera conscious and refused to have anything to do with facing the camera, so I found the right time to introduce her to the possibility of a life in acting. This is Aarti's take on that incident:

Trying to pick one memory from my experiences at Genesis is like trying to fit an elephant into a car. But since I have to pick one, I'll pick the one where we were shooting an ad for Rasna with Karisma Kapoor. We needed a living room set, birthday party decor, kids and, of course, a clown! Now, the clown we cast—I use that term loosely because we didn't actually cast him, we just decided to use our newest flunkey—he was tall, skinny and slightly creepy looking! Prahlad bounced him on sight, looked suitably angry for a few minutes, pointed his finger at me and bellowed, 'You will be the clown!'

Anyone who knows me even a little knows I'm mortified of being in front of the camera. So obviously, I made a big fuss. Needless to say, I had little choice in the matter and soon, Vidyadhar painted my face, put a wig on my head and that was that. I was suitably costumed and pushed out on to the set! I played the part and AD'd the film all at the same time—

dressed as a clown! I gave Lolo [Karisma] cues, dressed as a clown. I discussed the post schedule with the agency, dressed as a clown.

I think what I'm trying to say is that PK will push you out of your comfort zone, make you do crazy things and force you to do things you swore you wouldn't or were sure you couldn't. He showed me who I was and who I could be and taught me that it was okay to laugh at myself. It's a lesson I can never forget. I love you, PK. Thank you for the innumerable life lessons I can use till today. Being part of your team was one of the best experiences of my life. Sometimes, I still introduce myself as Aarti Patkar from Genesis.

Sam

Samina Motlekar—'Sam' to her friends and admirers—joined Genesis after her journalism course. She was, I believed, a good writer. She came in, fresh off the boat, with no clue about the business of film production. But she was spirited and confident even when clueless. She picked up the complicated maze of producing ad films, as there were at least forty vendors on any production. She also mastered the business of being able to calculate the cost of a film in a short amount of time. In two years, she was heading the office and was the chief executive producer. She eventually started her own production house, got tired of dealing with erratic clients and agencies, and went back to her first love—writing. She is now a successful writer of scripts for feature films and OTT projects.

The Tea Centre and Satoko Mitsui

One day, I walked into the tea centre, which Mama Kutty and the Genesis girls had set up in record time, and placed my hat on the baby grand piano. I looked around and saw a very elegant Japanese lady sipping green tea in a corner, against a lime-green chikan curtain. The hair on my forearms and the back of my neck stood up, and a frisson ran down my spine. I walked up to her and politely asked if she was Japanese. She said, 'Yes.' I continued, 'You are the lady Miyamoto Musashi painted 400 years ago in Japan.' She looked a bit startled and enquired, 'How do you know Miyamoto Musashi?' I thought a bit and said, 'I don't know, but I think he was my sensei.'

She looked gravely at me and said, 'He was my ancestor, and the lady he painted was my great-great-grandmother.'

I was gobsmacked. Sitting in front of me was a direct descendant of one of the greatest swordsmen of sixteenth-century Japan. Her name was Satoko Mitsui, and we became great friends. She also told me that the painting of her great-great-grandmother hung in the shrine for Miyamoto Musashi in the courtyard of her father's house in Tokyo and had never been publicly displayed. Satoko used to host a Japanese tea ceremony at the tea centre once every month.

The Star Girls

Sanvari Alagh spent all her holidays in her teen years with us. I suspect her father browbeat her into taking regular summer internships at Genesis. She was a bright, if entitled, teenager, always looking to find a shortcut, only to realize that we ate people looking for a quick fix for breakfast or threw them to the lions. For Sanvari, every day was a trial by fire where she was thrown into the deep end of production, and she had to sink or swim. And swim she did! Her eventual bestie and soul sister was an attractive, general's daughter, Rupali Kadyan. Bright as a newly minted coin and always looking for a corner to hide in, she was aided and abetted by many a willing protector, like Dhimant and Joel. Their metamorphosis into the Star girls (pun intended) was something to behold. From entitlement to hunger, focus and ambition.

Rupali's trial by fire took place at a denim jeans shoot where anything that could go wrong did go wrong. Everyone was running helter-skelter, and she faced the brunt of my ire as the main model injured his back during rehearsals, trying to show off to her while doing a somersault. That day, something shifted within her and suddenly that steely resolve that was always within her manifested itself. Being naturally gifted with multitasking and a high level of aesthetics, all she needed was that slight kick up her arse to become what she is today—a crack executive producer like her soul sister Sanvari. They were both poached by Star with a twenty fold raise in salary. They both worked closely as a part of the team that created *Kaun Banega Crorepati*.

Sanvari married her boss. She is now a top-level producer herself, while managing a bustling household of his, hers and ours. Rupali works with her husband and has taken their company, Contiloe, to a heady new level, while bringing up their two gorgeous girls and running a beautiful home.

This is one of the incidents which Rupali counts as a part of her learning curve:

> I was fresh out of one of Sophia's postgraduation course when I joined Genesis. Five months down the line, I was working on a commercial that required me to hire clothes from various boutiques. I took one outfit against an advance from a hip store. As is mostly the case, the shoot ran into overtime and I could only return the clothes late evening as opposed to early morning. I had also called to inform them of the same. When I went back that evening, the rude owner told me my full advance would be deducted. Totally panicked, as Cedric, our accountant, would have killed me, I grabbed a few extras off the hangers and ran out with all the clothes. I hailed a cab, got in and returned to office.
>
> I could hear the owner running after me down the street, shouting that she was going to call PK and I was going to regret everything. Sheepishly, I entered office where PK, looking a tad too serious, was awaiting my arrival. True to her word, the owner of the boutique had called him. I narrated the entire episode, waiting for my moment of judgement. I obviously hadn't spent enough time with him to anticipate the deafening laughter that ensued. He roared, patted me on the back and said my induction into Genesis was now complete.

The Three Musketeers

Uzer, Shujaat and Rumaan were known as the three musketeers of Genesis. They joined us at different times, but were the few outstanding men who survived the rigour of cleaning the ladies' loo with a toothbrush—in order to learn detailing. Uzer came from Dongri. He was a young, good-looking Pathan boy, who was remotely related to Karim Lala. He wanted to be a filmmaker and spent three very quiet years with us, flying below the radar and mostly out of my sight. But he was absorbing the business of film-making and production through every single pore like a sponge. The best part about Uzer was that he was mostly self-taught, but highly talented. His sense of colour, balance and graphic design was amazing.

The person who recognized this even before I did was Elsie Nanjee of Ambience, who is among the best graphic designers in this country in my opinion. She saw some of his scratch films, and immediately picked him out and asked who the boy was. I told her that he was one of my boys from Dongri. She commented that he was absolutely brilliant and that was when I started paying attention to Uzer. I realized that he was relatively shy at the time, but very keen and resilient. So, I started giving him more and more work. He took to it like a duck to water—initially, he was reluctant because he lacked the confidence to be able to hold his own on the set, but he learned the ropes very quickly. He has grown into becoming one of the best ad filmmakers in the country today.

Shujaat came as a trainee from Symbiosis University, Pune, and was extremely driven to become a filmmaker. He took everything that was thrown at him and not only survived his trial by fire, but excelled. Any job that I asked him to do was never too small or too big; he did them all with the same level of focus and enthusiasm. I once asked him and Uzer to follow young Prateik's nefarious activities and all the bad influences in his life, and to report them back to me.

Prateik had gone in and come out of rehab so many times that his grandmother was fed up and handed him over to Mitali and me in sheer exasperation. We were keeping him in our care. Uzer and Shujaat did a fantastic job and got a list of all the bad eggs around him and threatened them with dire consequences. This left young Prateik with no choice but to knuckle down and take his career seriously.

Shujaat wanted to make ad films, but his goal and dream was to make feature films, which he is finally doing now. He has taken quite well to long format, and his company made a lot of good ad films in its time, but is now focusing on OTT platforms. He has also done a feature film, *Rock On 2!* for Farhan Akhtar and is now making the first season of *Dongri to Dubai*. Genesis produced a television feature for Sanvari, which Shujaat directed and Sunita Ram was the executive producer, inspired by Roald Dahl's 'Lamb for the Slaughter', called *Bali*. Two ex-Genesis protégés, Ram Kapoor and Mandira Bedi, acted in it.

Rumaan came to us through Seema, who introduced me to him over the phone. I asked him what he wanted to do and what he had done so far. Rumaan told me that he had worked on the production of *Monsoon Wedding* and even played a small part in it. I had seen Mira Nair's *Monsoon Wedding* and thought it was an excellent piece of work. So, I asked him to find himself some transportation and land up in the office. Two days later, I got a call from Bombay Central. It was Rumaan. I told him to come to the office immediately since we weren't far from the station and we were in the thick of a production. Rumaan arrived with a large Delsey suitcase and started his first day of work at Genesis. He then found himself some digs very quickly and settled in. He has not looked back ever since.

Rumaan was probably one of the most sensitive, well-read and well-travelled youngsters, and he was a delight to work with. He understood immediately what was required. And what's great was that he didn't have trouble working under female bosses. In fact, he enjoyed it enormously. Rumaan is now on the verge of completing a really interesting script, which has taken him almost two years to write on a character whom he met totally by chance. And when that script is going to be presented to an OTT platform, we will see Rumaan at his best. Directing is such a natural thing for him that I'm surprised that he hasn't already done more work.

Of these three musketeers of Genesis, Uzer went on to set up his own company and do some outstanding work with some big brands. Covid-19 overtook Shujaat's production for a year and a half, but he managed to shoot through it all. Shujaat's team had made a huge sprawling film set of Mohammad Ali Road and the Dongri area—where it all started from. However, they had to dismantle it during Covid-19 and put it up again immediately afterward. He has only recently completed it and we are all waiting with bated breath to watch it when it releases.

Young Advait

Young Advait, all of seventeen years old, wide-eyed and overly enthusiastic, was sent from Mitali's office to Genesis to check if he had steel in his spine. He managed to escape all the usual rigours of initiation, as the girls in the office immediately adopted him and spoilt him silly. He barely stayed with us for a year, juggling his university lessons and our shoots, before he was offered a job as a production assistant on *Taare Zameen Par* by Sunita Ram, who thought he had potential. She was a tough taskmaster and put him through the ringer immediately. Advait could not handle the gruelling pace and post-production, so much so that he dropped out.

However, he had been noticed by Kiran Rao, who took him on for her directorial debut, *Dhobi Ghat*, where he did everything from casting, production and playing the role of assistant director—in true Genesis tradition. After this project, he was asked by Aamir to be his executive assistant. At the age of twenty-six, Advait Chandan wrote and directed his first feature, *Secret Superstar*, a small, sincere film with newbie actors, which became the surprise hit of the year. His marriage to Mitali's niece makes him family, so I guess we are stuck with him for life! Advait is well on his way to becoming a major force in both features and ad films, working in a top-notch production house, Chrome Pictures, run by Amit Sharma.

Pradeep Uppoor

Pradeep Uppoor was, for all practical purposes, our greatest support at Genesis. He was Ravi Uppoor's brother and had a company two floors above us called Neo Films and we always considered it an extension of Genesis. While we had a knack for rubbing people up the wrong way, Pradeep had a knack for soothing ruffled feathers. He was a great human being, generous to a fault and gave us lots of his time in trying to mend all the bridges that we had burnt. I also directed a lot of films for Pradeep and envied him for the fact that he had also produced renowned feature films, like *Aakrosh* with his buddy Manmohan Shetty. We lost him recently and it was a great gathering of all the people whose lives he had touched.

Night School

Irene, whom I had worked with at Lintas, one day stalked into my office with this cute little teenager. She came in bristling and angry, and for the life of me I couldn't figure out why. Naturally, I ducked for cover. She then deposited the young lady in the middle of my room and pointing a quivering finger at her, said, 'She has dropped out of college and refuses to go back! I don't know what to do with her; I am so fed up. You take her!'

I looked at her in great dismay and said, 'What have I done to deserve this?'

'You have taken on all the other problem children, now you take on mine!' she snapped, turned around and left. So we had very little choice in adopting Aadore. She was a fait accompli. I sat her down and asked her what she would like to do. She said, 'I want to work with you at Genesis!' I asked her, 'How badly do you want this?' She said, 'Very!' So, I made a deal with Aadore that she could attend office, learn the business of film-making, but after office, she would go to night college and finish her courses. She reluctantly agreed, and over the next two years, Aadore became very much a part of the office and cleared her graduation with a first class. She still looks like an eighteen-year-old, and is one of the top casting directors in the film industry today and works out of Goa.

Crashing Awards

Who receives a Lifetime Achievement Award at forty-nine years of age? It was as if the advertising fraternity was trying to send me a coded message. After all, most people received this award in their old age or when they were in the so-called happy hunting grounds. Of course, the event itself was very amusing—I had written my acceptance speech on a roll of toilet paper, which accidentally rolled off the podium and bounced down the steps towards the audience. And yes, I opened with, 'Oh shit, there goes my speech.' I reiterated to the audience that I had no intention of retiring peacefully and that I would go kicking, biting, screaming—if and when I went. The clan, the media and the universe somehow always connived to protect and support me, 'L'enfant terrible', who never grew up.

Thereafter, I continued the Genesis tradition of gatecrashing award nights with my motley crew of twenty. They would usually be Genesis rowdies and other production house lukkhas. The penultimate time was when the fraternity organized the Technicians Awards for Excellence in 2000 and they warned us that they were taking countermeasures so that we couldn't crash the function.

This was too much of a challenge to pass up on, so we planned the most elaborate gatecrash of all time, led by Anees Adenwala and Adarsh Vansay, with walkie-talkies to boot. We printed our own passes, we smuggled in our own table and chairs, and the pride of place was reserved for Dumbell, with an all-access crew pass, bow tie, etc. And boy, were the organizers pissed off.

Crete and the Nada Story

Mitali and I were invited to a food and wine festival in Greece, as part of the Indian media and chef contingent to introduce Greek produce to the world, organized by my dear friend Sudha, erstwhile MTV executive and economics professor. She is now running a popular destination magazine for the region. All the world-famous Michelin-star chefs were going to be there, and I wasn't going to miss the opportunity of sampling the best olive oils and sipping the best wine with them. We landed on the fabulous island of Crete, nestled in the azure-blue Mediterranean Sea, and checked into our fabulous villa by the beach. My enthusiastic wife, notebook in hand, left for the venue to collect the programme for the next five days.

Chef Gordon Ramsay's talk was a highlight that I immediately noted and he was going to cook-off against George Calombaris. It was going be delightful. All set for the day in my crisp white kurta and salwar, we walked through the abundant fresh-produce exhibition space to the conference hall. Sudha and Mitali, like good convent-educated girls, wrote copious notes as the talks progressed. Meanwhile, I had lost track of time as I waited for the famous chefs' workshops and desperately needed to relieve my bladder.

I rushed out, saw the men's restroom sign a floor below, went into the cubicle and pulled the nada of my pyjama. Oops, wrong end! It got hopelessly knotted. I desperately tried to open it as I peeped over my paunch. No such luck; the knot grew tighter. Bounding up the stairs, I called my wife (international call via Bombay), but there was no answer. I called Sudha next, who answered in hushed whispers as Gordon Ramsay was just being introduced. She darted out with great reluctance to see what the brouhaha was about.

I lifted up my kurta in the middle of the foyer and pointed to the offending Gordian knot. She looked at me with an arched eyebrow and asked, 'What?'

'Just open my nada please; kneel down and use your teeth if necessary!' I begged. I could see the picture of both of us in the middle of a busy foyer flash across her face—me with my kurta up, paunch out and her kneeling down with her face buried in my nether regions. She gave me a scathing look and walked off in a huff. In my desperation, I walked around some stalls, asking for a pair of scissors. No luck. From the corner of my eye, I spotted a cheese counter with a cheese knife to cut samples.

With hope lighting up my mind, I pretended to casually walk up and politely asked to taste the cheese, needing a preamble to jhaap the knife. I nonchalantly picked up the knife, mumbled something about returning it soon, bounded off with great speed to the restroom facilities and started sawing frantically at the offending nada. To my great relief, it came apart quickly and, as my pyjama collapsed around my knees, I let fly with acute respite.

When I lifted the pyjama to tie it back again, the two ends of said nada had disappeared into the multiple folds of the salwar. So I did the next best thing I could do, as I attempted to get back into the seminar via the bustling lobby. Sudha noticed me confidently enter the session, and ignored me as she rolled her eyes.

A confused Mits wrote a message to her in her notebook: What happened? Where is Prahlad?

Sudha wrote back: Don't ask, he is walking around with just his kurta and his hairy legs!!

'She's Italian and of noble blood,' he said.

One day in office, I had a visitor from Canada. He introduced himself as Biri. He was a cut surd and said that he had learnt the technique of making wine out of grape concentrate and would we be interested. Bloody hell, of course, we were interested considering that we consumed large quantities of wine on our open-house Saturdays. So we heard him out and invested in importing one barrel of Barolo grape concentrate from Canada (an Italian red grape variety). It got stuck at customs and we had declared it as fruit juice concentrate. They couldn't quite understand the difference between fruit juice concentrate and grape juice concentrate, since that was what was written across the barrel. They were twiddling their thumbs while we were frothing and fuming, because we didn't want to have the juice ferment in the warehouse.

I told the customs officer, 'Right now it is grape juice, but if you keep it any longer, it will become alcohol! If that happens, I am not willing to pay 200 per cent duty on the alcohol; so you can keep the barrel then and drink it at your own convenience.' The customs officer got very alarmed by my attitude and quickly released the barrel. We lugged it all the way to Goa to my house in Betim, and, under Biri's supervision, we started looking for a large vessel which we could use to dilute and ferment the grape juice.

There was no such vessel available, but instead I found an abandoned enamel bathtub in somebody's backyard. I bought it off them and lugged it to my living room in Betim, much to Biri's bemusement. When he realized that we were going to ferment his sacred grape juice in this slightly dented bathtub, he was horrified. But since we didn't have a choice, we proceeded to do precisely that. We poured the grape juice concentrate into the tub, diluted it with well water, not Bisleri, and put a starter in to kick-start the fermenting process. We covered the bathtub with enough plastic to make it airtight and waited for a month while it bubbled away to glory.

After a month, Biri tested the waters of the wine and pronounced it ready for bottling. There was one last process that was left, which was to filter and polish the wine, and it was just about palatable. Then we lugged the 200 bottles back to Bombay, and put them in a wine rack above the kitchen and proceeded to drink it over the next three months. We even invited a known sommelier to vet our home-grown vintage, knowing fully well that it was an unpedigreed 'plonk'.

Oozing charm from every pore, he oiled himself across the floor. He nosed, he swilled, he gargled and swallowed, and closed his eyes in meditative bliss as we held our collective breath. He opened his eyes wide and said, 'It's Italian, of noble blood from 1994!' We almost choked over Shankar's fish moilee while trying to keep a straight face. The moment we left, after a great repast and many quaffs of wine, all of us collectively collapsed laughing, and raised a toast and named our wine 'Mardi Gras!' (after the carnival). Two hundred bottles and two months later, nobody died, so we assumed that our exercise was a success.

Prahlad Kakar School of Branding and Entrepreneurship (PKSBE)

The entire curriculum of the Prahlad Kakar School of Branding and Entrepreneurship (PKSBE) came from our experiences and learnings at Genesis Film Production over the course of thirty-eight years. The curriculum was unconventional and unique. It was a combination of in-classroom teachings and real-world simulations delivered by industry professionals and entrepreneurs. It encouraged and nurtured young dreamers to dream big and follow their dreams. It took the stigma of fear and failure away.

Needless to say, the powers that be—i.e., the education board—rejected the curriculum because they were so immersed in academia and theory that they did not understand how important practical, real-world teachings can be. We started at Whistling Woods, thanks to the largesse and generosity of Subhash Ghai, who believed in us. Due to space constraints, we then moved to Narsee Monjee College, Juhu, where they allowed us some degree of autonomy, and whatever we did outside the accepted curriculum was entirely our responsibility.

The course grew so popular amongst students wanting a career in the creative and innovation fields that, by the second year, we had many more students than we could accommodate. Our faculty's engagement with the students was so high that with this success came its own problems. The board of the college felt threatened by the popularity of our course, as the student grapevine was abuzz. In fact, their BBM (Bachelor of Business Management) and management students wanted to shift mid-year to our course.

The course was designed to break down barriers and push students to think out of the box, and to empower and nurture them into becoming socially responsible, creative, passionate business leaders. All the founders of PKSBE believed in that implicitly and contributed their own personal experiences, enriching the course immensely. We were asked to leave the college as they wanted to take over the course and run it themselves. I didn't try to patent the curriculum because, to make it in any way successful, the people running the courses had to live and breathe the experience. And, in our present corridors of academia and teaching, this is nearly impossible.

It never ceases to amaze me how loyal the clan has remained to this date, and how they credit their success to me and have showered me with unconditional love, even though I feel they have given me much more than I could ever give them. I only taught them the craft, but they gave me the secret to eternal youth. Every product of Genesis became independent and entrepreneurial and carried the essential DNA of Genesis with them and each one of them in their own way, mentored many trainees in the Genesis tradition, which formed the nucleus of the clan. Even newbies like Garima Arora formed an extension of Genesis, with a successful production house called Entourage.

Mitali always wondered why clients gave me work, despite my exasperating and incorrigible behaviour, rude, with no filters. Years later, a repeat client approached her to say that he would be happy to give us the TVC project as long as he didn't have to deal with me! The backstory was that he had been an overzealous management trainee at one of our client's offices and he must have spoken out of turn and I must have chewed his head off for it. He carried it for many years, nursing the grudge until he became the boss and could actually call the shots. Now that he had become the head honcho in his organization, the roles had been reversed and he thought that he could now ban me from the set, which he proceeded to do with extreme prejudice!

Throughout my career, the media has always been interested in my slightly radical views on everything around us—from politics to the environment, and the right and the wrong of it. But I must say, while everyone is always complaining that the media misquotes them, they have always been very supportive and protective of me, and have always tempered down some of my outbursts and quotes, so that I don't land up in court or in jail!

A lot of people from the fifth estate also became friends and mentors in their own way. They always had my back, people like Sreenivasan Jain from NDTV, Arnab Goswami from Republic TV, Rajdeep Sardesai from CNBC, Rahul Shivshankar from Times Now and Rahul Kanwal from India Today. Pavan Lall, a bright young journalist, ex- Fortune magazine, has also been a close friend and sounding board, and he went on to write some very interesting books on financial scams and amazing entrepreneurs. I am also beholden and grateful to many journalists from the regional language media across the country for their tenacity and drive.

All in all, our journey has been about touching hearts, minds and funny bones. That is who we are and what we do. That has been our greatest learning and teaching, and that is what will continue through everyone whom we have mentored, no matter where they are. The legacy of Genesis is our body of work and the people who graduated through our portals—kicking, biting, screaming.

Fade to black.

Answer to Jean-Paul Sartre—I am the sum total of all the people who have stopped to touch my life and shape its direction.

Notes

Scan this QR code to access the detailed notes

About the Author

Prahlad Kakar is a renowned ad-film director and co-founder of Genesis Film Production, one of India's oldest and foremost ad-film production houses. He has ruled the advertising world with his brand of irreverent humour and memorable brand-building campaigns, and has created award-winning commercials for the most reputed corporates and agencies in India and the Asia-Pacific region.

About the Coauthor

Rupangi Sharma is an author, editor and edupreneur. She is the founder and CEO of EFG Learning, a Mumbai-based education consultancy. Her focus has been on the power of technology, storytelling and innovation, and their transformational role in education. Rupangi's recent books include *A Life of My Own* and *Young Indian Innovators, Entrepreneurs and Change-makers*.

HarperCollins *Publishers* India

At HarperCollins India, we believe in telling the best stories and finding the widest readership for our books in every format possible. We started publishing in 1992; a great deal has changed since then, but what has remained constant is the passion with which our authors write their books, the love with which readers receive them, and the sheer joy and excitement that we as publishers feel in being a part of the publishing process.

Over the years, we've had the pleasure of publishing some of the finest writing from the subcontinent and around the world, including several award-winning titles and some of the biggest bestsellers in India's publishing history. But nothing has meant more to us than the fact that millions of people have read the books we published, and that somewhere, a book of ours might have made a difference.

As we look to the future, we go back to that one word—a word which has been a driving force for us all these years.

Read.

Harper
Collins

HARPER
PERENNIAL

HARPER
BUSINESS

HARPER
BLACK

हार्पर
हिन्दी

HarperCollins
Children's Books

HARPER
DESIGN

HARPER
VANTAGE

Harper
Sport